Microsoft Windows Azure Development Cookbook

Over 80 advanced recipes for developing scalable
services with the Windows Azure platform

Neil Mackenzie

[PACKT] enterprise
PUBLISHING
professional expertise distilled

BIRMINGHAM - MUMBAI

Microsoft Windows Azure Development Cookbook

First published: August 2011

Production Reference: 2020811

Published by Packt Publishing Ltd.
Livery Place
35 Livery Street
Birmingham B3 2PB, UK.

ISBN 978-1-849682-22-0

www.packtpub.com

Cover Image by Jackson Myers (jax@rice.edu)

Credits

Author

Neil Mackenzie

Reviewers

Michael S. Collier

Maarten Balliauw

Gaurav Mantri

Brent Stineman

Acquisition Editor

Kerry George

Development Editor

Pallavi Madihalli Ramakrishna

Technical Editor

Azharuddin Sheikh

Project Coordinator

Vishal Bodwani

Indexer

Monica Ajmera Mehta

Proofreader

Aaron Nash

Production Coordinator

Shantanu Zagade

Cover Work

Shantanu Zagade

About the Author

Neil Mackenzie has worked with computers for nearly three decades. He started by doing large-scale numerical simulations for scientific research and business planning. Since then, he has primarily been involved in healthcare software, developing electronic medical record systems. He has been using Windows Azure since PDC 2008, and has used nearly all parts of the Windows Azure platform—including those parts that no longer exist. Neil is very active in the online Windows Azure community, in particular, contributing to the MSDN Windows Azure Forums. He is a Microsoft MVP for Windows Azure.

Neil tweets as @mknz and blogs at http://convective.wordpress.com/

I would like to thank all the people from whom I have learned Windows Azure. I would also like to thank the staff at Packt Publishing for nursing the project along and Brent Stineman for first suggesting my name to them. I have found invaluable comments from the technical reviewers which have immeasurably improved the book. Moreover, last, but not least, I would like to thank my wife, Claire, and children for suffering through all the late nights and lost weekends that went into the writing of the book.

About the Reviewers

Maarten Balliauw is a technical consultant in web technologies at RealDolmen, one of Belgium's biggest ICT companies. His interests are ASP.NET (MVC), for Windows Azure, and Windows Azure. He is a Microsoft Most Valuable Professional (MVP) ASP.NET and has published many articles in both PHP and .NET literature, such as MSDN magazine and PHP architect. Maarten is a frequent speaker at various national and international events, such as MIX (Las Vegas), TechDays, DPC, and so on. His blog can be found at http://blog.maartenballiauw.be.

Michael S Collier is a Windows Azure MVP and serves as a National Architect for Neudesic, a Microsoft SI partner that specializes in Windows Azure. He has nearly 11 years of experience building Microsoft-based applications for a wide range of clients. He spends his days serving as a developer or architect—helping clients succeed with the Microsoft development platform. He gets very "geeked up" about any new technology, tool, or technique that makes his development life easier. He spends most of his spare time reading technology blogs and exploring new development technologies. He is also an avid golfer and attempts to be good at shooters on the Xbox 360. His previous speaking engagements include Central Ohio Day of .NET, Central Ohio .NET Developers Group, Cloud Connections, and multiple Windows Azure Boot Camp events. He is also the Founder of the Central Ohio Cloud Computing User Group. He earned his Bachelor of Computer Science and Engineering from The Ohio State University. You can follow Michael on Twitter at www.twitter.com/MichaelCollier and he maintains his blog at www.MichaelSCollier.com.

Gaurav Mantri is the Founder and Head of Technology for Cerebrata Software Private Limited (http://www.cerebrata.com), an ISV based out of India specializing in building tools and services for Microsoft's Windows Azure Platform. He is also a Microsoft MVP for Windows Azure.

Brent Stineman is a solution architect specializing in cloud computing with Sogeti, USA. His 18+ year IT career has spanned technology from the mainframe to mobile devices. However, he has spent the bulk of the last 10 years working on Internet applications and distributed system development. Brent started working with the Windows Azure Platform early in its CTP phase and is now focused on helping colleagues and clients explore the promise of cloud computing.

I would like to thank Neil for asking me to be a part of this book's creation and all the wonderful members of the Microsoft Windows Azure Development Community. I hope this book will enrich the community as much as I've been enriched by it.

www.PacktPub.com

Support files, eBooks, discount offers and more

You might want to visit www.PacktPub.com for support files and downloads related to your book.

Did you know that Packt offers eBook versions of every book published, with PDF and ePub files available? You can upgrade to the eBook version at www.PacktPub.com and, as a print book customer, you are entitled to a discount on the eBook copy. Get in touch with us at service@packtpub.com for more details.

At www.PacktPub.com, you can also read a collection of free technical articles, sign up for a range of free newsletters, and receive exclusive discounts and offers on Packt books and eBooks.

http://PacktLib.PacktPub.com

Do you need instant solutions to your IT questions? PacktLib is Packt's online digital book library. Here, you can access, read, and search across Packt's entire library of books.

Why subscribe?

- ► Fully searchable across every book published by Packt
- ► Copy and paste, print, and bookmark content
- ► On demand and accessible via web browser

Free access for Packt account holders

If you have an account with Packt at www.PacktPub.com, you can use this to access PacktLib today and view nine entirely free books. Simply use your login credentials for immediate access.

Instant Updates on New Packt Books

Get notified! Find out when new books are published by following @PacktEnterprise on Twitter, or the *Packt Enterprise* Facebook page.

Table of Contents

Preface

The Windows Azure Platform is Microsoft's Platform-as-a-Service environment for hosting services and data in the cloud. It provides developers with on-demand compute, storage, and service connectivity capabilities that facilitate the hosting of highly-scalable services in Windows Azure datacenters across the globe.

This practical cookbook will show you advanced development techniques for building highly-scalable, cloud-based services using the Windows Azure Platform. It contains several practical, task-based, and immediately usable recipes covering a wide range of advanced development techniques for building highly scalable services to solve particular problems/ scenarios when developing these services on the Windows Azure Platform. The solutions are presented in a clear systematic manner and explained in great detail, which makes them good learning material for everyone who has experience of the Windows Azure Platform and wants to improve.

Packed with reusable, real-world recipes, the book starts by explaining the various access control mechanisms used in the Windows Azure platform. Next, you will see the advanced features of Windows Azure Blob storage, Windows Azure Table storage, and Windows Azure Queues. The book then dives deep into topics such as developing Windows Azure hosted services, using Windows Azure Diagnostics, managing hosted services with the Service Management API, using SQL Azure and the Windows Azure AppFabric Service Bus. You will see how to use several of the latest features such as VM roles, Windows Azure Connect, startup tasks, and the Windows Azure AppFabric Caching Service.

The Windows Azure Platform is changing rapidly with new features being released or previewed every few months. However, the core of the platform remains stable. This cookbook focuses on that core but, where appropriate, points out the direction the platform is moving in. Using this book, you can build advanced scalable cloud-based services with the Windows Azure Platform.

What this book covers

Chapter 1, Controlling Access in the Windows Azure Platform, shows you techniques that applications can use to authenticate against the Windows Azure Storage Service, the Windows Azure Service Management API, and the Windows Azure AppFabric Caching service. This authentication provides applications with secure access to the resources managed by these services. The chapter also shows how to control public access to Windows Azure blobs.

Chapter 2, Handling Blobs in Windows Azure, shows how to use the Windows Azure Storage Client library and the Windows Azure Storage Services REST API to access the Windows Azure Blob Service. It demonstrates various techniques for uploading and downloading block and page blobs. The chapter also shows how to use the Windows Azure Content Delivery Network (CDN) to optimize the distribution of blobs.

Chapter 3, Going NoSQL with Windows Azure Tables, shows how to use the Windows Azure Storage Client library and WCF Data Services to access the Windows Azure Table Service. It shows how to create a scalable data model and how to upload and download entities conforming to that model. The chapter also shows how to use the lightweight transaction capability provided by entity group transactions.

Chapter 4, Disconnecting with Windows Azure Queues, shows how to use the Windows Azure Storage Client Library to manage and access the Windows Azure Queue Service. It shows how to insert and retrieve messages from a queue. The chapter also shows how to handle poison messages.

Chapter 5, Developing Hosted Services for Windows Azure, shows how to develop and deploy an application as a Windows Azure hosted service. It shows how to create an appropriate service model for an application. For web roles, it shows how to use a custom domain name and implement HTTPS, as well as use the Windows Azure AppFabric Caching service to share session state. The chapter also shows how to use Windows Azure Connect and the Windows Azure MarketPlace DataMarket.

Chapter 6, Digging into Windows Azure Diagnostics, shows how to use Windows Azure Diagnostics to capture diagnostic data on a hosted service and persist it to the Windows Azure Storage Service. The chapter also shows how to access Windows Azure Diagnostics remotely, both to manage it and to access the diagnostic data for analysis.

Chapter 7, Managing Hosted Services with the Service Management API, shows how to use the Windows Azure Service Management REST API to manage a Windows Azure hosted service. It shows how to create and upgrade deployments of a hosted service, including how to modify the number of role instances for that service. The chapter also shows how to use the Windows Azure Platform PowerShell cmdlets to manage a Windows Azure hosted service.

Chapter 8, Using SQL Azure, shows how to use SQL Azure and, specifically, how to migrate to SQL Azure. It shows how to manage ADO.NET connections to SQL Azure and how to handle the connection failures that are more prevalent in that environment. The chapter also shows how to scale out a SQL Azure database into the Windows Azure Blob Service.

Chapter 9, Looking at the Windows Azure AppFabric, covers various features of the Windows Azure AppFabric. It shows how to use the relay and event capability of the Windows Azure AppFabric Service Bus. The chapter also shows how to use the Windows Azure AppFabric Caching service to scale out Windows Azure hosted services.

What you need for this book

This book requires you to have some exposure to Windows Azure and you need basic understanding of Visual Studio, C#, SQL, .NET development, XML, and web development concepts (HTTP, Services, and so on).

Who this book is for

If you are an experienced Windows Azure developer or architect who wants to understand advanced development techniques when building highly scalable services using the Windows Azure platform, then this book is for you.

Conventions

In this book, you will find a number of styles of text that distinguish between different kinds of information. Here are some examples of these styles, and an explanation of their meaning.

Code words in text are shown as follows: "We can include other contexts through the use of the `include` directive."

A block of code is set as follows:

```
String containerName = "chapter2";
String blobName = "DownloadBlobExample";
String fileName = Path.GetTempPath() + @"\Pippo";
DownloadBlob(containerName, blobName, fileName);
```

When we wish to draw your attention to a particular part of a code block, the relevant lines or items are set in bold:

```
String containerName = "chapter2";
String blobName = "DownloadBlobExample";
String fileName = Path.GetTempPath() + @"\BlobName";
DownloadBlob(containerName, blobName, fileName);
```

Any command-line input or output is written as follows:

```
# makecert -sky exchange -r -pe -a sha1 -len 2048 -sr localmachine
    -ss My -n "CN=Azure Service Management" AzureServiceManagement.cer
```

New terms and **important words** are shown in bold. Words that you see on the screen, in menus or dialog boxes for example, appear in the text like this: "On the Windows Azure Compute node, right click on an instance node and select **View IntelliTrace logs**".

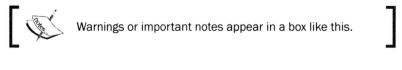

Warnings or important notes appear in a box like this.

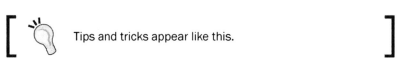

Tips and tricks appear like this.

Reader feedback

Feedback from our readers is always welcome. Let us know what you think about this book—what you liked or may have disliked. Reader feedback is important for us to develop titles that you really get the most out of.

To send us general feedback, simply send an e-mail to feedback@packtpub.com, and mention the book title via the subject of your message.

If there is a book that you need and would like to see us publish, please send us a note in the **SUGGEST A TITLE** form on www.packtpub.com or e-mail suggest@packtpub.com.

If there is a topic that you have expertise in and you are interested in either writing or contributing to a book, see our author guide on www.packtpub.com/authors.

Customer support

Now that you are the proud owner of a Packt book, we have a number of things to help you to get the most from your purchase.

Downloading the example code for this book

You can download the example code files for all Packt books you have purchased from your account at http://www.PacktPub.com. If you purchased this book elsewhere, you can visit http://www.PacktPub.com/support and register to have the files e-mailed directly to you.

Errata

Although we have taken every care to ensure the accuracy of our content, mistakes do happen. If you find a mistake in one of our books—maybe a mistake in the text or the code—we would be grateful if you would report this to us. By doing so, you can save other readers from frustration and help us improve subsequent versions of this book. If you find any errata, please report them by visiting http://www.packtpub.com/support, selecting your book, clicking on the **errata submission form** link, and entering the details of your errata. Once your errata are verified, your submission will be accepted and the errata will be uploaded on our website, or added to any list of existing errata, under the Errata section of that title. Any existing errata can be viewed by selecting your title from http://www.packtpub.com/support.

Piracy

Piracy of copyright material on the Internet is an ongoing problem across all media. At Packt, we take the protection of our copyright and licenses very seriously. If you come across any illegal copies of our works, in any form, on the Internet, please provide us with the location address or website name immediately so that we can pursue a remedy.

Please contact us at copyright@packtpub.com with a link to the suspected pirated material.

We appreciate your help in protecting our authors, and our ability to bring you valuable content.

Questions

You can contact us at questions@packtpub.com if you are having a problem with any aspect of the book, and we will do our best to address it.

1
Controlling Access in the Windows Azure Platform

In this chapter, we will cover:

- ▶ Managing Windows Azure Storage Service access keys
- ▶ Connecting to the Windows Azure Storage Service
- ▶ Using `SetConfigurationSettingPublisher()`
- ▶ Connecting to the storage emulator
- ▶ Managing access control for containers and blobs
- ▶ Creating a Shared Access Signature for a container or blob
- ▶ Using a container-level access policy
- ▶ Authenticating against the Windows Azure Service Management REST API
- ▶ Authenticating with the Windows Azure AppFabric Caching Service

Introduction

The various components of the **Windows Azure Platform** are exposed using Internet protocols. Consequently, they need to support authentication so that access to them can be controlled.

The **Windows Azure Storage Service** manages the storage of blobs, queues, and tables. It is essential that this data be kept secure, so that there is no unauthorized access to it. Each storage account has an account name and an access key which are used to authenticate access to the storage service. The management of these access keys is important. The storage service provides two access keys for each storage account, so that the access key not being used can be regenerated. We see how to do this in the *Managing Windows Azure Storage Service access keys* recipe.

The storage service supports **hash-based message authentication** (**HMAC**), in which a storage operation request is hashed with the access key. On receiving the request, the storage service validates it and either accepts or denies it. The **Windows Azure Storage Client** library provides several classes that support various ways of creating an HMAC, and which hide the complexity of creating and using one. We see how to use them in the *Connecting to the Windows Azure Storage Service* recipe. The `SetConfigurationSettingPublisher()` method has caused some programmer grief, so we look at it in the *Using SetConfigurationSettingPublisher()* recipe.

The **Windows Azure SDK** provides a compute emulator and a storage emulator. The latter uses a hard-coded account name and access key. We see the support provided for this in the *Connecting to the storage emulator* recipe.

Blobs are ideal for storing static content for web roles, so the storage service provides several authentication methods for access to containers and blobs. Indeed, a container can be configured to allow anonymous access to the blobs in it. Blobs in such a container can be downloaded without any authentication. We see how to configure this in the *Managing access control for containers and blobs* recipe.

There is a need to provide an intermediate level of authentication for containers and blobs, a level that lies between full authentication and anonymous access. The storage service supports the concept of a shared access signature, which is a pre-calculated authentication token and can be shared in a controlled manner allowing the bearer to access a specific container or blob for up to one hour. We see how to do this in the *Creating a shared access signature for a container or blob* recipe.

A shared access policy combines access rights with a time for which they are valid. A container-level access policy is a shared access policy that is associated by name with a container. A best practice is to derive a shared access signature from a container-level access policy. Doing this provides greater control over the shared access signature as it becomes possible to revoke it. We see how do this in the *Using a container-level access policy* recipe.

There is more to the Windows Azure Platform than storage. The **Windows Azure Service Management REST API** is a RESTful API that provides programmatic access to most of the functionality available on the Windows Azure Portal. This API uses X.509 certificates for authentication. Prior to use, the certificate must be uploaded, as a *management certificate*, to the Windows Azure Portal. The certificate must then be added as a certificate to each request made against the Service Management API. We see how to do this in the *Authenticating against the Windows Azure Service Management REST API* recipe.

The **Windows Azure AppFabric** services use a different authentication scheme, based on a service namespace and authentication token. In practice, these are similar to the account name and access key used to authenticate against the storage service, although the implementation is different. The Windows Azure AppFabric services use the **Windows Azure Access Control Service** (**ACS**) to perform authentication. However, this is abstracted away in the various SDKs provided for the services. We see how to authenticate to one of these services in the *Authenticating with the Windows Azure AppFabric Caching Service* recipe.

Managing Windows Azure Storage Service access keys

The data stored by the Windows Azure Storage Service must be secured against unauthorized access. To ensure that security, all storage operations against the table service and the queue service must be authenticated. Similarly, other than inquiry requests against public containers and blobs, all operations against the blob service must also be authenticated. The blob service supports public containers so that, for example, blobs containing images can be downloaded directly into a web page.

Each storage account has a primary access key and a secondary access key that can be used to authenticate operations against the storage service. When creating a request against the storage service, one of the keys is used along with various request headers to generate a 256-bit, hash-based message authentication code (HMAC). This HMAC is added as an *Authorization* request header to the request. On receiving the request, the storage service recalculates the HMAC and rejects the request if the received and calculated HMAC values differ. The Windows Azure Storage Client library provides methods that manage the creation of the HMAC and attaching it to the storage operation request.

There is no distinction between the primary and secondary access keys. The purpose of the secondary access key is to enable continued use of the storage service while the other access key is being regenerated. While the primary access key is used for authentication against the storage service, the secondary access key can be regenerated without affecting the service—and vice versa. This can be extremely useful in situations where storage access credentials must be rotated regularly.

As possession of the storage account name and access key is sufficient to provide full control over the data managed by the storage account, it is essential that the access keys be kept secure. In particular, access keys should never be downloaded to a client, such as a Smartphone, as that exposes them to potential abuse.

In this recipe, we will learn how to use the primary and secondary access keys.

Getting ready

This recipe requires a deployed Windows Azure hosted service that uses a Windows Azure storage account.

How to do it...

We are going to regenerate the secondary access key for a storage account and configure a hosted service to use it. We do this as follows:

1. Go to the Windows Azure Portal.
2. In the Storage Accounts section, regenerate the secondary access key for the desired storage account.
3. In the Hosted Services section, configure the desired hosted service and replace the value of `AccountKey` in the `DataConnectionString` setting with the newly generated secondary access key.

How it works...

In step 2, we can choose which access key to regenerate. It is important that we never regenerate the access key currently being used since doing so immediately renders the storage account inaccessible. Consequently, we regenerate only the secondary access key if the primary access key is currently in use—and vice versa.

In step 3, we upgrade the service configuration to use the access key we just generated. This change can be trapped and handled by the hosted service. However, it should not require the hosted service to be recycled. We see how to handle configuration changes in the *Handling changes to the configuration and topology of a hosted service* recipe in *Chapter 5*.

Connecting to the Windows Azure Storage Service

In a Windows Azure hosted service, the storage account name and access key are stored in the service configuration file. By convention, the account name and access key for data access are provided in a setting named `DataConnectionString`. The account name and access key needed for Windows Azure diagnostics **must** be provided in a setting named `Microsoft.WindowsAzure.Plugins.Diagnostics.ConnectionString`.

The `DataConnectionString` setting must be declared in the `ConfigurationSettings` section of the service definition file. However, unlike other settings, the connection string setting for Windows Azure diagnostics is implicitly defined when the diagnostics module is specified in the `Imports` section of the service definition file. Consequently, it must not be specified in the `ConfigurationSettings` section.

A best practice is to use different storage accounts for application data and diagnostic data. This reduces the possibility of application data access being throttled by competition for concurrent writes from the diagnostics monitor. It also provides a security boundary between application data and diagnostics data, as diagnostics data may be accessed by individuals who should have no access to application data.

In the Windows Azure Storage Client library, access to the storage service is through one of the *client* classes. There is one client class for each of Blob service, Queue service, and Table service—`CloudBlobClient`, `CloudQueueClient`, and `CloudTableClient` respectively. Instances of these classes store the pertinent endpoint, as well as the account name and access key.

The `CloudBlobClient` class provides methods to access containers list their contents and get references to containers and blobs. The `CloudQueueClient` class provides methods to list queues and to get a reference to the `CloudQueue` instance used as an entry point to the Queue service functionality. The `CloudTableClient` class provides methods to manage tables and to get the `TableServiceContext` instance used to access the **WCF Data Services** functionality used in accessing the Table service. Note that `CloudBlobClient`, `CloudQueueClient`, and `CloudTableClient` instances are not thread safe so distinct instances should be used when accessing these services concurrently.

The client classes must be initialized with the account name and access key, as well as the appropriate storage service endpoint. The `Microsoft.WindowsAzure` namespace has several helper classes. The `StorageCredentialsAccountAndKey` class initializes a `StorageCredential` instance from an account name and access key while the `StorageCredentialsSharedAccessSignature` class initializes a `StorageCredential` instance from a shared access signature. The `CloudStorageAccount` class provides methods to initialize an encapsulated `StorageCredential` instance directly from the service configuration file.

In this recipe, we will learn how to use `CloudBlobClient`, `CloudQueueClient`, and `CloudTableClient` instances to connect to the storage service.

Getting ready

This recipe assumes the application configuration file contains the following:

```
<appSettings>
  <add key="DataConnectionString"
    value="DefaultEndpointsProtocol=https;AccountName={ACCOUNT_NAME};
    AccountKey={ACCOUNT_KEY}"/>
  <add key="AccountName" value="{ACCOUNT_NAME}"/>
  <add key="AccountKey" value="{ACCOUNT_KEY}"/>
</appSettings>
```

> **Downloading the example code for this book**
>
> You can download the example code files for all Packt books you have purchased from your account at `http://www.PacktPub.com`. If you purchased this book elsewhere, you can visit `http://www.PacktPub.com/support` and register to have the files e-mailed directly to you.

We must replace {ACCOUNT_NAME} and {ACCOUNT_KEY} with appropriate values for the storage account name and access key.

How to do it...

We are going to connect to the Table service, the Blob service, and the Queue service to perform a simple operation on each. We do this as follows:

1. Add a new class named ConnectingToStorageExample to the project.
2. Add the following using statements to the top of the class file:

```
using Microsoft.WindowsAzure;
using Microsoft.WindowsAzure.StorageClient;
using System.Configuration;
```

3. Add the following method, connecting to the blob service, to the class:

```
private static void UseCloudStorageAccountExtensions()
{
    CloudStorageAccount cloudStorageAccount =
      CloudStorageAccount.Parse(
      ConfigurationManager.AppSettings[
      "DataConnectionString"]);

    CloudBlobClient cloudBlobClient =
      cloudStorageAccount.CreateCloudBlobClient();
    CloudBlobContainer cloudBlobContainer =
      cloudBlobClient.GetContainerReference(
      "{CONTAINER_NAME}");

    cloudBlobContainer.Create();
}
```

4. Add the following method, connecting to the Table service, to the class:

```
private static void UseCredentials()
{
    String accountName = ConfigurationManager.AppSettings[
        "AccountName"];
    String accountKey = ConfigurationManager.AppSettings[
        "AccountKey"];
    StorageCredentialsAccountAndKey storageCredentials =
        new StorageCredentialsAccountAndKey(
            accountName, accountKey);

    CloudStorageAccount cloudStorageAccount =
        new CloudStorageAccount(storageCredentials, true);
    CloudTableClient tableClient =
        new CloudTableClient(
            cloudStorageAccount.TableEndpoint.AbsoluteUri,
            storageCredentials);

    Boolean tableExists =
        tableClient.DoesTableExist("{TABLE_NAME}");
}
```

5. Add the following method, connecting to the Queue service, to the class:

```
private static void UseCredentialsWithUri()
{
    String accountName = ConfigurationManager.AppSettings[
        "AccountName"];
    String accountKey = ConfigurationManager.AppSettings[
        "AccountKey"];
    StorageCredentialsAccountAndKey storageCredentials =
        new StorageCredentialsAccountAndKey(
            accountName, accountKey);

    String baseUri =
        String.Format("https://{0}.queue.core.windows.net/",
            accountName);
    CloudQueueClient cloudQueueClient =
        new CloudQueueClient(baseUri, storageCredentials);
    CloudQueue cloudQueue =
        cloudQueueClient.GetQueueReference("{QUEUE_NAME}");

    Boolean queueExists = cloudQueue.Exists();
}
```

6. Add the following method, using the other methods, to the class:

```
public static void UseConnectionToStorageExample()
{
    UseCloudStorageAccountExtensions();
    UseCredentials();
    UseCredentialsWithUri();
}
```

How it works...

In steps 1 and 2, we set up the class.

In step 3, we implement the standard way to access the storage service using the Storage Client library. We use the static `CloudStorageAccount.Parse()` method to create a `CloudStorageAccount` instance from the value of the connection string stored in the configuration file. We then use this instance with the `CreateCloudBlobClient()` extension method to the `CloudStorageAccount` class to get the `CloudBlobClient` instance we use to connect to the Blob service. We can also use this technique with the Table service and the Queue service using the relevant extension methods for them: `CreateCloudTableClient()` and `CreateCloudQueueClient()` respectively. We complete this example by using the `CloudBlobClient` instance to get a `CloudBlobContainer` reference to a container and then fetch its attributes. We need to replace {CONTAINER_NAME} with the name for a container.

In step 4, we create a `StorageCredentialsAccountAndKey` instance directly from the account name and access key. We then use this to construct a `CloudStorageAccount` instance, specifying that any connection should use HTTPS. Using this technique, we need to provide the Table service endpoint explicitly when creating the `CloudTableClient` instance. We then use this to verify the existence of a table. We need to replace {TABLE_NAME} with the name for a table. We can use the same technique with the Blob service and Queue service by using the relevant `CloudBlobClient` or `CloudQueueClient` constructor.

In step 5, we use a similar technique except that we avoid the intermediate step of using a `CloudStorageAccount` instance and explicitly provide the endpoint for the Queue service. We use the `CloudQueueClient` instance created in this step to verify the existence of a queue. We need to replace {QUEUE_NAME} with the name of a queue. Note that we have hard-coded the endpoint for the Queue service.

In step 6, we add a method that invokes the methods added in the earlier steps.

Using SetConfigurationSettingPublisher()

The `CloudStorageAccount` class in the Windows Azure Storage Client library encapsulates a `StorageCredential` instance that can be used to authenticate against the Windows Azure Storage Service. It also exposes a `FromConfigurationSetting()` factory method that creates a `CloudStorageAccount` instance from a configuration setting.

This method has caused much confusion since, without additional configuration, it throws an `InvalidOperationException` with a message of "`SetConfigurationSettingPublisher` needs to be called before `FromConfigurationSetting()` can be used." Consequently, before using `FromConfigurationSetting()`, it is necessary to invoke `SetConfigurationSettingPublisher()` once. The intent of this method is that it can be used to specify alternate ways of retrieving the data connection string that `FromConfigurationSetting()` uses to initialize the `CloudStorageAccount` instance. This setting is process-wide, so is typically done in the `OnStart()` method of the `RoleEntryPoint` class for the role.

The following is a simple implementation for `SetConfigurationSettingPublisher()`:

```
CloudStorageAccount.SetConfigurationSettingPublisher(
(configName, configSetter) =>
{
   configSetter(RoleEnvironment.GetConfigurationSettingValue(
      configName));
});
```

There are several levels of indirection here, but the central feature is the use of a method that takes a `String` parameter specifying the name of the configuration setting and returns the value of that setting. In the example here, the method used is `RoleEnvironment.GetConfigurationSettingValue()`. The configuration-setting publisher can be set to retrieve configuration settings from any location including `app.config` or `web.config`.

The use of `SetConfigurationSettingPublisher()` is no longer encouraged. Instead, it is better to use `CloudStorageAccount.Parse()`, which takes a data connection string in canonical form and creates a `CloudStorageAccount` instance from it. We see how to do this in the *Connecting to the Windows Azure Storage Service* recipe.

In this recipe, we will learn how to set and use a configuration-setting publisher to retrieve the data connection string from a configuration file.

How to do it...

We are going to add an implementation for `SetConfigurationSettingPublisher()` to a worker role. We do this as follows:

1. Create a new cloud project.

2. Add a worker role to the project.

3. Add the following to the `WorkerRole` section of the `ServiceDefinition.csdef` file:

```
<ConfigurationSettings>
    <Setting name="DataConnectionString" />
</ConfigurationSettings>
```

4. Add the following to the `ConfigurationSettings` section of the `ServiceConfiguration.cscfg` file:

```
<Setting name="DataConnectionString" value="DefaultEndpointsProtoc
ol=https;AccountName={ACCOUNT_NAME};AccountKey={ACCOUNT_KEY}"/>
```

5. Replace `WorkerRole.Run()` with the following:

```
public override void Run()
{
    UseFromConfigurationSetting("{CONTAINER_NAME}");

    while (true)
    {
        Thread.Sleep(10000);
        Trace.WriteLine("Working", "Information");
    }
}
```

6. Replace `WorkerRole.OnStart()` with the following:

```
public override bool OnStart()
{
    ServicePointManager.DefaultConnectionLimit = 12;

    CloudStorageAccount.SetConfigurationSettingPublisher(
      (configName, configSetter) =>
    {
        configSetter(RoleEnvironment.GetConfigurationSettingValue(
        configName));
    });

    return base.OnStart();
}
```

7. Add the following method, implicitly using the configuration setting publisher, to the `WorkerRole` class:

```
private void UseFromConfigurationSetting(String containerName)
{
    CloudStorageAccount cloudStorageAccount =
      CloudStorageAccount.FromConfigurationSetting(
        "DataConnectionString");

    CloudBlobClient cloudBlobClient =
      cloudStorageAccount.CreateCloudBlobClient();
    CloudBlobContainer cloudBlobContainer =
      cloudBlobClient.GetContainerReference(containerName);

    cloudBlobContainer.Create();
}
```

How it works...

In steps 1 and 2, we set up the project.

In steps 3 and 4, we define and provide a value for the `DataConnectionString` setting in the service definition and service configuration files. We must replace `{ACCOUNT_NAME}` and `{ACCOUNT_KEY}` with appropriate values for the account name and access key.

In step 5, we modify the `Run()` method to invoke a method that accesses the storage service. We must provide an appropriate value for `{CONTAINER_NAME}`.

In step 6, we modify the `OnStart()` method to set a configuration setting publisher for the role instance. We set it to retrieve configuration settings from the service configuration file.

In step 7, we invoke `CloudStorageAccount.FromConfigurationSetting()`, which uses the configuration setting publisher we added in step 6. We then use the `CloudStorageAccount` instance to create `CloudBlobClient` and `CloudBlobContainer` instances that we use to create a new container in blob storage.

Connecting to the storage emulator

The Windows Azure SDK provides a **compute emulator** and a **storage emulator** that work in a development environment to provide a local emulation of Windows Azure hosted services and storage services. There are some differences in functionality between storage services and the storage emulator. Prior to Windows Azure SDK v1.3, the storage emulator was named development storage.

By default, the storage emulator uses SQL Server Express, but it can be configured to use SQL Server.

An immediate difference is that the storage emulator supports only one account name and access key. The account name is hard-coded to be `devstoreaccount1`. The access key is hard-coded to be:

```
Eby8vdM02xNOcqFlqUwJPLlmEtlCDXJ1OUzFT50uSRZ6IFsuFq2UVErCz4I6tq/
K1SZFPTOtr/KBHBeksoGMGw==
```

Another difference is that the storage endpoints are constructed differently for the storage emulator. The storage service uses URL subdomains to distinguish the endpoints for the various types of storage. For example, the endpoint for the Blob service for a storage account named *myaccount* is:

```
myaccount.blob.core.windows.net
```

The endpoints for the other storage types are constructed similarly by replacing the word `blob` with either `table` or `queue`.

This differentiation by subdomain name is not used in the storage emulator which is hosted on the local host at `127.0.0.1`. Instead, the storage emulator distinguishes the endpoints for various types of storage through use of different ports. Furthermore, the account name, rather than being part of the subdomain, is provided as part of the URL. Consequently, the endpoints used by the storage emulator are as follows:

 ▸ `127.0.0.1:10000/devstoreaccount1`   `Blob`
 ▸ `127.0.0.1:10001/devstoreaccount1`   `Queue`
 ▸ `127.0.0.1:10002/devstoreaccount1`   `Table`

The Windows Azure Storage Client library hides much of this complexity but an understanding of it remains important in case something goes wrong. The account name and access key are hard-coded into the Storage Client library, which also provides simple access to an appropriately constructed `CloudStorageAccount` object.

The Storage Client library also supports a special value for the `DataConnectionString` in the service configuration file. Instead of specifying the account name and access key, it is sufficient to specify the following:

```
UseDevelopmentStorage=true
```

For example, this is specified as follows in the service configuration file:

```
<Setting name="DataConnectionString" value="UseDevelopmentStorage=true
" />
```

This value can also be used for the `Microsoft.WindowsAzure.Plugins.Diagnostics.` `ConnectionString` data connection string required for Windows Azure Diagnostics.

The `CloudStorageAccount.Parse()` and `CloudStorageAccount.` `FromConnectionString()` methods handle this value in a special way to create a `CloudStorageAccount` object that can be used to authenticate against the storage emulator.

In this recipe, we will learn how to connect to the storage emulator.

Getting ready

This recipe assumes the following is in the application configuration file:

```
<appSettings>
   <add key="DataConnectionString"
        value="UseDevelopmentStorage=true"/>
</appSettings>
```

How to do it...

We are going to connect to the storage emulator in various ways and perform some operations on blobs. We do this as follows:

1. Add a class named `StorageEmulatorExample` to the project.

2. Add the following `using` statements to the top of the class file:

   ```
   using Microsoft.WindowsAzure;
   using Microsoft.WindowsAzure.StorageClient;
   using System.Configuration;
   ```

3. Add the following private members to the class:

   ```
   private String containerName;
   private String blobName;
   ```

4. Add the following constructor to the class:

   ```
   StorageEmulatorExample(String containerName, String blobName)
   {
   this.containerName = containerName;
   this.blobName = blobName;
   }
   ```

5. Add the following method, using the configuration file, to the class:

   ```
   private void UseConfigurationFile()
   {
      CloudStorageAccount cloudStorageAccount =
        CloudStorageAccount.Parse(
   ```

```
    ConfigurationManager.AppSettings[
    "DataConnectionString"]);

  CloudBlobClient cloudBlobClient =
    cloudStorageAccount.CreateCloudBlobClient();
  CloudBlobContainer cloudBlobContainer =
    cloudBlobClient.GetContainerReference(containerName);
  cloudBlobContainer.Create();
}
```

6. Add the following method, using an explicit storage account, to the class:

```
private void CreateStorageCredential()
{
  String baseAddress =
    "http://127.0.0.1:10000/devstoreaccount1";
  String accountName = "devstoreaccount1";
  String accountKey =
"Eby8vdM02xNOcqFlqUwJPLlmEtlCDXJ1OUzFT50uSRZ6IFsuFq2UVErCz4I6tq/
K1SZFPTOtr/KBHBeksoGMGw==";
  StorageCredentialsAccountAndKey storageCredentials = new
    StorageCredentialsAccountAndKey(accountName, accountKey);

  CloudBlobClient cloudBlobClient =
    new CloudBlobClient(baseAddress, storageCredentials);
  CloudBlobContainer cloudBlobContainer =
    cloudBlobClient.GetContainerReference(containerName);
  CloudBlockBlob cloudBlockBlob =
    cloudBlobContainer.GetBlockBlobReference(blobName);

  cloudBlockBlob.UploadText("If we shadows have offended.");
  cloudBlockBlob.Metadata["{METADATA_KEY}"] =
    "{METADATA_VALUE}";
  cloudBlockBlob.SetMetadata();
}
```

7. Add the following method, using the `CloudStorageAccount.DevelopmentStorageAccount` property, to the class:

```
private void UseDevelopmentStorageAccount()
{
  CloudStorageAccount cloudStorageAccount =
    CloudStorageAccount.DevelopmentStorageAccount;

  CloudBlobClient cloudBlobClient =
    cloudStorageAccount.CreateCloudBlobClient();
  CloudBlobContainer cloudBlobContainer =
    cloudBlobClient.GetContainerReference(containerName);
```

```
CloudBlockBlob cloudBlockBlob =
   cloudBlobContainer.GetBlockBlobReference(blobName);

cloudBlockBlob.FetchAttributes();
BlobAttributes blobAttributes = cloudBlockBlob.Attributes;
String metadata =
   blobAttributes.Metadata["{METADATA_KEY}"];
}
```

8. Add the following method, using the methods added earlier, to the class:

```
public static void UseStorageEmulatorExample()
{
    String containerName = "{CONTAINER_NAME}";
    String blobName = "{BLOB_NAME}";

    StorageEmulatorExample example =
       new StorageEmulatorExample(containerName, blobName);

    example.UseConfigurationFile();
    example.CreateStorageCredential();
    example.UseDevelopmentStorageAccount();
}
```

How it works...

In steps 1 and 2, we set up the class. In step 3, we add some private members for the container name and blob name, which we initialize in the constructor we add in step 4.

In step 5, we retrieve a data connection string from a configuration file and pass it into `CloudStorageAccount.Parse()` to create a `CloudStorageAccount` instance. We use this to get references to a `CloudBlobContainer` instance for the specified container. We use this to create the container.

In step 6, we create a `StorageCredentialsAccountAndKey` instance from the explicitly provided storage emulator values for account name and access key. We use the resulting `StorageCredential` to initialize a `CloudStorageClient` object, explicitly providing the storage emulator endpoint for blob storage. We then create a reference to a blob, upload some text to the blob, define some metadata for the blob, and finally update the blob with it. We must replace {METADATA_KEY} AND {METADATA_VALUE} with actual values.

In step 7, we initialize a `CloudStorageAccount` from the hard-coded `CloudStorageAccount` property exposed by the class. We then get a `CloudBlockBlob` object, which we use to retrieve the properties stored on the blob and retrieve the metadata we added in step 6. We should replace {METADATA_KEY} with the same value that we used in step 6.

In step 8, we add a helper method that invokes each of the methods we added earlier. We must replace {CONTAINER_NAME} and {BLOB_NAME} with appropriate names for the container and blob.

There's more...

Fiddler is a program that captures HTTP traffic, which makes it very useful for diagnosing problems when using the Windows Azure Storage Service. Its use is completely transparent when cloud storage is being used. However, the data connection string must be modified if you want Fiddler to be able to monitor the traffic. The data connection string must be changed to the following:

```
UseDevelopmentStorage=true;DevelopmentStorageProxyUri=http://ipv4.
fiddler
```

Fiddler can be downloaded from the following URL:

```
http://www.fiddler2.com/fiddler2/
```

Managing access control for containers and blobs

The Windows Azure Storage Service authenticates all requests against the Table service and Queue service. However, the storage service allows the possibility of unauthenticated access against the Blob service. The reason is that blobs provide an ideal location for storing large static content for a website. For example, the images in a photo-sharing site could be stored as blobs and downloaded directly from the Blob service without being transferred through a web role.

Public access control for the Blob service is managed at the container level. The Blob service supports the following three types of access control:

- ▶ No public read access in which all access must be authenticated
- ▶ Public read access which allows blobs in a container to be readable without authentication
- ▶ Full public read access in which authentication is not required to read the container data and the blobs contained in it

No public read access is the same access control as for the Queue service and Table service. The other two access control types both allow anonymous access to a blob, so that, for example, the blob can be downloaded into a browser by providing its full URL.

In the Windows Azure Storage Client library, the `BlobContainerPublicAccessType` enumeration specifies the three types of public access control for a container. The `BlobContainerPermissions` class exposes two properties: `PublicAccess` specifying a member of the `BlobContainerPublicAccessType` enumeration and `SharedAccessPolicies` specifying a set of shared access policies. The `SetPermissions()` method of the `CloudBlobContainer` class is used to associate a `BlobContainerPermissions` instance with the container. The `GetPermissions()` method retrieves the access permissions for a container.

In this recipe, we will learn how to specify the level of public access control for containers and blobs managed by the Blob service.

Getting ready

This recipe assumes the following is in the application configuration file:

```
<appSettings>
    <add key="DataConnectionString"
value="DefaultEndpointsProtocol=https;AccountName={ACCOUNT_NAME};Accou
ntKey={ACCOUNT_KEY}"/>
</appSettings>
```

We must replace {ACCOUNT_NAME} and {ACCOUNT_KEY} with appropriate values for the account name and access key.

How to do it...

We are going to specify various levels of public access control for a container. We do this as follows:

1. Add a new class named `BlobContainerPublicAccessExample` to the project.

2. Add the following `using` statements to the top of the class file:

    ```
    using Microsoft.WindowsAzure;
    using Microsoft.WindowsAzure.StorageClient;
    using System.Configuration;
    using System.Net;
    ```

3. Add the following method, setting public access control for a container, to the class:

    ```
    public static void CreateContainerAndSetPermission(
      String containerName, String blobName,
      BlobContainerPublicAccessType publicAccessType )
    {
      CloudStorageAccount cloudStorageAccount =
        CloudStorageAccount.Parse(
        ConfigurationManager.AppSettings[
    ```

```
    "DataConnectionString"]);
CloudBlobClient cloudBlobClient =
  cloudStorageAccount.CreateCloudBlobClient();

CloudBlobContainer blobContainer =
  new CloudBlobContainer(containerName, cloudBlobClient);
blobContainer.Create();

BlobContainerPermissions blobContainerPermissions =
  new BlobContainerPermissions()
{
    PublicAccess = publicAccessType
};
blobContainer.SetPermissions(blobContainerPermissions);

CloudBlockBlob blockBlob =
  blobContainer.GetBlockBlobReference(blobName);
blockBlob.UploadText("Has been changed glorious summer");
}
```

4. Add the following method, retrieving a blob, to the class:

```
public static void GetBlob(
  String containerName, String blobName)
{
  CloudStorageAccount cloudStorageAccount =
    CloudStorageAccount.Parse(
    ConfigurationManager.AppSettings[
    "DataConnectionString"]);
  Uri blobUri = new Uri(cloudStorageAccount.BlobEndpoint +
    containerName + "/" + blobName);

  HttpWebRequest httpWebRequest =
    (HttpWebRequest)HttpWebRequest.Create(blobUri);
  httpWebRequest.Method = "GET";
  using (HttpWebResponse response =
    (HttpWebResponse)httpWebRequest.GetResponse())
  {
    String status = response.StatusDescription;
  }
}
```

5. Add the following method, using the method we just added, to the class:

```
public static void UseBlobContainerPublicAccessExample()
{
    CreateContainerAndSetPermission("container1", "blob1",
        BlobContainerPublicAccessType.Blob);

    CreateContainerAndSetPermission("container2", "blob2",
        BlobContainerPublicAccessType.Container);

    CreateContainerAndSetPermission("container3", "blob3",
        BlobContainerPublicAccessType.Off);
}
```

How it works...

In steps 1 and 2, we set up the class.

In step 3, we add a method that creates a container and blob, and applies a public access policy to the container. We create a `CloudBlobClient` instance from the data connection string in the configuration file. We then create a new container using the name passed in to the method. Then, we create a `BlobContainerPermissions` instance with the `BlobContainerPublicAccessType` passed into the method and set the permissions on the container. Note that we must create the container before we set the permissions because `SetPermissions()` sets the permissions directly on the container. Finally, we create a blob in the container.

In step 4, we use an `HttpWebRequest` instance to retrieve the blob without providing any authentication. This request causes a **404 (Not Found)** error when the request attempts to retrieve a blob that has not been configured for public access. Note that when constructing `blobUri` for the storage emulator, we must add a / into the path after `cloudStorageAccount.BlobEndpoint` because of a difference in the way the Storage Client library constructs the endpoint for the storage emulator and the storage service. For example, we need to use the following for the storage emulator:

```
Uri blobUri = new Uri(cloudStorageAccount.BlobEndpoint + "/" +
    containerName + "/" + blobName);
```

In step 5, we add a method that invokes the `CreateContainerAndSetPermission()` method once for each value of the `BlobContainerPublicAccessType` enumeration. We then invoke the method twice, to retrieve blobs from different container. The second invocation leads to a **404** error since `container3` has not been configured for unauthenticated public access.

See also

▸ The recipe named *Creating a Shared Access Signature for a container or blob* in this chapter

Creating a Shared Access Signature for a container or blob

The Windows Azure Blob Service supports fully authenticated requests, anonymous requests, and requests authenticated by a temporary access key referred to as a Shared Access Signature. The latter allows access to containers or blobs to be limited to only those in possession of the Shared Access Signature.

A Shared Access Signature is constructed from a combination of:

▸ Resource (container or blob)

▸ Access rights (read, write, delete, list)

▸ Start time

▸ Expiration time

These are combined into a string from which a 256-bit, hash-based message authentication code (HMAC) is generated. An access key for the storage account is used to seed the HMAC generation. This HMAC is referred to as a shared access signature. The process of generating a Shared Access Signature requires no interaction with the Blob service. A shared access signature is valid for up to one hour, which limits the allowable values for the start time and expiration time.

When using a Shared Access Signature to authenticate a request, it is submitted as one of the query string parameters. The other query parameters comprise the information from which the shared access signature was created. This allows the Blob service to create a Shared Access Signature, using the access key for the storage account, and compare it with the Shared Access Signature submitted with the request. A request is denied if it has an invalid Shared Access Signature.

An example of a storage request for a blob named `theBlob` in a container named `chapter1` is:

```
GET /chapter1/theBlob
```

An example of the query string parameters is:

```
st=2011-03-22T05%3A49%3A09Z
&se=2011-03-22T06%3A39%3A09Z
&sr=b
&sp=r
&sig=GLqbiDwYweXW4y2NczDxmWDzrJCc89oFfgBMTieGPww%3D
```

The `st` parameter is the start time for the validity of the Shared Access Signature. The `se` parameter is the expiration time for the validity of the Shared Access Signature. The `sr` parameter specifies that the Shared Access Signature is for a blob. The `sp` parameter specifies that the Shared Access Signature authenticates for read access only. The `sig` parameter is the Shared Access Signature. A complete description of these parameters is available on MSDN at the following URL:

```
http://msdn.microsoft.com/en-us/library/ee395415.aspx
```

Once a Shared Access Signature has been created and transferred to a client, no further verification of the client is required. It is important, therefore, that the Shared Access Signature be created with the minimum period of validity and that its distribution be restricted as much as possible. It is not possible to revoke a Shared Access Signature created in this manner.

In this recipe, we will learn how to create and use a Shared Access Signature.

Getting ready

This recipe assumes the following is in the application configuration file:

```
<appSettings>
    <add key="DataConnectionString"
value="DefaultEndpointsProtocol=https;AccountName={ACCOUNT_NAME};Accou
ntKey={ACCOUNT_KEY}"/>
    <add key="AccountName" value="{ACCOUNT_NAME}"/>
    <add key="AccountKey" value="{ACCOUNT_KEY}"/>
</appSettings>
```

We must replace {ACCOUNT_NAME} and {ACCOUNT_KEY} with appropriate values for the account name and access key.

How to do it...

We are going to create and use Shared Access Signatures for a blob. We do this as follows:

1. Add a class named `SharedAccessSignaturesExample` to the project.

2. Add the following `using` statements to the top of the class file:

```
using Microsoft.WindowsAzure;
using Microsoft.WindowsAzure.StorageClient;
using System.Configuration;
using System.Net;
using System.IO;
using System.Security.Cryptography;
```

3. Add the following private members to the class:

```
private String blobEndpoint;
private String accountName;
private String accountKey;
```

4. Add the following constructor to the class:

```
SharedAccessSignaturesExample()
{
   CloudStorageAccount cloudStorageAccount =
     CloudStorageAccount.Parse(
     ConfigurationManager.AppSettings[
     "DataConnectionString"]);
   blobEndpoint =
     cloudStorageAccount.BlobEndpoint.AbsoluteUri;
   accountName = cloudStorageAccount.Credentials.AccountName;


   StorageCredentialsAccountAndKey accountAndKey =
     cloudStorageAccount.Credentials as
     StorageCredentialsAccountAndKey;
   accountKey =
     accountAndKey.Credentials.ExportBase64EncodedKey();
}
```

5. Add the following method, creating a container and blob, to the class:

```
private void CreateContainerAndBlob(
  String containerName, String blobName)
{
  CloudStorageAccount cloudStorageAccount =
    CloudStorageAccount.Parse(
    ConfigurationManager.AppSettings[
      "DataConnectionString"]);
  CloudBlobClient cloudBlobClient =
    cloudStorageAccount.CreateCloudBlobClient();
  CloudBlobContainer cloudBlobContainer =
    new CloudBlobContainer(containerName, cloudBlobClient);
  cloudBlobContainer.Create();
  CloudBlockBlob cloudBlockBlob =
    cloudBlobContainer.GetBlockBlobReference(blobName);
  cloudBlockBlob.UploadText("This weak and idle theme.");
}
```

6. Add the following method, getting a Shared Access Signature, to the class:

```
private String GetSharedAccessSignature(
  String containerName, String blobName)
{
    SharedAccessPolicy sharedAccessPolicy =
      new SharedAccessPolicy()
    {
      Permissions = SharedAccessPermissions.Read,
      SharedAccessStartTime =
        DateTime.UtcNow.AddMinutes(-10d),
      SharedAccessExpiryTime =
        DateTime.UtcNow.AddMinutes(40d)
    };

    CloudStorageAccount cloudStorageAccount =
      CloudStorageAccount.Parse(
        ConfigurationManager.AppSettings[
        "DataConnectionString"]);
    CloudBlobClient cloudBlobClient =
      cloudStorageAccount.CreateCloudBlobClient();
    CloudBlobContainer cloudBlobContainer =
      new CloudBlobContainer(containerName, cloudBlobClient);
    CloudBlockBlob cloudBlockBlob =
      cloudBlobContainer.GetBlockBlobReference(blobName);

    String sharedAccessSignature =
      cloudBlockBlob.GetSharedAccessSignature(
        sharedAccessPolicy);

    return sharedAccessSignature;
}
```

7. Add the following method, creating a Shared Access Signature, to the class:

```
private String CreateSharedAccessSignature(
  String containerName, String blobName, String permissions)
{
    String iso8061Format = "{0:yyyy-MM-ddTHH:mm:ssZ}";
    DateTime startTime = DateTime.UtcNow;
    DateTime expiryTime = startTime.AddHours(1d);
    String start = String.Format(iso8061Format, startTime);
    String expiry = String.Format(iso8061Format, expiryTime);
    String stringToSign =
      String.Format("{0}\n{1}\n{2}\n/{3}/{4}\n",
      permissions, start, expiry, accountName, containerName);

    String rawSignature = String.Empty;
```

```
    Byte[] keyBytes = Convert.FromBase64String(accountKey);
    using (HMACSHA256 hmacSha256 = new HMACSHA256(keyBytes))
    {
        Byte[] utf8EncodedStringToSign =
          System.Text.Encoding.UTF8.GetBytes(stringToSign);
        Byte[] signatureBytes =
          hmacSha256.ComputeHash(utf8EncodedStringToSign);
        rawSignature = Convert.ToBase64String(signatureBytes);
    }

    String sharedAccessSignature =
      String.Format("?st={0}&se={1}&sr=c&sp={2}&sig={3}",
        Uri.EscapeDataString(start),
        Uri.EscapeDataString(expiry),
        permissions,
        Uri.EscapeDataString(rawSignature));

    return sharedAccessSignature;
}
```

8. Add the following method, authenticating with a Shared Access Signature, to the class:

```
private void AuthenticateWithSharedAccessSignature(
  String containerName, String blobName,
  String sharedAccessSignature)
{
    StorageCredentialsSharedAccessSignature storageCredentials
      = new StorageCredentialsSharedAccessSignature(
        sharedAccessSignature);
    CloudBlobClient cloudBlobClient =
      new CloudBlobClient(blobEndpoint, storageCredentials);

    CloudBlobContainer cloudBlobContainer =
      new CloudBlobContainer(containerName, cloudBlobClient);
    CloudBlockBlob cloudBlockBlob =
      cloudBlobContainer.GetBlockBlobReference(blobName);
    String blobText = cloudBlockBlob.DownloadText();
}
```

9. Add the following method, using a Shared Access Signature, to the class:

```
private void UseSharedAccessSignature(
  String containerName, String blobName,
  String sharedAccessSignature)
{
    String requestMethod = "GET";
    String urlPath = String.Format("{0}{1}/{2}{3}",
```

```
    blobEndpoint, containerName, blobName,
      sharedAccessSignature);
  Uri uri = new Uri(urlPath);
  HttpWebRequest request =
    (HttpWebRequest)WebRequest.Create(uri);
  request.Method = requestMethod;
  using (HttpWebResponse response =
    (HttpWebResponse)request.GetResponse())
  {
    Stream dataStream = response.GetResponseStream();
    using (StreamReader reader =
      new StreamReader(dataStream))
    {
      String responseFromServer = reader.ReadToEnd();
    }
  }
}
```

10. Add the following method, using the methods added earlier, to the class:

```
public static void UseSharedAccessSignaturesExample()
{
  String containerName = "{CONTAINER_NAME}";
  String blobName = "{BLOB_NAME}";

  SharedAccessSignaturesExample example =
    new SharedAccessSignaturesExample();

  example.CreateContainerAndBlob(containerName, blobName);

  String sharedAccessSignature1 =
    example.GetSharedAccessSignature(
      containerName, blobName);
  example.AuthenticateWithSharedAccessSignature(
      containerName, blobName, sharedAccessSignature1);

  String sharedAccessSignature2 =
    example.CreateSharedAccessSignature(
      containerName, blobName, "rw");
  example.UseSharedAccessSignature(
    containerName, blobName, sharedAccessSignature2);
}
```

How it works...

In steps 1 and 2, we set up the class. In step 3, we add some private members for the blob endpoint, as well as the account name and access key which we initialize in the constructor we add in step 4. In step 5, we create a container and upload a blob to it.

In step 6, we use the `GetSharedAccessSignature()` method of the `CloudBlockBlob` class to get a shared access signature based on a `SharedAccessPolicy` we pass into it. In this `SharedAccessPolicy`, we specify that we want read access on a blob from 10 minutes earlier to 40 minutes later than the current time. The fuzzing of the start time is to minimize any risk of the time on the local machine being too far out of sync with the time on the storage service. This approach is the easiest way to get a shared access signature.

In step 7, we construct a Shared Access Signature from first principles. This version does not use the Storage Client library. We generate a string to sign from the account name, desired permissions, start, and expiration time. We initialize an `HMACSHA256` instance from the access key, and use this to generate an HMAC from the string to sign. We then create the remainder of the query string while ensuring that the data is correctly URL encoded.

In step 8, we use a shared access signature to initialize a `StorageCredentialsSharedAccessSignature` instance, which we use to create a `CloudBlobClient` instance. We use this to construct the `CloudBlobContainer` and `CloudBlobClient` instances we use to download the content of a blob.

In step 9, we use `HttpWebRequest` and `HttpWebResponse` objects to perform an anonymous download of the content of a blob. We construct the query string for the request using the Shared Access Signature and direct the request to the appropriate blob endpoint. Note that when constructing `urlPath` for the storage emulator, we must add a / between `{0}` and `{1}` because of a difference in the way the Storage Client library constructs the endpoint for the storage emulator and the storage service. For example, we need to use the following for the storage emulator:

```
String urlPath = String.Format("{0}/{1}/{2}{3}",
    blobEndpoint, containerName, blobName,
    sharedAccessSignature);
```

In step 10, we add a helper method that invokes all the methods we added earlier. We must replace `{CONTAINER_NAME}` and `{BLOB_NAME}` with appropriate names for the container and blob.

There's more...

In step 7, we could create a Shared Access Signature based on a container-level access policy by replacing the definition of `stringToSign` with the following:

```
String stringToSign = String.Format(
  "\n\n\n/{0}/{1}\n{2}", accountName, containerName, policyId);
```

`policyId` specifies the name of a container-level access policy.

See also

▸   The recipe named *Using a container-level access policy* in this chapter

Using a container-level access policy

A shared access policy comprises a set of permissions (read, write, delete, list) combined with start and expiration times for validity of the policy. There are no restrictions on the start and expiration times for a shared access policy. A container-level access policy is a shared access policy associated by name with a container. A maximum of five container-level access policies can be associated simultaneously with a container, but each must have a distinct name.

A container-level access policy improves the management of shared access signatures. There is no way to retract or otherwise disallow a standalone shared access signature once it has been created. However, a shared access signature created from a container-level access policy has validity dependent on the container-level access policy. The deletion of a container-level access policy causes the revocation of all shared access signatures derived from it and they can no longer be used to authenticate a storage request. As they can be revoked at any time, there are no time restrictions on the validity of a shared access signature derived from a container-level access policy.

The container-level access policies for a container are set and retrieved as a `SharedAccessPolicies` collection of named `SharedAccessPolicy` objects. The `SetPermissions()` and `GetPermissions()` methods of the `CloudBlobContainer` class set and retrieve container-level access policies. A container-level access policy can be removed by retrieving the current `SharedAccessPolicies`, removing the specified policy, and then setting the `SharedAccessPolicies` on the container again.

A shared access signature is derived from a container-level access policy by invoking the `CloudBlobContainer.GetSharedAccessSignature()` passing in the name of the container-level access policy and an empty `SharedAccessPolicy` instance. It is not possible to modify the validity of the shared-access signature by using a non-empty `SharedAccessPolicy`.

In this recipe, we will learn how to manage container-level access policies and use them to create shared access signatures.

Getting ready

This recipe assumes the following is in the application configuration file:

```
<appSettings>
  <add key="DataConnectionString"
value="DefaultEndpointsProtocol=https;AccountName={ACCOUNT_NAME};Accou
ntKey={ACCOUNT_KEY}"/>
</appSettings>
```

We must replace {ACCOUNT_NAME} and {ACCOUNT_KEY} with appropriate values for the account name and access key.

How to do it...

We are going to create, use, modify, revoke, and delete a container-level access policy. We do this as follows:

1. Add a class named ContainerLevelAccessPolicyExample to the project.

2. Add the following using statements to the top of the class file:

    ```
    using Microsoft.WindowsAzure;
    using Microsoft.WindowsAzure.StorageClient;
    using System.Configuration;
    ```

3. Add the following private members to the class:

    ```
    private Uri blobEndpoint;
    private CloudBlobContainer cloudBlobContainer;
    ```

4. Add the following constructor to the class:

    ```
    ContainerLevelAccessPolicyExample()
    {
       CloudStorageAccount cloudStorageAccount =
         CloudStorageAccount.Parse(
         ConfigurationManager.AppSettings[
         "DataConnectionString"]);
       blobEndpoint = cloudStorageAccount.BlobEndpoint;

       CloudBlobClient cloudBlobClient =
         cloudStorageAccount.CreateCloudBlobClient();
       cloudBlobContainer =
         new CloudBlobContainer(containerName, cloudBlobClient);
       cloudBlobContainer.Create();
    }
    ```

5. Add the following method, creating a container-level access policy, to the class:

```
private void AddContainerLevelAccessPolicy(String policyId)
{
    DateTime startTime = DateTime.UtcNow;
    SharedAccessPolicy sharedAccessPolicy =
      new SharedAccessPolicy()
    {
        Permissions = SharedAccessPermissions.Read |
          SharedAccessPermissions.Write,
        SharedAccessStartTime = startTime,
        SharedAccessExpiryTime = startTime.AddDays(3d)
    };

    BlobContainerPermissions blobContainerPermissions =
      new BlobContainerPermissions();
    blobContainerPermissions.SharedAccessPolicies.Add(
      policyId, sharedAccessPolicy);

    blobContainer.SetPermissions(blobContainerPermissions);
}
```

6. Add the following method, getting a shared access signature using the container-level access policy, to the class:

```
private String GetSharedAccessSignature(String policyId)
{
    SharedAccessPolicy sharedAccessPolicy =
      new SharedAccessPolicy();
    String sharedAccessSignature =
      cloudBlobContainer.GetSharedAccessSignature(
        sharedAccessPolicy, policyId);

    return sharedAccessSignature;
}
```

7. Add the following method, modifying the container-level access policy, to the class:

```
private void ModifyContainerLevelAccessPolicy(String policyId)
{
    BlobContainerPermissions blobContainerPermissions =
      cloudBlobContainer.GetPermissions();

    DateTime sharedAccessExpiryTime =
      (DateTime)blobContainerPermissions.SharedAccessPolicies[
        policyId].SharedAccessExpiryTime;
    blobContainerPermissions.SharedAccessPolicies[
      policyId].SharedAccessExpiryTime =
```

```
        sharedAccessExpiryTime.AddDays(1d);

    blobContainer.SetPermissions(blobContainerPermissions);
}
```

8. Add the following method, revoking a container-level access policy, to the class:

```
private void RevokeContainerLevelAccessPolicy(String policyId)
{
    BlobContainerPermissions containerPermissions =
        cloudBlobContainer.GetPermissions();

    SharedAccessPolicy sharedAccessPolicy =
        containerPermissions.SharedAccessPolicies[policyId];
    containerPermissions.SharedAccessPolicies.Remove(policyId);
    containerPermissions.SharedAccessPolicies.Add(
        policyId + "1", sharedAccessPolicy);

    cloudBlobContainer.SetPermissions(containerPermissions);
}
```

9. Add the following method, deleting all container-level access policies, to the class:

```
private void DeleteContainerLevelAccessPolicies()
{
    BlobContainerPermissions blobContainerPermissions =
        new BlobContainerPermissions();

    blobContainer.SetPermissions(blobContainerPermissions);
}
```

10. Add the following method, using the methods added earlier, to the class:

```
public static void UseContainerLevelAccessPolicyExample()
{
    String containerName = "{CONTAINER_NAME}";
    String policyId = "{POLICY_NAME}";

    ContainerLevelAccessPolicyExample example =
        new ContainerLevelAccessPolicyExample(containerName);

    example.AddContainerLevelAccessPolicy(policyId);
    String sharedAccessSignature1 =
        example.GetSharedAccessSignature(policyId);

    example.ModifyContainerLevelAccessPolicy(policyId);
    String sharedAccessSignature2 =
        example.GetSharedAccessSignature(policyId);
```

```
        example.RevokeContainerLevelAccessPolicy(policyId);
        String sharedAccessSignature3 =
            example.GetSharedAccessSignature(policyId + "1");

        example.DeleteContainerLevelAccessPolicies();
    }
```

How it works...

In steps 1 and 2, we set up the class. In step 3, we add some private members which we initialize in the constructor we add in step 4. We also create a container in the constructor.

In step 5, we create a `SharedAccessPolicy` instance and add it to the `SharedAccessPolicies` property of a `BlobContainerPermissions` object. Finally, we pass this and a policy name into a `SetPermissions()` method of the `CloudBlobContainer` class to create a container-level access policy name for the container.

In step 6, we get a shared access signature for a container with a specified container-level access policy. We initialize a `CloudStorageAccount` from the application configuration and use this to get a `CloudBlobContainer` instance for a specified container. Finally, we pass the policy name into the `CloudBlobContainer.GetSharedAccessSignature()` method to get a shared access signature for the container.

In step 7, we again get a `CloudBlobContainer` instance for the container and invoke `GetPermissions()` on it to retrieve the shared access policies for the container. We then add one day to the expiration date for a specified container-level access policy. Finally, we invoke `CloudBlobContainer.SetPermissions()` to update the container-level access policies for the container.

In step 8, we revoke an existing container-level access policy and create a new container-level policy with the same `SharedAccessPolicy` and a new policy name. We again use `GetPermissions()` to retrieve the shared access policies for the container and then invoke the `Remove()` and `Add()` methods of the `SharedAccessPolicies` class to perform the revocation. Finally, we invoke `CloudBlobContainer.SetPermissions()` to update the container-level access policies for the container.

In step 9, we delete all container-level access policies for a container. We create a default `BlobContainerPermissions` instance and pass this into `CloudBlobContainer.SetPermissions()` to remove all the container-level access policies for the container.

In step 10, we add a helper method that invokes all the methods we added earlier. We need to replace `{CONTAINER_NAME}` and `{POLICY_NAME}` with the names of a container and a policy for it.

Authenticating against the Windows Azure Service Management REST API

The Windows Azure Portal provides a user interface for managing Windows Azure hosted services and storage accounts. The Windows Azure Service Management REST API provides a RESTful interface that allows programmatic control of hosted services and storage accounts. It supports most, but not all, of the functionality provided in the Windows Azure Portal.

The Service Management API uses an X.509 certificate for authentication. This certificate must be uploaded as a *management certificate* to the Windows Azure Portal. Unlike service certificates, management certificates are not deployed to role instances. Consequently, if the Service Management API is to be accessed from an instance of a role, it is necessary to upload the certificate twice: as a management certificate for authentication and as a server certificate that is deployed to the instance. The latter also requires appropriate configuration in the service definition and service configuration files.

A management certificate can be self-signed because it is used only for authentication. As Visual Studio uses the Service Management API to upload and deploy packages, it contains tooling supporting the creation of the certificate. This is an option on the **Publish** dialog. A management certificate can also be created using `makecert` as follows:

```
C:\Users\Administrator>makecert -r -pe -sky exchange
-a sha1 -len 2048 -ss my -n "CN=Azure Service Management"
AzureServiceManagement.cer
```

This creates an X.509 certificate and installs it in the Personal (My) branch of the Current User level of the certificate store. It also creates a file named `AzureServiceManagement.cer` containing the certificate in a form that can be uploaded as a management certificate to the Windows Azure Portal. The certificate is self-signed (-r), with an exportable private key (-pe), created with the SHA-1 hash algorithm (-a), a 2048-bit key (-len), and with a key type of exchange (-sky).

Once created, the certificate must be uploaded to the **Management Certificates** section of the Windows Azure Portal. This section is at the subscription level—not the service level—as the Service Management API has visibility across all hosted services and storage accounts under the subscription.

In this recipe, we will learn how to authenticate to the Windows Azure Service Management REST API.

How to do it...

We are going to authenticate against the Windows Azure Service Management REST API and retrieve the list of hosted services for the subscription. We do this as follows:

1. Add a class named `ServiceManagementExample` to the project.

2. Add the following using statements to the top of the class file:

```
using System.Net;
using System.IO;
using System.Xml.Linq;
using System.Security.Cryptography.X509Certificates;
```

3. Add the following private members to the class:

```
XNamespace ns = "http://schemas.microsoft.com/windowsazure";
String apiVersion = "2011-02-25";
String subscriptionId;
String thumbprint;
```

4. Add the following constructor to the class:

```
ServiceManagementExample(
   String subscriptionId, String thumbprint)
{
   this.subscriptionId = subscriptionId;
   this.thumbprint = thumbprint;
}
```

5. Add the following method, retrieving the client authentication certificate from the certificate store, to the class:

```
private static X509Certificate2 GetX509Certificate2(
   String thumbprint)
{
   X509Certificate2 x509Certificate2 = null;
   X509Store store =
      new X509Store("My", StoreLocation.CurrentUser);
   try
   {
      store.Open(OpenFlags.ReadOnly);
      X509Certificate2Collection x509Certificate2Collection =
         store.Certificates.Find(
            X509FindType.FindByThumbprint, thumbprint, false);
      x509Certificate2 = x509Certificate2Collection[0];
   }
   finally
   {
      store.Close();
   }
   return x509Certificate2;
}
```

6. Add the following method, creating a web request, to the project:

```
private HttpWebRequest CreateHttpWebRequest(
  Uri uri, String httpWebRequestMethod)
{
    X509Certificate2 x509Certificate2 =
      GetX509Certificate2(thumbprint);

    HttpWebRequest httpWebRequest =
       (HttpWebRequest)HttpWebRequest.Create(uri);
    httpWebRequest.Method = httpWebRequestMethod;
    httpWebRequest.Headers.Add("x-ms-version", apiVersion);
    httpWebRequest.ClientCertificates.Add(x509Certificate2);
    httpWebRequest.ContentType = "application/xml";

    return httpWebRequest;
}
```

7. Add the following method, invoking a Get Services operation on the Service Management API, to the class:

```
private IEnumerable<String> GetHostedServices()
{
    String responseFromServer = String.Empty;
    XElement xElement;

    String uriPath = String.Format(
"https://management.core.windows.net/{0}/services/hostedservices",
subscriptionId);
    Uri uri = new Uri(uriPath);

    HttpWebRequest httpWebRequest =
      CreateHttpWebRequest(uri, "GET");
    using (HttpWebResponse response =
      (HttpWebResponse)httpWebRequest.GetResponse())
    {
      Stream responseStream = response.GetResponseStream();
      xElement = XElement.Load(responseStream);
    }

    IEnumerable<String> serviceNames =
      from s in xElement.Descendants(ns + "ServiceName")
      select s.Value;

    return serviceNames;
}
```

8. Add the following method, invoking the methods added earlier, to the class:

```
public static void UseServiceManagementExample()
{
    String subscriptionId = "{SUBSCRIPTION_ID}";
    String thumbprint = "{THUMBPRINT}";

    ServiceManagementExample example =
        new ServiceManagementExample(subscriptionId, thumbprint);
    IEnumerable<String> serviceNames =
        example.GetHostedServices();
    List<String> listServiceNames =
        serviceNames.ToList<String>();
}
```

How it works...

In steps 1 and 2, we set up the class. In step 3, we add some private members including the `subscriptionId` and `thumbprint` that we initialize in the constructor we add in step 4. The `ns` member specifies the namespace used in the XML data returned by the Service Management API. In `apiVersion`, we specify the API version sent with each request to the Service Management API. The supported versions are listed on MSDN at `http://msdn.microsoft.com/en-us/library/gg592580.aspx`. Note that the API version is updated whenever new operations are added and that an operation can use a newer API version than the one it was released with.

In step 5, we retrieve the X.509 certificate we use to authenticate against the Service Management API. We use the certificate thumbprint to find the certificate in the Personal/Certificates (My) branch of the Current User level of the certificate store.

In step 6, we create and initialize the `HttpWebRequest` used to submit an operation to the Service Management API. We add the X.509 certificate to the request. We also add an `x-ms-version` request header specifying the API version of the Service Management API we are using.

In step 7, we submit the request to the Service Management API. We first construct the appropriate URL, which depends on the particular operation to be performed. Then, we make the request and load the response into a `XElement`. We query this `XElement` to retrieve the names of the hosted services created for the subscription and return them in an `IEnumerable<String>`.

In step 8, we add a helper method that invokes each of the methods we added earlier. We must replace `{SUBSCRIPTION_ID}` with the subscription ID for the Windows Azure subscription and replace `{THUMBPRINT}` with the thumbprint of the management certificate. These can both be found on the Windows Azure Portal.

There's more...

The **Microsoft Management Console** (**MMC**) can be used to navigate the certificate store to view and, if desired, export an X.509 certificate. In MMC, the *Certificates* snap-in provides the choice of navigating through either the Current User or Local Machine level of the certificate store. The `makecert` command used earlier inserts the certificate in the Personal branch of the Current User level of the certificate store. The export certificate wizard can be found by selecting the certificate **All Tasks** on the right-click menu, and then choosing **Export....** This wizard supports export both with and without a private key. The former creates the `.CER` file needed for a management certificate while the latter creates the password-protected `.PFX` file needed for a service certificate for a hosted service.

The thumbprint is one of the certificate properties that are displayed in the MMC certificate snap-in. However, the snap-in displays the thumbprint as a space-separated, lower-case string. When using the thumbprint in code, it must be converted to an upper-case string with no spaces.

Authenticating with the Windows Azure AppFabric Caching Service

The Windows Azure AppFabric Caching Service provides a hosted data cache along with local caching of that data. It provides a cloud-hosted version of the Windows Server AppFabric Caching Service.

All access to the caching service must be authenticated using a service namespace and an authentication token. These are generated on the Windows Azure Portal. The service namespace is similar to the account name used with the storage services. It forms the base of the service URL used in accessing the caching service.

The Windows Azure **Access Control Service** (**ACS**) is used to authenticate requests to the caching service. However, the complexity of this is abstracted by the caching service SDK. A `DataCacheSecurity` instance is constructed from the authentication token. To reduce the likelihood of the authentication token remaining in memory in an accessible form, the `DataCacheSecurity` constructor requires that it be passed in as a `SecureString` rather than a simple `String`. This `DataCacheSecurity` instance is then added to a `DataCacheFactoryConfiguration` instance. This is used to initialize the `DataCacheFactory` used to create the `DataCache` object used to interact with the caching service.

In this recipe, we will learn how to authenticate to the Windows Azure AppFabric Caching Service.

Getting ready

This recipe uses the Windows Azure AppFabric SDK. It also requires the creation—on the Windows Azure Portal—of a namespace for the Windows Azure AppFabric Caching Service. We see how to do this in the *Creating a namespace for the Windows Azure AppFabric* recipe in *Chapter 9*.

How to do it...

We are going to authenticate against the Windows Azure AppFabric Caching Service and cache an item in the service. We do this as follows:

1. Add a class named `AppFabricCachingExample` to the project.

2. Add the following assembly references to the project:

```
Microsoft.ApplicationServer.Caching.Client
Microsoft.ApplicationServer.Caching.Core
```

3. Add the following `using` statements to the top of the class file:

```
using Microsoft.ApplicationServer.Caching;
using System.Security;
```

4. Add the following private members to the class:

```
Int32 cachePort = 22233;
String hostName;
String authenticationToken;
DataCache dataCache;
```

5. Add the following constructor to the class:

```
AppFabricCachingExample
   (String hostName, String authenticationToken)
{
   this.hostName = hostName;
   this.authenticationToken = authenticationToken;
}
```

6. Add the following method, creating a `SecureString`, to the class:

```
static private SecureString CreateSecureString(String token)
{
   SecureString secureString = new SecureString();
   foreach (char c in token)
   {
      secureString.AppendChar(c);
   }
   secureString.MakeReadOnly();
   return secureString;
}
```

7. Add the following method, initializing the cache, to the class:

```
private void InitializeCache()
{
    DataCacheSecurity dataCacheSecurity =
      new DataCacheSecurity(CreateSecureString(
        authenticationToken), false);

    List<DataCacheServerEndpoint> server =
      new List<DataCacheServerEndpoint>();
    server.Add(new DataCacheServerEndpoint(
      hostName, cachePort));

    DataCacheTransportProperties dataCacheTransportProperties =
      new DataCacheTransportProperties()
    {
      MaxBufferSize = 10000,
      ReceiveTimeout = TimeSpan.FromSeconds(45)
    };

    DataCacheFactoryConfiguration dataCacheFactoryConfiguration
      = new DataCacheFactoryConfiguration()
    {
      SecurityProperties = dataCacheSecurity,
      Servers = server,
      TransportProperties = dataCacheTransportProperties
    };

    DataCacheFactory myCacheFactory =
      new DataCacheFactory(dataCacheFactoryConfiguration);
    dataCache = myCacheFactory.GetDefaultCache();
}
```

8. Add the following method, inserting an entry to the cache, to the class:

```
private void PutEntry( String key, String value)
{
    dataCache.Put(key, value);
}
```

9. Add the following method, retrieving an entry from the cache, to the class:

```
private String GetEntry(String key)
{
    String playWright = dataCache.Get(key) as String;
    return playWright;
}
```

10. Add the following method, invoking the methods added earlier, to the class:

```
public static void UseAppFabricCachingExample()
{
    String hostName = "{SERVICE_NAMESPACE}.cache.windows.net";
    String authenticationToken = "{AUTHENTICATION_TOKEN}";

    String key = "{KEY}";
    String value = "{VALUE}";

    AppFabricCachingExample example =
        new AppFabricCachingExample();

    example.InitializeCache();
    example.PutEntry(key, value);
    String theValue = example.GetEntry(key);
}
```

How it works...

In steps 1 through 3, we set up the class. In step 4, we add some private members to hold the caching service endpoint information and the authentication token. We initialize these in the constructor we add in step 5.

In step 6, we add a method that creates a `SecureString` from a normal `String`. The authentication token used when working with the caching service SDK must be a `SecureString`. Typically, this would be initialized in a more secure fashion than from a private member.

In step 7, we first initialize the objects used to configure a `DataCacheFactory` object. We need to provide the authentication token and the caching service endpoint. We specify a `ReceiveTimeout` of less than 1 minute to reduce the possibility of an error caused by stale connections. We use the `DataCacheFactory` to get the `DataCache` for the default cache for the caching service. Note that in this recipe, we did not configure a local cache.

In step 8, we insert an entry in the cache. Note that we use `Put()` rather than `Add()` here, as `Add()` throws an error if the item is already cached. We retrieve it from the cache in step 9.

In step 10, we add a helper method that invokes each of the methods we added earlier. We must replace {SERVICE_NAMESPACE} and {AUTHENTICATION_TOKEN} with actual values for the caching service namespace and authentication token that we created on the Windows Azure Portal. We can replace {KEY} and {VALUE} with appropriate values.

2
Handling Blobs in Windows Azure

In this chapter, we will cover:

- ▶ Setting properties and metadata for a blob
- ▶ Using blob directories
- ▶ Creating and using a blob snapshot
- ▶ Creating and using the root container for blobs
- ▶ Uploading blocks to a block blob
- ▶ Uploading a VHD into a page blob
- ▶ Downloading a blob asynchronously
- ▶ Optimizing blob uploads and downloads
- ▶ Using retry policies with blob operations
- ▶ Copying a blob with the Windows Azure Storage Service REST API
- ▶ Leasing a blob using the Protocol classes in the Windows Azure Storage Client Library
- ▶ Using the Windows Azure Content-Delivery Network (CDN)

Introduction

The **Windows Azure Blob Service** is the Windows Azure Storage Service feature that manages the storage of file-based entities referred to as blobs. In this chapter, we will focus on the Blob service. In the next two chapters, we will look at the other storage services: the Table service and the Queue service.

The definitive way to access the storage service is through the Windows Azure Storage Service REST API. The Windows Azure Storage Client library is a high-level managed library, included in the Windows Azure SDK, which abstracts the RESTful interface into a set of classes. The Windows Azure Storage Client Protocol classes contained in the Storage Client library expose functionality not provided in the core library classes. Specifically, the protocol classes provide access to the underlying `HttpWebRequest` object used to invoke the RESTful operations.

Nearly all the recipes in this chapter use the Storage Client library. Scattered through the recipes are examples of how to use it for basic operations, such as creating a container and uploading blobs. However, we use the RESTful interface in the *Copying a blob with the Windows Azure Storage Service REST API* recipe. It is worthwhile to have some knowledge of the Storage Service REST API because it is informative to look at the raw REST operations sent over the wire to the storage service when debugging problems with storage operations. We use the Protocol classes in the *Leasing a blob using the Protocol classes in the Windows Azure Storage Client Library* recipe.

There are two types of blob: block blobs optimized for streaming and page blobs optimized for random access. In the *Uploading blocks to a block blob* recipe, we see how to increase control over the uploading of a block blob by uploading individual blocks and then committing them to create the block blob. In the *Uploading a VHD into a page blob* recipe, we see how to improve the upload performance by uploading only non-empty pages. The primary use case for page blobs is the storage of VHDs, which can then be attached as an Azure Drive to a role instance.

Blobs can have both properties and metadata associated with them. The properties comprise standard HTTP header fields that provide additional information to clients downloading the blobs. The metadata comprises a sequence of arbitrary name-value pairs. In the *Setting properties and metadata for a blob* recipe, we see how to use properties and metadata.

The Blob service supports the creation of a blob snapshot to provide a read-only version of the content of a blob when the snapshot is created. A blob can be rolled-back to an earlier state by copying the snapshot over it. An important use case for a snapshot is when its base blob is a VHD page blob. A writable VHD page blob can be attached as an Azure Drive to only one instance at a time. However, a read-only VHD blob snapshot can be attached simultaneously to an unlimited number of instances. The *Creating and using a blob snapshot* recipe shows us blob snapshots in action.

The Blob service stores blobs in a simple two-level hierarchy of containers and blobs. In the *Using blob directories* recipe we use the directory support provided by the Blob service to simulate a more complex hierarchy mimicking directories in a file system. In the *Creating and using the root container for blobs* recipe we see how to create a root directory that allows blobs to appear to be located at the root of the hierarchy and not inside a container. This allows cross-domain policy files to be stored as blobs.

The Storage Client library provides both synchronous and asynchronous versions of almost all methods that access the storage service. The asynchronous methods adhere to the common language runtime **Asynchronous Programming Model** (**APM**). In the *Downloading a blob asynchronously* recipe, we see how easy it is to use the asynchronous methods to download a blob. In the *Optimizing blob uploads and downloads* recipe, we see how to use the Task Parallel library provided in .NET Framework 4 to improve the performance of blob uploads and downloads by performing operations in parallel.

A storage operation against the storage service may fail for various reasons. Consequently, the Storage Client library provides built-in support for retries of failed operations. In the *Using retry policies with blob operations* recipe, we see how to parameterize existing retry behavior and implement custom retry functionality.

The Windows Azure Content Delivery Network (CDN) can be used to cache blobs closer to the user. This significantly improves the download performance of blobs. In the *Using the Windows Azure Content-Delivery Network (CDN)* recipe, we see how to use the CDN. We also see how to configure custom domains for both the Blob service and the CDN.

Setting properties and metadata for a blob

The Windows Azure Blob Service allows metadata and properties to be associated with a blob. The metadata comprises a sequence of developer-defined, name-value pairs. The properties comprise HTTP request headers including: *Cache-Control*, *Content-Encoding*, *Content-MD5*, and *Content-Type*. The Blob service also supports metadata and properties for blob containers. Requesting a download of the blob attributes—its metadata and properties—is an efficient way of checking blob existence as only a small amount of data is downloaded.

The Blob service uses the *Content-MD5* property to validate blob upload. When specified, the *Content-MD5* property must be set to the base64-encoded value of the MD5 hash of the blob data. The Blob service returns an error if this value does not match the value it calculates from the uploaded blob content.

In this recipe, we will learn how to set and get blob properties and metadata. We will also learn how to calculate the *Content-MD5* property.

How to do it...

We are going to create a blob and add some metadata and the *Content-MD5* property to it. We will then fetch the attributes of the blob to retrieve the property and metadata. We do this as follows:

1. Add a new class named `PropertiesMetadataExample` to the project.
2. Set the Target Framework for the project to .NET Framework 4.

3. Add the following assembly references to the project:

```
Microsoft.WindowsAzure.StorageClient
System.Configuration
```

4. Add the following using statements to the top of the class file:

```
using Microsoft.WindowsAzure;
using Microsoft.WindowsAzure.StorageClient;
using System.Configuration;
using System.Security.Cryptography;
using System.Collections.Specialized;
```

5. Add the following member to the class:

```
CloudBlobClient cloudBlobClient;
```

6. Add the following constructor to the class:

```
public PropertiesMetadataExample()
{
  CloudStorageAccount cloudStorageAccount =
    CloudStorageAccount.Parse(
    ConfigurationManager.AppSettings[
    "DataConnectionString"]);
  cloudBlobClient =
    cloudStorageAccount.CreateCloudBlobClient();
}
```

7. Add the following method, uploading a blob as a `Byte` array, to the class:

```
private void UploadByteArray(
  String containerName, String blobName)
{
  CloudBlobContainer cloudBlobContainer =
    cloudBlobClient.GetContainerReference(containerName);
  cloudBlobContainer.CreateIfNotExist();

  Byte[] blobData = { 0x41, 0x7A, 0x75, 0x72, 0x65 };
  CloudBlockBlob cloudBlockBlob =
    cloudBlobContainer.GetBlockBlobReference(blobName);
  cloudBlockBlob.Metadata["TodayIs"] = "Wednesday";
  cloudBlockBlob.Attributes.Properties.ContentMD5 =
    CalculateMD5Hash(blobData);
  cloudBlockBlob.UploadByteArray(blobData);
}
```

8. Add the following method, retrieving blob attributes, to the class:

```
private void FetchAttributes(String containerName,
  String blobName)
{
  CloudBlobContainer cloudBlobContainer =
    cloudBlobClient.GetContainerReference(containerName);
  CloudBlockBlob cloudBlockBlob =
    cloudBlobContainer.GetBlockBlobReference(blobName);

  cloudBlockBlob.FetchAttributes();

  BlobProperties blobProperties =
    cloudBlockBlob.Attributes.Properties;
  NameValueCollection blobMetadata =
    cloudBlockBlob.Attributes.Metadata;
  foreach (String key in blobMetadata)
  {
    String value = blobMetadata[key];
  }
}
```

9. Add a method, calculating the MD5 hash, to the class:

```
private static String CalculateMD5Hash(Byte[] bytes)
{
  MD5 md5 = MD5.Create();
  Byte[] md5Hash = md5.ComputeHash(bytes);
  String base64EncodedMD5Hash =
    Convert.ToBase64String(md5Hash);

  return base64EncodedMD5Hash;
}
```

10. Add the following method, using the methods added earlier, to the class:

```
public static void UsePropertiesMetadataExample()
{
  String containerName = "{CONTAINER_NAME}";
  String blobName = "{BLOB_NAME}";

  PropertiesMetadataExample example = new
    PropertiesMetadataExample();
  example.UploadByteArray(containerName, blobName);
  example.FetchAttributes(containerName, blobName);
}
```

11. Add the following to the `configuration` section of `app.config`:

```
<appSettings>
  <add key="DataConnectionString"
    value="DefaultEndpointsProtocol=http;
    AccountName={ACCOUNT_NAME};AccountKey={ACCOUNT_KEY}"/>
</appSettings>
```

How it works...

In steps 1 through 4, we set up the class. In step 5, we add a member to hold the `CloudBlobClient` instance we initialize in the constructor we add in step 6. We initialize the `CloudStorageAccount` instance from `app.config`.

In step 7, we add a method that creates a blob out of a `Byte` array, adds the calculated *Content-MD5* property to the blob, and associates some metadata, named `TodayIs`, with the blob. In step 8, we add a method that retrieves the attributes of a blob and iterates over any metadata associated with it.

In step 9, we add the method that calculates the base64-encoded MD5 hash for a `Byte[]`.

In step 10, we add a method that invokes the methods we added to the class. We must replace `{CONTAINER_NAME}` and `{BLOB_NAME}` with appropriate container and blob names.

In step 11, we add the connection string to the `app.config` configuration file. We must replace `{ACCOUNT_NAME}` and `{ACCOUNT_KEY}` with actual values for account name and access key.

Using blob directories

The Windows Azure Blob Service uses a simple organizational structure for containers and blobs. A storage account has zero or more containers each of which contains zero or more blobs. Containers contain only blobs and may not contain other containers. There is no hierarchy for containers.

The Windows Azure Storage Service REST API provides support for a simulation of a hierarchical directory structure through an ability to parse blob names containing a special delimiter character and navigate the list of blobs while taking account of that delimiter. This delimiter is the forward-slash symbol (/). The Windows Azure Storage Client library exposes this feature through the `CloudBlobDirectory` class.

The `CloudBlobDirectory` class provides methods allowing blobs to be enumerated in a way that takes account of the directory structure built into the naming convention used. A blob name can include multiple levels of directory.

A `CloudBlobDirectory` object can be created using either `CloudBlobClient.GetDirectoryReference()` or `CloudBlobContainer.GetDirectoryReference()`. The `CloudBlobDirectory` object refers to a particular level in the directory hierarchy. The blobs and directories in this directory can be retrieved using the synchronous `ListBlobs()` method, the asynchronous `BeginListBlobsSegmented()` method, and `EndListBlobsSegmented()`. The directory list can be pages through using the `ListBlobsSegmented()` method.

The various methods to list blobs provide the list as an `IEnumerable<IListBlobItem>`. The `IListBlobItem` interface is actually the base interface for `CloudBlob`, `CloudBlockBlob`, `CloudPageBlob`, and `CloudBlobDirectory`. Consequently, any given item in the list could be from any of these classes, so care must be taken that the item is handled correctly. This is similar to the way in which a file needs to be handled differently from a subdirectory when processing the contents of a directory in a file system.

The `CloudBlobDirectory` class also exposes methods that retrieve a strongly typed `CloudBlockBlob`, `CloudPageBlob`, or `CloudBlobDirectory` with a specified name that may include multiple levels in the directory hierarchy.

In this recipe, we will learn how to generate a list of the contents of a directory and traverse a directory hierarchy.

How to do it...

We are going to list the top-level contents of a directory. Then we will get the top-level directories and list their contents. We do this as follows:

1. Add a new class named `BlobDirectoryExample` to the project.
2. Set the Target Framework for the project to .NET Framework 4.
3. Add the following assembly references to the project:

    ```
    Microsoft.WindowsAzure.StorageClient
    System.Configuration
    ```

4. Add the following `using` statements to the top of the class file:

    ```
    using Microsoft.WindowsAzure;
    using Microsoft.WindowsAzure.StorageClient;
    using System.Configuration;
    ```

5. Add the following member to the class:

    ```
    private CloudBlobContainer cloudBlobContainer;
    ```

6. Add the following constructor to the class:

```
public BlobDirectoryExample(String containerName)
{
  CloudStorageAccount cloudStorageAccount =
    CloudStorageAccount.Parse(
    ConfigurationManager.AppSettings[
    "DataConnectionString"]);
  CloudBlobClient cloudBlobClient =
    cloudStorageAccount.CreateCloudBlobClient();
  cloudBlobContainer =
    cloudBlobClient.GetContainerReference(containerName);
}
```

7. Add a method, creating a container and adding blobs to it, to the class:

```
private void CreateContainerAndBlobs(String containerName)
{
  cloudBlobContainer.CreateIfNotExist();
  CreateBlob("Yosemite/ElCapitan");
  CreateBlob("Yosemite/ElCapitan/TheNose");
  CreateBlob("Yosemite/ElCapitan/SalatheWall");
  CreateBlob("Yosemite/HalfDome");
  CreateBlob("Yosemite/HalfDome/NorthRidge");
  CreateBlob("Yosemite/HalfDome/NorthWestFace");
  CreateBlob("Yosemite/HalfDome/Trail");
}
```

8. Add a method, uploading a blob, to the class:

```
private void CreateBlob(String blobName)
{
  CloudBlockBlob cloudBlockBlob =
    cloudBlobContainer.GetBlockBlobReference(blobName);
  cloudBlockBlob.UploadText("To be, or not to be");
}
```

9. Add a method, listing the top-level directory items, to the class:

```
private void ListTopLevelItems(String directoryName)
{
  CloudBlobDirectory cloudBlobDirectory =
    cloudBlobContainer.GetDirectoryReference(directoryName);

  IEnumerable<IListBlobItem> blobItems =
    cloudBlobDirectory.ListBlobs();
  foreach (IListBlobItem blobItem in blobItems)
  {
    Uri uri = blobItem.Uri;
  }
}
```

10. Add a method, traversing the directory tree, to the class:

```
private void TraverseDirectoryTree(String directoryName)
{
  CloudBlobDirectory cloudBlobDirectory =
    cloudBlobContainer.GetDirectoryReference(
    directoryName);

  IEnumerable<IListBlobItem> blobItems =
    cloudBlobDirectory.ListBlobs();
  foreach (CloudBlobDirectory cloudBlobDirectoryItem in
    blobItems.OfType<CloudBlobDirectory>())
  {
    Uri uri = cloudBlobDirectoryItem.Uri;

    IEnumerable<CloudBlockBlob> leafBlobs =
      cloudBlobDirectoryItem.ListBlobs().OfType<CloudBlockBlob>();
    foreach (CloudBlockBlob leafBlockBlob in leafBlobs)
    {
      Uri leafUri = leafBlockBlob.Uri;
    }
  }
}
```

11. Add the following method, using the methods added earlier, to the class:

```
public static void UseBlobDirectoryExample()
{
  String containerName = "{CONTAINER_NAME}";
  String directoryName = "Yosemite";

  BlobDirectoryExample blobDirectoryExample =
    new BlobDirectoryExample(containerName);
   blobDirectoryExample.CreateContainerAndBlobs(
      containerName);
  blobDirectoryExample.ListTopLevelItems(directoryName);
  blobDirectoryExample.TraverseDirectoryTree(directoryName);
}
```

12. Add the following to the `configuration` section of `app.config`:

```
<appSettings>
  <add key="DataConnectionString"
    value="DefaultEndpointsProtocol=http;
    AccountName={ACCOUNT_NAME};AccountKey={ACCOUNT_KEY}"/>
</appSettings>
```

How it works...

In steps 1 through 4, we set up the `BlobDirectoryExample` class. In step 5, we add a member which we initialize in the constructor we add in step 6.

In step 7, we create a container and then invoke `CreateBlob()` multiple times to create the blobs we use in the example. In step 8, we add `CreateBlob()` to upload a blob.

In step 9, we add a `ListTopLevelItems()` method that uses a `CloudBlobContainer` object for the current container to retrieve a `CloudBlobDirectory` object for the specified directory. We then invoke `CloudBlobDirectory.ListBlobs()` to generate a directory listing query which we invoke and enumerate. With the example blobs created earlier, this corresponds to the directory listing of *Yosemite* that retrieves two blobs and two directories.

In step 10, we add a `TraverseDirectoryTree()` method that uses a `CloudBlobContainer` object for the current container to retrieve a `CloudBlobDirectory` object for the specified directory. We then use `CloudBlobDirectory.ListBlobs()` to generate a directory listing query which we invoke and enumerate over while restricting the enumeration to only `CloudBlobDirectory` objects. We then use these `CloudBlobDirectory` objects as the base of separate invocations `CloudBlobDirectory.ListBlobs()` to retrieve lists of their contents.

In step 11, we add a method to use the methods we added earlier. We must replace `{CONTAINER_NAME}` with an appropriate container name.

In step 12, we add the connection string to the `app.config` configuration file. We must replace `{ACCOUNT_NAME}` and `{ACCOUNT_KEY}` with actual values for account name and access key.

Creating and using a blob snapshot

The Windows Azure Blob Service supports the creation of read-only snapshots of a blob. A storage account is billed only for those blocks and pages in a snapshot that differ from those in the underlying blob. A blob snapshot is useful in providing a backup for a blob as it can be used to reset the blob to an earlier state. Indeed, multiple snapshots can be made over time allowing a historic record to be kept of changes to a blob.

An important use case for blob snapshots is provided by the Azure Drive feature. An Azure Drive is a page blob comprising an NTFS-formatted VHD that can be attached to a hosted service role instance and accessed as an NTFS drive. To avoid read-write conflicts, a single VHD page blob can be attached to only one instance at a time. However, a blob snapshot is read-only, allowing no possibility of write contention, so an arbitrary number of instances can attach a VHD snapshot simultaneously.

A blob snapshot is created using the `CloudBlob.CreateSnapshot()` method. Each snapshot of a blob is distinguished by its creation time that must be provided to operations accessing the snapshot. A snapshot created at a particular `datetime` is addressed by appending a `snapshot={datetime}` query string to the URL identifying the underlying blob.

For example, the following is the complete URL for a snapshot taken on `11/25/2010` of a blob named `SnapshotsExample`:

```
http://myaccountname.blob.core.windows.net/ chapter2/SnapshotsExample
?snapshot=2010-11-25T02:02:40.1680568Z
```

The storage account is named `myaccountname` and the container is named `chapter2`.

In this recipe, we will learn how to create and use blob snapshots.

How to do it...

We are going to create a blob and create a snapshot of it. We are then going to download the snapshot. We do this as follows:

1. Add a new class named `SnapshotsExample` to the project.

2. Set the Target Framework for the project to .NET Framework 4.

3. Add the following assembly references to the project:

   ```
   Microsoft.WindowsAzure.StorageClient
   System.Configuration
   ```

4. Add the following `using` statements to the top of the class file:

   ```
   using Microsoft.WindowsAzure;
   using Microsoft.WindowsAzure.StorageClient;
   using System.Configuration;
   using System.IO;
   ```

5. Add the following private member to the class:

   ```
   private CloudBlobClient cloudBlobClient;
   ```

6. Add the following constructor to the class:

   ```
   public SnapshotsExample()
   {
     CloudStorageAccount cloudStorageAccount =
       CloudStorageAccount.Parse(
       ConfigurationManager.AppSettings[
       "DataConnectionString"]);
     cloudBlobClient =
       cloudStorageAccount.CreateCloudBlobClient();
   }
   ```

7. Add the following method, creating the container and a blob, to the class:

```
private void CreateContainerAndBlob(
  String containerName, String blobName)
{
  CloudBlobContainer cloudBlobContainer =
    cloudBlobClient.GetContainerReference(containerName);
  cloudBlobContainer.CreateIfNotExist();

  CloudBlockBlob cloudBlockBlob =
    cloudBlobContainer.GetBlockBlobReference(blobName);
  cloudBlockBlob.UploadText("To be, or not to be");
}
```

8. Add the following method, making a snapshot of the blob, to the class:

```
private DateTime MakeSnapshot(
  String containerName, String blobName)
{
  CloudBlobContainer cloudBlobContainer =
    cloudBlobClient.GetContainerReference(containerName);
  CloudBlockBlob cloudBlockBlob =
    cloudBlobContainer.GetBlockBlobReference(blobName);

  CloudBlob snapshot = cloudBlockBlob.CreateSnapshot();
  return (DateTime)snapshot.SnapshotTime;
}
```

9. Add the following method, retrieving the snapshot, to the class:

```
private void GetSnapshot(String containerName,
  String blobName, DateTime snapshotTime)
{
  String uriFix = "";
  if (cloudBlobClient.Credentials.AccountName ==
    "devstoreaccount1")
  {
    uriFix = "/";
  }
  String blobUri =
    String.Format("{0}{1}{2}/{3}?snapshot={4:O}",
    cloudBlobClient.BaseUri, uriFix, containerName, blobName,
    snapshotTime);
  CloudBlockBlob cloudBlockBlob =
    new CloudBlockBlob(blobUri, cloudBlobClient);

  using (MemoryStream memoryStream = new MemoryStream())
  {
```

```
    cloudBlockBlob.DownloadToStream(memoryStream);
    memoryStream.Position = 0;

    using (StreamReader streamReader =
      new StreamReader(memoryStream))
    {
      String blobText = streamReader.ReadToEnd();
    }
  }
}
```

10. Add the following method, using the methods added earlier, to the class:

```
public static void UseSnapshotsExample()
{
  String containerName = "{CONTAINER_NAME}";
  String blobName = "{BLOB_NAME}";

  SnapshotsExample example = new SnapshotsExample();
  example.CreateContainerAndBlob(containerName, blobName);

  DateTime snapshotTime =
    example.MakeSnapshot(containerName, blobName);
  example.GetSnapshot(containerName, blobName, snapshotTime);
}
```

11. Add the following to the `configuration` section of `app.config`:

```
<appSettings>
  <add key="DataConnectionString"
    value="UseDevelopmentStorage=true"/>
</appSettings>
```

How it works...

In steps 1 through 4, we set up the recipe. In step 5, we add a private member storing a `CloudBlobClient` that we initialize in the constructor we add in step 6. This constructor retrieves the storage account information from the `app.config` file. In step 7, we create a container and upload the blob to it.

In step 8, we invoke the `CreateSnapshot()` method to make a snapshot of the blob. We return the `SnapshotTime` because we need it later to access the snapshot. In step 9, we perform a fix to account for the different ways the Storage Client Library constructs endpoints for the storage service and the storage emulator. We then construct the full URI, including the `snapshot` query parameter, and use it to download the snapshot using `DownloadToStream()`.

In step 10, we invoke the methods added earlier to create a blob, make a snapshot, and retrieve it. We must replace {CONTAINER_NAME} and {BLOB_NAME} with the name of the container and blob we want to use.

In step 11, we add the connection string to the app.config configuration file.

CloudDrive.Snapshot()

The CloudDrive class has a Snapshot() method which creates a snapshot of the VHD page blob backing the current CloudDrive object. This method is needed because the Azure Drive simulation in the compute emulator is not integrated with the storage emulator. Consequently, neither VHD page blobs nor VHD snapshots are visible to the Azure Drive simulation. The specialized CloudDrive.Snapshot() method can be used to create snapshots of Azure Drives in the compute emulator.

Creating and using the root container for blobs

The Windows Azure Blob Service supports a simple two-level hierarchy for blobs. There is a single level of containers, each of which may contain zero or more blobs. Containers may not contain other containers.

In the Blob service, a blob resource is addressed as follows:

```
http://{account}.blob.core.windows.net/{container}/{blob}
```

{account}, {container}, and {blob} represent the name of the storage account, container, and blob.

This addressing convention works for most uses of blobs. However, when using Silverlight the runtime requires that a cross-domain policy file reside at the root of the domain and not beneath a container, as would be the case with the standard addressing for blobs. The cross-domain policy file allows a web client to access data from more than one domain at a time. (http://msdn.microsoft.com/en-us/library/cc197955(VS.95).aspx) Microsoft added support for a root container, named $root, to the Blob service, so that it could host cross-domain policy files.

The root container name does not need to be provided when retrieving blobs contained in it. For example, the following is a valid address for a blob named crossdomain.xml stored in the root container:

```
http://{account}.blob.core.windows.net/crossdomain.xml
```

The Silverlight runtime is able to access this blob and use it as a cross-domain policy file.

Note that the names of root-container blobs must not contain the / symbol to avoid any confusion with blobs being named to simulate a directory tree.

In this recipe, we will learn how to create and use the root container for a storage account.

Getting ready

We need to create a file that we will upload using the recipe. As we do not rely on this file being a cross-domain policy file, we can actually use any file for the recipe.

How to do it...

We are going to create a root container and upload a cross-domain policy file to it. We do this as follows:

1. Add a new class named `RootContainerExample` to the project.

2. Set the Target Framework for the project to.NET Framework 4.

3. Add the following assembly references to the project:

   ```
   Microsoft.WindowsAzure.StorageClient
   System.Configuration
   ```

4. Add the following `using` statements to the top of the class file:

   ```
   using Microsoft.WindowsAzure;
   using Microsoft.WindowsAzure.StorageClient;
   using System.Configuration;
   ```

5. Add the following method, uploading the cross-domain policy file, to the class:

   ```
   private static void UploadCrossDomainPolicyFile(
      String fileName)
   {
     String rootContainerName = "$root";
     String crossDomainPolicyName = "crossdomain.xml";
     CloudStorageAccount cloudStorageAccount =
       CloudStorageAccount.Parse(
       ConfigurationManager.AppSettings[
       "DataConnectionString"]);

     CloudBlobClient cloudBlobClient =
       cloudStorageAccount.CreateCloudBlobClient();
     CloudBlobContainer cloudBlobContainer =
       cloudBlobClient.GetContainerReference(
       rootContainerName);
     cloudBlobContainer.CreateIfNotExist();
   ```

```
    CloudBlockBlob cloudBlockBlob =
      cloudBlobContainer.GetBlockBlobReference(
      crossDomainPolicyName);
    cloudBlockBlob.UploadFile(fileName);
  }
```

6. Add the following method, using `UploadCrossDomainPolicyFile()`, to the class:

```
public static void UseRootContainerExample()
{
  String crossDomainPolicyFilename = "{PATH_TO_FILE}";
  UploadCrossDomainPolicyFile(crossDomainPolicyFilename);
}
```

7. Add the following to the `configuration` section of `app.config`:

```
<appSettings>
  <add key="DataConnectionString"
    value="UseDevelopmentStorage=true"/>
</appSettings>
```

How it works...

In steps 1 through 4, we set up the recipe.

In step 5, we create the root container, with the special name `$root`, and then use `UploadFile()` to upload the cross-domain policy file into it.

In step 6, we invoke the `UploadCrossDomainPolicyFile()` method we added in step 4. We must replace `{PATH_TO_FILE}` with the actual path to the file.

In step 7, we add the connection string to the `app.config` configuration file.

See also

▶ In the *Using blob directories* recipe in this chapter, we see how to simulate a directory hierarchy for blobs inside a container.

Uploading blocks to a block blob

The Windows Azure Blob Service supports two types of blobs: block blobs optimized for streaming, and page blobs optimized for random access. Block blobs are so named because they comprise blocks and can be updated by either replacing the entire blob or by replacing individual blocks. Page blobs can be updated by either replacing the entire blob or by modifying individual pages.

A block blob can be up to 200 GB, and comprises blocks that can be up to 4 MB. Block blobs larger than 64 MB must be uploaded in blocks and then a list of uploaded blocks must be *committed* to create the blob. The various upload methods in the `CloudBlob` class handle this two-phase process automatically. However, there are times when it is worthwhile taking direct control of the block upload and commit process. These include: uploading very large blobs, performing parallel uploads of blocks, or updating individual blocks.

At any given time, a block blob can comprise a set of committed blocks and a set of uncommitted blocks. Only the committed blocks are visible when the blob is accessed. The block blob can be updated by committing some mixture of the committed and uncommitted blocks. Any uncommitted blocks are garbage collected seven days after the last time blocks were committed to the block blob.

In this recipe, we will learn how to upload individual blocks and commit them to a block blob.

How to do it...

We are going to upload some blocks and commit them as a block blob. Then we are going to upload some more blocks to the same blob and retrieve the block list to confirm that the blob comprises a mixture of committed blocks and uncommitted blocks. Finally, we are going to commit the latest blocks and confirm that all the blocks in the blob have been committed. We do this as follows:

1. Add a new class named `UploadBlockBlobsExample` to the project.

2. Set the Target Framework for the project to .NET Framework 4.

3. Add the following assembly references to the project:

    ```
    Microsoft.WindowsAzure.StorageClient
    System.Configuration
    ```

4. Add the following `using` statements to the top of the class file:

    ```
    using Microsoft.WindowsAzure;
    using Microsoft.WindowsAzure.StorageClient;
    using System.Configuration;
    ```

5. Add the following member to the class:

    ```
    private CloudBlockBlob cloudBlockBlob;
    ```

6. Add the following constructor to the class:

    ```
    public UploadBlockBlobsExample(String containerName,
      String blobName)
    {
      CloudStorageAccount cloudStorageAccount =
        CloudStorageAccount.Parse(
        ConfigurationManager.AppSettings[
        "DataConnectionString"]);
    ```

```
CloudBlobClient cloudBlobClient =
  cloudStorageAccount.CreateCloudBlobClient();

CloudBlobContainer cloudBlobContainer =
  cloudBlobClient.GetContainerReference(containerName);
cloudBlobContainer.CreateIfNotExist();
cloudBlockBlob =
  cloudBlobContainer.GetBlockBlobReference(blobName);
}
```

7. Add the following methods, uploading blobs, to the class:

```
private IEnumerable<String> UploadBlocks(Int32 numberOfBlocks)
{
  String[] base64EncodedBlockIds =
    new String[numberOfBlocks];
  for (Int32 blockId = 0; blockId < numberOfBlocks;
    blockId++)
  {
    base64EncodedBlockIds[blockId] =
      PutBlockFromStream(blockId);
  }

  return base64EncodedBlockIds;
}


private String PutBlockFromStream(Int32 blockId)
{
  String base64EncodedBlockId = Convert.ToBase64String(
    System.BitConverter.GetBytes(blockId));
  String blobText = new String('z', 1000);
  UTF8Encoding utf8Encoding = new UTF8Encoding();
  using (MemoryStream memoryStream = new
    MemoryStream(utf8Encoding.GetBytes(blobText)))
  {
    cloudBlockBlob.PutBlock(base64EncodedBlockId,
      memoryStream, null);
  }
  return base64EncodedBlockId;
}
```

8. Add the following methods, handling block lists, to the class:

```
private void PutBlockList(IEnumerable<String> blockList)
{
  cloudBlockBlob.PutBlockList(blockList);
}
```

```
private void GetBlockList()
{
  IEnumerable<ListBlockItem> listBlockItems =
    cloudBlockBlob.DownloadBlockList(
    BlockListingFilter.All);
  foreach (ListBlockItem item in listBlockItems)
  {
    Boolean committed = item.Committed;
    String name = item.Name;
    Int64 size = item.Size;
  }
}
```

9. Add the following method, using the methods added earlier, to the class:

```
public static void UseUploadBlockBlobsExample()
{
  String containerName = "{CONTAINER_NAME}";
  String blobName = "{BLOB_NAME}";

  UploadBlockBlobsExample example =
    new UploadBlockBlobsExample(containerName, blobName);

  IEnumerable<String> base64EncodedBlockIds =
    example.UploadBlocks(20);
  example.PutBlockList(base64EncodedBlockIds);

  base64EncodedBlockIds = example.UploadBlocks(10);
  example.GetBlockList();
  example.PutBlockList(base64EncodedBlockIds);
  example.GetBlockList();
}
```

10. Add the following to the configuration section of `app.config`:

```
<appSettings>
  <add key="DataConnectionString"
    value="DefaultEndpointsProtocol=http;
    AccountName={ACCOUNT_NAME};AccountKey={ACCOUNT_KEY}"/>
</appSettings>
```

How it works...

In steps 1 through 4, we set up the `UploadBlockBlobsExample` class. In step 5, we add a member storing a `CloudBlockBlob` instance that we initialize in the constructor we add in step 6.

The UploadBlocks() method we add in step 7 iterates over the specified number of blocks and invokes the PutBlockFromStream() method. UploadBlocks() passes the loop counter in as a block ID. PutBlockFromStream() converts the integer into the required Base64 format. For the sake of simplicity, we then create a memory stream based on a simple String and invoke the CloudBlockBlob.PutBlob() method to upload the block with the specified Base64 block ID. PutBlockFromStream() returns the Base64 block ID to UploadBlocks() which, in turn, returns an IEnumerable<String> containing the sequence of block IDs.

In step 8, we add a PutBlockList() method that simply defers to the CloudBlockBlob.PutBlockList(). The GetBlockList() method invokes the CloudBlockBlob.DownloadBlockList() method to retrieve the list of committed blocks. We then iterate over the list to observe various properties of it.

In step 9, we add a method that uses the methods we created earlier. We upload 20 blocks and commit them to a block blob. Then we upload another 10 blocks and invoke the GetBlockList() method to verify that we have 20 committed and 10 uncommitted blocks. Finally, we commit the 10 blocks and confirm with another call to GetBlockList() that these blocks have replaced the blob with 20 blocks. We must replace {CONTAINER_NAME} and {BLOB_NAME} with an appropriate container name and blob name.

In step 10, we add the connection string to the app.config configuration file. We must replace {ACCOUNT_NAME} and {ACCOUNT_KEY} with actual values for the account name and access key.

See also

▶ We see how to improve upload performance for blobs in the *Optimizing blob uploads and downloads* recipe in this chapter.

▶ We see how to upload page blobs in the *Uploading a VHD into a page blob* recipe in this chapter.

Uploading a VHD into a page blob

An instance of a Windows Azure role comprises several virtual disks (VHD) deployed into a virtual machine. One VHD contains the Guest OS; another contains the role package, while the third is a writable VHD containing the local resources of the instance.

Windows Azure provides the Azure Drive feature whereby an arbitrary VHD, contained in a page blob, can be attached to an instance and then accessed as an NTFS drive. This VHD must be an NTFS-formatted, fixed-size VHD. The VHD can be created directly as a page blob or uploaded like any other page blob.

The **Disk Management** snap-in for the Microsoft Management Console (MMC) can be used to create and format a VHD on a local system. Once attached to the local system, files can be copied to, or created on the file system of the VHD just as they can with any hard drive. The VHD can then be detached from the local system and uploaded as a page blob to the Windows Azure Blob Service.

A page blob, which may have a maximum size of 1 TB, comprises a sequence of 512-byte pages. All writes to a page blob must be aligned with a page boundary. There is no charge for an empty page in a page blob. There is no need to upload empty pages in the VHD, which means that bandwidth need not be wasted uploading empty pages. The Blob service identifies these empty pages when a download of one of them is requested and it merely injects a page full of 0x0 bytes into the response stream.

Uploads to block blobs comprise a two-step process: upload the blocks and commit the blocks to the blob. Uploading a page blob is a single step process: write one or more 512-byte pages to the blob. Once uploaded, these pages immediately form part of the blob. This can cause problems if multiple writers are writing to the page blob simultaneously. The Windows Azure Storage Service REST API provides support for a sequence number that can be used to control which writer wins a contest to write to a single page. This functionality is not exposed in the Windows Azure Storage Client library.

In the Storage Client library, the `CloudPageBlob` class provides various methods supporting page blob uploads. `CloudPageBlob` is derived from `CloudBlob`. Note that the upload methods in `CloudBlob` class are not supported for `CloudPageBlob`. Instead, `CloudPageBlob` provides synchronous and asynchronous `WritePages()` methods specifically for uploading page blobs. Additionally, there are synchronous and asynchronous forms of the `GetPageRanges()` method that returns an `IEnumerable<PageRange>` of the non-empty page ranges in the blob.

In this recipe, we will learn how to upload a VHD into a page blob.

Getting ready

We use the disk management snap-in to create and format a VHD on the local system that we will upload with the recipe. There is more documentation on the disk management snap-in at `http://technet.microsoft.com/en-us/library/dd979539(WS.10).aspx`.

We launch disk management by clicking on **Start**, typing `diskmgmt.msc` in the **Search** box, and then pressing *Enter*. The **Create VHD** and **Attach VHD** operations are on the **Actions** menu.

We use the disk management snap-in for the following tasks:

- ▶ Creating VHD—as "fixed size" with a specified size in the specified location
- ▶ Initializing disk with a master boot record
- ▶ Creating a "new simple volume" formatted with NTFS with a specified drive letter

▸ Copying files and directories to the specified drive

▸ Detaching VHD

If the VHD already exists, then we use the disk management snap-in for the following tasks:

▸ Attaching the VHD

▸ Copying files and directories to the specified drive

▸ Detaching VHD

How to do it...

We are going to create a page blob and upload a VHD into it. We do this as follows:

1. Add a new class named `UploadVhdExample` to the project.

2. Set the Target Framework for the project to .NET Framework 4.

3. Add the following assembly references to the project:

```
Microsoft.WindowsAzure.StorageClient
System.Configuration
```

4. Add the following `using` statements to the top of the class file:

```
using Microsoft.WindowsAzure;
using Microsoft.WindowsAzure.StorageClient;
using System.Configuration;
using System.IO;
```

5. Add the following members to the class:

```
private const Int32 pageSize = 0x200; // 512 bytes
private const Int32 uploadSize = 0x100000; // 1MBytes
private CloudBlobClient cloudBlobClient;
```

6. Add the following constructor to the class:

```
public UploadVhdExample()
{
  CloudStorageAccount cloudStorageAccount =
    CloudStorageAccount.Parse(
    ConfigurationManager.AppSettings[
    "DataConnectionString"]);
  cloudBlobClient =
    cloudStorageAccount.CreateCloudBlobClient();
}
```

7. Add the following method, uploading a VHD, to the class:

```
private void UploadCloudDrive(
  String containerName, String blobName, String vhdPath)
{
  CloudBlobContainer cloudBlobContainer =
    cloudBlobClient.GetContainerReference(containerName);
  cloudBlobContainer.CreateIfNotExist();

  CloudPageBlob cloudPageBlob =
    cloudBlobContainer.GetPageBlobReference(blobName);
  cloudPageBlob.Properties.ContentType =
    "binary/octet-stream";

  using (FileStream fileStream =
    new FileStream(vhdPath, FileMode.Open))
  {
    Int32 blobSize = (Int32)fileStream.Length;
    if ((blobSize % pageSize) != 0)
    {
      throw new ApplicationException(
        "Page blob size must be a multiple of page size");
    }
    cloudPageBlob.Create(blobSize);

    Int32 pageBlobOffset = 0;
    Int32 numberIterations = blobSize / uploadSize;
    for (Int32 i = 0; i < numberIterations; i++)
    {
      pageBlobOffset = UploadPages(
        fileStream, cloudPageBlob, pageBlobOffset);
    }

    pageBlobOffset = UploadFooter(
      fileStream, cloudPageBlob, pageBlobOffset);
  }
}
```

8. Add the following method, uploading pages to a page blob, to the class:

```
private Int32 UploadPages(FileStream fileStream,
  CloudPageBlob cloudPageBlob, Int32 pageBlobOffset)
{
  Byte[] buffer = new Byte[uploadSize];
  Int32 countBytesRead = fileStream.Read(
    buffer, 0, uploadSize);
  Int32 countBytesUploaded = 0;
```

```
      Int32 bufferOffset = 0;
      Int32 rangeStart = 0;
      Int32 rangeSize = 0;
      while (bufferOffset < uploadSize)
      {
        Boolean nextPageIsLast =
          bufferOffset + pageSize >= uploadSize;
        Boolean nextPageHasData =
          NextPageHasData(buffer, bufferOffset);
        if (nextPageHasData)
        {
          if (rangeSize == 0)
          {
            rangeStart = bufferOffset;
          }
          rangeSize += pageSize;
        }

        if ((rangeSize > 0) && (!nextPageHasData ||
          nextPageIsLast))
        {
          using (MemoryStream memoryStream =
            new MemoryStream(buffer, rangeStart, rangeSize))
          {
            cloudPageBlob.WritePages(
              memoryStream, pageBlobOffset + rangeStart);
            countBytesUploaded += rangeSize;
            rangeSize = 0;
          }
        }
        bufferOffset += pageSize;
      }
      pageBlobOffset += uploadSize;

      return pageBlobOffset;
    }
```

9. Add the following method, uploading the VHD footer, to the class:

```
   private Int32 UploadFooter(FileStream fileStream,
     CloudPageBlob cloudPageBlob, Int32 pageBlobOffset)
   {
     const Int32 numberFooterBytes = 512;
     Byte[] footerBytes = new Byte[numberFooterBytes];
     Int32 countBytesRead = fileStream.Read(
       footerBytes, 0, numberFooterBytes);
```

```
using (MemoryStream memoryStream =
  new MemoryStream(footerBytes))
{
  cloudPageBlob.WritePages(memoryStream, pageBlobOffset);
  pageBlobOffset += numberFooterBytes;
}
return pageBlobOffset;
}
```

10. Add the following method, verifying a page contains data, to the class:

```
private Boolean NextPageHasData(Byte[] buffer,
  Int32 bufferOffset)
{
  for (Int32 i = bufferOffset; i < bufferOffset + pageSize; i++)
  {
    if (buffer[i] != 0x0)
    {
      return true;
    }
  }
  return false;
}
```

11. Add the following method, using the methods added earlier, to the class:

```
public static void UseUploadVhdExample()
{
  String containerName = "{CONTAINER_NAME}";
  String blobName = "{BLOB_NAME}";
  String pathName = @"{PATH_TO_THE_VHD}";
  UploadVhdExample example = new UploadVhdExample();
  example.UploadCloudDrive(
    containerName, blobName, pathName);
}
```

12. Add the following to the `configuration` section of `app.config`:

```
<appSettings>
  <add key="DataConnectionString"
    value="DefaultEndpointsProtocol=http;
    AccountName={ACCOUNT_NAME};AccountKey={ACCOUNT_KEY}"/>
</appSettings>
```

How it works...

In steps 1 through 4, we set up the class. In step 5, we define various constants and the `CloudBlobClient` we use to access the Blob service. We initialize this in the constructor we add in step 6.

In step 7, we add the method that controls the upload process. We open a `FileStream` on the VHD and create a page blob the same size as the VHD. We then iterate over the VHD file in increments of 1 MB, invoking `UploadPages()` to upload the data in each 1 MB window. Finally, we invoke `UploadFooter()` to upload the VHD footer.

In step 8, we add the `UploadPages()` method to upload non-empty pages to the page blob. We read the VHD into a buffer in 1 MB chunks. We then look for ranges of 512-byte pages containing some data and upload only these ranges. Remember, we do not need to upload empty pages. The tricky part of this process is identifying the end of a range when we come across an empty page or reach the end of the buffer.

In step 9, we add the `UploadFooter()` method to upload the 512-byte VHD footer. We simply load the footer into a `Byte[]` buffer and create a `MemoryStream` on it. We then invoke `WritePages()` to upload this to the page blob.

In Step 10, we add a method that returns `false` if every byte of a specified 512-byte page of a buffer is 0x0; otherwise, `NextPageHasData()` returns `true`.

In step 11, we add a method to use the methods added earlier. We must replace `{CONTAINER_NAME}` and `{BLOB_KEY}` with actual values for account name and access key. We must also replace `{PATH_TO_THE_VHD}` with the actual path to a VHD.

In step 12, we add the connection string to the `app.config` configuration file. We must replace `{ACCOUNT_NAME}` and `{ACCOUNT_KEY}` with actual values for the account name and access key.

There's more...

When uploading an arbitrary file that—unlike the VHD—is not an integral multiple of the upload buffer, we need to handle correctly the final chunk that is smaller than the size of the upload buffer.

See also

▸   See the *Uploading blocks to a block blob* recipe to see how to upload a block blob.

Downloading a blob asynchronously

The Windows Azure Storage Client library provides synchronous and asynchronous versions of nearly all the methods that access the Windows Azure Storage Service.

The asynchronous methods follow the **common language runtime (CLR) Asynchronous Programming Model (APM)**. In this model, asynchronous methods for an *action* are defined as a pair named `BeginAction` and `EndAction`. The asynchronous operation is initiated through a call to `BeginAction` and is cleaned up by a call to `EndAction`. `BeginAction` has a parameter that is a callback delegate and `EndAction` must be invoked in that delegate.

This apparent complexity can be greatly simplified through the use of a lambda expression to represent the callback delegate. Furthermore, local variables defined in the method containing the lambda expression are available inside the lambda expression. This removes any difficulty caused by a need to pass variables into the delegate. Using a lambda expression, instead of a callback delegate, makes using the asynchronous methods almost as simple as using the synchronous methods.

In this recipe, we will learn how to use asynchronous methods to download a blob into a file.

How to do it...

We are going to download a blob asynchronously. We do this as follows:

1. Add a new class named `DownloadBlobExample` to the project.
2. Set the Target Framework for the project to .NET Framework 4.
3. Add the following assembly references to the project:
   ```
   Microsoft.WindowsAzure.StorageClient
   System.Configuration
   ```
4. Add the following `using` statements to the top of the class file:
   ```
   using Microsoft.WindowsAzure;
   using Microsoft.WindowsAzure.StorageClient;
   using System.Configuration;
   using System.Net;
   using System.IO;
   ```
5. Add the following method, creating a container and blob, to the class:
   ```
   private static void CreateContainerAndBlob(
     String containerName, String blobName)
   {
     CloudStorageAccount cloudStorageAccount =
       CloudStorageAccount.Parse(
       ConfigurationManager.AppSettings[
   ```

```
      "DataConnectionString"]);
  CloudBlobClient cloudBlobClient =
    cloudStorageAccount.CreateCloudBlobClient();

  CloudBlobContainer cloudBlobContainer =
    cloudBlobClient.GetContainerReference(containerName);
  cloudBlobContainer.CreateIfNotExist();

  CloudBlockBlob cloudBlockBlob =
    cloudBlobContainer.GetBlockBlobReference(blobName);
  cloudBlockBlob.UploadText("To be, or not to be");
}
```

6. Add the following method, downloading a blob, to the class:

```
private static void DownloadBlob(String containerName,
  String blobName, String fileName)
{
  CloudStorageAccount cloudStorageAccount =
    CloudStorageAccount.Parse(
    ConfigurationManager.AppSettings[
    "DataConnectionString"]);
  CloudBlobClient cloudBlobClient =
    cloudStorageAccount.CreateCloudBlobClient();

  CloudBlobContainer cloudBlobContainer =
    cloudBlobClient.GetContainerReference(containerName);
  CloudBlockBlob cloudBlockBlob =
    cloudBlobContainer.GetBlockBlobReference(blobName);

  FileStream fileStream = new FileStream(fileName,
    FileMode.Append);
  IAsyncResult iAsyncResult =
    cloudBlockBlob.BeginDownloadToStream(fileStream,
    (result) =>
    {
      cloudBlockBlob.EndDownloadToStream(result);
      fileStream.Close();
    },
    null);
  return;
}
```

7. Add the following method, using the methods added earlier, to the class:

```
public static void UseDownloadBlobExample()
{
   String containerName = "{CONTAINER_NAME}";
   String blobName = "{BLOB_NAME}";
   String fileName = Path.GetTempPath() + @"\{FILE_NAME}";

   CreateContainerAndBlob(containerName, blobName);
   DownloadBlob(containerName, blobName, fileName);
}
```

8. Add the following to the `configuration` section of `app.config`:

```
<appSettings>
  <add key="DataConnectionString"
    value="UseDevelopmentStorage=true"/>
</appSettings>
```

How it works...

In steps 1 through 4, we set up the class. In step 5, we initialize a `CloudStorageAccount` from `app.config` and use it to create a `CloudBlobClient` instance. We use this to create a container and a blob.

In step 6, we follow the same route to get a `CloudBlockBlob` reference to the blob. We use it to invoke the `BeginDownloadToStream()` method. We pass this a lambda expression, instead of a callback delegate, and invoke `EndDownloadToStream()` in the lambda expression to clean up the asynchronous call. We use the ability to refer to local objects from inside the lambda expression to close the `FileStream` used in the download.

In step 7, we add a method that sets the parameters for the call to `DownloadBlob()`. We download the blob to a `temp` directory. We must replace `{CONTAINER_NAME}` and `{BLOB_NAME}` with appropriate container and blob names, and `{FILE_NAME}` with the file name.

In step 8, we add the connection string to the `app.config` configuration file.

Optimizing blob uploads and downloads

Large blobs need to be uploaded to the Windows Azure Blob Service, either in blocks for block blobs or in pages for page blobs. Similarly, blobs can be downloaded in byte ranges. These operations can be implemented in parallel using different threads to upload or download different parts of the blob.

The Blob service has a scalability target for throughput of about 60 MB per second for an individual blob. This creates a limit to how much performance improvement can be achieved through parallelizing operations on a blob. When contemplating parallelization, it is always worth testing the actual workload to ensure that any expected performance gain is in fact realized.

.NET Framework 4 includes the Parallel Extensions to .NET that simplifies the task of parallelizing operations. These provide parallel versions of the traditional `for` and `foreach` statements. The `Parallel.For` and `Parallel.ForEach` methods can be dropped in almost as replacements for `for` and `foreach`.

In this recipe, we will learn how to use `Parallel.For` to improve the upload and download performance of a block blob.

How to do it...

We are going to upload a 2 MB block blob in 200 KB blocks and then download it in 200 KB batches. This small blob size is used purely for demonstration purposes. We will use `Parallel.For` to parallelize both the upload and the download. We do this as follows:

1. Add a new class named `ParallelizationExample` to the project.

2. Set the Target Framework for the project to .NET Framework 4.

3. Add the following assembly references to the project:

    ```
    Microsoft.WindowsAzure.StorageClient
    System.Configuration
    ```

4. Add the following `using` statements to top of the class file:

    ```
    using Microsoft.WindowsAzure;
    using Microsoft.WindowsAzure.StorageClient;
    using System.Configuration;
    using System.Net;
    using System.IO;
    using System.Threading.Tasks;
    ```

5. Add the following private members to the class:

    ```
    private Int32 numberOfBlocks = 10;
    private Int32 batchSize = 200000;
    private String containerName;
    private String blobName;
    private CloudBlobClient cloudBlobClient;
    ```

6. Add the following constructor to the class:

```
public ParallelizationExample(String containerName, String
  blobName)
{
  CloudStorageAccount cloudStorageAccount =
    CloudStorageAccount.Parse(
    ConfigurationManager.AppSettings[
    "DataConnectionString"]);
  cloudBlobClient =
    cloudStorageAccount.CreateCloudBlobClient();
  this.containerName = containerName;
  this.blobName = blobName;
}
```

7. Add the following method, uploading a blob in blocks, to the class:

```
private void ParallelUpload()
{
  CloudBlobContainer cloudBlobContainer =
    cloudBlobClient.GetContainerReference(containerName);
  cloudBlobContainer.CreateIfNotExist();

  CloudBlockBlob cloudBlockBlob =
    cloudBlobContainer.GetBlockBlobReference(blobName);

  String[] base64EncodedBlockIds =
    new String[numberOfBlocks];

  ParallelLoopResult parallelLoopResult =
    Parallel.For(0, numberOfBlocks, i =>
    {
      String base64EncodedBlockId = Convert.ToBase64String(
        System.BitConverter.GetBytes(i));
      String blobText = new String('z', batchSize);
      UTF8Encoding utf8Encoding = new UTF8Encoding();
      using (MemoryStream memoryStream =
        new MemoryStream(utf8Encoding.GetBytes(blobText)))
      {
        cloudBlockBlob.PutBlock(base64EncodedBlockId,
          memoryStream, null);
      }
      base64EncodedBlockIds[i] = base64EncodedBlockId;
    });
  cloudBlockBlob.PutBlockList(base64EncodedBlockIds);

  return;
}
```

8. Add the following method, downloading the blob, to the class:

```
private void ParallelDownload()
{
  CloudBlobContainer cloudBlobContainer =
    cloudBlobClient.GetContainerReference(containerName);
  // This prevents an additional operation to check integrity
  cloudBlobClient.UseIntegrityControlForStreamReading =
    false;
  // This limits the download range to that requested.
  cloudBlobClient.ReadAheadInBytes = 0;
  CloudBlockBlob cloudBlockBlob =
    cloudBlobContainer.GetBlockBlobReference(blobName);

  Byte[] bytes = new Byte[batchSize * numberOfBlocks];
  Int32 numberOfDownloads = bytes.Count<Byte>() / batchSize;

  ParallelLoopResult parallelLoopResult =
    Parallel.For(0, numberOfDownloads, i =>
    {
      Int32 bufferStart = i * batchSize;
      using (BlobStream blobStream =
        cloudBlockBlob.OpenRead())
      {
        blobStream.Seek(bufferStart, SeekOrigin.Begin);
        blobStream.Read(bytes, bufferStart, batchSize);
      }
    });
  return;
}
```

9. Add the following method, using the methods added earlier:

```
public static void UseParallelizationExample()
{
  String containerName = "{CONTAINER_NAME}";
  String blobName = "{BLOB_NAME}";

  ServicePointManager.DefaultConnectionLimit = 5;

  ParallelizationExample example =
    new ParallelizationExample(containerName, blobName);
  example.ParallelUpload();
  example.ParallelDownload();
}
```

10. Add the following to the `configuration` section of `app.config`:

```
<appSettings>
  <add key="DataConnectionString"
    value="DefaultEndpointsProtocol=http;
    AccountName={ACCOUNT_NAME};AccountKey={ACCOUNT_KEY}"/>
</appSettings>
```

How it works...

In steps 1 through 4, we set up the `ParallelizationExample` class. In step 5, we add some constants used in the example: `numberOfBlocks` indicates the number of blocks we upload to the blob and `batchSize` indicates their size. We also define some private members that we initialize in the constructor we add in step 6.

In step 7, we add the method to upload the blob. This uses a `Parallel.For` loop to upload blocks in parallel. When the loop completes, the uploaded blocks are committed to create the blob.

In step 8, we add the method to download the blob. We set `CloudBlobClient.UseIntegrityControlForStreamReading` to `false` to prevent an unnecessary storage operation that request the block list. We also set `CloudBlobClient.ReadAheadInBytes` to `0`, so that the correct range of bytes in the blob is downloaded. Then, we use a `Parallel.For` loop to download the blob in parallel.

In step 9, we add a static method to use methods we created earlier. We set `ServicePointManager.DefaultConnectionLimit` to `5` to allow a maximum of five uploads and downloads to be performed in parallel. The default value for `ServicePointManager.DefaultConnectionLimit` is `2`. The Visual Studio 2010 templates for cloud projects set this value to `12`.

In step 10, we add the connection string to the `app.config` configuration file. We must replace `{ACCOUNT_NAME}` and `{ACCOUNT_KEY}` with actual values for account name and access key.

There's more...

Windows Azure provides several instance sizes for VMs, ranging in size from one shared core through eight cores. The network throughput and VM memory also increase with instance size. These values affect the performance improvement provided by parallelization. When investigating parallelization, the effort required to merge separate downloads should also be taken into consideration.

See also

> ▸ The eXtreme Computing Group of Microsoft Research maintains the Azurescope website (`http://azurescope.cloudapp.net/Default.aspx`). This contains a lot of material on optimizing access to the Blob service.

> ▸ Rob Gillen has done a lot of research on accessing the Blob service. He has published a blog post on choosing the optimal blob size for uploads at `http://weblogs.asp.net/rgillen/archive/2010/04/26/external-file-upload-optimizations-for-windows-azure.aspx`

Using retry policies with blob operations

A storage operation accessing the Windows Azure Storage Service can fail in various ways. For example, there could be an unexpected timeout if the storage service is moving a partition for performance reasons. It is advisable, therefore, to code defensively in the assumption that failure could occur unexpectedly.

The Windows Azure Storage Client library supports defensive coding by providing a retry policy for operations to the storage service. This is done by default, but the retry policy classes support parameterization and customization of the process.

`CloudBlobClient` has a `RetryPolicy` property. A storage operation on a `CloudBlob` object has a retry policy associated with it through the `RetryPolicy` property of its `BlobRequestOptions` parameter. These `RetryPolicy` properties provide access to a `RetryPolicy` delegate that returns a `ShouldRetry` delegate which specifies whether or not a retry should be attempted.

The `RetryPolicies` class provides several `RetryPolicy` delegates. The `NoRetry` delegate does not perform retries; the `Retry` delegate performs a number of retries with a fixed interval between them, while the `RetryExponential` performs a number of retries with an exponential back off time between them (that is, the interval between successive retries roughly doubles). By default, a `RetryExponential` delegate is associated with a `CloudBlobClient` and with any storage operation using that `CloudBlobClient`. This default may be overridden for an individual `CloudBlob` storage operation by associating a `RetryPolicy` with the storage operation.

The configurability provided by the `RetryPolicies` delegates is sufficient for most cases. However, the `ShouldRetry` delegate can be used if more control is needed. For example, none of the `RetryPolicy` delegates provided in `RetryPolicies` uses the `Exception` thrown by a failed operation.

In this recipe, we will see various uses of retry policies. We will see how to have no retry policy, have a non-default retry policy, and how to customize the retry process.

How to do it...

We are going to use various retry policies when uploading a 1 MB blob. We do this as follows:

1. Add a new class named `RetryPoliciesExample` to the project.

2. Set the Target Framework for the project to .NET Framework 4.

3. Add the following assembly references to the project:

   ```
   Microsoft.WindowsAzure.StorageClient
   System.Configuration
   ```

4. Add the following `using` statements to the top of the class file:

   ```
   using Microsoft.WindowsAzure;
   using Microsoft.WindowsAzure.StorageClient;
   using System.Configuration;
   using System.Threading;
   ```

5. Add the following members to the class:

   ```
   private String blobText = new String('z', 1000000);
   private CloudBlockBlob cloudBlockBlob;
   ```

6. Add the following constructor to the class:

   ```
   public RetryPoliciesExample(String containerName,
     String blobName)
   {
     CloudStorageAccount cloudStorageAccount =
       CloudStorageAccount.Parse(
       ConfigurationManager.AppSettings[
       "DataConnectionString"]);
     CloudBlobClient cloudBlobClient =
       cloudStorageAccount.CreateCloudBlobClient();
     CloudBlobContainer cloudBlobContainer =
       cloudBlobClient.GetContainerReference(containerName);
     cloudBlobContainer.CreateIfNotExist();

     cloudBlockBlob =
       cloudBlobContainer.GetBlockBlobReference(blobName);
   }
   ```

7. Add the following method, uploading a blob with no retry policy, to the class:

   ```
   private void UploadWithNoRetry()
   {
     BlobRequestOptions blobRequestOptions =
       new BlobRequestOptions();
     blobRequestOptions.Timeout = TimeSpan.FromSeconds(10);
     blobRequestOptions.RetryPolicy = RetryPolicies.NoRetry();
     cloudBlockBlob.UploadText(blobText, new UTF8Encoding(),
       blobRequestOptions);
   }
   ```

8. Add the following method, uploading a blob using an exponential retry policy, to the class:

```
private void UploadWithModifiedRetry()
{
  TimeSpan deltaBackOff = TimeSpan.FromSeconds(20);
  BlobRequestOptions blobRequestOptions =
    new BlobRequestOptions();
  blobRequestOptions.Timeout = TimeSpan.FromSeconds(10);
  blobRequestOptions.RetryPolicy =
    RetryPolicies.RetryExponential(5, deltaBackOff);
  cloudBlockBlob.UploadText(blobText, new UTF8Encoding(),
    blobRequestOptions);
}
```

9. Add the following method, uploading a blob with a custom retry policy, to the class:

```
private void UploadWithCustomRetry()
{
  ShouldRetry shouldRetry =
    cloudBlockBlob.ServiceClient.RetryPolicy();

  BlobRequestOptions blobRequestOptions =
    new BlobRequestOptions();
  blobRequestOptions.Timeout = TimeSpan.FromSeconds(10);
  blobRequestOptions.RetryPolicy = RetryPolicies.NoRetry();

  Int32 moreThanDefaultRetryCount =
    RetryPolicies.DefaultClientRetryCount + 1;
  TimeSpan delay;
  for (Int32 retryCount = 0; retryCount <
    moreThanDefaultRetryCount; retryCount++)
  {
    try
    {
      cloudBlockBlob.UploadText(blobText,
        new UTF8Encoding(), blobRequestOptions);
    }
    catch (StorageServerException e)
    {
      if (e.ErrorCode == StorageErrorCode.ServiceTimeout &&
        shouldRetry(retryCount, e, out delay))
      {
        Thread.Sleep(delay);
      }
      else
      {
```

```
        throw;
      }
    }
  }
}
```

10. Add the following method, using the methods just added, to the class:

```
public static void UseRetryPoliciesExample()
{
  String containerName = "chapter2";
  String blobName = "RetriesBlob";

  RetryPoliciesExample retryPoliciesExample =
    new RetryPoliciesExample(containerName, blobName);

  retryPoliciesExample.UploadWithNoRetry();

  retryPoliciesExample.UploadWithModifiedRetry();

  retryPoliciesExample.UploadWithCustomRetry();
}
```

11. Add the following to the `configuration` section of `app.config`:

```
<appSettings>
  <add key="DataConnectionString"
  value="DefaultEndpointsProtocol=http;
  AccountName={ACCOUNT_NAME};AccountKey={ACCOUNT_KEY}"/>
</appSettings>
```

How it works...

In this recipe, we use a short timeout of 10 seconds when uploading a 1 MB blob with the deliberate intent of making the upload operation fail, so that we can see various retry policies in action. The blob size can be increased if the upload speed is sufficiently fast that the upload succeeds without the retry policy being invoked. This recipe should be used with the storage service rather than the storage emulator to take advantage of the slower connection speeds on the Internet.

In steps 1 through 4, we set up the class. In step 5, we initialize the `String` we will upload to the blob and define a `CloudBlockBlob` instance that we initialize in the constructor we add in step 6. We also create a container in the constructor.

In step 7, we upload a blob while using no retry policy. We do this by creating a `BlobRequestOptions` instance and assigning a `NoRetry()` delegate to the `RetryPolicy` of the `BlobRequestOption` for the `CloudBlob.UploadText()` operation. When this method is invoked, it makes a single call to the Blob service. It throws an exception if the operation times out.

In step 8, we upload a blob while using an exponential retry policy. We do this by creating a `BlobRequestOptions` instance and assigning a `RetryExponential()` delegate to the `RetryPolicy` of the `BlobRequestOption` for the `CloudBlob.UploadText()` operation. This retry policy performs five retries of a failed operation with a 20 second back off interval. These differ from the default of three retries and 30 seconds for the back off interval.

In step 9, we upload a blob using a custom retry policy. We capture the default retry policy and turn off the retry policy for the `CloudBlob.UploadText()` operation. We then create a loop to invoke `CloudBlob.UploadText()` multiple times, if necessary. If an exception is thrown, then we check it and if it is a timeout exception, we invoke the `ShouldRetry()` delegate to see if we should retry the operation. We throw an exception if we do not retry the operation.

In step 10, we add a method that invokes the three upload methods. For the purpose of demonstrating the retry policy, ideally each of these methods should fail.

In step 11, we add the connection string to the `app.config` configuration file. We must replace `{ACCOUNT_NAME}` and `{ACCOUNT_KEY}` with actual values for account name and access key.

There's more...

The description and examples in this recipe are specific to blobs. However, the retry policy classes may also be used when using the Storage Client library to access the Table service and the Queue service.

Transient Fault Handling Framework

The Windows Azure AppFabric Customer Advisory Team has made the source code and pre-compiled assemblies for the *Transient Fault Handling Framework for Azure Storage, Service Bus,* and *SQL Azure* available on the MSDN Code Gallery This comprises a set of classes that can be used to detect transient failures and retry storage operations. We see how to use this in the *Handling connection failures to SQL Azure* recipe.

The Transient Fault Handling Framework can be downloaded from the following URL:

```
http://archive.msdn.microsoft.com/appfabriccat/Release/
ProjectReleases.aspx?ReleaseId=5011
```

Copying a blob with the Windows Azure Storage Service REST API

RESTful APIs have become a common way to expose services to the Internet since Roy Fielding first described them in his Ph.D. thesis (`http://www.ics.uci.edu/~fielding/pubs/dissertation/top.htm`). The basic idea is that a service exposes resources that can be accessed through a small set of operations. The only operations allowed are those named for and which behave like the HTTP verbs—`DELETE`, `GET`, `HEAD`, `MERGE`, `POST`, and `PUT`. Although this appears to be very simplistic, RESTful interfaces have proven to be very powerful in practice.

An immediate benefit of a RESTful interface is cross-platform support as regardless of platform an application capable of issuing HTTP requests can invoke RESTful operations. The Windows Azure Platform exposes almost all its functionality exclusively through a RESTful interface, so that it can be accessed from any platform.

In particular, the Windows Azure Storage Service REST API provides the definitive way to access the Windows Azure Storage Service. The Windows Azure Storage Client Library is a managed .NET library that uses the Storage Service REST API. This means that the Storage Client library supports only those storage operations exposed by the Storage Service REST API.

In practice, the availability of the Storage Client library means that there is not much reason to use the Storage Service REST API in a managed .NET environment. However, the Storage Service REST API is worth knowing about for various reasons. An attempt to perform low-level analysis of operations sent to the storage service requires an understanding of the Storage Service REST API because it operates at the raw HTTP level that tools, such as Fiddler operate at. This is helpful when diagnosing issues with storage operations against storage service. Another reason is that the MSDN documentation for the Storage Service REST API is more definitive and more comprehensive than that for the Storage Client library. This helps in understanding why features behaves the way they do.

In a managed .NET environment, the Storage Service REST API is invoked through the `HttpWebRequest` and `HttpWebResponse` classes. Each storage operation must be authenticated using a hash-based message authentication code (HMAC) header. The HMAC is generated by using the storage account access key to initialize an `HMACSHAS256` object which is then used to create a hash of the request headers. The storage service rejects any storage operation not accompanied by a valid HMAC header unless the operation is on a publicly accessible container or blob.

The Storage Service REST API (and the Storage Client library) supports the ability to copy a blob from one container to another. Indeed, the two blobs can even be in different storage accounts.

In this recipe, we will learn how to use the Storage Service REST API to invoke the
`Copy Blob` operation.

How to do it...

We are going to copy a blob using both the Storage Service REST API and the Storage Client
library. We do this as follows:

1. Add a new class named `CopyBlobExample` to the project.

2. Set the Target Framework for the project to .NET Framework 4.

3. Add the following assembly references to the project:

    ```
    Microsoft.WindowsAzure.StorageClient
    System.Configuration
    ```

4. Add the following `using` statements to the top of the class file:

    ```
    using Microsoft.WindowsAzure;
    using Microsoft.WindowsAzure.StorageClient;
    using System.Configuration;
    using System.Net;
    using System.Security.Cryptography;
    using System.Globalization;
    ```

5. Add the following private members to the class:

    ```
    private static String devAccountName= "devstoreaccount1";
    private static String devAccountKey=
      "Eby8vdM02xNOcqFlqUwJPLlmEtlCDXJlOUzFT50uSRZ6IFsuFq2UVErCz4I6tq
      /K1SZFPTOtr/KBHBeksoGMGw==";

    private static String cloudEndPointFormat =
      "http://{0}.blob.core.windows.net/";
    private static String localEndPointFormat =
      "http://127.0.0.1:{0:D}/{1}/";
    private static String sharedKey = "SharedKey";
    ```

6. Add the following method, creating the containers and source blob, to the class:

    ```
    private static void SetupRecipe(String fromContainerName,
      String fromBlobName, String toContainerName)
    {
      CloudStorageAccount cloudStorageAccount =
        CloudStorageAccount.Parse(
        ConfigurationManager.AppSettings[
        "DataConnectionString"]);
      CloudBlobClient cloudBlobClient =
        cloudStorageAccount.CreateCloudBlobClient();
    ```

```
    CloudBlobContainer fromContainer =
      cloudBlobClient.GetContainerReference(fromContainerName);
    fromContainer.CreateIfNotExist();
    CloudBlob fromBlob =
      fromContainer.GetBlockBlobReference(fromBlobName);
    fromBlob.UploadText("To sleep, perchance to dream ");

    CloudBlobContainer toContainer =
      cloudBlobClient.GetContainerReference(toContainerName);
    toContainer.CreateIfNotExist();
}
```

7. Add the following method, copying a blob using the Storage Service REST API,
    to the class:

```
private static void CopyBlobWithRest(
  String accountName, String accountKey,
  String fromContainerName, String fromBlobName,
  String toContainerName, String toBlobName)
{
  String urlPath = String.Format("{0}/{1}",
    toContainerName, toBlobName);
  String storageServiceVersion = "2009-09-19";
  String dateInRfc1123Format =DateTime.UtcNow.ToString(
    "R", CultureInfo.InvariantCulture);

  String copySourceName = String.Format("/{0}/{1}/{2}",
    accountName, fromContainerName, fromBlobName);

  String requestMethod = "PUT";
  String contentEncoding = String.Empty;
  String contentLanguage = String.Empty;
  String contentLength = "0";
  String contentMD5 = String.Empty;
  String contentType = String.Empty;
  String date = String.Empty;
  String ifModifiedSince = String.Empty;
  String ifMatch = String.Empty;
  String ifNoneMatch = String.Empty;
  String ifUnmodifiedSince = String.Empty;
  String range = String.Empty;
  String canonicalizedHeaders = String.Format(
    "x-ms-copy-source:{0}\nx-ms-date:{1}\nx-ms-version:{2}",
    copySourceName, dateInRfc1123Format,
    storageServiceVersion);
```

```
String canonicalizedResource =
  GetCanonicalizedResource(accountName, urlPath);

String stringToSign = String.Format(
  "{0}\n{1}\n{2}\n{3}\n{4}\n{5}\n{6}\n{7}\n{8}\n{9}\n{10}\
  n{11}\n{12}\n{13}",
  requestMethod,
  contentEncoding,
  contentLanguage,
  contentLength,
  contentMD5,
  contentType,
  date,
  ifModifiedSince,
  ifMatch,
  ifNoneMatch,
  ifUnmodifiedSince,
  range,
  canonicalizedHeaders,
  canonicalizedResource);

String authorizationHeader = CreateAuthorizationHeader(
  stringToSign, accountName, accountKey);

String blobEndpoint = GetBlobEndpoint(accountName);
Uri uri = new Uri(blobEndpoint + urlPath);
HttpWebRequest request =
  (HttpWebRequest)WebRequest.Create(uri);
request.Method = requestMethod;
request.Headers.Add("x-ms-copy-source", copySourceName);
request.Headers.Add("x-ms-date", dateInRfc1123Format);
request.Headers.Add("x-ms-version", storageServiceVersion);
request.Headers.Add("Authorization", authorizationHeader);
request.ContentLength = 0;

using (HttpWebResponse response =
  (HttpWebResponse)request.GetResponse())
{
  HttpStatusCode statusCode = response.StatusCode;
}
}
```

8. Add the following methods, handling differences in the endpoint format for the storage emulator and the storage service, to the class:

```
private static String GetBlobEndpoint(String accountName)
{
  String blobEndpoint;
  if (accountName == devAccountName)
  {
    blobEndpoint = String.Format(
      localEndPointFormat, 10000, accountName);
  }
  else
  {
    blobEndpoint = String.Format(
      cloudEndPointFormat, accountName);
  }
  return blobEndpoint;
}


private static String GetCanonicalizedResource(
  String accountName, String urlPath)
{
  String canonicalizedResource;
  if (accountName == devAccountName)
  {
    canonicalizedResource = String.Format("/{0}/{0}/{1}",
      accountName, urlPath);
  }
  else
  {
    canonicalizedResource = String.Format("/{0}/{1}",
      accountName, urlPath);
  }
  return canonicalizedResource;
}
```

9. Add the following method, creating the authorization header, to the class:

```
private static String CreateAuthorizationHeader(
  String canonicalizedString, String accountName,
  String accountKey)
{
  String signature = string.Empty;
  Byte[] key = Convert.FromBase64String(accountKey);
  using (HMACSHA256 hmacSha256 = new HMACSHA256(key))
  {
```

```
    Byte[] dataToHmac =
      Encoding.UTF8.GetBytes(canonicalizedString);
    signature = Convert.ToBase64String(
      hmacSha256.ComputeHash(dataToHmac));
  }

  String authorizationHeader = String.Format("{0} {1}:{2}",
    sharedKey, accountName, signature);
  return authorizationHeader;
}
```

10. Add the following method, using the Storage Client Library to copy a blob, to the class:

```
private static void CopyBlobWithLibrary(
  String fromContainerName, String fromBlobName,
  String toContainerName, String toBlobName)
{
  CloudStorageAccount cloudStorageAccount =
    CloudStorageAccount.Parse(
    ConfigurationManager.AppSettings[
    "DataConnectionString"]);
  CloudBlobClient cloudBlobClient =
    cloudStorageAccount.CreateCloudBlobClient();

  CloudBlobContainer toCloudBlobContainer =
    cloudBlobClient.GetContainerReference(toContainerName);
  CloudBlob toCloudBlob =
    toCloudBlobContainer.GetBlobReference(toBlobName);

  CloudBlobContainer fromCloudBlobContainer =
    cloudBlobClient.GetContainerReference(fromContainerName);
  CloudBlob fromCloudBlob =
    fromCloudBlobContainer.GetBlobReference(fromBlobName);

  toCloudBlob.CopyFromBlob(fromCloudBlob);
}
```

11. Add the following method, using the methods added earlier, to the class:

```
public static void UseCopyBlobExample()
{
  String accountName = devAccountName;
  String accountKey = devAccountKey;

  String fromContainerName = "{FROM_CONTAINER}";
  String fromBlobName = "{FROM_BLOB}";
  String toContainerName = "{TO_CONTAINER}";
  String toBlobNameRest = "{TO_BLOB_REST}";
```

```
String toBlobNameLibrary = "{TO_BLOB_LIBRARY}";

SetupRecipe( fromContainerName, fromBlobName,
  toContainerName);
CopyBlobWithRest(accountName, accountKey,
  fromContainerName, fromBlobName,
  toContainerName, toBlobNameRest);
CopyBlobWithLibrary(fromContainerName, fromBlobName,
  toContainerName, toBlobNameLibrary);
}
```

12. Add the following to the `configuration` section of `app.config`:

```
<appSettings>
  <add key="DataConnectionString"
    value="UseDevelopmentStorage=true"/>
</appSettings>
```

How it works...

In steps 1 through 4, we set up the recipe. In step 5, we add some members with various constants. These include the hard-coded account name and access key for the storage emulator which we covered in the *Connecting to the storage emulator* recipe in Chapter 1. In step 6, we get a `CloudBlobClient` instance and use that to create source and destination containers, as well as the blob we copy elsewhere in the recipe.

In step 7, we add the `CopyBlobWithRest()` method, which uses the Storage Service REST API to copy a blob. We first initialize some variables and constants and then use these to create `canonicalizedHeaders` and `canonicalizedResource` strings. We provide `2009-09-19` as the version for the Storage Service REST API. We create `stringToSign` from a combination of various (potential) request headers, a canonicalized header, and a canonicalized resource. We invoke the `CreateAuthorizationHeader()` method to create an `Authorization` request header. We then create the `HttpWebRequest` and assign some request headers to it. Finally, we submit the `Copy Blob` request to the Blob service and retrieve the response as an `HttpWebResponse`.

In step 8, we add two methods to handle slight differences in the way endpoints are created for the storage service and the storage emulator.

In step 9, we add a method that creates an HMAC token from the canonicalized request string and the account name and access key.

In step 10, we add a method that uses the Storage Client library to copy a blob. This simply gets references to the source and destination blobs and then invokes `CopyFromBlob()` on the destination blob.

In step 11, we provide names for the source and destination containers, and the blob we copy. Then, we invoke `SetupRecipe()` to create them. Finally, we invoke `CopyBlobWithRest()` and `CopyBlobWithLibrary()` to copy the source blob using the Storage Service REST API and the Storage Client library respectively. If we wish to use the storage service rather than the storage emulator, then we must provide the appropriate account name and access key both in this method and in `app.config`.

In step 12, we add the connection string to the `app.config` configuration file. We see how to modify the configuration file in the *Connecting to the Windows Azure storage service* recipe.

There's more...

An application such as Fiddler that captures the actual HTTP request and response sent over the wire is useful in solving problems with the Storage Service REST API. Indeed, it is also useful in solving problems with the Storage Client library because it allows us to view the actual REST request sent to the Blob service by the Storage Client library. Fiddler can be downloaded from `http://www.fiddler2.com/fiddler2/`.

Using the REST API with the Queue service and Table service

Note that the Storage Service REST API can also be used in a similar manner with the Queue service and the Table service. Although the latter service is authenticated slightly differently, the general idea is the same.

See also

▶ We show a higher-level use of `HttpWebRequest` in the *Leasing a blob using the Protocol classes in the Windows Azure Storage Client Library* recipe in this chapter.

Leasing a blob using the Protocol classes in the Windows Azure Storage Client Library

The Windows Azure Storage Service REST API provides the definitive way to access the Windows Azure Storage Service. It provides platform independence for the storage service allowing it to be accessed from any platform capable of using a RESTful interface.

Microsoft also provides the Windows Azure Storage Client Library that simplifies access to the storage service from a managed .NET environment. The high-level classes in this library are in the `Microsoft.WindowsAzure.StorageClient` namespace. These classes hide from the complexity of dealing with the raw `HttpWebRequest` and `HttpWebResponse` classes used with the Storage Service REST API. However, this simplicity comes at the cost of hiding some features of the storage service.

The Storage Client library also provides a set of lower-level managed classes in the `Microsoft.WindowsAzure.StorageClient.Protocol` namespace that expose the `HttpWebRequest` and `HttpWebResponse` objects used to connect to the storage service. These Protocol classes provide access to features in the Storage Service REST API that are not included in the Storage Client library. Usually, we never need to access the Protocol classes.

An important feature not supported in the high-level Storage Client library classes is *leasing a blob*. A blob can be leased for a minute at a time, so that only the holder of the lease has write access to the blob. This is particularly useful with page blobs as they can be updated with random writes. Indeed, the Azure Drive feature uses leases to ensure that only one instance at a time can mount VHD page blob as an Azure Drive.

There are four blob-leasing actions:

1. Acquire
2. Renew
3. Release
4. Break

The `Acquire` action is invoked on a blob to acquire a one-minute lease on it. This lease is identified by a lease ID that must be presented with any operation which modifies the blob. The `Renew` action renews an existing lease for another minute. The `Release` action ends the lease immediately, so that the blob can be updated without presenting the lease ID. The `Break` action ends the lease, but does not allow the blob to be updated until the expiration of the current lease period.

`BlobRequest` is the core class in the Protocol namespace. It provides a set of static factory methods that create an `HttpWebRequest` object for a specific Storage Service REST API operation. For example, the `BlobRequest.Lease()` method creates and initializes an `HttpWebRequest` object for the `Lease Blob` operation. The `BlobRequest` class also provides a `SignRequest()` method, which adds the appropriate Blob service authorization header to the request.

In this recipe, we will learn how to lease blobs using the classes in the Protocol namespace.

How to do it...

We are going to lease a blob, write data to it, and then release the lease on it. We do this as follows:

1. Add a new class named `LeaseBlobsExample` to the project.
2. Set the Target Framework for the project to .NET Framework 4.
3. Add the following assembly references to the project:
   ```
   Microsoft.WindowsAzure.StorageClient
   System.Configuration
   ```

4. Add the following `using` statements to the top of the class file:

```
using Microsoft.WindowsAzure;
using Microsoft.WindowsAzure.StorageClient;
using Microsoft.WindowsAzure.StorageClient.Protocol;
using System.Net;
using System.IO;
```

5. Add the following `enum` definition after the namespace declaration:

```
public enum EndLease
{
  Break,
    Release
}
```

6. Add the following members to the class:

```
private static String devStorageAccount = "devstoreaccount1";
private static String devStorageKey =
  "Eby8vdM02xNOcqFlqUwJPLlmEtlCDXJ1OUzFT50uSRZ6IFsuFq2UVErCz4I6tq
  /K1SZFPTOtr/KBHBeksoGMGw==";

private String cloudEndpointFormat =
  "http://{0}.blob.core.windows.net/";
private String localEndpointFormat =
  "http://127.0.0.1:{0:D}/{1}/";

private Uri uri;
private Uri endpointUri;
private Credentials credentials;
private String leaseId;
```

7. Add the following constructor to the class:

```
public LeaseBlobsExample(String accountName,
  String accountKey, String containerName, String blobName)
{
  String blobEndPoint = GetBlobEndpoint(accountName);
  blobUri = new Uri(String.Format("{0}{1}/{2}",
    blobEndPoint, containerName, blobName));
  endpointUri = new Uri(blobEndPoint);
  credentials = new Credentials(accountName, accountKey);
}
```

8. Add the following method, creating a container and the blob, to the class:

```
private void CreateContainerAndBlob(
  String containerName, String blobName)
{
  StorageCredentialsAccountAndKey storageCredentials =
    new StorageCredentialsAccountAndKey(
    credentials.AccountName,
    credentials.ExportBase64EncodedKey());

  CloudBlobClient cloudBlobClient =
    new CloudBlobClient(endpointUri, storageCredentials);

  CloudBlobContainer cloudBlobContainer =
    cloudBlobClient.GetContainerReference(containerName);
  cloudBlobContainer.CreateIfNotExist();

  CloudBlockBlob cloudBlockBlob =
    cloudBlobContainer.GetBlockBlobReference(blobName);
  cloudBlockBlob.UploadText("The slings and arrows");
}
```

9. Add the following method, handling differences between the storage emulator and the storage service, to the class:

```
private String GetBlobEndpoint(String accountName)
{
  String blobEndpoint = String.Format(
    cloudEndpointFormat, accountName);
  if (accountName == devAccountName)
  {
    blobEndpoint = String.Format(localEndpointFormat,
      10000, accountName);
  }
  return blobEndpoint;
}
```

10. Add the following methods, managing a lease, to the class:

```
private void AcquireLease()
{
  HttpWebRequest acquireLeaseRequest =
    BlobRequest.Lease(blobUri, 30, LeaseAction.Acquire,
    null);
  BlobRequest.SignRequest(acquireLeaseRequest, credentials);

  using (HttpWebResponse response =
    acquireLeaseRequest.GetResponse() as HttpWebResponse)
```

```
    {
      leaseId = response.Headers["x-ms-lease-id"];
    }
  }
}


private void RenewLease()
{
  HttpWebRequest renewLeaseRequest =
    BlobRequest.Lease(blobUri, 30, LeaseAction.Renew,
    leaseId);
  BlobRequest.SignRequest(renewLeaseRequest, credentials);

  using (HttpWebResponse response =
    renewLeaseRequest.GetResponse() as HttpWebResponse)
  {
    leaseId = response.Headers["x-ms-lease-id"];
  }
}


private void ReleaseOrBreakLease(EndLease endLease)
{
  HttpWebRequest releaseLeaseRequest =
    BlobRequest.Lease(blobUri, 30,
    endLease == EndLease.Release ? LeaseAction.Release :
    LeaseAction.Break, leaseId);
  BlobRequest.SignRequest(releaseLeaseRequest, credentials);

  using (HttpWebResponse response =
    releaseLeaseRequest.GetResponse() as HttpWebResponse)
  {
    HttpStatusCode httpStatusCode = response.StatusCode;
  }
}
```

11. Add the following method, writing text to a blob, to the class:

```
private void WriteTextToBlob(String blobText)
{
  BlobProperties blobProperties = new BlobProperties();
  HttpWebRequest putRequest = BlobRequest.Put(blobUri, 30,
    blobProperties, BlobType.BlockBlob, leaseId, 0);

  using (Stream stream = putRequest.GetRequestStream())
  {
    UTF8Encoding utf8Encoding = new UTF8Encoding();
```

```
      Byte[] bytes = utf8Encoding.GetBytes(blobText);
      stream.Write(bytes, 0, bytes.Length);
    }
    BlobRequest.SignRequest(putRequest, credentials);

    using (HttpWebResponse response =
      putRequest.GetResponse() as HttpWebResponse)
    {
      HttpStatusCode httpStatusCode = response.StatusCode; ;
    }
  }
}
```

12. Add the following method, using the lease-management functionality, to the class:

```
public static void UseLeaseBlobsExample()
{
  String accountName = devAccountName;
  String accountKey = devAccountKey;
  String containerName = "{CONTAINER_NAME}";
  String blobName = "{BLOB_NAME}";

  LeaseBlobsExample leaseBlobsExample =
    new LeaseBlobsExample(accountName, accountKey,
    containerName, blobName);

  leaseBlobsExample.CreateContainerAndBlob(
    containerName, blobName);

  leaseBlobsExample.WriteTextToBlob("To be, or not to be");
  leaseBlobsExample.AcquireLease();
  leaseBlobsExample.WriteTextToBlob("that is the question");
  leaseBlobsExample.ReleaseOrBreakLease(EndLease.Release);
}
```

How it works...

In steps 1 through 4, we set up the class. In step 5, we add an enum allowing us to distinguish between a Break and Release action for a lease. We add some members to the class in step 6 and initialize them in the constructor we add in step 7.

In step 8, we create a StorageCredentialsAccountAndKey by extracting the account name and access key from the Credentials object we initialized in the constructor. We use it to initialize the CloudBlockClient instance we use to create the container and blob.

In step 9, we add a method that handles differences in the construction of storage service and storage emulator endpoints.

The lease-management methods we add in step 10 all follow the same rubric. We invoke a `BlobRequest.Lease()` method specifying the desired lease action and, when needed, the lease ID. We then add the required authorization headers using `BlobRequest.SignRequest()`. Finally, we submit the operation to the Blob service by invoking `HttpWebRequest.GetResponse()`. The response to a successful `Lease` or `Renew` action contains the lease ID in the `x-ms-lease-id` response header.

The `WriteTextToBlob()` method we added add in step 11 is implemented similarly. We invoke `BlobRequest.Put()` to create the `HttpWebRequest` object for the *Put Blob* operation. We need to perform any necessary modifications to the request—in this case, writing to the request stream—before adding the authorization headers with `BlobRequest.SignRequest()`. This is essentially the model for the other factory methods in the `BlobRequest` class.

In step 12, we add a simple method to use the methods we added earlier. We lease a blob, write a few words to it, and then release the lease. We must replace `{CONTAINER_NAME}` and `{BLOB_NAME}` with appropriate container and blob names. If we wish to use the storage service, rather than the storage emulator, then we must provide appropriate values for `accountName` and `accountKey`.

There's more...

The Protocol classes can be used with both blobs and queues. However, the table functionality in the Storage Client library is built on **WCF Data Services** rather than the Protocol classes.

Using a blob lease as a singleton ticket

Another use of a blob lease is as a ticket to ensure that only one instance of a role can perform some task. When an instance starts, it tries to lease the blob and, if successful, becomes the ticket holder and can perform any tasks associated with that status. It can then renew the lease repeatedly to ensure that no other instance can acquire the lease and become the ticket holder. If the instance is recycled, then the lease expires after one minute, allowing another instance to acquire it and become the ticket holder.

See also

 ▸ You can see how to use the Storage Service REST API in the *Using the Windows Azure Storage Service REST API to copy a blob* recipe.

Using the Windows Azure Content-Delivery Network (CDN)

The Windows Azure Blob Service is hosted in a small number of Windows Azure datacenters worldwide. The Windows Azure Content-Delivery Network (CDN) is a service that enhances end user experience by caching blobs in more than 20 strategic locations across the World.

After the CDN is enabled for a storage account, a CDN endpoint can be used, instead of the storage-account endpoint, to access a cached version of publicly accessible blobs in the storage account. The CDN endpoint is location aware, and a request to the CDN endpoint is directed automatically to the closest CDN location. If the blob is not currently cached there, then the CDN retrieves the blob from the Blob service endpoint and caches it before satisfying the request.

The cache-control property of the blob can be used to specify a time-to-live in the cache. Otherwise, the CDN uses a heuristic based on how old the blob is and caches the blob, for the shorter of 72 hours or 20% of the time since the blob was last modified.

A custom domain can be associated with a CDN endpoint. As with a custom domain for a storage account, this provides a convenient alias for the CDN endpoint. When configuring a custom domain for either a CDN or a storage account, it is necessary to validate the custom domain by demonstrating access to the DNS records for the domain.

The endpoints for the Blob service and the CDN are as follows:

- `http://{account_name}.blob.core.windows.net`
- `http://{CDN_name}.vo.msecnd.net`

`{CDN_name}` is the unique identifier that the Windows Azure Portal uses to specify the CDN for the storage account. When the account name and CDN endpoints are associated with custom domains, they could be addressed as, for example:

- `http://blobs.{domain}.com`
- `http://cdn.{domain}.com`

In this recipe, we will learn how to enable a CDN for a Blob service endpoint, and associate a custom domain with it.

How to do it...

We are going to enable the CDN and validate it. Then, we will add a custom domain to it. We do this as follows:

1. On the Windows Azure Portal, select the storage account and click on **Enable CDN**.
2. On the Windows Azure Portal, select the newly created CDN and click on **Add Domain**. In the popup dialog, enter the desired custom domain.
3. On the CNAME management page of your DNS provider, add a new CNAME mapping the portal-provided validation domain to the CNAME verification domain.
4. On the Windows Azure Portal, select the custom domain for the CDN and click on **Validate Domain**.
5. On the CNAME management page of your DNS provider, delete the CNAME mapping from the portal-provided validation domain to the CNAME verification domain.
6. On the CNAME management page of your DNS provider, add a new CNAME mapping the desired custom domain to the CDN endpoint.

How it works...

In step 1, we use the Windows Azure Portal to enable the CDN for a specific storage account and in step 2, we add a custom domain to it.

In steps 3 and 4, we demonstrate our control over the custom domain through a validation process. The Windows Azure Portal provides a specific validation domain that we must use to create a CNAME mapping from the custom domain to the Windows Azure custom-domain verification endpoint. We then go back to the Windows Azure Portal and validate the domain.

Having validated the custom domain, we remove the validation CNAME mapping in step 5. Finally, in step 6, we add the CNAME mapping from our custom domain to the CDN endpoint.

Note that it can take some time for the CNAME mapping for the custom domain to percolate through the DNS system. It can then take some time for the CDN to recognize the custom domain.

There's more...

We add a custom domain for a storage account endpoint in exactly the same way, except that we specify the Blob service endpoint for the storage account instead of the CDN endpoint.

3
Going NoSQL with Windows Azure Tables

In this chapter, we will cover:

- ▶ Creating a table
- ▶ Creating a data model and context for an entity
- ▶ Using entity group transactions
- ▶ Diagnosing problems when using the Table service
- ▶ Handling concurrency with the Table service
- ▶ Choosing a PartitionKey and RowKey for a table
- ▶ Using continuation tokens and server-side paging
- ▶ Performing asynchronous queries
- ▶ Performing queries in parallel
- ▶ Handling the `WritingEntity` and `ReadingEntity` events

Introduction

The **Windows Azure Table Service** is the Windows Azure Storage Service feature that provides cost-effective scalable storage of entities. In this chapter, we focus on the Table service. In related chapters, we look at the other storage services: the Blob service and the Queue service.

During the last three decades, relational databases have become the dominant data system. Relational databases are transaction-oriented and implement **ACID** semantics in which database transactions are **a**tomic, **c**onsistent, **i**solated, and **d**urable. These are important considerations for a data system where data fidelity is absolute, such as those used in a financial system. However, large-scale data systems implementing ACID semantics are extremely expensive.

In the last decade, there has been a growing interest in creating cost-effective, large-scale data systems. This interest is driven primarily by the data mining needs of social websites that generate enormous amounts of click-stream data. Much of this data is read-only, so there is less emphasis on support for transactions. Furthermore, these data systems typically do not provide support for SQL, so they are referred to as **NoSQL** systems—with the *No* being an acronym for *not only*.

Some NoSQL data systems implement BASE semantics (**b**asically **a**vailable, **s**oft state, **e**ventually consistent) rather than ACID semantics. The idea being that a change to stored data does not have to be immediately consistent across the data system as long as it is eventually consistent.

The Table service is the NoSQL data system provided by the Windows Azure Platform. It provides large-scale storage at a cost significantly lower than that provided by SQL Azure—the relational database provided in the Windows Azure Platform.

The Table service uses storage accounts to provide an authentication boundary. Each storage account can store up to 100 TB of data. The Table service stores all data in one or more tables. Unlike a relational database, these tables have no schema and each entity stored in the table defines its own schema. We see how to create a table in the *Creating a table* recipe.

An entity is a collection of properties and their associated values. The Primary Key for a table is the combination of two properties: the `PartitionKey` and the `RowKey` that must be present in each entity stored in the table. The Table service uses the `PartitionKey` to provide scalability and the `RowKey` to ensure uniqueness for a given `PartitionKey`. The entities in a table with the same `PartitionKey` comprise a partition. We consider this further in the *Choosing a PartitionKey and RowKey for a table* recipe.

The Windows Azure Storage Service REST API provides the definitive interface to the Table service. The Windows Azure SDK contains the Windows Azure Storage Client library which is a high-level, managed .NET API for the Table service that hides the underlying Storage Service REST interface. The Storage Client library extends the WCF Data Services Client library with functionality specific to the Table service such as authentication, server-side paging, and automated retry logic. All the recipes in this chapter use the Storage Client library.

The Storage Client library follows the WCF Data Services paradigm and associates table entities with a model class. To some extent, this imposes a schema on the table although many model classes could be associated with a single table. It uses a context to track instances of the model class, which represent entities to be inserted in the table or retrieved from the table. We go further into this in the *Creating a data model and context for an entity* recipe. In the *Handling the WritingEntity and ReadingEntity events* recipe, we go deep into how a context converts instance data of the model class to and from the entity data stored in the atom entry used in the RESTful storage operations against the Table service.

The Table service provides limited support for ACID semantics. Up to 100 storage operations against the same partition may be batched into a single entity group transaction, and performed as a single transaction in which either all operations succeed or all operations are rejected. We consider these in the *Using entity group transactions* recipe. Note that the Table service does not implement BASE semantics because it uses hard state, with all data changes being strongly consistent.

Optimistic concurrency is a technique used in NoSQL data systems to avoid the scalability problems caused by data being locked to prevent simultaneous updates by different clients. The Table service implements optimistic concurrency by providing an **entity tag** (**ETag**) with each entity it returns to a client. A subsequent update succeeds only if the current ETag is provided. This provides a lightweight, and scalable, way to manage concurrent updates to an entity. We look at optimistic concurrency in the *Handling concurrency with the Table service* recipe.

The Table service supports the concept of server-side paging in which no more than 1,000 entities are returned in response to a query. When this throttling occurs, the Table service also returns continuation tokens that the client can use to reissue the query for the next page of data. We show this in the *Using continuation tokens and server-side paging* recipe.

The Storage Client library provides both synchronous and asynchronous versions of nearly all methods accessing the Table service. Asynchronous queries are introduced in the *Performing asynchronous queries* recipe. We follow this up by looking at how asynchronous queries can improve query performance in the *Performing queries in parallel* recipe. The *Using continuation tokens and server-side paging* recipe also contains examples of asynchronous queries.

As in any software system, many things can go wrong when developing a service or application using the Table service. In the *Diagnosing problems when using the Table service* recipe, we look at various ways of gathering more information and diagnosing problems when using the Table service.

The examples used in the recipe are developed in a simple WPF project.

Creating a table

The Windows Azure Table Service supports a simple two-level hierarchy. There is a single level of tables each of which contains zero or more entities. An entity can have up to 255 properties, including three system-defined properties, and there is no requirement that different entities in the same table have the same properties. This feature makes the Table service schemaless. The only requirement of entities in a table is that the combination of PartitionKey and RowKey is distinct for each entity in a table. Consequently, when a table is created, the only required information is its name.

The Windows Azure Storage Client library contains a `CloudTableClient` class that provides a set of synchronous and asynchronous methods supporting the creation and deletion of tables. It also supports the listing of the tables associated with a Windows Azure Storage Service storage account.

In this recipe, we will learn how to use the synchronous methods to create and delete tables as well as list them.

How to do it...

We are going to create two tables, list the tables, and then delete a table. We do this as follows:

1. Add a new class named `TablesExample` to the project.
2. Set the Target Framework for the project to .NET Framework 4.
3. Add the following assembly references to the project:
   ```
   Microsoft.WindowsAzure.StorageClient
   System.Configuration
   ```
4. Add the following `using` statements to the top of the class file:
   ```
   using Microsoft.WindowsAzure;
   using Microsoft.WindowsAzure.StorageClient;
   using System.Configuration;
   ```
5. Add the following member to the class:
   ```
   private CloudTableClient cloudTableClient;
   ```
6. Add the following constructor to the class:
   ```
   TablesExample()
   {
       CloudStorageAccount cloudStorageAccount =
           CloudStorageAccount.Parse(
           ConfigurationManager.AppSettings[
           "DataConnectionString"]);
       cloudTableClient =
           cloudStorageAccount.CreateCloudTableClient();
   }
   ```

7. Add the following method, creating a table, to the class:

```
public void CreateTable(String tableName,
    Boolean checkExistence = false)
{
    if (checkExistence)
    {
        cloudTableClient.CreateTableIfNotExist(tableName);
    }
    else
    {
        cloudTableClient.CreateTable(tableName);
    }
    Boolean doesTableExist =
        cloudTableClient.DoesTableExist(tableName);
}
```

8. Add the following method, deleting a table, to the class:

```
public void DeleteTable(String tableName)
{
    cloudTableClient.DeleteTable(tableName);
    Boolean doesTableExist =
        cloudTableClient.DoesTableExist(tableName);
}
```

9. Add the following method, listing the tables, to the class:

```
protected void ListTables(String tableNamePrefix)
{
    // Does a local filter
    IEnumerable<String> listTablesPrefix =
        cloudTableClient.ListTables(tableNamePrefix);
    Int32 countListTablesPrefix =
        listTablesPrefix.Count<String>();

    IEnumerable<String> listTables =
        cloudTableClient.ListTables();
    Int32 countListTables = listTables.Count<String>();
}
```

10. Add the following method to the class:

```
public static void UseTablesExample()
{
    TablesExample example = new TablesExample();
    example.CreateTable("Stars");
    example.CreateTable("Planets", true);
```

```
        example.ListTables("P");

        example.DeleteTable("Planets");
    }
```

11. Add the following to the **configuration** section of `app.config`:

```
<appSettings>
    <add key="DataConnectionString" value="DefaultEndpointsProtocol=
        http;AccountName={ACCOUNT_NAME};AccountKey={ACCOUNT_KEY}"/>
</appSettings>
```

How it works...

In steps 1 through 4, we set up the class. In step 5, we add a private member to store the `CloudTableClient` instance used to connect to the Table service. We initialize this in the constructor we add in step 6.

In step 7, we add a method that shows two ways to create a table. The first invokes `CreateTableIfNotExist()`, which creates the table only if it does not already exist. Note that this is not (currently) an atomic operation, so it is possible for it to fail if two threads invoke it simultaneously. The second invokes `CreateTable()`, which throws an exception if the table already exists. In step 8, we add a method that deletes a table. Note that, unlike many other methods in the Storage Client library, the `CreateTable()` and `DeleteTable()` do not come in versions that implement automatic retries in the event of failure.

In step 9, we add a method to list all the tables in the storage account. It does so in two different ways: with and without using a prefix. In practice, both of these invoke the same operation in the Storage Service REST API and the Storage Client library performs the requested prefix filtering on the client.

In step 10, we add a simple method to use the methods we added earlier. We create a couple of tables, list all the tables in the storage account, and then delete one of the tables.

In step 11, we add the connection string to the `app.config` configuration file. We must replace `{ACCOUNT_NAME}` and `{ACCOUNT_KEY}` with actual values for account name and access key.

Creating a data model and context for an entity

The Windows Azure Storage Client library uses WCF Data Services to invoke table operations in the Windows Azure Storage Services REST API. The library has methods providing functionality specific to the Windows Azure Table Service, such as retry functionality allowing methods to be retried automatically in the event of failure and continuation functionality supporting server-side paging.

In the Storage Client library, instances of a model class represent entities of a table. When saving an instance to a table, the Storage Client library creates a property in the entity for each public property of the instance. The model class must contain the Primary Key properties for the entity: `PartitionKey` and `RowKey`. An entity can have no more than 252 user-defined properties. Furthermore, if it is used to store query results, then the model class must have a default constructor taking no parameters. The Storage Client library provides the `TableServiceEntity` class as a convenient base class from which to derive model classes.

The Storage Client library supports only the following datatypes for entities:

- Byte[]
- Boolean
- DateTime
- Double
- Guid
- Int32
- Int64
- String

Both the `Byte[]` and `String` are limited to no more than 64 KB. Note that the Storage Client library automatically converts `DateTime` values to the local time zone when retrieving entities. Each entity has a maximum size of 1 MB.

WCF Data Services use `DataServiceContext` to expose storage operations and queries, as well as to track entities used in these storage operations and queries. Entities are tracked by adding them as new entities using `DataServiceContext.AddObject()`, or attaching them to the context with the `DataServiceContext.AttachTo()` method that provides additional functionality for updating entities. Entities returned by queries are also tracked. Any changes to tracked entities are submitted as individual storage operations when the `SaveChanges()` method is invoked on the context. When a context is used only for queries, performance can be improved by turning off tracking by setting `DataServiceContext.MergeOption` to `MergeOption.NoTracking`. We see more about **MergeOption** in the *Handling concurrency with the Table service* recipe.

The Storage Client library contains a `TableServiceContext` class, derived from `DataServiceContext`, which adds retry functionality to the synchronous and asynchronous `SaveChanges()` methods through the provision of `SaveChangesWithRetries()` methods. It can be convenient to create a model-dependent class derived from `TableServiceContext`. This can be generalized by creating a generic class parameterized by the type of the model class. Doing so simplifies the text of queries and provides type-safe methods for managing entities.

The following two code fragments demonstrate this simplification:

```
from c in tableServiceContext.CreateQuery<Country>("Country")
from c in countryContext.GenericEntities
```

The first example explicitly uses a `TableServiceContext` to create a query, while the second uses a generic context class exposing a `GenericEntities` property encapsulating the `CreateQuery<Country>()` method.

Contexts should not be reused. That is, unrelated storage operations should use different contexts.

In this recipe, we will learn how to create a model class and an associated context class and use them to perform various storage operations and queries.

How to do it...

We are going to create a model class to describe the entities stored in a table and a context class to manage access to these entities. We create an extension class to provide a factory method to create instances of the context class. Finally, we add a class with several methods demonstrating the use of the model class both with a `TableServiceContext` and the generic context class we added. We do this as follows:

1. Add a new class named `ModelContextExample` to the project.

2. Set the Target Framework for the project to.NET Framework 4.

3. Add the following assembly references to the project:

   ```
   Microsoft.WindowsAzure.StorageClient
   System.Configuration
   System.Data.Services.Client
   ```

4. Add the following `using` statements to the top of the class file:

   ```
   using Microsoft.WindowsAzure;
   using Microsoft.WindowsAzure.StorageClient;
   using System.Configuration;
   using System.Data.Services.Common;
   ```

5. Add the following model class declaration, for the model class, after the namespace declaration for the class file:

   ```
   [DataServiceKey("PartitionKey", "RowKey")]
   public class Country
   {
       private readonly String partitionKey = "country";

       public String PartitionKey { get; set; }
       public String RowKey { get; set; }
   ```

```
public DateTime Timestamp { get; set; }
public String CapitalCity { get; set; }
public Int64 Population { get; set; }

public Country() { }

public Country(String name, String capitalCity,
    Int64 population)
{
    PartitionKey = partitionKey;
    RowKey = name;
    CapitalCity = capitalCity;
    Population = population;
}
}
```

6. Add the following class declaration, for the generic context class, after the model class declaration:

```
public class GenericContext<T> : TableServiceContext
{
    public String TableName {get; set;}

    public GenericContext(
        String baseAddress, StorageCredentials credentials)
        : base(baseAddress, credentials)
    {
        Type type = typeof(T);
        TableName = type.Name;
    }

    public void AddEntity(T entity)
    {
        AddObject(TableName, entity);
    }

    public IQueryable<T> GenericEntities
    {
        get { return CreateQuery<T>(TableName); }
    }
}
```

7. Add the following class declaration, exposing a factory method for the generic-context class:

```
public static class GenericContextExtensions
{
    public static GenericContext<T> GetGenericContext<T>(
        this CloudTableClient cloudTableClient)
    {
        GenericContext<T> genericContext =
            new GenericContext<T>(
                cloudTableClient.BaseUri.ToString(),
                cloudTableClient.Credentials);
        return genericContext;
    }
}
```

8. Add the following private member to the `ModelContextExample` class:

```
private CloudTableClient cloudTableClient;
```

9. Add the following constructor to the `ModelContextExample` class:

```
private ModelContextExample(String tableName)
{
    CloudStorageAccount cloudStorageAccount =
        CloudStorageAccount.Parse(
        ConfigurationManager.AppSettings[
        "DataConnectionString"]);
    cloudTableClient =
        cloudStorageAccount.CreateCloudTableClient();
    cloudTableClient.CreateTableIfNotExist(tableName);
}
```

10. Add the following method to the `ModelContextExample` class:

```
private void UseTableServiceContext()
{
    TableServiceContext tableServiceContext =
        cloudTableClient.GetDataServiceContext();

    tableServiceContext.AddObject("Country",
        new Country("Australia", "Canberra", 22558947));
    tableServiceContext.AddObject("Country",
        new Country("India", "New Delhi", 1189914000));
    tableServiceContext.SaveChangesWithRetries();

    CloudTableQuery<Country> query =
        (from c in tableServiceContext.CreateQuery<Country>(
        "Country")
```

```
        where c.PartitionKey == "country" &&
            c.RowKey == "Australia"
        select c).AsTableServiceQuery<Country>();

    Country country = query.FirstOrDefault<Country>();

    tableServiceContext.DeleteObject(country);
    tableServiceContext.SaveChangesWithRetries();
}
```

11. Add the following method to the `ModelContextExample` class:

```
private void UseGenericContext()
{
    GenericContext<Country> countryContext =
        cloudTableClient.GetGenericContext<Country>();
    countryContext.AddEntity(
        new Country("France", "Paris", 63900000));
    countryContext.AddEntity(
        new Country("Italy", "Rome", 59600000));
    countryContext.SaveChangesWithRetries();

    CloudTableQuery<Country> query =
        (from c in countryContext.GenericEntities
          where c.PartitionKey == "country" &&
              c.RowKey == "France"
         select c).AsTableServiceQuery<Country>();

    Country country = query.FirstOrDefault<Country>();

    country.Population += 100000;
    countryContext.UpdateObject(country);
    countryContext.SaveChangesWithRetries();
}
```

12. Add the following method to the `ModelContextExample` class:

```
public static void UseModelContextExample()
{
    String tableName = "Country";
    ModelContextExample example =
        new ModelContextExample (tableName);
    example.UseTableServiceContext();
    example.UseGenericContext();
}
```

13. Add the following to the configuration section of `app.config`:

```
<appSettings>
  <add key="DataConnectionString" value="DefaultEndpointsProtocol=
http;AccountName={ACCOUNT_NAME};AccountKey={ACCOUNT_KEY}"/>
</appSettings>
```

How it works...

In steps 1 through 4, we set up the `ModelContextExample` class.

In step 5, we add a model class named `Country` to represent entities describing various properties of countries. The `PartitionKey` is always set to *country* for entities created using this class. The `RowKey` is set to the name of the country. The `Timestamp` is one of the three system properties present in each entity. In practice, it is not needed in the model class. There are two constructors: one being the required parameterless constructor and the other fully initializing an instance of the model class. We decorate the class with the `DataServiceKey` attribute to specify the Primary Key for entities. The Storage Client library contains the `TableServiceEntity` class that can be used as a base for the model class.

In step 6, we add a generic-context class, `GenericContext<T>`, derived from `TableServiceContext`. We infer the table name from the name of the `Type`. The constructor for this class simply invokes the base class constructor. We add a type-safe method to add objects to the context. Finally, we add a property, `GenericEntities`, returning an `IQueryable<T>` which we use to simplify the syntax for queries.

In step 7, we add a utility class named `GenericContextExtensions` that exposes a factory method to create `GenericContext<T>` instances. This mimics the `GetServiceContext()` factory method in the `CloudTableClient` class. It is a trivial exercise to extend this class to provide additional type-safe methods for update, delete, and so on.

In step 8, we add a private member to the `ModelContextExample` class to store the `CloudTableClient` we use to connect to the Table service. We initialize this in the constructor we add in step 9. We also create the `Country` table there.

In step 10, we add a method that uses a `TableServiceContext` to add several entities to the `Country` table. It then queries the table to retrieve a single entity and deletes that entity from the table.

In step 11, we add a method that uses `GenericContext<Country>` to add several entities to the `Country` table. It then queries the table to retrieve a single entity and updates that entity in the table.

In step 12, we add a method that uses the methods we added in steps 10 and 11.

In step 13, we add the connection string to the `app.config` configuration file. We must replace `{ACCOUNT_NAME}` and `{ACCOUNT_KEY}` with actual values for account name and access key.

TableServiceEntity class

The Storage Client library contains a `TableServiceEntity` class that can be used as a base class for the model class. It contains properties for the `PartitionKey`, `RowKey`, and `Timestamp`. Using the `TableServiceEntity` class, the model class in this recipe can be replaced with the following:

```
public class Country : TableServiceEntity
{
    private readonly String partitionKey = "country";

    public String CapitalCity { get; set; }
    public Int64 Population { get; set; }

    public Country() { }

    public Country(String name, String capitalCity,
      Int64 population)
    {
        PartitionKey = partitionKey;
        RowKey = name;
        CapitalCity = capitalCity;
        Population = population;
    }
}
```

See also

▶   The _Using entity group transactions_ recipe in this chapter shows entities being explicitly tracked in a context.

Using entity group transactions

The Windows Azure Table Service supports entity group transactions in which, a group of storage operations on entities with the same `PartitionKey` are handled atomically. That is, if any operation in the group fails, then all the operations are rolled back. Unlike transactions in a traditional SQL database, entity group transactions cannot span tables or even partitions.

A single entity group transaction is limited to no more than 100 storage operations and a total size of 4 MB. An individual entity can be used only once in an entity group transaction. Any combination of create, update, and delete operations can be contained in an entity group transaction. Alternatively, it can contain only query operations. However, an entity group transaction may not combine queries with create, update, and delete operations.

The concept of entity group transactions exists in the WCF Data Services that the table functionality of the Storage Client library is based on. In WCF Data Services, entity group transactions are referred to as **batch operations**.

The default behavior when a `SaveChanges()` or `SaveChangesWithRetries()` method is invoked on a context is that any changes to entities tracked by the context are submitted to the Table service one storage operation at a time. Specifying a `SaveChangesOptions.Batch` parameter for these methods causes all the changes to be submitted as a single entity group transaction.

Regardless of how many individual storage operations a single entity group transaction contains, it is billed as a single storage operation. This can bring considerable cost savings over performing the storage operations individually.

In this recipe, we will learn how to use entity group transactions.

Getting ready

This recipe uses a model class named `Country` that is declared in the preceding *Creating a data model and context for an entity* recipe.

How to do it...

We are going to create some contexts of type `TableServiceContext`. We are then going to show one entity group transaction inserting two entities in a table and another entity group transaction that updates one entity and deletes another from the same table. We do this as follows:

1. Add a new class named `EntityGroupTransactionsExample` to the project.
2. Set the Target Framework for the project to.NET Framework 4.
3. Add the following assembly references to the project:

   ```
   Microsoft.WindowsAzure.StorageClient
   System.Configuration
   System.Data.Services.Client
   ```

4. Add the following `using` statements to the top of the class file:

```
using Microsoft.WindowsAzure;
using Microsoft.WindowsAzure.StorageClient;
using System.Configuration;
using System.Data.Services.Client;
```

5. Add the following private members to the EntityGroupTransactionsExample class:

```
private CloudTableClient cloudTableClient;
private String tableName = "Country";
```

6. Add the following constructor to the class:

```
public EntityGroupTransactionsExample()
{
   CloudStorageAccount cloudStorageAccount =
      CloudStorageAccount.Parse(
         ConfigurationManager.AppSettings[
         "DataConnectionString"]);
   cloudTableClient =
      cloudStorageAccount.CreateCloudTableClient();
   cloudTableClient.CreateTableIfNotExist(tableName);
}
```

7. Add the following method, showing an insert-only entity group transaction, to the class:

```
public void BatchInsert()
{
   TableServiceContext tableServiceContext =
      cloudTableClient.GetDataServiceContext();

   Country pakistan = new Country(
      "Pakistan", "Islamabad", 171365000);
   tableServiceContext.AddObject(tableName, pakistan);

   Country bangladesh = new Country(
      "Bangladesh", "Dhaka", 149715000);
   tableServiceContext.AddObject(tableName, bangladesh);

   tableServiceContext.SaveChangesWithRetries(
      SaveChangesOptions.Batch);
}
```

8. Add the following method, showing a mixed-operation entity group transaction, to the class:

```
public void MixedBatch()
{
    TableServiceContext tableServiceContext =
        cloudTableClient.GetDataServiceContext();

    Country turkey = new Country(
        "Turkey", "Istanbul", 72561312);
    tableServiceContext.AddObject(tableName, turkey);

    Country pakistan = new Country(
        "Pakistan", "Islamabad", 171000000);
    tableServiceContext.AttachTo(tableName, pakistan, "*");
    tableServiceContext.UpdateObject(pakistan);

    Country bangladesh = new Country() {
        PartitionKey = "country", RowKey = "Bangladesh" };
    tableServiceContext.AttachTo(tableName, bangladesh, "*");
    tableServiceContext.DeleteObject( bangladesh);

    tableServiceContext.SaveChangesWithRetries(
        SaveChangesOptions.Batch);
}
```

9. Add the following method, invoking the other methods, to the class:

```
public static void UseEntityGroupTransactionsExample()
{
    EntityGroupTransactionsExample example =
        new EntityGroupTransactionsExample();
    example.BatchInsert();
    example.MixedBatch();
}
```

10. Add the following to the configuration section of `app.config`:

```
<appSettings>
  <add key="DataConnectionString" value="DefaultEndpointsProtocol=
http;AccountName={ACCOUNT_NAME};AccountKey={ACCOUNT_KEY}"/>
</appSettings>
```

How it works...

In steps 1 through 4, we set up the `EntityGroupTransactionsExample` class. In step 5, we add private members to the `ModelContextExample` class to store the `CloudTableClient` we use to connect to the Table service and provide the name of the table we use. We initialize the `CloudTableClient` instance in the constructor we add in step 6.

In step 7, we add a `BatchInsert()` method. In it, we create a new context. Then, we create two entities and add them to the context with `AddObject()` before invoking `SaveChangesW ithRetries(SaveChangesOptions.Batch)` to send the appropriate insert operations to the Table service as a single entity group transaction.

In step 8, we add a `MixedBatch()` method. In it, we create a new context and use it to update one entity and delete another. As we are performing storage operations on existing entities, we need to take into account the optimistic concurrency provided by the Table service. We do this by using `AttachTo()` with an ETag of `"*"` to have the context track the entities. This special ETag value allows us to override the optimistic concurrency used by the Table service and make it update or delete this entity in the table. A valid ETag must be provided when updating or deleting objects. A valid value is one returned with the entity as the result of a query or the special value of `"*"` as in this example.

After attaching the entities, we use `UpdateObject()` with one entity and `DeleteObject()` with the other to indicate which storage operation should be used. Finally, we invoke `SaveCh angesWithRetries(SaveChangesOptions.Batch)` to send the appropriate update and delete operations to the Table service as a single entity group transaction.

In step 9, we add a method that uses the methods we added in steps 7 and 8.

In step 10, we add the connection string to the `app.config` configuration file. We must replace `{ACCOUNT_NAME}` and `{ACCOUNT_KEY}` with actual values for the account name and access key.

See also

- We introduced contexts in the *Creating a data model and context for an entity* recipe. We discuss the optimistic concurrency used by the Table service in the *Handling concurrency with the Table service* recipe.

Diagnosing problems when using the Table service

The Windows Azure Table Service is cloud based. In the Windows Azure SDK, Microsoft provides a storage emulator which runs in the development environment and can be used for local development and testing. This emulator uses Microsoft SQL Server Express rather than the **Distributed File System** used by the Table service. The storage emulator can also be configured to use Microsoft SQL Server.

There are some circumstances in which the storage emulator and the Table service behave differently. Consequently, when problems are identified while developing with the storage emulator, it is often useful to check whether the problem exists when using the Table service. This is particularly true when there is a problem with an edge-case use of tables.

The Windows Azure Storage Service REST API is the definitive way to interact with the Table service. The Windows Azure Storage Client library is a high-level .NET library that sits on top of the Storage Service REST API. The Windows Azure diagnostics capability can be used to log any exceptions thrown by the Storage Client library. However, the error messages contained in these exceptions tend to be less complete than those returned by the Storage Service REST API.

A utility like *Fiddler*, that allows us to inspect HTTP traffic, can be helpful in identifying problems when developing against either the Table service or the storage emulator. Fiddler makes it easy to verify that the correct REST operations are invoked and to check the request and response headers and payloads. These can be compared with the MSDN documentation in the Windows Azure Storage Service REST API. Fiddler also provides direct access to any error message returned by the Storage Service REST API.

No special configuration is required to use Fiddler with the Table service. Fiddler merely needs to be running to capture all the network traffic to and from the Azure Table Service. However, a special connection string must be provided when using Fiddler with the storage emulator. In this case, the data connection string must be set to the following:

```
UseDevelopmentStorage=true;DevelopmentStorageProxyUri=http://ipv4.
fiddler
```

Although Fiddler is useful in identifying problems, it can itself introduce problems when used with the storage emulator, for example, when an entity is added to a context both directly and as the result of a query. Normally, the Storage Client library would merge the two entities into a single tracked entity. However, when Fiddler is used against the storage emulator, it modifies the URL used to identify the queried entity and this prevents the Storage Client library from correctly identifying and merging the two versions of the entity.

The Windows Azure SDK provides additional logging for the storage emulator. The logs generated by this include the SQL statements the storage emulator sends to Microsoft SQL Server (Express). The information logged can be helpful in diagnosing problems in using the storage emulator.

This logging is configured in the following configuration file:

`%LocalAppData%\DevelopmentStorage\DevelompentStorage.config`

It is off by default, but may be enabled by setting the value of the `LoggingEnabled` element to `true`. Note the misspelling in the file name. This logging should normally be disabled because it can generate a lot of data.

In this recipe, we will learn how to diagnose problems when developing against the Table service or the storage emulator.

How to do it...

We are going to install Fiddler and use it to help us diagnose problems when using either the Table service or the storage emulator. We do this as follows:

1. Download Fiddler from `http://www.fiddler2.com/fiddler2/`.
2. Install Fiddler.
3. Configure the `DataConnectionString`, if using the Storage Client library and the storage emulator. We don't need to change this if we are accessing the Table service. When using the storage emulator, we set the `DataConnectionString` to the following:

   `UseDevelopmentStorage=true;DevelopmentStorageProxyUri=http://ipv4.fiddler`

4. Start Fiddler.
5. Run the application.
6. In Fiddler, we select a HTTP session with an error and go to the **Inspectors** tab. We then look at the **Raw** view for both request and response and identity any unexpected behavior.

How it works...

In steps 1 and 2, we download and install Fiddler. The modification to `DataConnectionString` in step 3 allows the Storage Client library to use the Fiddler proxy.

In steps 4 through 6, we use Fiddler to intercept network traffic to the Storage Service or storage emulator, and investigate any issues. We can compare the request and response payloads with the MSDN documentation for the Storage Service REST API to identify any discrepancies between the documented and actual payloads.

There's more...

Fiddler is also helpful in diagnosing problems with the Windows Azure Blob Service or Windows Azure Queue Service.

Handling concurrency with the Table service

The Windows Azure Table Service supports optimistic concurrency for entity updates. Each entity has an associated entity tag (ETag) that changes whenever the entity is updated. A storage operation that updates or deletes an entity will succeed only if it provides either the current ETag or the special ETag value of "*", which forces the change to be accepted by the Windows Azure Table service.

A context, either `TableServiceContext` or `DataServiceContext`, keeps a list of the entities it is currently tracking. This list includes objects added to the context with `TableServiceContext.AddObject()` or attached through `TableServiceContext.AttachTo()`. Unless configured otherwise, the entities returned by a query are also tracked. Any modification to a tracked entity is submitted as the appropriate storage operation to the Table service when `DataServiceContext.SaveChanges()` or `TableServiceContext.SaveChangesWithRetries()` is invoked.

The `TableServiceContext.MergeOption` property can be used to specify the way a tracked entity is affected when the same entity is retrieved from a table. This property takes the following values in the `MergeOption` enumeration: `AppendOnly`, `NoTracking`, `OverwriteChanges`, and `PreserveChanges`.

With a `MergeOption.AppendOnly` context, an entity tracked by the context is not updated when the same entity is retrieved by a query. Other entities retrieved by the query are added to the list of entities tracked by the context. As the ETag of an existing entity is also not updated, any update storage operation for the entity will probably fail because of an invalid ETag. This is the default value of `DataServiceContext.MergeOption`.

With a `MergeOption.NoTracking` context, entities retrieved by a query are not added to the list of entities tracked by the context. This can provide a performance improvement if these queried entities are not used in other storage operations. As the ETag of an existing entity is also not updated, any update storage operation for the entity will probably fail because of an invalid ETag.

With a `MergeOption.OverwriteChanges` context, an entity tracked by the context is updated completely when the same entity is retrieved by a query. Other entities retrieved by the query are added to the list of entities tracked by the context. As the ETag of an existing entity is updated, any update storage operation for the entity will probably succeed. However, any modifications made to the tracked entity before the query will have been lost when it was overwritten.

With a `MergeOption.PreserveChanges` context, only the ETag of an entity tracked by the context is updated when the same entity is retrieved by a query. The remaining properties remain untouched. Other entities retrieved by the query are added to the list of entities tracked by the context. As the ETag of an existing entity is updated, any update storage operation for the entity will probably succeed. Any modifications made to the tracked entity, before the query, are preserved.

As the Table service uses optimistic concurrency, it is not possible to guarantee the success of a storage operation with a specific ETag on a context. This is because another context may have performed a storage operation that changed the current ETag for an entity, thereby invalidating the ETag on the first context. The special ETag value of "*" can be used to force an update regardless of current ETag value.

In this recipe, we will learn how to use `DataServiceContext.MergeOption` to manage optimistic concurrency for update and delete storage operations with the Table service.

Getting ready

This recipe uses a model class named `Country` that is declared in the *Creating a data model and context for an entity* recipe in this chapter.

How to do it...

For each value of the `MergeOption` enumeration, we are going to create a context and assign its `MergeOption` property to that value. We are then going to look at the effect on tracked entities when the same entity is retrieved by a query on the same context. We will also look at the effect of using the special "*" ETag value. We do this as follows:

1. Add a new class named `OptimisticConcurrencyExample` to the project.

2. Set the Target Framework for the project to.NET Framework 4.

3. Add the following assembly references to the project:

   ```
   Microsoft.WindowsAzure.StorageClient
   System.Configuration
   System.Data.Services.Client
   ```

4. Add the following `using` statements to the top of the class file:

   ```
   using Microsoft.WindowsAzure;
   using Microsoft.WindowsAzure.StorageClient;
   using System.Configuration;
   using System.Data.Services.Client;
   ```

5. Add the following private members to the class:

```
private CloudTableClient cloudTableClient;
private String tableName = "Country";
```

6. Add the following constructor to the class:

```
public OptimisticConcurrencyExample()
{
   CloudStorageAccount cloudStorageAccount =
      CloudStorageAccount.Parse(
      ConfigurationManager.AppSettings[
      "DataConnectionString"]);
   cloudTableClient =
      cloudStorageAccount.CreateCloudTableClient();
   cloudTableClient.CreateTableIfNotExist(tableName);
}
```

7. Add the following method, adding an entry to the table named `Country`, to the class:

```
public void AddCountry(String name, String capitalCity,
   Int64 population)
{
   TableServiceContext tableServiceContext =
      cloudTableClient.GetDataServiceContext();

   Country country = new Country(
      name, capitalCity, population);
   tableServiceContext.AddObject(tableName, country);
   tableServiceContext.SaveChangesWithRetries();
}
```

8. Add the following method, used to try out the various `MergeOption` values, to the class:

```
public void ModifyEntity(MergeOption mergeOption)
{
   TableServiceContext tableServiceContext =
      cloudTableClient.GetDataServiceContext();
   tableServiceContext.MergeOption = mergeOption;

   Country norway = new Country("Norway", "Oslo", 4920000);
   tableServiceContext.AttachTo(tableName, norway);
   tableServiceContext.UpdateObject(norway);

   CloudTableQuery<Country> query = (
      from c in
      tableServiceContext.CreateQuery<Country>(tableName)
      select c).AsTableServiceQuery<Country>();

   List<Country> countries = query.ToList<Country>();

   tableServiceContext.SaveChangesWithRetries();
}
```

9. Add the following method, forcing an update, to the class:

```
public void ForceUpdate()
{
    TableServiceContext tableServiceContext =
        cloudTableClient.GetDataServiceContext();

    Country norway = new Country("Norway", "Oslo", 4900000);
    tableServiceContext.AttachTo(tableName, norway, "*");
    tableServiceContext.UpdateObject(norway);

    tableServiceContext.SaveChangesWithRetries();
}
```

10. Add the following method, invoking the other methods, to the class:

```
public static void UseOptimisticConcurrencyExample()
{
    OptimisticConcurrencyExample example =
        new OptimisticConcurrencyExample();
    example.AddCountry("Norway", "Oslo", 4918900);
    example.ForceUpdate();
    example.ModifyEntity(MergeOption.PreserveChanges);
    example.ModifyEntity(MergeOption.OverwriteChanges);
    // Next two fail
    //example.ModifyEntity(MergeOption.AppendOnly);
    //example.ModifyEntity(MergeOption.NoTracking);
}
```

11. Add the following to the configuration section of `app.config`:

```
<appSettings>
    <add key="DataConnectionString" value="DefaultEndpointsProtocol=
http;AccountName={ACCOUNT_NAME};AccountKey={ACCOUNT_KEY}"/>
</appSettings>
```

How it works...

In steps 1 through 4, we set up the OptimisticConcurrencyExample class. In step 5, we add private members to the OptimisticConcurrencyExample class to store the CloudTableClient we use to connect to the Table service and provide the name of the table we use. We initialize the CloudTableClient instance in the constructor we add in step 6.

In step 7, we add a method to add an entity to the table named `Country`. In doing so, we use `SaveChangesWithRetries()` so that we retry the save operation using the default exponential backoff `RetryPolicy`. We see more about the default `RetryPolicy` in the *Using retry policies with blob operations* recipe in Chapter 2.

In step 8, we add the `ModifyEntity()` method which we use to try out the various settings for `DataServiceContext.MergeOption`. In this method, we create a context and set its `MergeOption` property to the value passed in the parameter. We then attach an entity to the context and specify that the entity is an update to an existing entity. The ETag associated with the entity is null. We then retrieve all the entities in the `Country` table, including this entity, and invoke the update storage operation by calling `SaveChangesWithRetries()`. The optimistic concurrency used by the Table service may cause this storage operation to fail with an invalid ETag value.

In step 9, we add the `ForceUpdate()` method which uses the special `"*"` ETag value to force an update to the entity in the table regardless of any change made by other contexts.

In step 10, we add a `UseOptimisticConcurrencyExample()` method to try out the various `MergeOption` values. `ForceUpdate()` always succeeds and the entity is correctly updated in the table.

When invoked with `MergeOption.PreserveChanges`, the `ModifyEntity()` method successfully updates the table with the values the entity was initialized with. When invoked with `MergeOption.OverwriteChanges`, the `ModifyEntity()` method successfully updates the table with the values retrieved by the query. However, the values the entity was initialized with are not used in the update.

When invoked with `MergeOption.AppendOnly` or `MergeOption.NoTracking`, the `ModifyEntity()` method fails because the ETag value sent with the storage operation is the null value associated with the original entity in the context. When used with `MergeOption.NoTracking`, the entities retrieved by the query are not added to the list of entities tracked by the context.

In step 11, we add the connection string to the `app.config` configuration file. We must replace `{ACCOUNT_NAME}` and `{ACCOUNT_KEY}` with actual values for account name and access key.

There's more...

When using the methods in this recipe, we have to be wary of the consequences of using a proxy, like Fiddler, to inspect the network traffic to the storage emulator. This causes the context to fail to recognize that a queried entity is the same entity as one already tracked by the context. This leads to unexpected and unwanted consequences. We look at this in the *Diagnosing problems when using the Table service* recipe in this chapter.

> ▶ We introduce contexts in the *Creating a data model and context for an entity* recipe. There are additional examples of using optimistic concurrency in the *Using entity group transactions* recipe.

Choosing a PartitionKey and RowKey for a table

The Primary Key for a table in the Windows Azure Table Service is the combination of `PartitionKey` and `RowKey`. These properties are not symmetric in that the `PartitionKey` and `RowKey` serve different purposes. The `PartitionKey` provides scalability for a table while the `RowKey` ensures uniqueness for a given value of `PartitionKey`.

A set of entities with the same `PartitionKey` in a table is referred to as a partition. The Table service has a scalability target for a partition that is lower than that for the storage account. Consequently, performance can be improved by ensuring that data access is distributed across partitions. It is important that the `PartitionKey` is designed, so that performance is optimized for the actual workload of a service.

An anti-pattern for the design of the `PartitionKey` is the *append* pattern in which the `PartitionKey` is created, so that all entities inserted in some interval of time are inserted in the same partition. For example, the `PartitionKey` created from the current date. This pattern distributes entities across many partitions, which is good, but it also ensures that all inserts are made to a single partition. This has a negative impact on scalability because little benefit is gained from the Table service load balancing partitions, as all inserts go to a single partition.

A solution to this anti-pattern is to create a compound `PartitionKey` comprising the current date and some bucket identifier. This means that instead of inserting entities in a single partition at a time, distinct entities are distributed among a set of date-dependent buckets. Simple algorithms for choosing the bucket include round robin (for example, 1, 2, 3, 4, 5) or random (for example, 3, 5, 2, 1, 4). This provision of multiple buckets (or partitions) for inserts allows the Table service to load balance partitions to improve performance.

When a query is executed against a table, the resulting entities are ordered by `PartitionKey` then `RowKey`. The Table service does not support any other index. Consequently, if entities must be retrieved in a particular order, the `RowKey` must be constructed to facilitate that order. An interesting case is where entities must be retrieved in reverse chronological order. Each `DateTime` has an associated `Ticks` property specifying the number of ticks since the earliest `DateTime`. A chronological order for the `RowKey` can be achieved by using the `Ticks` count for a `DateTime` for the `RowKey`.

A reverse chronological ordering can be achieved by subtracting the number of `Ticks` from the `Ticks` count for the maximum value of `DateTime`. For example, the following calculates the number of ticks remaining from now until the maximum number of ticks:

```
DateTime.MaxValue.Ticks - DateTime.UtcNow.Ticks
```

When converted to a `String`, as required for the `RowKey`, this requires 19 characters to ensure that all possible values can be represented. The `Ticks` count can be converted as follows:

```
String.Format("{0:D19}",
    DateTime.MaxValue.Ticks - DateTime.UtcNow.Ticks);
```

This creates a 19 character `String` that, when used for the `RowKey`, creates a reverse chronological ordering.

In this recipe, we will learn how to create a `PartitionKey` that avoids the *append* anti-pattern. We will also learn how to create a `RowKey` that generates a reverse chronological ordering.

How to do it...

We are going to create a model class. Then, we are going to add two methods: one uses a `PartitionKey` designed to avoid the append anti-pattern and the other uses a `RowKey` constructed from `DateTime.Ticks`, so that the entities are stored in reverse chronological order. We do this as follows:

1. Add a new class named `PartitionKeyRowKeyExample`to the project.

2. Set the Target Framework for the project to.NET Framework 4.

3. Add the following assembly references to the project:
   ```
   Microsoft.WindowsAzure.StorageClient
   System.Configuration
   System.Data.Services.Client
   ```

4. Add the following `using` statements to the top of the class file:
   ```
   using Microsoft.WindowsAzure;
   using Microsoft.WindowsAzure.StorageClient;
   using System.Configuration;
   using System.Data.Services.Common;
   ```

5. Add the following model class after the namespace declaration:
   ```
   public class Comment : TableServiceEntity
   {
       public String Text { get; set; }
       public Comment() { }
   }
   ```

6. Add the following method, focused on the `PartitionKey`, to the class:

```
private static void AppendWithPartitionKey()
{
    TableServiceContext tableServiceContext =
        cloudTableClient.GetDataServiceContext();

    DateTime now = DateTime.UtcNow;
    String randomBucketPartitionKey =
        String.Format("{0:yyyyMMdd}-{1}", now, now.Ticks & 0x7);

    Comment comment = new Comment
    {
        PartitionKey = randomBucketPartitionKey,
        RowKey = "Shakespeare",
        Text = "To be, or not to be"
    };

    tableServiceContext.AddObject("Comment", comment);
    tableServiceContext.SaveChangesWithRetries();

    CloudTableQuery<Comment> query =
        (from entity in
         tableServiceContext.CreateQuery<Comment>(
            "Comment")
         where entity.PartitionKey == randomBucketPartitionKey
         select entity).AsTableServiceQuery<Comment>();

    List<Comment> comments = query.Execute().ToList();
}
```

7. Add the following method, focused on the `RowKey`, to the class:

```
private static void UseTicksForRowKey()
{
    TableServiceContext tableServiceContext =
        cloudTableClient.GetDataServiceContext();

    // Max tick value is 19 digits
    String reverseTicksRowKey = String.Format("{0:D19}",
        DateTime.MaxValue.Ticks - DateTime.UtcNow.Ticks);

    Comment comment = new Comment
    {
        PartitionKey = "play",
        RowKey = reverseTicksRowKey,
        Text = "Hamlet"
```

```
    };

    tableServiceContext.AddObject("Comment", comment);
    tableServiceContext.SaveChangesWithRetries();

    CloudTableQuery<Comment> query =
        (from entity in
        tableServiceContext.CreateQuery<Comment>(
        "Comment")
        where entity.PartitionKey == "play"
        && entity.RowKey.CompareTo(reverseTicksRowKey) >= 0
        select entity).AsTableServiceQuery<Comment>();

    List<Comment> comments = query.Execute().ToList();
}
```

8. Add the following method, using the methods added earlier, to the class:

```
public static void UsePartitioningExample()
{
    PartitioningExample.AppendWithPartitionKey();
    PartitioningExample.UseTicksForRowKey();
}
```

9. Add the following to the configuration section of `app.config`:

```
<appSettings>
    <add key="DataConnectionString" value="DefaultEndpointsProtocol=
    http;AccountName={ACCOUNT_NAME};AccountKey={ACCOUNT_KEY}"/>
</appSettings>
```

How it works...

In steps 1 through 4, we set up the `PartitionKeyRowKeyExample` class.

In step 5, we add a model class named `Comment`.

The `AppendWithPartitionKey()` method we add in step 6 shows how to construct a random bucket identifier that we can use for the `PartitionKey` and so avoid the append pattern. We add a random element by constructing an integer between 0 and 7 from the last three bits of `now.Ticks`. We insert an entity using this key and then retrieve it with a simple query.

The `UseTicksForRowKey()` method we add in step 7 shows how to create a `RowKey` that implements a reverse chronological ordering. We insert an entity using this key, and then retrieve it with a simple query.

In step 8, we add a method that uses the methods we added earlier.

In step 9, we add the connection string to the `app.config` configuration file. We must replace {`ACCOUNT_NAME`} and {`ACCOUNT_KEY`} with actual values for account name and access key.

Using continuation tokens and server-side paging

The Windows Azure Table Service uses **partition servers** to manage the entities stored in a table. One partition server manages all the entities with the same `PartitionKey` in the table. However, entities with different values of `PartitionKey` may be managed by different partition servers. This distribution of entities among partition servers is, in general, transparent to clients of the Table service. This partitioning scheme is central to the scalability of the Table service.

When processing a query, the Table service submits the query to the first partition server (ordered by `PartitionKey`) that manages entities satisfying any filter on `PartitionKey`. It then returns the first page of up to 1,000 entities retrieved by the partition server. The Table service inserts two headers: `x-ms-continuation-NextPartitionKey` and (a possibly null) `x-ms-continuation-NextRowKey` into the response if there are additional results. These headers comprise the continuation tokens for the query.

Any remaining results can be retrieved one page at a time by adding the continuation tokens as request headers to the query. The Table service uses these continuation tokens to start the query processing at the correct page. This may be on the current partition server or the next partition server if the previous query had returned all the entities it managed that matched the query. The client can reuse the continuation tokens if a previously requested page of data is needed. This paging functionality is referred to as server-side paging.

Note that it is possible that a query execution returns no entities, but does return a continuation token indicating that there are additional results. This can happen if a query spans multiple partition servers but the current partition server has found no entities matching the query.

The Storage Client library supports manual handling of continuation tokens with the `DataServiceQuery<T>` class and supports automated handling of continuation tokens with the `CloudTableQuery<T>` class. If a large number of entities satisfy a query invoked using a synchronous method of the `CloudTableQuery<T>` class, then the method may not return for a considerable time.

When invoking `Execute()` on a `DataServiceQuery<T>`, the result can be cast into a `QueryOperationResponse` from which the continuation tokens, if present, can be extracted. The `DataServiceQuery<T>.AddQueryOption()` method can be used to add the continuation token to a subsequent invocation of the query if the additional results are required.

The `AsTableServiceQuery<T>()` method in the `TableServiceExtensionMethods` class can be used to convert a `DataServiceQuery<T>` into a `CloudTableQuery<T>`. For example, with a model class named `Country`, the following creates a `CloudTableQuery<C ountry>`:

```
CloudTableQuery<Country> query =
    (from c in tableServiceContext.CreateQuery<Country>(
    "Country")
    select c).AsTableServiceQuery<Country>();
```

The `CloudTableQuery<T>` class supports retries. It also provides synchronous execution of queries through the `Execute()` method and asynchronous execution through the `BeginExecuteSegmented()` and `EndExecuteSegmented()` methods.

In this recipe, we will learn how to handle server-side paging.

Getting ready

This recipe uses a model class named `Country` that is declared in the *Creating a data model and context for an entity* recipe in this chapter.

How to do it...

We are going to invoke a query in two different ways. In one, we use `DataServiceQuery` and explicitly handle any continuation tokens we receive when executing the query. In the other, we use `CloudTableQuery` to handle the continuation tokens for us. We do this as follows:

1. Add a class named `ContinuationTokensExample` to the project.
2. Set the Target Framework for the project to.NET Framework 4.
3. Add the following assembly references to the project:
   ```
   Microsoft.WindowsAzure.StorageClient
   System.Configuration
   System.Data.Services.Client
   ```

4. Add the following `using` statements to the top of the class file:
   ```
   using Microsoft.WindowsAzure;
   using Microsoft.WindowsAzure.StorageClient;
   using System.Configuration;
   using System.Data.Services.Client;
   ```

5. Add the following private member to the class:

```
private CloudTableClient cloudTableClient;
private String tableName = "Country";
```

6. Add the following constructor to the class:

```
public ContinuationTokensExample()
{
    CloudStorageAccount cloudStorageAccount =
        CloudStorageAccount.Parse(
        ConfigurationManager.AppSettings[
        "DataConnectionString"]);
    cloudTableClient =
        cloudStorageAccount.CreateCloudTableClient();
    cloudTableClient.CreateTableIfNotExist(tableName);
}
```

7. Add the following method, uploading entities, to the class:

```
public void AddEntities()
{
    TableServiceContext tableServiceContext =
        cloudTableClient.GetDataServiceContext();

    for (Int32 i = 1; i < 100; i++)
    {
        tableServiceContext.AddObject(tableName,
            new Country(String.Format("{0}_{1}", tableName, i),
                "Capital", 1000000));
    }
    tableServiceContext.SaveChangesWithRetries(
        SaveChangesOptions.Batch);
}
```

8. Add the following method, using `DataServiceQuery`, to the class:

```
public void UseContinuationTokens()
{
    TableServiceContext tableServiceContext =
        cloudTableClient.GetDataServiceContext();

    var continuationToken = new
        { PartitionKey = String.Empty, RowKey = String.Empty };
    do
    {
        DataServiceQuery<Country> query =
            (from c in tableServiceContext.CreateQuery<Country>(
            "Country").Take(5)
```

```
                  select c) as DataServiceQuery<Country>;

      if (continuationToken.PartitionKey != String.Empty)
      {
         query = query.AddQueryOption("NextPartitionKey",
            continuationToken.PartitionKey);
      }
      if (continuationToken.RowKey != String.Empty)
      {
         query = query.AddQueryOption("NextRowKey",
            continuationToken.RowKey);
      }

      QueryOperationResponse response =
         query.Execute() as QueryOperationResponse;

      foreach (Country country in response)
      {
         String countryName = country.RowKey;
      }

      if (response.Headers.ContainsKey(
         "x-ms-continuation-NextPartitionKey"))
      {
         String nextPartitionKey = response.Headers[
            "x-ms-continuation-NextPartitionKey"];
         String nextRowKey = response.Headers[
            "x-ms-continuation-NextRowKey"];

         continuationToken = new {
            PartitionKey = nextPartitionKey,
            RowKey = nextRowKey };
      }
      else
      {
         continuationToken = null;
      }
   }
   while (continuationToken != null);
}
```

9. Add the following method, using `CloudTableQuery`, to the class:

```
public void UseCloudTableQuery()
{
    TableServiceContext tableServiceContext =
        cloudTableClient.GetDataServiceContext();

    CloudTableQuery<Country> query =
        (from c in tableServiceContext.CreateQuery<Country>(
            "Country").Take(5)
          select c).AsTableServiceQuery<Country>();
    IEnumerable<Country> countries = query.Execute();

    foreach (Country country in countries)
    {
        String countryName = country.RowKey;
    }
}
```

10. Add the following method, invoking the other methods, to the class:

```
public static void UseContinuationTokensExample()
{
    ContinuationTokensExample example =
        new ContinuationTokensExample();
    example.UseContinuationTokens();
    example.UseCloudTableQuery();
}
```

11. Add the following to the configuration section of `app.config`:

```
<appSettings>
    <add key="DataConnectionString" value="DefaultEndpointsProtocol=
http;AccountName={ACCOUNT_NAME};AccountKey={ACCOUNT_KEY}"/>
</appSettings>
```

How it works...

In steps 1 through 4, we set up the `ContinuationTokensExample` class. In step 5, we add a couple of private members to the class: one specifying the name of the `Country` table and the other containing the `CloudTableClient` that we initialize in the constructor we add in step 6. In step 7, we add 100 entities to the `Country` table. We use `SaveChangesWithRetries()` to take advantage of the default exponential backoff `RetryPolicy`, and we use `SaveChangesOptions.Batch` to use an entity group transaction and upload all the operations as a single REST operation.

In step 8, we add the `UseContinuationTokens()` method. After creating a context, we initialize an instance, `continuationToken`, of an anonymous type we use later to store the continuation tokens returned by the query. We then use a `while` loop which runs as long as the query execution returns continuation tokens. In the loop, we create a query that returns all the entities in the table named `Country` in pages of five entities at a time. If `continuationToken` has non-empty properties, then we add them as options to the query before executing it. We then loop over the entities returned by the query. Finally, we check the response headers to see if they include continuation tokens and, if so, set the properties of `continuationToken` to them.

For the purposes of demonstration, we use `Take(5)` in the query to limit the page size to 5. Doing so makes it easier to see the individual page requests when using a network utility such as Fiddler.

In step 9, we add the `UseCloudTableQuery()` method. We first create a context. Then, we create the query and use `AsTableServiceQuery<T>()` to convert it to a `CloudTableQuery<T>`. We then execute the query and iterate over the results. Note that `AsTableServiceQuery<T>()` is a method in the `TableServiceExtensionMethods` class in the Storage Client library.

In step 10, we add a method that uses the methods we added in steps 8 and 9.

In step 11, we add the connection string to the `app.config` configuration file. We must replace `{ACCOUNT_NAME}` and `{ACCOUNT_KEY}` with actual values for account name and access key.

See also

- ▸ We use the asynchronous `CloudTableQuery<T>` methods in the *Performing asynchronous queries* recipe in this chapter.

Performing asynchronous queries

The Windows Azure Storage Client library uses the common language runtime (CLR) Asynchronous Programming Model to provide asynchronous versions of nearly all the methods that access Windows Azure Storage Service. The asynchronous methods that download lists (entities, tables, and so on) typically come in a matched pair named `BeginRequestSegmented()` and `EndRequestSegmented()` where `Request` indicates the specific request and the `Segmented` suffix indicates that the results are returned as a result segment which may not contain the complete result set. Essentially, these methods page through the data one result segment at a time.

The `CloudTableQuery<T>` class exposes the `BeginExecuteSegmented()` and `EndExecuteSegmented()` methods to implement query execute functionality. `BeginExecuteSegmented()` takes a parameter specifying the callback method in which `EndExecuteSegmented()` must be called to clean up resources used in the asynchronous call. The code can be simplified by using a lambda expression in place of the callback method.

`EndExecuteSegmented()` returns a `ResultSegment<T>` which contains the current page of results, as well as any continuation tokens returned by the Table service. It also exposes a `HasMoreResults` property that can be used to control a loop over subsequent synchronous calls to `ResultSegment<T>.GetNext()` to retrieve the remaining pages of data. The `GetNext()` method automates the handling of the continuation tokens the Table service requires to generate subsequent pages of data.

In this recipe, we will learn how to use asynchronous queries to retrieve the result segments resulting from server-side paging.

Getting ready

This recipe uses a model class named `Country` that is declared in the *Creating a data model and context for an entity* recipe in this chapter.

How to do it...

We are going to execute `CloudTableQuery<T>` using the asynchronous `BeginExecuteSegmented()` and `EndExecuteSegmented()` methods. We do this as follows:

1. Add a class named `AsynchronousQueriesExample` to the project.
2. Set the Target Framework for the project to.NET Framework 4.
3. Add the following assembly references to the project:

   ```
   Microsoft.WindowsAzure.StorageClient
   System.Configuration
   System.Data.Services.Client
   ```

4. Add the following `using` statements to the top of the class file:

   ```
   using Microsoft.WindowsAzure;
   using Microsoft.WindowsAzure.StorageClient;
   using System.Configuration;
   using System.Data.Services.Client;
   ```

5. Add the following private members to the class:

   ```
   private CloudTableClient cloudTableClient;
   private String tableName = "Country";
   ```

6. Add the following constructor to the class:

```
public AsynchronousQueriesExample()
{
    CloudStorageAccount cloudStorageAccount =
      CloudStorageAccount.Parse(
      ConfigurationManager.AppSettings[
      "DataConnectionString"]);
    cloudTableClient =
      cloudStorageAccount.CreateCloudTableClient();
    cloudTableClient.CreateTableIfNotExist(tableName);
}
```

7. Add the following method, uploading entities, to the class:

```
public void AddEntities()
{
    TableServiceContext tableServiceContext =
      cloudTableClient.GetDataServiceContext();

    for (Int32 i = 1000; i < 1100; i++)
    {
        tableServiceContext.AddObject(tableName,
          new Country(String.Format("{0}_{1}", tableName, i),
          "Capital", 1000000));
    }
    tableServiceContext.SaveChangesWithRetries(
      SaveChangesOptions.Batch);
}
```

8. Add the following method, demonstrating asynchronous server-side paging, to the class:

```
public void InvokeAsynchronousQuery()
{
    TableServiceContext tableServiceContext =
      cloudTableClient.GetDataServiceContext();

    List<Country> countries = new List<Country>();

    CloudTableQuery<Country> query =
      (from c in tableServiceContext.CreateQuery<Country>(
          tableName).Take(5)
        select c).AsTableServiceQuery<Country>();
    query.BeginExecuteSegmented( (result) =>
    {
        ResultSegment<Country> resultSegment =
          query.EndExecuteSegmented(result);
```

```
        countries.AddRange(resultSegment.Results);
        while (resultSegment.HasMoreResults)
        {
            resultSegment = resultSegment.GetNext();
            countries.AddRange(resultSegment.Results);
        }
    }
    , null);
}
```

9. Add the following method using the methods we added earlier:

```
public static void UseAsynchronousQueriesExample()
{
    AsynchronousQueriesExample example = new
        AsynchronousQueriesExample();
    example.AddEntities();
    example.InvokeAsynchronousQuery();
}
```

10. Add the following to the configuration section of `app.config`:

```
<appSettings>
    <add key="DataConnectionString" value="DefaultEndpointsProtocol=
    http;AccountName={ACCOUNT_NAME};AccountKey={ACCOUNT_KEY}"/>
</appSettings>
```

How it works...

In steps 1 through 4, we set up the `AsynchronousQueriesExample` class. In step 5, we add a couple of private members to the class: one specifying the name of the `Country` table and the other containing the `CloudTableClient` that we initialize in the constructor we add in step 6. In step 7, we add 100 entities to the `Country` table. We use `SaveChangesWithRetries()` to take advantage of the default exponential backoff `RetryPolicy`, and we use `SaveChangesOptions.Batch` to use an entity group transaction and upload all the operations as a single REST operation.

In step 8, we add the `InvokeAsynchronousQuery()` method to invoke query execution asynchronously. First, we create a context and use it to create a `CloudTableQuery`. For demonstration purposes, we use the LINQ `Take()` operator to limit each result segment to five entities. Then, we execute it with the asynchronous `BeginExecuteSegmented` while using a lambda expression for the callback method.

In the lambda expression, we clean up the asynchronous call by invoking `EndExecuteSegmented()`. This returns a `ResultSegment` giving us access to the results, which we add to a `List`. We then use `ResultSegment.HasMoreResults` to control a loop that uses `ResultSegment.GetNext()` to retrieve subsequent result segments.

In step 9, we add a method that uses the methods we added earlier.

In step 10, we add the connection string to the `app.config` configuration file. We must replace `{ACCOUNT_NAME}` and `{ACCOUNT_KEY}` with actual values for account name and access key.

See also

- There are additional examples of asynchronous queries in the *Performing queries in parallel* recipe in this chapter.
- We see how to use the Storage Client library to download blobs asynchronously in the *Downloading a blob asynchronously* recipe in Chapter 2.

Performing queries in parallel

The performance of a query against a table in the Windows Azure Table Service is critically dependent on whether or not the `PartitionKey` and `RowKey` are provided. The only index on a table is the combination of `PartitionKey` and `RowKey`. The most performant query, and the only one guaranteed not to result in a continuation token, is one specifying both `PartitionKey` and `RowKey`. A query specifying the `PartitionKey` but not the `RowKey` results in a scan of all the entities with that `PartitionKey`. A query specifying the `RowKey` but not the `PartitionKey` is processed sequentially by each partition server. A query specifying neither `PartitionKey` nor `RowKey` results in a scan of the entire table regardless of any filters in the query.

The Table service provides lower scalability targets for simultaneous queries within a single partition than it does for simultaneous queries against different partitions. Consequently, it can be more efficient to break a multipartition query up and execute queries in parallel against each partition.

One curiosity is that the query optimiser does not optimize queries involving a logical `Or` operator. Using an `Or` operator causes a scan of all entities. In this case, it may also be worthwhile removing the `Or` by executing individual queries for each side of the `Or` operator simultaneously.

In this recipe, we will learn how to execute parallel queries.

Getting ready

This recipe uses a model class named `Country` that is declared in the *Creating a data model and context for an entity* recipe in this chapter.

How to do it...

We are going to create two queries using different ranges for the `RowKey`. We will then execute them asynchronously. We will use a `ManualResetEvent`, so that the calling method waits for the completion of the two queries. We do this as follows:

1. Add a class named `ParallelQueriesExample` to the project.

2. Set the Target Framework for the project to.NET Framework 4.

3. Add the following assembly references to the project:

   ```
   Microsoft.WindowsAzure.StorageClient
   System.Configuration
   System.Data.Services.Client
   ```

4. Add the following `using` statements to the top of the class file:

   ```
   using Microsoft.WindowsAzure;
   using Microsoft.WindowsAzure.StorageClient;
   using System.Configuration;
   using System.Data.Services.Client;
   using System.Threading;
   ```

5. Add the following static members to the class:

   ```
   private static Int32 queryExecutionCount;
   private static ManualResetEvent manualResetEvent =
       new ManualResetEvent(false);
   private static String tableName = "Country"
   ```

6. Add the following method, uploading entities, to the class:

   ```
   public static void SetupRecipe()
   {
       CloudStorageAccount cloudStorageAccount =
         CloudStorageAccount.Parse(
         ConfigurationManager.AppSettings[
         "DataConnectionString"]);
       CloudTableClient cloudTableClient =
         cloudStorageAccount.CreateCloudTableClient();
       cloudTableClient.CreateTableIfNotExist(tableName);

       TableServiceContext tableServiceContext =
         cloudTableClient.GetDataServiceContext();
   ```

```
tableServiceContext.AddObject(
   tableName, new Country("France", "Paris", 65000000));
tableServiceContext.AddObject(
   tableName, new Country("Germany", "Berlin", 82000000));
tableServiceContext.AddObject(
   tableName, new Country("Norway", "Oslo", 5000000));
tableServiceContext.AddObject(
   tableName, new Country("Portugal", "Lisbon", 1100000));

tableServiceContext.SaveChangesWithRetries(
   SaveChangesOptions.Batch);
}
```

7. Add the following callback method to the class:

```
private static void BeginExecuteSegmentedIsDone(IAsyncResult
result)
{
   CloudTableQuery<Country> query =
      result.AsyncState as CloudTableQuery<Country>;

   ResultSegment<Country> resultSegment =
      query.EndExecuteSegmented(result);

   List<Country> countries =
      resultSegment.Results.ToList<Country>();
   while (resultSegment.HasMoreResults)
   {
      resultSegment = resultSegment.GetNext();
      countries.AddRange(resultSegment.Results);
   }
   if (Interlocked.Decrement(ref queryExecutionCount) < 1)
   {
      manualResetEvent.Set();
   }
}
```

8. Add the following method to the class:

```
public static void UseParallelQueriesExample()
{
   SetupRecipe();
   CloudStorageAccount cloudStorageAccount =
      CloudStorageAccount.Parse(
      ConfigurationManager.AppSettings[
      "DataConnectionString"]);
   CloudTableClient cloudTableClient =
      cloudStorageAccount.CreateCloudTableClient();
```

```
TableServiceContext tableServiceContext1 =
    cloudTableClient.GetDataServiceContext();
TableServiceContext tableServiceContext2 =
    cloudTableClient.GetDataServiceContext();


CloudTableQuery<Country> query1 = (
    from c in tableServiceContext1.CreateQuery<Country>(
        tableName)
    where c.PartitionKey == "country"
    && c.RowKey.CompareTo("N") >= 0
    && c.RowKey.CompareTo("O") <  0
    select c
    ).AsTableServiceQuery<Country>();



CloudTableQuery<Country> query2 = (
    from c in tableServiceContext2.CreateQuery<Country>(
        tableName)
    where c.PartitionKey == "country"
    && c.RowKey.CompareTo("F") >= 0
    && c.RowKey.CompareTo("G") < 0
    select c
    ).AsTableServiceQuery<Country>();

queryExecutionCount = 2;

query1.BeginExecuteSegmented(
    new AsyncCallback(BeginExecuteSegmentedIsDone), query1);

query2.BeginExecuteSegmented(
    new AsyncCallback(BeginExecuteSegmentedIsDone), query2);

manualResetEvent.WaitOne();
}
```

9. Add the following to the configuration section of `app.config`:

```
<appSettings>
  <add key="DataConnectionString" value="DefaultEndpointsProtocol=
http;AccountName={ACCOUNT_NAME};AccountKey={ACCOUNT_KEY}"/>
</appSettings>
```

How it works...

In steps 1 through 4, we set up the `ParallelQueriesExample` class. In step 5, we add some private members to the class. `queryExecutionCount` tracks the number of currently executing queries and is used to control the signaling of the `ManualResetEvent` we define in `manualResetEvent`. The final member stores the name of the `Country` table. In step 6, we setup the recipe by creating the table and uploading a few entities to it. We use `SaveChangesWithRetries()` to take advantage of the default exponential backoff `RetryPolicy`, and we use `SaveChangesOptions.Batch` to use an entity group transaction and upload all the operations as a single REST operation.

In step 7, we add a callback method named `BeginExecuteSegmentedIsDone()`. This method invokes `CloudTableQuery<T>.EndExecuteSegmented()` to complete the asynchronous call. It then creates a list of the countries retrieved by the query. The `ResultSegment<T>.HasMoreResults` property is used to control a `while` loop that pages through any remaining query results. When both queries have completed, indicated by the `queryExecutionCount` going to 0, we set the state of the `ManualResetEvent` to signaled, so that the `UseParallelQueriesExample()` method can continue.

In step 8, we add a method named `UseParallelQueriesExample()` to demonstrate the invocation of parallel queries. We initialize two separate contexts and then create a query on each of them that use the same `PartitionKey`, but different ranges for the `RowKey`. We then execute the two queries asynchronously using `CloudTableQuery<T>.BeginExecuteSegmented()`. Finally, we invoke `WaitOne()` on the `ManualResetEvent`, so that execution pauses for this method until the queries complete successfully and the event state is set to signaled. Note that the full performance benefit of using parallel queries would be gained by performing them against different partitions.

In step 9, we add the connection string to the `app.config` configuration file. We must replace {ACCOUNT_NAME} and {ACCOUNT_KEY} with actual values for account name and access key.

See also

▶ There are additional examples of asynchronous queries in the *Performing asynchronous queries* recipe in this chapter.

Handling the WritingEntity and ReadingEntity events

The Windows Azure Table Service exposes a RESTful interface in which an entity is represented as an **atom** entry. In saving an instance to a table, the Windows Azure Storage Client library serializes the instance into an atom entry before invoking the appropriate REST operation on the Table service. Similarly, when retrieving an entity from a table, the Storage Client library deserializes the atom entry into an instance of the model class.

The Table service supports a limited set of simple datatypes for the properties of entities. These datatypes are listed in the *Creating a data model and context for an entity* recipe. By default, the Storage Client library serializes an instance of a model class by converting each public property of one of the supported datatypes into an element in an atom entry. Deserialization simply reverses this process.

The Storage Client library exposes extension points, the `WritingEntity` and `ReadingEntity` events, which can be used to modify the default behavior of serialization and deserialization. An argument of type `ReadingWritingEntityEventArgs` is passed into the `WritingEntity` and `ReadingEntity` handlers. This argument provides access to both the instance properties and the atom entry allowing them to be inspected and modified as desired.

The following is an example of an atom entry:

```
<entry
    xmlns:d="http://schemas.microsoft.com/ado/2007/08/
        dataservices"
    xmlns:m="http://schemas.microsoft.com/ado/2007/08/
        dataservices/metadata"
    xmlns="http://www.w3.org/2005/Atom">
    <title />
    <author>
      <name />
    </author>
    <updated>2011-01-03T08:56:59.70075Z</updated>
    <id />
    <content type="application/xml">
      <m:properties>
        <d:PartitionKey>M</d:PartitionKey>
        <d:RowKey>Mercier and Camier</d:RowKey>
        <d:Timestamp m:type="Edm.DateTime">
            0001-01-01T00:00:00</d:Timestamp>
        <d:Title>Mercier and Camier</d:Title>
        <d:LastName>Beckett</d:LastName>
        <d:FirstName>Samuel</d:FirstName>
        <d:Birthday m:type="Edm.DateTime">
            1906-04-13T00:00:00</d:Birthday>
      </m:properties>
    </content>
</entry>
```

This atom entry represents an entity with the required properties: `PartitionKey`, `RowKey`, and `Timestamp`, as well as the specific properties: `Title`, `LastName`, `FirstName`, and `Birthday`. A type attribute must be specified for any element where the instance property is not of type `String`. The `WritingEntity` and `ReadingEntity` event handlers must use the correct namespaces when the atom entry is inspected and modified.

In this recipe, we will learn how to use the `WritingEntity` and `ReadingEntity` event handlers to modify the default serialization and deserialization behavior when saving and retrieving data from a table.

How to do it...

We are going to create a model class named `Book` with a public property of a type, `Author`, not supported by the Table service. We are then going to insert a book entity into a table by handling the `WritingEntity` event to serialize the unsupported property into properties the Table service can handle. Finally, we query the table and handle the `ReadingEntity` event to deserialize the retrieved entity into an instance of `Book`:

1. Add a class named `ReadingWritingEntityExample`.

2. Set the Target Framework for the project to.NET Framework 4.

3. Add the following assembly references to the project:

   ```
   Microsoft.WindowsAzure.StorageClient
   System.Configuration
   System.Data.Services.Client
   ```

4. Add the following `using` statements to the top of the class file:

   ```
   using Microsoft.WindowsAzure;
   using Microsoft.WindowsAzure.StorageClient;
   using System.Configuration;
   using System.Globalization;
   using System.Data.Services.Client;
   using System.Xml.Linq;
   ```

5. Add the `Author` class after the namespace declaration:

   ```
   public class Author
   {
      public String FirstName { get; set; }
      public String LastName { get; set; }
      public DateTime Birthday { get; set; }
   }
   ```

6. Add the `Book` class after the preceding class declaration:

   ```
   public class Book : TableServiceEntity
   {
      public String Title { get; set; }
      public Author Author { get; set; }

      public Book() { }
   ```

```
public Book( String title, Author author)
{
    PartitionKey = title.Substring(0, 1);
    RowKey = title;
    Title = title;
    Author = author;
}
}
```

7. Add the following members to the `ReadingWritingEntityExample` class:

```
private CloudTableClient cloudTableClient;
private XNamespace d =
    "http://schemas.microsoft.com/ado/2007/08/dataservices";
private XNamespace m =
    "http://schemas.microsoft.com/ado/2007/08/dataservices/
    metadata";
```

8. Add the following constructor to the `ReadingWritingEntityExample` class:

```
public ReadingWritingEntityExample()
{
    CloudStorageAccount cloudStorageAccount =
        CloudStorageAccount.Parse(
        ConfigurationManager.AppSettings[
        "DataConnectionString"]);
    cloudTableClient =
        cloudStorageAccount.CreateCloudTableClient();
    cloudTableClient.CreateTable(tableName);
}
```

9. Add the following method, insert a `Book` into the table, to the class:

```
public void AddBook(String title, Author author)
{
    TableServiceContext tableServiceContext =
        cloudTableClient.GetDataServiceContext();
    tableServiceContext.WritingEntity +=
        new EventHandler<ReadingWritingEntityEventArgs>(
        SerializeAuthor);

    Book book = new Book( title, author);
    tableServiceContext.AddObject( "Book", book);
    tableServiceContext.SaveChangesWithRetries();
}
```

10. Add the following method, serializing an entity, to the class:

```
private void SerializeAuthor(Object sender,
   ReadingWritingEntityEventArgs args)
{
   Book book = args.Entity as Book;
   XElement lastName =
      new XElement(d + "LastName", book.Author.LastName);
   XElement firstName =
      new XElement(d + "FirstName", book.Author.FirstName);
   XElement birthday =
      new XElement(d + "Birthday", book.Author.Birthday);
   birthday.Add(new XAttribute(m + "type", "Edm.DateTime"));

   XElement properties = args.Data.Descendants(
      m + "properties").First();
   properties.Add(lastName);
   properties.Add(firstName);
   properties.Add(birthday);
   XElement author = properties.Element(d + "Author");
   author.Remove();
}
```

11. Add the following method, retrieving `Book` entities from the table, to the class:

```
public void QueryBooks()
{
   TableServiceContext tableServiceContext =
      cloudTableClient.GetDataServiceContext();
   tableServiceContext.ReadingEntity += new
      EventHandler<ReadingWritingEntityEventArgs>(
      DeserializeAuthor);

   CloudTableQuery<Book> query =
      (from c in tableServiceContext.CreateQuery<Book>("Book")
      select c).AsTableServiceQuery<Book>();
   List<Book> books = query.Execute().ToList();
   foreach (Book b in books)
   {
      String lastName = b.Author.LastName;
      String firstName = b.Author.FirstName;
      String title = b.Title;
   }
}
```

12. Add the following method, deserializing an entity, to the class:

```
private void DeserializeAuthor(Object sender,
    ReadingWritingEntityEventArgs args)
{
    XElement properties = args.Data.Descendants(
        m + "properties").First();
    XElement firstName = properties.Element(d + "FirstName");
    XElement lastName = properties.Element(d + "LastName");
    XElement birthday = properties.Element(d + "Birthday");

    Book book = args.Entity as Book;
    book.Author = new Author
    {
        LastName = lastName.Value,
        FirstName = firstName.Value,
// Fixes automatic conversion from UTC to local time
        Birthday = DateTime.Parse(
        birthday.Value, null, DateTimeStyles.AdjustToUniversal)
    };
}
```

13. Add the following method, using the previously added methods, to the class:

```
public static void UseReadingWritingEntityExample()
{
    ReadingWritingEntityExample example =
        new ReadingWritingEntityExample();
    Author samuelBeckett = new Author
        { LastName = "Beckett", FirstName = "Samuel",
          Birthday = new DateTime(1906, 4, 13) };
    example.AddBook("Mercier and Camier", samuelBeckett);
    example.QueryBooks();
}
```

14. Add the following to the configuration section of `app.config`:

```
<appSettings>
  <add key="DataConnectionString" value="DefaultEndpointsProtocol=
http;AccountName={ACCOUNT_NAME};AccountKey={ACCOUNT_KEY}"/>
</appSettings>
```

How it works...

In steps 1 through 4, we set up the `ReadingWritingEntityExample` class.

In step 5, we add the `Author` class we use to provide an unsupported type in a property we add to the model class, `Book`, in step 6.

In step 7, we add a private member for the `CloudTableClient` we use to access the Table service. We also define private members to store the namespaces we use when parsing the atom entry transferred to and from the Table service. In step 8, we initialize the `CloudTableClient`.

The `AddBook()` method we add in step 9 inserts an instance of the `Book` class into the table. We do this by creating a context and assigning the `SerializeAuthor()` method to be a handler for the `WritingEntity` event. We then create a `Book` instance and save it to the table.

In step 10, we add the `SerializeAuthor()` handler which uses the `Book` instance passed in as an argument to initialize XElements, with the appropriate namespace, for each of the three properties in the `Author` property of the `Book` instance. We then add these XElements to the appropriate location in the atom entry sent to the Table service. Note that elements not representing strings need an attribute specifying the type, as with the birthday XElement. Finally, we remove the `Author` element from the atom entry, so that this invalid element is not sent to the Table service.

The `QueryBooks()` method we add in step 11 retrieves entities from the table. We do this by creating a context and assigning the `DeserializeAuthor()` method as a handler for the `ReadingEntity` event. We then create and execute a query against the table before iterating over the retrieved entities.

In step 12, we add the `DeserializeAuthor()` handler in which we get the values needed to create an `Author` instance out of the atom entry retrieved by the query. We then create the `Author` instance and assign it to the `Author` property of the `Book` instance passed in as an argument to the handler.

In step 13, we add a method that uses the methods we added earlier.

In step 14, we add the connection string to the `app.config` configuration file. We must replace {`ACCOUNT_NAME`} and {`ACCOUNT_KEY`} with actual values for account name and access key.

See also

▶ We learn more about the data model used by the Table service in the *Creating a data model and context for an entity* recipe in this chapter.

4

Disconnecting with Windows Azure Queues

In this chapter, we will cover:

- ▸ Managing Windows Azure queues
- ▸ Adding messages to a queue
- ▸ Retrieving messages from a queue
- ▸ Storing large amounts of data for a message
- ▸ Implementing a backoff when polling a queue
- ▸ Identifying and handling poison messages

Introduction

The **Windows Azure Queue Service** is the Windows Azure Storage Service feature that manages Windows Azure queues and the messages in them. A queue facilitates scalability of a Windows Azure hosted service by allowing disconnected communication between roles in the hosted service, allowing the roles to scale independently of each other. Indeed, they do not even need to be active at the same time.

More generally, the Queue service provides a coherent way to manage the processing of a task comprising several steps. For example, a long-lived task could be broken up into steps and the status of these steps managed using queues. We look at this in the *Managing Windows Azure queues* recipe.

The Queue service provides a two-level hierarchy comprising queues and the messages in them. The only limit on the size of a queue is the 100 TB limit for a storage service account. An individual message may store up to 8192 bytes of data. A queue stores a message for a maximum of seven days, after which it deletes the message. Typically, the consumer of a message deletes it after use. We see how to add messages in the *Adding messages to a queue* recipe. In the *Storing large amounts of data for a message* recipe, we see how to get around the 8192-byte limit for message content.

The Queue service provides best-effort FIFO queues. They are only best effort FIFO as the Queue service does not guarantee message-retrieval order. Furthermore, a message may be retrieved more than once from a queue. When a message is retrieved from a queue, it is made invisible to other consumers for a specified TimeSpan. If the message has not been deleted from the queue when that TimeSpan expires, then it is once again made visible to other message consumers. One of these other consumers may get the message and start processing it. This leads to the possibility of two (or more) consumers processing the same message simultaneously. Consequently, any processing based on a message must be idempotent (that is, the result of processing a message must be the same no matter how often the message is processed) even when the message is being processed more than once at the same time. We see how to get a message from a queue in the *Retrieving messages from a queue* recipe.

Adding and retrieving messages are billable storage transactions. When a tight loop is used to poll a queue containing no messages, these storage transaction charges can increase rapidly. We see how to mitigate this problem in the *Implementing a backoff when polling a queue* recipe.

One problem that arises with queues is that a corrupt message may cause the message consumer to fail in a way that prevents it deleting the message. This means that the message keeps reappearing on the queue causing message consumers to fail repeatedly. Such a message is referred to as a **poison message**. We see how to deal with such messages in the *Identifying and handling poison messages* recipe.

The example code provided with this chapter uses a simple WPF project.

Managing Windows Azure queues

A Windows Azure Queue Service queue provides a way to decouple the connection between two roles, so that one role can request another role to perform some task. The producing role inserts into the queue a message containing the details of the request. The consuming role polls the queue and, on getting the message, performs the associated task. If necessary, the consuming role can insert a message in another queue indicating the completion of the task.

A more general view is that the Queue service provides a way to manage the processing of a task, so that it is more robust against failure. Windows Azure is a scalable system and it is possible that a component of the system could fail at any time, causing the loss of any work in progress. The extent of this loss can be minimized by breaking the task into individual steps. The loss of work-in-progress for an individual step is less significant than that of the overall task. The Queue service supports this functionality by providing a coherent way to track the work status of a task through the insertion of a message in a queue to indicate the completion of a step and allow the next step to start.

Depending on the nature of the task, one role in a Windows Azure hosted service could complete all the steps, so that a single queue can be used, with individual messages indicating the next step to be performed. Alternatively, the scalability requirements of the hosted service may lead to different roles performing different steps in the task. A distinct queue should be used for each pair of roles involved in the task. This allows the approximate message count of the queue to be used in evaluating how many instances of the roles are needed to maintain the queue at an acceptable length.

The Windows Azure Storage Service partitions data to provide scalability and has a lower scalability target for data in a single partition than for a storage account. The Queue service stores each queue in its own partition. The scalability target for a single queue is 500 messages per second while the scalability target for an entire storage account is up to 5,000 messages per second. Consequently, scalability may be improved by using multiple queues.

In the Windows Azure Storage Client library, the `CloudQueue` class provides both synchronous and asynchronous methods to manage queues and the messages in them. These include methods to create, delete, and clear queues. Although queues may have metadata associated with them, only the queue name is needed to create a queue. The queue name may comprise only lowercase letters, numbers, and the dash character.

In this recipe, we will learn how to manage queues.

How to do it...

We are going to create a queue, look at some of its attributes, and then delete the queue. We do this as follows:

1. Add a new class named `CreateQueueExample` to the project.
2. Set the Target Framework for the project to .NET Framework 4.
3. Add the following assembly references to the project:
   ```
   Microsoft.WindowsAzure.StorageClient
   System.Configuration
   ```

4. Add the following using statements to the top of the class file:

```
using Microsoft.WindowsAzure;
using Microsoft.WindowsAzure.StorageClient;
using System.Configuration;
```

5. Add the following private member to the class:

```
private CloudQueueClient cloudQueueClient;
```

6. Add the following constructor to the class:

```
public CreateQueueExample()
{
    CloudStorageAccount cloudStorageAccount =
        CloudStorageAccount.Parse(
        ConfigurationManager.AppSettings[
        "DataConnectionString"]);
    cloudQueueClient =
        cloudStorageAccount.CreateCloudQueueClient();
}
```

7. Add the following method, creating a queue, to the class:

```
public void CreateQueue(String queueName)
{
    CloudQueue cloudQueue =
        cloudQueueClient.GetQueueReference(queueName);
    cloudQueue.Create();
}
```

8. Add the following method, retrieving queue information, to the class:

```
public void GetQueueInformation(String queueName)
{
    CloudQueue cloudQueue =
        cloudQueueClient.GetQueueReference(queueName);
    Int32 approximateMessageCount =
        cloudQueue.RetrieveApproximateMessageCount();
    cloudQueue.FetchAttributes();
    Uri uri = cloudQueue.Attributes.Uri;
    foreach ( String key in cloudQueue.Metadata.Keys)
    {
        String metadataValue = cloudQueue.Metadata[key];
    }
}
```

9. Add the following method, deleting the queue, to the class:

```
public void DeleteQueue(String queueName)
{
    CloudQueue cloudQueue =
        cloudQueueClient.GetQueueReference(queueName);
    cloudQueue.Delete();
}
```

10. Add the following method, using the methods added earlier, to the class:

```
public static void UseCreateQueueExample()
{
    String queueName = "{QUEUE_NAME}";
    CreateQueueExample example = new CreateQueueExample();
    example.CreateQueue(queueName);
    example.GetQueueInformation(queueName);
    example.DeleteQueue(queueName);
}
```

11. Add the following to the configuration section of `app.config`:

```
<appSettings>
    <add key="DataConnectionString"
        value="UseDevelopmentStorage=true"/>
</appSettings>
```

How it works...

In steps 1 through 4, we set up the class. In step 5, we add a private member to store the `CloudQueueClient` object used to connect to the Queue service. We initialize this in the constructor we add in step 6.

In step 7, we add a method that initializes a `CloudQueue` object and uses it to create a queue.

In step 8, we add a method that initializes a `CloudQueue` object and uses it to retrieve the approximate message count of the queue. We then retrieve and look at the queue attributes, including the Uri and any metadata associated with the queue.

In step 9, we add a method that initializes a `CloudQueue` object and uses it to delete a queue.

In step 10, we add a method that invokes the methods we added earlier. We need to replace `{QUEUE_NAME}` with an appropriate name for a queue.

In step 11, we add the storage emulator connection string to the `app.config` configuration file.

Adding messages to a queue

The `CloudQueue` class in the Windows Azure Storage Client Library provides both synchronous and asynchronous methods to add a message to a queue. A message comprises up to 8192 bytes of data. By default, the Storage Client library Base64 encodes message content to ensure that the request payload containing the message is valid XML. This encoding adds overhead that reduces the actual maximum size of a message. The Windows Azure SDK v1.3 added an `EncodeMessage` property to CloudQueue allowing a message, the content of which is already valid XML, to be sent without being Base64 encoded.

Each message added to a queue has a time-to-live property after which it is deleted automatically. The maximum, and default, time-to-live value is 7 days.

In this recipe, we will learn how to add messages to a queue.

How to do it...

We are going to create a queue and add some messages to it. We do this as follows:

1. Add a new class named `AddMessagesExample` to the project.
2. Set the Target Framework for the project to.NET Framework 4.
3. Add the following assembly references to the project:

    ```
    Microsoft.WindowsAzure.StorageClient
    System.Configuration
    ```

4. Add the following `using` statements to the top of the class file:

    ```
    using Microsoft.WindowsAzure;
    using Microsoft.WindowsAzure.StorageClient;
    using System.Configuration;
    ```

5. Add the following private member to the class:

    ```
    private CloudQueue cloudQueue;
    ```

6. Add the following constructor to the class:

    ```
    public AddMessagesExample(String queueName)
    {
        CloudStorageAccount cloudStorageAccount =
            CloudStorageAccount.Parse(
            ConfigurationManager.AppSettings[
            "DataConnectionString"]);
        CloudQueueClient cloudQueueClient =
            cloudStorageAccount.CreateCloudQueueClient();
        cloudQueue = cloudQueueClient.GetQueueReference(queueName);
        cloudQueue.CreateIfNotExist();
    }
    ```

7. Add the following method, adding two messages, to the class:

```
public void AddMessages()
{
    String content1 = "Do something";
    CloudQueueMessage message1 = new CloudQueueMessage(content1);
    cloudQueue.AddMessage(message1);

    String content2 = "Do something else";
    CloudQueueMessage message2 = new CloudQueueMessage(content2);
    cloudQueue.AddMessage(message2, TimeSpan.FromDays(1.0));
}
```

8. Add the following method, using the `AddMessage()` method, to the class:

```
public static void UseAddMessagesExample()
{
    String queueName = "actions";
    AddMessagesExample example = new AddMessagesExample(queueName);
    example.AddMessages();
}
```

9. Add the following to the configuration section of `app.config`:

```
<appSettings>
    <add key="DataConnectionString"
        value="UseDevelopmentStorage=true"/>
</appSettings>
```

How it works...

In steps 1 through 4, we set up the class. In step 5, we add a private member to store the `CloudQueue` object used to interact with the Queue service. We initialize this in the constructor we add in step 6, where we also create the queue.

In step 7, we add a method that adds two messages to a queue. We create two `CloudQueueMessage` objects. We add the first message to the queue with the default time-to-live of seven days, and we add the second with a time-to-live of one day.

In step 8, we add a method that invokes the methods we added earlier.

In step 9, we add the storage emulator connection string to the `app.config` configuration file.

Retrieving messages from a queue

The `CloudQueue` class in the Windows Azure Storage Client Library provides both synchronous and asynchronous methods to retrieve messages from a queue. The `GetMessage()` method retrieves a message from a queue while the `GetMessages()` method retrieves up to 32 messages at a time. `GetMessages()` reduces the number of storage operations used to access a queue and can improve scalability of a Windows Azure Hosted Service.

Messages retrieved in this way have a visibility timeout during which they cannot be retrieved by additional calls to the Windows Azure Queue Service. The maximum visibility timeout for a message is 2 hours and the default is 30 seconds. This visibility timeout enhances the durability of a hosted service. If a consumer fails while processing a message, then the expiration of the visibility timeout causes the message to be visible once again on the queue from which another consumer can retrieve it.

One consequence of the visibility timeout is that if a consumer fails to process a message before the visibility timeout expires, another consumer may retrieve the message and start processing it. This can cause problems if message processing is not idempotent, that is, the same result arises whenever a message is processed.

The Queue service also uses optimistic concurrency to manage message deletion. When a message is retrieved, it includes a pop receipt that must be provided to delete the message from the queue. Even after the visibility timeout expires, the pop receipt remains valid until the message is next retrieved from the queue. In the Windows Azure Storage Client Library, the `CloudQueueMessage.DeleteMessage()` method is used to delete messages.

The Queue service supports the concept of peeking at a message. This allows a consumer to retrieve a message while leaving it visible to other consumers of the queue. Consequently, a consumer can retrieve and delete a message that another consumer is peeking at. The Queue service does not generate a pop receipt when a message is peeked at, so the consumer peeking at the message is unable to delete it from the queue. The Storage Client library has `PeekMessage()` and `PeekMessages()` methods in the `CloudQueue` class. These mimic the functionality of the equivalent `GetMessage()` and `GetMessages()` methods.

In this recipe, we will learn how to retrieve messages from a queue.

How to do it...

We are going to add some messages to a queue. We do this as follows:

1. Add a new class named `GetMessagesExample` to the project.
2. Set the Target Framework for the project to .NET Framework 4.

3. Add the following assembly references to the project:

```
Microsoft.WindowsAzure.StorageClient
System.Configuration
```

4. Add the following `using` statements to the top of the class file:

```
using Microsoft.WindowsAzure;
using Microsoft.WindowsAzure.StorageClient;
using System.Configuration;
```

5. Add the following private member to the class:

```
private CloudQueue cloudQueue;
```

6. Add the following constructor to the class:

```
public GetMessagesExample(String queueName)
{
    CloudStorageAccount cloudStorageAccount =
        CloudStorageAccount.Parse(
        ConfigurationManager.AppSettings[
        "DataConnectionString"]);
    CloudQueueClient cloudQueueClient =
        cloudStorageAccount.CreateCloudQueueClient();
    cloudQueue = cloudQueueClient.GetQueueReference(queueName);
}
```

7. Add the following method, setting up the recipe, to the class:

```
public void SetupRecipe()
{
    cloudQueue.CreateIfNotExist();
    for (Int32 i = 0; i < 100; i++)
    {
        String content = String.Format("Message_{0}", i);
        CloudQueueMessage message = new CloudQueueMessage(content);
        cloudQueue.AddMessage(message);
    }
}
```

8. Add the following method, retrieving a message, to the class:

```
public void GetMessage()
{
    Int32 messageCount =
        cloudQueue.RetrieveApproximateMessageCount();
    CloudQueueMessage cloudQueueMessage =
        cloudQueue.GetMessage();
    if (cloudQueueMessage != null)
```

```
        {
            String messageText = cloudQueueMessage.AsString;
            // use message
            cloudQueue.DeleteMessage(cloudQueueMessage);
        }
    }
```

9. Add the following method, peeking at a message, to the class:

```
public void PeekMessage()
{
    CloudQueueMessage cloudQueueMessage =
        cloudQueue.PeekMessage();
}
```

10. Add the following method, retrieving 20 messages, to the class:

```
public void GetMessages()
{
    IEnumerable<CloudQueueMessage> cloudQueueMessages =
        cloudQueue.GetMessages(20);
    foreach (CloudQueueMessage message in cloudQueueMessages
    {
        String messageText = message.AsString;
        // use message
        cloudQueue.DeleteMessage(message);
    }
}
```

11. Add the following method, using the methods added earlier, to the class:

```
public static void UseGetMessagesExample()
{
    String queueName = "actions";
    GetMessagesExample example =
        new GetMessagesExample(queueName);
    example.SetupRecipe();
    example.GetMessage();
    example.PeekMessage();
    example.GetMessages();
}
```

12. Add the following to the configuration section of `app.config`:

```
<appSettings>
    <add key="DataConnectionString"
        value="UseDevelopmentStorage=true"/>
</appSettings>
```

How it works...

In steps 1 through 4, we set up the class. In step 5, we add a private member to store the `CloudQueue` object used to interact with the Queue service. We initialize this in the constructor we add in step 6. In step 7, we add a method to set up the recipe by creating a queue and adding 100 messages to it.

In step 8, we add a `GetMessage()` method that retrieves the approximate message count for the queue. It then requests a message from the queue. If a message is retrieved, we then get its content as a `String`, use the message, and finally delete it. In step 9, we add a method that peeks at a message. In this case, we cannot delete the message because `PeekMessage()` does not retrieve the pop receipt for the message. In step 10, we add a method that retrieves up to 20 messages, processes them, and then deletes them.

In step 11, we add a method that uses other methods in the class.

In step 12, we add the storage emulator connection string to the `app.config` configuration file.

Storing large amounts of data for a message

The Windows Azure Queue Service supports messages containing up to 8192 bytes of data. There are obvious cases where this is not sufficient to store the data associated with a message. For example, the message could be a request to process an image or a video.

The solution is to use the Windows Azure Blob Service to store the data in a blob and store the URL of the blob in the message. When the message is retrieved, the blob can be retrieved and processed appropriately. If the data is associated only with the message, then the blob should be deleted after use. The same technique can also be used with the Windows Azure Table Service being used to store the data in a table.

In this recipe, we will learn how to store large amounts of data for a message.

How to do it...

We are going to add a message to a queue. The content of the message is the URI to a blob containing large amounts of data. We then retrieve the message and access the contents of the blob, for further processing, before deleting the message and the blob. We do this as follows:

1. Add a new class named `LargeDataExample` to the project.
2. Set the Target Framework for the project to.NET Framework 4.

3. Add the following assembly references to the project:

    ```
    Microsoft.WindowsAzure.StorageClient
    System.Configuration
    ```

4. Add the following using statements to the top of the class file:

    ```
    using Microsoft.WindowsAzure;
    using Microsoft.WindowsAzure.StorageClient;
    using System.Configuration;
    ```

5. Add the following private members to the class:

    ```
    private CloudQueue cloudQueue;
    private CloudBlobClient cloudBlobClient;
    ```

6. Add the following constructor to the class:

    ```
    public LargeDataExample(String queueName, String containerName)
    {
        CloudStorageAccount cloudStorageAccount =
            CloudStorageAccount.Parse(
            ConfigurationManager.AppSettings[
            "DataConnectionString"]);
        CloudQueueClient cloudQueueClient =
            cloudStorageAccount.CreateCloudQueueClient();
        cloudQueue = cloudQueueClient.GetQueueReference(queueName);
        cloudBlobClient = cloudStorageAccount.CreateCloudBlobClient();
    }
    ```

7. Add the following method, setting up the recipe, to the class:

    ```
    public String SetupRecipe(String containerName, String blobName)
    {
        cloudQueue.CreateIfNotExist();

        CloudBlobContainer cloudBlobContainer =
            cloudBlobClient.GetContainerReference(containerName);
        cloudBlobContainer.CreateIfNotExist();
        CloudBlockBlob cloudBlockBlob =
            cloudBlobContainer.GetBlockBlobReference(blobName);
        cloudBlockBlob.UploadText("Large amount of data");
        return cloudBlockBlob.Uri.AbsoluteUri;
    }
    ```

8. Add the following method, linking a message to a blob, to the class:

```
public void AddLargeMessage(String blobUrl)
{
    CloudQueueMessage cloudQueueMessage =
        new CloudQueueMessage(blobUrl);
    cloudQueue.AddMessage(cloudQueueMessage);
}
```

9. Add the following method, processing a large message, to the class:

```
public void ProcessLargeMessage()
{
    CloudQueueMessage cloudQueueMessage = cloudQueue.GetMessage();
    if (cloudQueueMessage != null)
    {
        String blobUri = cloudQueueMessage.AsString;
        CloudBlockBlob cloudBlockBlob =
            cloudBlobClient.GetBlockBlobReference(blobUri);
        String blobText = cloudBlockBlob.DownloadText();
        // Process blobText
        cloudBlockBlob.Delete();
        cloudQueue.DeleteMessage(cloudQueueMessage);
    }
}
```

10. Add the following method, using the methods added previously, to the class:

```
public static void UseLargeDataExample()
{
    String queueName = "largedata";
    String containerName = "largedata";
    String blobName = "largeblob";

    LargeDataExample example = new LargeDataExample(queueName);
    String blobUrl = example.SetupRecipe(containerName, blobName);

    example.AddLargeMessage(blobUrl);
    example.ProcessLargeMessage();
}
```

11. Add the following to the configuration section of `app.config`:

```
<appSettings>
    <add key="DataConnectionString"
        value="UseDevelopmentStorage=true"/>
</appSettings>
```

How it works...

In steps 1 through 4, we set up the class. In step 5, we add private members for the CloudQueue and CloudBlobClient objects we use to interact with the storage service. We initialize these in the constructor we add in step 6. In step 7, we add a method to create the queue and a container. We then upload a blob to the container. The intent is that this blob simulates, for the purpose of demonstration, a blob whose content is too large to fit in a message.

In step 8, we implement the AddLargeMessage() method, in which we add a message whose content is the complete URI of the blob we uploaded in step 7. The idea is that all the messages in this queue would contain a URI to a large blob.

In step 9, we retrieve a message from the queue. We extract the blob URI from the message content and download the blob. We then simulate the processing of the data in the blob. Finally, we use the Storage Client library to delete the blob and the message.

In step 10, we add a method that uses other methods in the class.

In step 11, we add the storage emulator connection string to the app.config configuration file.

Implementing a backoff when polling a queue

When using a Windows Azure Queue Service queue to drive processing, the simplest technique is for a consumer to poll the queue and initiate processing when it retrieves a message. This works well when the queue contains messages. However, when the queue is empty for an extended period, it can lead to unnecessary storage operations.

The Queue service has a scalability target of 500 messages per second corresponding to 1.8 million messages per hour. At the standard billing rate for storage operations ($0.01/10 K operations), this amounts to $1.80 per hour, which is an order of magnitude more expensive than the cost of a compute hour. Consequently, when the queue is empty, it may be worth implementing a backoff strategy to throttle the polling of the queue.

The basic idea is that once a consumer finds the queue to be empty, it should introduce a wait interval between successive polls of the queue. This reduces the polling frequency. If the queue remains empty, then it can further increase the wait interval. The consumer should not increase the wait interval to a level where there would be a significant delay when messages are added to the queue. The consumer can reset the wait interval when it retrieves a message from the queue.

In this recipe, we will learn how to implement a backoff when polling an empty queue.

How to do it...

We are going to poll an empty queue and, on detecting several get message requests that fail to retrieve a message, we are going to increase the backoff interval. We repeat the process until we hit an upper limit for the backoff interval. We do this as follows:

1. Add a new class named `BackoffExample` to the project.

2. Set the Target Framework for the project to.NET Framework 4.

3. Add the following assembly references to the project:

```
Microsoft.WindowsAzure.StorageClient
System.Configuration
```

4. Add the following `using` statements to the top of the class file:

```
using Microsoft.WindowsAzure;
using Microsoft.WindowsAzure.StorageClient;
using System.Configuration;
using System.Threading;
```

5. Add the following constants to the class:

```
public const Int32 minimumBackoff = 10;
public const Int32 maximumBackoff = 10000;
```

6. Add the following private member to the class:

```
private CloudQueue cloudQueue;
```

7. Add the following property to the class:

```
private Int32 backoff = minimumBackoff;
public Int32 Backoff
{
   get { return backoff; }
   set {
      backoff = value > maximumBackoff ?
         maximumBackoff : value;
      backoff = backoff < minimumBackoff ?
         minimumBackoff : backoff;
   }
}
```

8. Add the following constructor to the class:

```
public BackoffExample(String queueName)
{
   CloudStorageAccount cloudStorageAccount =
      CloudStorageAccount.Parse(
```

```
        ConfigurationManager.AppSettings[
        "DataConnectionString"]);
    CloudQueueClient cloudQueueClient =
        cloudStorageAccount.CreateCloudQueueClient();
    cloudQueue = cloudQueueClient.GetQueueReference(queueName);
    cloudQueue.CreateIfNotExist();

    CloudQueueMessage cloudQueueMessage =
        new CloudQueueMessage("Some message");
    cloudQueue.AddMessage(cloudQueueMessage);
}
```

9. Add the following method, processing a message, to the class:

```
public Boolean ProcessMessage()
{
    CloudQueueMessage cloudQueueMessage =
        cloudQueue.GetMessage();
    if (cloudQueueMessage != null)
    {
        String messageText = cloudQueueMessage.AsString;
        // use message
        cloudQueue.DeleteMessage(cloudQueueMessage);
    }

    return cloudQueueMessage != null;
}
```

10. Add the following method, using the methods added previously, to the class:

```
public static void UseBackoffExample()
{
    String queueName = "backoff";
    BackoffExample example = new BackoffExample(queueName);

    Int32 noMessageCount = 0;
    for (Int32 i = 0; i < 100; i++)
    {
        if (example.ProcessMessage())
        {
            example.Backoff = BackoffExample.minimumBackoff;
            noMessageCount = 0;
        }
        else
        {
            if (++noMessageCount > 1)
            {
```

```
                        example.Backoff *= 10;
                        noMessageCount = 0;
                    }
                }
                Thread.Sleep(example.Backoff);
            }
        }
```

11. Add the following to the configuration section of `app.config`:

```xml
<appSettings>
    <add key="DataConnectionString"
        value="UseDevelopmentStorage=true"/>
</appSettings>
```

How it works...

In steps 1 through 4, we set up the class. In step 5, we add constants to specify the minimum and maximum backoff. In step 6, we add a private member for the `CloudQueue` object we use to interact with the Queue service.

In step 7, we add the `Backoff` property that stores the number of milliseconds we wait for the current backoff. The setter restricts `Backoff` to be between the minimum and maximum values specified in step 5.

In step 8, we add a constructor in which we initialize the `CloudQueue` private member we added in step 6. We also create the queue and add a message to it.

In step 9, we add a `ProcessMessage()` method, in which we retrieve a message from the queue. We return a `Boolean` to indicate whether we retrieved a message.

In step 10, we use a loop to invoke `ProcessMessage()` to poll the queue. At the end of each loop, we wait for the number of milliseconds specified by `Backoff`. Initially, we use the `minimumBackoff` specified for the class. If we detect two sequential `ProcessMessage()` calls failing to retrieve a message, then we increase the `Backoff` by a factor of 10. This process repeats until we reach the maximum allowed `Backoff`. If we retrieve a message, then we set the backoff to the minimum and reset `noMessageCount` to 0.

In step 11, we add the storage emulator connection string to the `app.config` configuration file.

Identifying and handling poison messages

The standard way to use a Windows Azure Queue Service queue is to retrieve a message, do some processing based on the message, and then delete the message from the queue. A problem arises if the content of the message causes an error during processing that prevents the consumer from deleting the message from the queue. When the message once again becomes visible on the queue, another consumer will retrieve it, and the failure process begins again. Such a message is referred to as a poison message because it poisons the queue and prevents messages in it from being processed. When there is only a single consumer, a poison message can completely block processing of the queue.

A poison message has to be identified, removed from the queue, and logged for subsequent investigation. A convenient way to log the poison message is to insert it in a poison message queue where it is not processed in a way that causes problems. When a consumer requests a message, the Queue service provides a dequeue count specifying the number of times the message has been dequeued. If this count exceeds some application-specific value, then the message can be identified as a poison message and diverted into poison message handling. The Windows Azure Storage Client library exposes the dequeue count as `CloudQueueMessage.DequeueCount`.

In this recipe, we will learn how to handle poison messages in a queue.

How to do it...

We are going to add some messages, including a poison message, to a queue. We will then retrieve the messages, identify the poison message, and divert it to a poison message queue.

1. Add a new class named `PoisonMessagesExample` to the project.
2. Set the Target Framework for the project to.NET Framework 4.
3. Add the following assembly references to the project:

   ```
   Microsoft.WindowsAzure.StorageClient
   System.Configuration
   ```

4. Add the following `using` statements to the top of the class file:

   ```
   using Microsoft.WindowsAzure;
   using Microsoft.WindowsAzure.StorageClient;
   using System.Configuration;
   using System.IO;
   using System.Runtime.Serialization.Formatters.Binary;
   using System.Threading;
   ```

5. Add the following class declaration after the namespace declaration:

```
[Serializable]
public class SomeClass
{
    public String Action { get; set; }

    public SomeClass() { }

    public static SomeClass ToSomeClass(Byte[] bytes)
    {
        SomeClass someObject = new SomeClass();
        using (MemoryStream memoryStream =
          new MemoryStream(bytes))
        {
            BinaryFormatter formatter = new BinaryFormatter();
            someObject =
                formatter.Deserialize(memoryStream) as SomeClass;
        }
        return someObject;
    }

    public static Byte[] ToByte(SomeClass someObject)
    {
        Byte[] bytes;
        using (MemoryStream memoryStream = new MemoryStream())
        {
            BinaryFormatter formatter = new BinaryFormatter();
            formatter.Serialize(memoryStream, someObject);
            bytes = memoryStream.ToArray();
        }
        return bytes;
    }
}
```

6. Add the following private member to the `PoisonMessagesExample` class:

```
private CloudQueue cloudQueue;
```

7. Add the following constructor to the `PoisonMessagesExample` class:

```
public PoisonMessagesExample(String queueName)
{
    CloudStorageAccount cloudStorageAccount =
        CloudStorageAccount.Parse(
        ConfigurationManager.AppSettings[
        "DataConnectionString"]);
```

```
CloudQueueClient cloudQueueClient =
    cloudStorageAccount.CreateCloudQueueClient();
cloudQueue = cloudQueueClient.GetQueueReference(queueName);
cloudQueue.CreateIfNotExist();

CloudQueue poisonQueue =
    cloudQueueClient.GetQueueReference("poisoned");
poisonQueue.CreateIfNotExist();
}
```

8. Add the following method, adding a message, to the `PoisonMessagesExample` class:

```
public void AddMessage()
{
    SomeClass someObject = new SomeClass()
        { Action = "MonteCarloSimulation" };

    Byte[] message = SomeClass.ToByte(someObject);

    CloudQueueMessage cloudQueueMessage =
        new CloudQueueMessage(message);
    cloudQueue.AddMessage(cloudQueueMessage);
}
```

9. Add the following method, adding a poison message, to the `PoisonMessagesExample` class:

```
public void AddPoisonMessage()
{
    String message = "Poison message";
    CloudQueueMessage cloudQueueMessage =
        new CloudQueueMessage(message);
    cloudQueue.AddMessage(cloudQueueMessage);
}
```

10. Add the following method, processing a message, to the `PoisonMessagesExample` class:

```
public void ProcessMessage()
{
    CloudQueueMessage cloudQueueMessage =
        cloudQueue.GetMessage(
        TimeSpan.FromSeconds(1));
    if (cloudQueueMessage == null)
    {
        return;
    }
}
```

```
SomeClass someObject;
try
{
    someObject =
        SomeClass.ToSomeClass(cloudQueueMessage.AsBytes);
    // use message
    cloudQueue.DeleteMessage(cloudQueueMessage);
}
catch
{
    Int32 dequeueCount = cloudQueueMessage.DequeueCount;
    if (dequeueCount > 3)
    {
        CloudQueueClient cloudQueueClient =
            cloudQueue.ServiceClient;
        CloudQueue poisonQueue =
            cloudQueueClient.GetQueueReference(
            "poisoned");
        poisonQueue.AddMessage(cloudQueueMessage);
        cloudQueue.DeleteMessage(cloudQueueMessage);
    }
}
}
```

11. Add the following method, using the methods added earlier, to the `PoisonMessagesExample` class:

```
public static void UsePoisonMessagesExample()
{
    String queueName = "tasks";
    PoisonMessagesExample example =
        new PoisonMessagesExample(queueName);
    example.AddMessage();
    example.AddPoisonMessage();
    for (Int32 i = 0; i < 10; i++)
    {
        example.ProcessMessage();
        Thread.Sleep(2000);
    }
}
```

12. Add the following to the configuration section of `app.config`:

```
<appSettings>
    <add key="DataConnectionString"
      value="UseDevelopmentStorage=true"/>
</appSettings>
```

How it works...

In steps 1 through 4, we set up the recipe. In step 5, we add a class named `SomeClass` that we use to serialize the content of a message. The class contains a single property, `Action`, which specifies the action we take to process the message. `SomeClass` uses a `BinaryFormatter` to serialize an instance to and from a `Byte[]`.

In step 6, we add a private member to store the `CloudQueue` object used to interact with the Queue service. We initialize this in the constructor we add in step 7, in which we also create a message queue and a poisoned message queue.

In step 8, we add the `AddMessage()` method that adds a message to the queue. This method constructs an object of type `SomeClass` and then serializes it to a `Byte[]`, which we use as the content of the good message we add to the queue.

In step 9, we add the `AddPoisonMessage()` method that adds a poison message to the queue. We simply add a message to the queue whose content is not of the expected `SomeClass` type.

In step 10, we add the `ProcessMessage()` method that processes a single message. On retrieving a message, we create a `SomeClass` object from the message content. We use a very short visibility timeout of 1 second for demonstration purposes, so that the poison messages become visible without undue delay. On success, we use the message and then delete it from the queue. In the event of an error creating the `SomeClass` object, we check the `Dequeue` count of the message and if it is greater than 3, we add the message to the poison message queue and delete it from the `tasks` queue.

In step 11, we add the `UsePoisonMessagesExample()` method to use the methods added earlier. We invoke `AddMessage()` and `AddPoisonMessage()` to add a good and poison message to the `tasks` queue. Then, we enter a loop that invokes `ProcessMessage()` and sleeps for 2 seconds. The pause is to ensure that the visibility timeout for the message expires, so that the poison message is visible when the `GetMessage()` is invoked.

In step 12, we add the storage emulator connection string to the `app.config` configuration file.

5
Developing Hosted Services for Windows Azure

In this chapter, we will cover:

- ▸ Choosing the service model for a hosted service
- ▸ Choosing which Windows Azure storage type to use
- ▸ Configuring the service model for a hosted service
- ▸ Hosting multiple websites in a web role
- ▸ Providing a custom domain name for a hosted service
- ▸ Implementing HTTPS in a web role
- ▸ Sharing session state with the Windows Azure AppFabric Caching Service
- ▸ Using local storage in an instance
- ▸ Using startup tasks in a Windows Azure role
- ▸ Managing upgrades and changes to a hosted service
- ▸ Handling changes to the configuration and topology of a hosted service
- ▸ Using an Azure Drive in a hosted service
- ▸ Using the Azure Drive simulation in the development environment
- ▸ Using a VM Role
- ▸ Using Windows Azure Connect
- ▸ Consuming data from the Windows Azure MarketPlace DataMarket
- ▸ Using Web Deploy with Windows Azure

Introduction

Windows Azure is the paradigm of the **Platform-as-a-Service** model (**PaaS**) of cloud computing. A hosted service can be developed and deployed to any of several Windows Azure data centers located across the World. A service hosted in Windows Azure can leverage the high scalability and reduced administrative benefits of the PaaS model.

A hosted service is an administrative and security boundary. Administrative because applications in it are packaged and deployed as a whole, and security because the hosted service is accessible from outside only through load-balanced endpoints. An application deployed into a hosted service comprises a set of roles, instances of which are deployed to virtual machines (VM) to implement service functionality.

A role is the scalability unit of a hosted service in that it provides vertical scaling, through the use of a larger VM size for instances of the role, and horizontal scaling through the elastic deployment of a workload-dependent number of instances. The **service model** of a hosted service defines the roles used in the service, as well as their configuration. It is specified in the following two XML files:

- ▸ The service definition file (`ServiceDefinition.csdef`)
- ▸ The service configuration file (`ServiceConfiguration.cscfg`)

In the *Choosing the service model for a hosted service* recipe, we see how to choose which roles to use in a hosted service. We see how to configure the service model in the *Configuring the service model for a hosted service* recipe.

Major changes to the service model, such as adding new endpoints, require that the application be deleted and redeployed. Minor changes, such as to configuration settings or the number of instances (a topology change), can be accomplished through either an in-place upgrade or a Virtual IP (VIP) swap. In an in-place upgrade, the instances are upgraded in groups to ensure that the hosted service remains available during the upgrade, although served by fewer instances. In a VIP swap, the load balancer configuration is changed, so that it forwards traffic to the instances in the staging slot rather than the production slot. We look at the various types of service upgrade in the *Managing upgrades and changes to a hosted service* recipe. We see how to handle these changes in code in the *Handling changes to the configuration and topology of a hosted service* recipe.

With the Windows Azure SDK v1.3 release, Windows Azure introduced the use of full IIS in web roles rather than the hosted web core used previously. This provides many advantages, with the most important being the ability to host multiple websites in a single web role. This feature has been requested often because it allows a web role to host many low-traffic websites, something that was previously cost-prohibitive. We see how to do this in the *Hosting multiple websites in a web role* recipe. A web role exposes a single VIP address in the `cloudapp.net` domain, so different websites hosted by the role must use different URLs pointing to that VIP address. We see how to map a custom URL to the `cloudapp.net` domain in the *Providing a custom domain name for a hosted service* recipe. A website can also expose an HTTPS endpoint to allow secure communication. We see how to do this in the *Implementing HTTPS in a web role* recipe.

A hosted service implements horizontal scalability of a web role by changing the number of instances. All traffic to a web role is load balanced using a round-robin algorithm. This means that IIS session state must be sharable across the instances. We see how to do this in the *Sharing session state with the Windows Azure AppFabric Caching Service* recipe.

The Windows Azure Platform provides several types of storage that a hosted service can use. This varies from relational with SQL Azure, to NoSQL with the Windows Azure Table Service, and to queues and blobs with the Windows Azure Queue Service and Windows Azure Blob Service respectively. We see how to select an appropriate storage type for a hosted service in the *Choosing which Windows Azure storage type to use* recipe.

There are two types of storage available locally to an instance: local storage and Azure Drive. Local storage is space on a local drive of the instance that it has read-write access to. This space is only semi-durable in that it does not survive when an instance is moved. We see how to use this space in the *Using local storage in an instance* recipe. An Azure Drive is a virtual hard disk (VHD) stored as a page blob, in the Blob service, and which an instance can mount locally as an NTFS-formatted disk. We see how to do this in the *Using an Azure Drive in a hosted service* recipe. The development environment provides an Azure Drive simulation and we see how to use this in the *Using the Azure Drive simulation in the development environment* recipe.

Windows Azure provides a Guest OS with an application-hosting environment into which an application can be injected. The Guest OS is hardened, and the hosted service has only limited access to it. This matches the statelessness of an instance because any changes made to it are lost when it is reimaged or moved. The Windows Azure SDK v1.3 release relaxed the hardening in several ways: the ability to run a role with elevated privilege; the use of startup tasks to modify the application-hosting environment; and a VM Role allowing a customized Guest OS to be used in a role. We see how to use startup tasks in the *Using startup tasks in an Azure role* recipe. We learn about VM roles in the *Using a VM Role* recipe.

A hosted service represents a security boundary in which the instances of the service are contained in a virtual network inaccessible from outside. The Windows Azure SDK v1.3 release introduced Windows Azure Connect, which allows local machines to be added to the virtual network of the hosted service. An important use case for Windows Azure Connect is to allow a Windows Azure web role to access a Microsoft SQL Server database stored in a corporate datacenter. We learn about Windows Azure Connect in the *Using Windows Azure Connect* recipe.

The **Windows Azure MarketPlace DataMarket** provides a way for owners of datasets to expose them to consumers in a standard way. It supports subscription, so that commercial dataset providers can charge for data access. Some providers, such as Governments, can use the DataMarket as an effective way to expose datasets without charge. The DataMarket exposes data as OData, making it easy to consume. It also provides strongly typed classes to simplify access to the datasets. We see how to use the DataMarket in the *Consuming data from the Windows Azure MarketPlace DataMarket* recipe.

The deployment of an application to a Windows Azure Hosted Service typically takes 10 minutes or longer. This has frustrated many developers who have grown used to much quicker deployments. Microsoft has provided Visual Studio tooling allowing Web Deploy to be used to deploy changes to a web role in only a few seconds. We see how to do this in the *Using Web Deploy in Windows Azure* recipe.

> Note that at the time of writing, the following features are still in CTP or beta:
> ▸ VM role
> ▸ Azure Drive
> ▸ Windows Azure Connect

Choosing the service model for a hosted service

Cloud services are classified typically as **infrastructure-as-a-service (IaaS)**, **platform-as-a-service (PaaS)**, and **software-as-a service (SaaS)**. In the IaaS model, the core service provided is a virtual machine (VM) with a Guest OS. The customer is responsible for everything about the Guest OS, including hardening it and adding any required software. Amazon Elastic Cloud Compute (EC2) is the paradigm for IaaS. In the PaaS model, the core service provided is a VM with a hardened Guest OS and an application-hosting environment. The customer is responsible only for the service injected into that environment. In the SaaS model, a service is exposed over the Internet and the customer merely has to access it.

Windows Azure is the paradigm for PaaS. As such, Windows Azure provides a high-level, application-hosting environment modeled on services, roles, and instances. The specification of the roles in the service is referred to as the service model.

A hosted service provides the management and security boundary for a set of roles. It is the management boundary because a hosted service is deployed, started, stopped, and deleted as a unit. A hosted service represents a security boundary because roles can expose input endpoints to the public Internet, but they can also expose internal endpoints that are visible only to other roles in the service.

Roles are the scalability unit for a hosted service, as they provide vertical scaling through increasing the instance size and horizontal scaling through increasing the number of instances. Each role is deployed as one or more instances. The number of deployed instances for a role scales independently of other roles. For example, one role could have two instances deployed while another has two hundred. Furthermore, the compute capacity (or size) of each deployed instance is specified at the role level, so that all instances of a role have the same size, though instances of different roles may have different sizes.

The application functionality of a role is deployed to individual instances that provide the compute capability for the hosted service. Each instance is hosted on its own virtual machine (VM). An instance is stateless because any changes made to it following deployment will not survive an instance failure and will be lost. Note that the word *role* is used frequently where the word *instance* should be used.

A central driver of interest in cloud computing has been the realization that horizontal scalability, by adding commodity servers, is significantly more cost effective than vertical scalability achieved through increasing the power of a single server. As do other cloud platforms, the Windows Azure Platform emphasizes horizontal scalability over vertical scalability. The ability to increase and decrease the number of deployed instances to match workload is described as *elasticity*.

Prior to the release of Windows Azure SDK v1.3, the guest OS that hosts an instance was completely locked down with only a small set of changes allowed. For example, additional software could be deployed only if it could be **XCOPY** installed and required no registry changes. These restrictions led to a flexible, though constrained, application environment. The Windows Azure SDK v1.3 release relaxed some of these constraints. It added startup tasks that are batch scripts or executable programs invoked each time an instance starts. Startup tasks modify the hosting environment by, for example, installing additional software.

Windows Azure supports three types of roles: web role, worker role, and VM role. The web and worker roles are central to the PaaS model of Windows Azure. While the VM role moves the Windows Azure Platform down the stack towards an IaaS model, the contents of a VM role are still tightly controlled so that, for example, it cannot host an arbitrary Guest OS.

Prior to Windows Azure SDK v1.3, a web role was implemented using hosted web core and could support only a single website. With Windows Azure SDK v1.3, a web role hosts websites using full IIS. A web role can now host multiple websites with a single endpoint using host headers to distinguish them. An instance of a web role implements two processes: the web role running code that interacts with the Azure fabric and the process that runs IIS. Note that it is still possible to use hosted web core for a web role.

A worker role hosts a long-running service and essentially, replicates the functionality of a Windows service. Otherwise, the only real difference between a worker role and a web role is that a web role hosts IIS. Furthermore, a worker role can also be used to host web servers other than IIS.

With Windows Azure SDK v1.3, Windows Azure added the VM role. For this type of role, the customized Windows Server 2008 R2 virtual machine can be created locally then uploaded as a VHD to Windows Azure, where is it is associated with a hosted service. This customized VHD then acts as the Guest OS image and can include any software needed for the hosted service. While it is possible to install software on web and worker roles, a much wider variety of software can be installed on a VM role. We learn more about VM roles in the *Using a VM role* recipe in this chapter.

With the VM role, it appears that Windows Azure is heading down the platform stack towards IaaS. A lot of existing software cannot be ported immediately into web and worker roles, but can be installed directly into a VM role and thereby migrated to Windows Azure.

The most common practice is to use web and worker roles, invoking startup tasks to install software, rather than VM roles. This provides the best way to maximize the administrative and cost savings provided by the PaaS model of Windows Azure. Additionally, software packages may not always work well with the stateless, scale out infrastructure provided by Windows Azure.

In this recipe, we will learn how to choose the service model for a hosted service.

How to do it...

We are going to see how to choose which role types to use in a hosted service. We do this as follows:

1. We choose a web role if we are deploying one or more IIS websites to the hosted service.

2. We choose a worker role if we are deploying one or more websites, not using IIS, to the hosted service.

3. We choose a worker role if we are deploying long-running tasks to the hosted service.

4. We choose separate roles if we are deploying significant tasks with different scalability requirements.

5. We choose a VM role if the complexity of any modifications to the VM is beyond that achievable in a web or worker role. These include installations that:
    - Take more than 5 minutes to complete
    - Are fragile or prone to failure
    - Require human intervention
    - Require complex configuration

6. We choose a larger instance size if the role can effectively and fully use the increased number of cores, memory, local storage, or network capacity.

How it works...

In step 1, we choose a web role because hosting IIS websites is the only reason web roles exist. In step 2, we need to use a worker role because web roles are not able to host web servers other than IIS. In step 3, we choose a worker role because hosting long-running tasks is the primary reason worker roles exist.

In step 4, we distribute functionality among different roles to allow us to match functionality with scalability. For example, we could have one worker role with two instances; to satisfy the SLA, manage another worker role with 10 instances. Each role gets enough resources to perform its assigned tasks.

In step 5, we use a VM role because we are changing the VM environment in a way that is too complicated to achieve in a worker role, even using startup tasks. The best practice is that we should use a web or worker role, if possible, rather than use a VM role and become responsible for its additional administration burden.

In step 6, we look at vertical scalability and consider the appropriate instance size. Note that for small installations, we should favor horizontal scalability over vertical scalability because, for example, although eight small instances cost the same as one extra-large instance, the latter does not benefit from an SLA.

Choosing which Windows Azure storage type to use

The Windows Azure Platform supports various storage types:

- ▶ Blobs
- ▶ Tables
- ▶ Queues
- ▶ Local storage
- ▶ Azure Drive
- ▶ SQL Azure

The Windows Azure Blob Service supports the storage of two types of blobs: *block* supporting streamed access and *page* supporting random read-write access. The maximum size of a block blob is 200 GB and the maximum size of a page blob is 1 TB. Block blobs can be used to host streaming content for websites and exposed through the **Windows Azure Content Delivery Network** (**CDN**). The primary use case for page blobs is the storage of the virtual hard drive (VHD) used to back an Azure Drive. We can see more about blobs in *Chapter 2, Handling Blobs in Windows Azure*.

The Windows Azure Table Service provides for the schemaless storage of structured data, providing a NoSQL like feature in the Windows Azure Platform. A Windows Azure storage account can have many tables with each table comprising a collection of entities. Each entity has a Primary Key of `PartitionKey` and `RowKey`, as well as a `Timestamp` property used for optimistic concurrency. Windows Azure tables are schemaless, so the restrictions on the properties of an entity relate to overall size of the entity, and the datatypes supported for the entities. The Table service does not currently support indexes other than the Primary Key and does not support referential integrity. It provides limited support for transactions. We can see more about tables in *Chapter 3, Going NoSQL with Windows Azure Tables*.

The Windows Azure Queue Service provides queue capability to Windows Azure. The primary use case is to allow disconnected communication between roles, but queues can also be used to manage the workflow of multistep tasks. The Queue service provides a best-effort FIFO queue. A message, of up to 8 KB, can be added to the queue and remains there until it is deleted or for a maximum of seven days.

The pattern for using a queue is that one or more instances poll the queue. Once retrieved, a message remains on the queue but is rendered invisible to other callers until its visibility timeout expires after which it once again becomes visible. Any processing based on getting a message should be completed and the message deleted from the queue before the timeout expires. It is possible that a message is retrieved more than once, so it is important that any task performed is idempotent, that is, the same outcome occurs regardless of how many times the message is retrieved. We can see more about queues in *Chapter 4, Disconnecting with Windows Azure Queues*.

Each instance of a Windows Azure role has read-write access to an instance-size dependent quantity of local disk storage. Local storage for the role is defined in the service definition file. An instance can retrieve the root path to local storage and has full control over the contents of this reserved area of local disk. Regular file and directory methods may be used to read and write to local storage. This is only semi-durable in that it does not survive the move of an instance from one VM to another. We can see more about local storage in the *Using local storage in an instance* recipe in this chapter.

The Azure Drive feature allows an instance to mount, as an NTFS drive, a VHD stored as a page blob. Once mounted, the instance has full read-write access to the drive. All non-buffered/flushed writes to the Azure Drive are committed immediately to the page blob. Local storage can be configured for use as a read cache for an Azure Drive. A limitation is that only one instance at a time can mount a VHD page blob as a writable Azure Drive. However, an unlimited number of instances can mount simultaneously a VHD page blob snapshot as a read-only Azure Drive. We see more about Azure Drive in the *Using an Azure Drive in an instance* recipe and the *Using the Azure Drive simulation in the development fabric* recipe.

SQL Azure is a version of Microsoft SQL Server running in a Windows Azure data center. The maximum size of a SQL Azure database is currently 50 GB. SQL Azure uses the same TDS protocol as SQL Server, so it is possible to switch an application from using SQL Server to SQL Azure merely by changing the connection string. SQL Azure exposes most, but not all, Microsoft SQL Server functionality. However, SQL Azure does provide full ACID semantics in a cloud environment. We can see more about SQL Azure in *Chapter 8, Using SQL Azure.*

Windows Azure blobs and tables provide cost-effective, highly scalable storage. They achieve this by being non-relational and providing only limited indexing capability. SQL Azure exposes relational functionality with ACID semantics, but at the cost of being significantly more expensive and less scalable than Windows Azure blobs and tables.

In this recipe, we will learn how to choose which storage type to use in a hosted service.

How to do it...

We are going to see how to choose which storage type to use in a hosted service. We do this as follows:

1. We choose Windows Azure blobs if we want to stream large quantities of data (block blob) or perform random read-write access to a large file (page blob).
2. We choose Windows Azure tables if we want cost-effective, highly scalable storage of entities when we are willing to accept the query limitations.
3. We choose SQL Azure if we want to use a relational database.
4. We can choose to combine SQL Azure with one or both of Windows Azure blobs and Windows Azure tables if we want to combine the indexing capability of SQL Azure with the scalable content of blob containers and tables.
5. We choose Windows Azure queues when we need to implement disconnected communication between processes.
6. We choose local storage if we need NTFS access to a semi-durable local disk.
7. We choose Azure Drive if we need NTFS access to a durable disk.

How it works...

In steps 1 through 3, we choose Windows Azure blobs, Windows Azure tables, and SQL Azure respectively because these are their core use cases. In step 4, we consider the possibility of combining them by vertically partitioning the data, so that (for example) a SQL Azure database stores references to images stored as blobs. This combination helps mitigate the size limitations of SQL Azure in a cost-effective and highly scalable way.

In step 5, we choose Windows Azure queues because this is the core use case.

The primary distinction between steps 6 and 7 is durability. Local storage is convenient if we want high-speed access to a local disk and we are not too concerned about durability. Azure Drive provides durable storage with slower access, because it is over a network (the backing store is a Windows Azure blob), unless and until data is cached in local storage. Another advantage of Azure Drive is that the same data can be made visible in a read-only manner to more than one instance at a time.

Configuring the service model for a hosted service

The service model for a hosted service in Windows Azure is specified in two XML files: the service definition file (`ServiceDefinition.csdef`) and the service configuration file (`ServiceConfiguration.cscfg`). These files are part of the Windows Azure project.

The service definition file specifies the roles used in the hosted service. There can be at most five roles in a hosted service. For each role, the service definition file specifies: the instance size; the available endpoints; the public key certificates; the pluggable modules used in the role; the startup tasks; the local resources; and the runtime execution context. The service definition file also contains the declaration of any custom configuration settings used in a role. For a web role running full IIS, the service definition file contains the IIS configuration.

All instances of a role have the same size, chosen from extra-small to extra-large. Each role may specify a number of input endpoints and internal endpoints. Input endpoints are accessible over the Internet and are load balanced, using a round-robin algorithm, across all instances of the role. Internal endpoints are accessible only by instances of any role in the hosted service. They are not load balanced. A hosted service can have up to 25 input endpoints distributed among all roles, and up to five internal endpoints per role.

An **X.509** public key certificate can be uploaded to a hosted service either directly on the Windows Azure Portal or by using the Windows Azure Service Management REST API. The service definition file specifies which public key certificates, if any, are to be deployed with the role, as well as the certificate store where they are put. A public key certificate can be used to configure an HTTPS endpoint, but can also be accessed from code.

Pluggable modules were introduced with Windows Azure SDK v1.3, so that functionality, such as Windows Azure Diagnostics, could be imported into VM roles. However, pluggable modules are used with all role types. Only those pluggable modules configured for a role are available inside the role. The Windows Azure tooling for Visual Studio can be used to manage configuration of the other pluggable modules. The pluggable modules available in Windows Azure SDK v1.3 are:

- **Connect** to inject Azure Connect
- **Diagnostics** to inject Windows Azure Diagnostics
- **RemoteAccess** to inject remote desktop capability
- **RemoteForwarder** to inject the forwarding capability used to support remote desktop

Startup tasks are scripts or executables that run each time an instance starts and which modify the runtime environment of the instance, up to and including the installation of required software. The runtime execution context specifies whether the role runs with limited privileges (default) or with elevated privileges that provide complete administrative capabilities. Note that in a web role running full IIS, the runtime execution context applies only to the web role and does not affect IIS, which runs in a separate process with restricted privileges.

In a web role running full IIS, the `Sites` element in the service definition file contains the IIS configuration for the role. It specifies the endpoint bindings, virtual applications, virtual directories, and host headers for the various websites hosted by the web role. The *Hosting multiple websites in a web role* recipe in this chapter contains more information about this configuration.

The service definition file is uploaded to Windows Azure as part of the Windows Azure package. Although some changes to the service definition file can be implemented by upgrading the application deployed to the hosted service, most changes require that the existing application be deleted and a new one deployed.

The service configuration file specifies the number of instances of each role. It also specifies the values of any custom-configuration settings, as well as those for any pluggable modules imported in the service definition file.

Applications developed using the .NET Framework, typically store application configuration settings in an `app.config` or `web.config` file. Hosted services can also use these files. However, changes to these files require the redeployment of the entire service package. Windows Azure allows custom configuration settings to be specified in the service configuration file, where they can be modified without redeploying the application. Any service configuration setting that could be changed while the hosted service is running should be stored in the service configuration file. These custom configuration settings must be declared in the service definition file. The Windows Azure SDK provides a `RoleEnvironment.GetConfigurationSetting()` method that can be used to access the values of custom configuration settings.

The service configuration file is uploaded separately from the Windows Azure package and can be modified independently of it. Changes to the service configuration file can be implemented either directly on the Windows Azure Portal or through upgrading the hosted service. The service configuration can also be upgraded using the Windows Azure Service Management REST API. The handling of service upgrades is described in the *Managing upgrades and updates to a hosted service recipe* and the *Handling changes to the configuration and topology of a hosted service* recipe.

In this recipe, we will learn how to configure the service model for a hosted service.

Getting ready

To use this recipe, we need to have created a Windows Azure hosted service and deployed an application to it.

How to do it...

We are going to see how to implement various changes to the service definition and service configuration files. We do this as follows:

1. We implement a change in the service configuration for the hosted service on the Windows Azure Portal.

2. We add a new custom-configuration setting by declaring it in the `ConfigurationSettings` section of the service definition file, `ServiceDefinition.csdef`, and providing its value in the `ConfigurationSettings` section of the service configuration file, `ServiceConfiguration.cscfg`. We deploy the amended configuration by upgrading the hosted service.

3. We modify the endpoints exposed by the hosted service by editing the service definition file. We enable these endpoint changes by deleting the existing application deployed to the hosted service and deploying the updated application into it.

How it works...

Performing the change described in step 1 directly on the Windows Azure Portal without redeploying the hosted service is the primary reason behind having a service configuration file. We can also use the Windows Azure Service Management REST API to upload a new configuration. Alternatively, we can upgrade the hosted service by including a modified service configuration file.

When we perform the change described in step 2, we need to rebuild the application and deploy it through an upgrade.

The service definition change described in step 3 affects the load balancer and consequently requires that we delete the existing application and deploy a newer version.

There's more...

Most changes to the service definition file require that the application be deleted and redeployed, which involves bringing the hosted service down until the upgrade is completed. One way to reduce the impact of such an upgrade for a web role is to deploy the upgraded application as a new-hosted service and repoint the CNAME record to the new service. It takes some time for CNAME records to migrate through DNS, so the two services must run simultaneously for a while. We can delete the old service once the new CNAME mapping has percolated across DNS. *Providing a custom domain name for a hosted service* recipe in this chapter shows how to use a CNAME record with a hosted service.

Handling upgrades and configuration changes

We see how to manage upgrades in the *Managing upgrades and changes to a hosted service* recipe. We can see how to handle configuration changes in code in the *Handling changes to the configuration and topology of a hosted service* recipe.

Storing Configuration in Azure storage

The custom-configuration settings supported by Windows Azure provide a convenient and coherent way to configure a hosted service. However, this custom configuration is restricted to simple name-value pairs. A hosted service could use the Windows Azure Storage Service to store more sophisticated configuration in either blobs or tables.

Hosting multiple websites in a web role

Microsoft released Windows Azure as a production service in February 2010. A common complaint was that it was too expensive to develop small websites because a web role could support only a single website. The cause of this limitation was that a web role hosted a website using hosted web core rather than full IIS.

With the Windows Azure SDK v1.3 release, Windows Azure added support for full IIS for web roles. This means that a single web role can host multiple websites. However, all of these websites share the same Virtual IP (VIP) address, and a CNAME record must be used to map the domain name of the website to the `servicename.cloudapp.net` URL for the web role. Each website is then distinguished inside IIS by its distinct host header. The *Providing a custom domain name for a hosted service* recipe in this chapter shows how to use a CNAME record to map a custom domain to a hosted service domain. Note that full IIS is also available on worker roles.

A new `Sites` element in the service definition file (`ServiceDefinition.csdef`) is used to configure multiple websites. This element contains one child `Site` element for each website hosted by the web role. Each `Site` element has two attributes: `name` distinguishing the configuration and `physicalDirectory` specifying the physical directory for the website. Note that multiple websites can reference the same physical directory. Each `Site` element has a `Bindings` child element that contains a set of `Binding` child elements, each of which identifies an endpoint used by the website and the host header used to distinguish the website. Each endpoint must correspond to an input endpoint specified in the `EndPoints` declaration for the web role. It is possible to define virtual applications and virtual directories for a website by using the `VirtualApplication` and `VirtualDirectory` elements respectively. This configuration is a subset of standard IIS configuration.

The following example shows a fragment of a service definition file for a web role hosting two websites:

```
<WebRole name="MultipleWebsites">
    <Sites>
        <Site name="WebsiteOne" physicalDirectory="..\Web">
            <Bindings>
                <Binding name="HttpIn" endpointName="HttpIn"
                    hostHeader="www.websiteone.com" />
            </Bindings>
        </Site>
        <Site name="WebsiteTwo" physicalDirectory="..\Web">
            <VirtualApplication name="Payment"
                physicalDirectory="..\..\Payment">
                <VirtualDirectory name="Scripts"
                physicalDirectory="..\Web\Scripts" />
            </VirtualApplication>
            <Bindings>
                <Binding name="HttpIn" endpointName="HttpIn"
                hostHeader="www.websitetwo.com" />
                <Binding name="HttpsIn" endpointName="HttpsIn"
                hostHeader="www.websitetwo.com" />
            </Bindings>
        </Site>
    </Sites>
    <Endpoints>
        <InputEndpoint name="HttpIn" protocol="http"
            port="80" />
        <InputEndpoint name="HttpsIn" protocol="https"
            port="443" />
    </Endpoints>
    <ConfigurationSettings />
</WebRole>
```

This configuration specifies that the web role hosts two websites: www.websiteone.com and www.websitetwo.com. They share the same physical directory, but www.websitetwo.com also uses a virtual application with its own virtual directory. Both websites are accessible using HTTP, but www.websitetwo.com also exposes an HTTPS endpoint.

In this recipe, we will learn how to host multiple websites in a single Windows Azure web role.

How to do it...

We are going to see how to implement two websites in a hosted service. We do this as follows:

1. Use Visual Studio to create an empty Cloud project.
2. Add a web role to the project (accept default name of WebRole1).

 The changes in steps 3 through 8 affect the service definition file, ServiceDefinition.csdef:

3. Set the name attribute of the Site element to WebSiteOne.
4. Add a physicalDirectory attribute with value ..\WebRole1 to the Site element.
5. Add a hostHeader attribute, with value www.websiteone.com, to the Binding element for the Site.
6. Copy the entire Site element and paste it under itself.
7. Change the name attribute of the new Site element to WebsiteTwo.
8. Change the hostHeader attribute of the new Site element to www.websitetwo.com.
9. Add the following entries to the hosts file in %SystemRoot%\system32\drivers\etc:

   ```
   127.0.0.1    www.websiteone.com
   127.0.0.1    www.websitetwo.com
   ```

10. Build and run the hosted service.
11. Change the URL in the browser to www.websiteone.com and refresh.
12. Change the URL in the browser to www.websitetwo.com and refresh.

How it works...

On completing the steps, the `WebRole` element in the `ServiceDefinition.csdef` file should be as follows:

```
<WebRole name="WebRole1">
  <Sites>
    <Site name="WebsiteOne" physicalDirectory="..\WebRole1">
      <Bindings>
        <Binding name="Endpoint1" endpointName="Endpoint1"
          hostHeader="www.websiteone.com"/>
      </Bindings>
    </Site>
    <Site name="WebsiteTwo" physicalDirectory="..\WebRole1">
      <Bindings>
        <Binding name="Endpoint1" endpointName="Endpoint1"
          hostHeader="www.websitetwo.com"/>
      </Bindings>
    </Site>
  </Sites>
  <Endpoints>
    <InputEndpoint name="Endpoint1"
      protocol="http" port="80" />
  </Endpoints>
  <Imports>
    <Import moduleName="Diagnostics" />
  </Imports>
</WebRole>
```

In steps 1 and 2, we create a cloud project with a web role.

In steps 3 and 4, we configure the `Site` element for the first website. In step 3 we provide a distinct name for the element and in step 4, we specify the physical directory for the website.

In step 5, we configure the `Binding` element for the `Site` by specifying the host header we use to distinguish the website.

In step 6, we create the `Site` element for the second website. In steps 7 and 8, we complete the configuration of the second website by providing a name for its configuration and specifying the host header that we use to distinguish the website. Note that in this example, we use the same physical directory for both websites.

In step 9, we modify the `hosts` file, so that we can use the configured host headers as URLs.

We build and run the hosted service in step 10. We will encounter an error in the browser, because there is no default website at 127.0.0.1:81 (or whatever port the Windows Azure Compute Emulator has assigned to the hosted service). In steps 11 and 12, we confirm this by replacing the 127.0.0.1 in the browser URL with the URLs we configured as host headers for the two websites.

Note that although we only created two websites in this example, we could have configured additional websites.

There's more...

When we use this hosted service, we must use CNAME records to map the two domains to the `ourservice.cloudapp.net` URL of our hosted service. Just as we cannot access the hosted service locally as 127.0.0.1, so we cannot access the hosted service at `ourservice.cloudapp.net`. We see how to do use CNAME to do this mapping in the *Providing a custom domain name for a hosted service* recipe in this chapter.

Providing a custom domain name for a hosted service

A hosted service can expose an input endpoint to the Internet. This endpoint has a load-balanced Virtual IP (VIP) address which remains constant as long as the hosted service exists.

Each VIP has an associated domain of the form `servicednsprefix.cloudapp.net`. The `servicednsprefix` is specified when the hosted service is created, and is not changeable following creation. A hosted service may be reached over the Internet with the following URL: `servicednsprefix.cloudapp.net`. All hosted services exist under the `cloudapp.net` domain.

The DNS system supports a CNAME record that maps one domain to another. This allows, for example, `www.servicename.com` to be mapped to `servicednsprefix.cloudapp.net`. The DNS system also supports an A record that maps a domain to a fixed IP address. Unfortunately, reliable use of an A record is not possible with a hosted service because the IP address can change if the hosted service is deleted and redeployed.

It is not possible to acquire a public key certificate for the `cloudapp.net` domain as Microsoft controls it. Consequently, a CNAME is needed to map a custom domain to a `cloudapp.net` domain when HTTPS is used. We see how to do this in the *Implementing HTTPS in a web role* recipe.

A similar issue exists when configuring hosted services to use the Windows Azure AppFabric Access Control Service (ACS). It is not possible to configure ACS to use a `cloudapp.net` domain as a callback URL. Again, a CNAME record can be used to map a custom domain to `cloudapp.net` and this custom domain can be used as a callback URL.

In this recipe, we will learn how to use CNAME to map a custom domain to a hosted service domain.

Getting ready

To use this recipe, we need to control a custom domain (for example, `customdomain.com`) and have created a hosted service (for example, `theservice.cloudapp.net`).

How to do it...

We are going to see how to use CNAME to map a custom domain to a hosted service. We do this as follows:

1. On the domain-forwarding page of your DNS provider, forward `customdomain.com` to `www.customdomain.com`.

2. On the CNAME management page of your DNS provider, add a new CNAME mapping `www.customdomain.com` to `theservice.cloudapp.net`.

How it works...

In step 1, we configure forwarding so that the root `customdomain.com` is forwarded automatically to `www.customdomain.com`.

In step 2, we implement the CNAME mapping from our custom domain to our hosted service at `ourservice.cloudapp.net`.

There's more...

CNAME records can also be used to provide custom domains for Windows Azure Storage Service and Windows Azure Content Delivery Network (CDN) endpoints. We see how to use CNAME to map a custom domain to a Storage service endpoint and a CDN endpoint in the *Using the Azure content-delivery network (CDN)* recipe.

This is particularly convenient when the Blob service is used to store images for a website. For example, a CNAME record can be used to map `images.servicename.com` to `servicename.blob.core.windows.net` while a separate CNAME record can be used to map `www.servicename.com` to `servicename.cloudapp.net`. Note that a custom domain cannot be used when accessing the Blob service using HTTPS.

Using the hosts file to map domains

The equivalent of a CNAME mapping in the development environment is a `hosts` file entry that maps `servicename.com` to 127.0.0.1. The `hosts` file is located in `%SystemRoot%\system32\drivers\etc`. Modifying the `hosts` file is helpful when integrating ACS with a hosted service, as it lets us use a real service domain in the development environment. For example, adding the following entry to the `hosts` file maps `servicename.com` to 127.0.0.1:

```
127.0.0.1  servicename.com
```

Note that we need to remember to remove this entry from the `hosts` file on the development machine after the application is deployed to the Windows Azure datacenter. Otherwise, we will not be able to access the real `servicename.com` domain from the development machine.

Implementing HTTPS in a web role

A Windows Azure web role can be configured to expose an HTTPS endpoint for a website. This requires that an X.509 public key certificate be uploaded, as a service certificate, to the hosted service and the web role configured to use it.

The following steps are used to implement HTTPS for a web role:

- Acquire a public key certificate for the custom domain of the web role.
- Upload the certificate to the hosted service.
- Add the certificate to the web role configuration.
- Configure the website endpoint to use the certificate.

The use of HTTPS requires that the website be configured to use a public key certificate. It is not possible to acquire a public key certificate for the `cloudapp.net` domain as Microsoft owns that domain. Consequently, a custom domain must be used when exposing an HTTPS endpoint. The *Providing a custom domain name for a hosted service* recipe shows how to map a custom domain to the `cloudapp.net` domain. For production use, a certification authority (CA) must issue the certificate to ensure that its root certificate is widely available. For test purposes, a self-signed certificate is sufficient.

The certificate must be uploaded to the hosted service using either the Windows Azure Portal or the Windows Azure Service Management REST API. Note that this upload is to the *Certificates* section for the hosted service and not to the *Management Certificates* section for the Windows Azure subscription. As a service certificate must contain both public and private keys, it is uploaded as a password-protected PFX file.

The configuration for the certificate is split between the service definition file, `ServiceDefinition.csdef`, and the service configuration file, `ServiceConfiguration.cscfg`. The logical definition and deployment location of the certificate is specified in the service definition file. The thumbprint of the actual certificate is specified in the service configuration file, so that the certificate can be renewed or replaced without redeploying the hosted service. In both cases, for each web role there is a hierarchy comprising a `Certificates` child to the `WebRole` element that, in turn, includes a set of one or more `Certificate` elements each referring to a specific certificate.

In this recipe, we will learn how to implement HTTPS in a web role.

How to do it...

We are going to see how to implement an HTTPS endpoint in a web role using a test (self-signed) certificate. We do this as follows:

The first stage is creating a test certificate and uploading it to the hosted service:

1. Use the **Server Certificates** section of IIS 7 to create a self-signed certificate and give it a friendly name of `Thebes` (for example).

2. Open the Microsoft Management Console by typing `mmc` in the **Run** windows of the **Start** menu, and use the **Certificate** snap-in, specifying the **Local Machine** level.

3. In the **Personal/Certificates** branch, right click on the certificate with the friendly name of `Thebes` and select **All Tasks/Export** to open the Certificate Export Wizard.

4. Complete the Wizard choosing to export the private key (and otherwise accepting default values), providing a password, and a location for the PFX file.

5. On the Windows Azure Portal, select the **Certificates** section for the hosted service and click on **Add certificate**.

6. Upload the public key certificate by providing the location for the PFX file and its password.

The next stage is configuring a hosted service to use the certificate:

7. Use Visual Studio to create an empty cloud project.

8. Add a web role to the project (accept default name of `WebRole1`).

9. Add the following as a child to the `WebRole` element in the `ServiceDefinition.csdef` file:

```
<Certificates>
  <Certificate name="Thebes"
     storeLocation="LocalMachine" storeName="My"/>
</Certificates>
```

10. Add the following as a child to the `InputEndpoints` element in the `ServiceDefinition.csdef` file:

```
<InputEndpoint name="HttpsIn"
    protocol="https" port="443" certificate="Thebes" />
```

11. Add the following as a child to the `Bindings` element in the `ServiceDefinition.csdef` file:

```
<Binding name="HttpsIn" endpointName="HttpsIn" />
```

12. Add the following as a child to the `Role` element in the `ServiceConfiguration.cscfg` file:

```
<Certificates>
   <Certificate name="Thebes"
      thumbprint="THUMBPRINT OF UPLOADED CERTIFICATE"
      thumbprintAlgorithm="sha1"/>
</Certificates>
```

13. Build the application and deploy it into the hosted service.

The final stage is verifying that we can use HTTPS:

14. Use a browser to access the web role using HTTPS.

15. Choose to ignore the certificate error, caused by our use of a test certificate, and view the certificate.

How it works...

In steps 1 through 6, we create and upload our test certificate. We need to export the certificate as a password-protected PFX file, so that it contains both the public and private keys for the certificate.

In steps 7 and 8, we create a cloud project with a web role.

In steps 9 through 11, we specify the linkage between web role bindings, endpoints, and the certificate. In step 9, we specify the certificate store on each instance into which the Azure Fabric deploys the certificate. In step 10, we declare an HTTPS endpoint, using the certificate, on port 443. In step 11, we link the web role to the endpoint.

In step 12, we configure the actual certificate uploaded as the one we use. Doing this in the `ServiceConfiguration.cscfg` file allows us to update the certificate as needed without redeploying the hosted service. Note that we need to provide the thumbprint of the certificate we use. This is conveniently available in the **Certificate** properties displayed on the Azure portal. The thumbprint is a string of the form `609EE257361E5CABC80A07B23CDAD43B29A0DE91`.

In step 13, we build the application and deploy it into the hosted service. We verify that that we can use HTTPS in steps 14 and 15. We are using a test certificate for which there is no root certificate in the browser, which consequently causes the browser to issue a warning. For demonstration purposes, we ignore the error and look at the certificate properties to confirm it to be the test certificate.

There's more...

We can use IIS to generate a **certificate signing request** (**CSR**), which we can send to a certification authority (CA). We do this by opening the **Server Certificates** section of IIS and clicking on **Create Certificate Request**. When generating the request, we specify in the **Common Name** field the fully qualified domain name for the custom domain, for example, www.ourcustomdomain.com. After the CA issues the certificate, we click on **Complete Certificate Request** in the **Server Certificates** section of IIS to import the certificate into the *My* certificate store of the *Local Machine* level.

From there, we can upload and deploy the CA-issued certificate by starting at step 2 of the recipe.

Using makecert to create a test certificate

We can invoke the makecert command from the Visual Studio command prompt, as follows, to create a test certificate and install it in the Personal (*My*) branch of the Local Machine level of the certificate store:

```
C:\Users\Administrator>makecert -r -pe -sky exchange
-a sha1 -len 2048 -sr localmachine -ss my
-n "CN=www.ourservice.com"
```

This test certificate has a subject name of www.ourservice.com.

Sharing session state with the Windows Azure AppFabric Caching Service

Windows Azure supports the elastic provision of web and application services. The number of role instances used to provide these services can be varied to match the current demand for them. Furthermore, the instances of a web role are located behind a load balancer that forwards traffic to them using a round-robin algorithm.

The load balancer does not support session stickiness, which can cause problems when session state is used on a web role. Each web page provided to the user may come from a different instance of the web role, so some means must be provided so that all the instances can access the same session state. In the context of a web role, obvious choices for the session state store are Windows Azure tables or SQL Azure. However, neither of these provide for the local caching of data.

The Windows Azure AppFabric Caching Service is a Windows Azure-hosted version of the Windows Server AppFabric Caching Service (formerly known as Velocity). The Windows Azure version provides most of the functionality of the Windows Server version, but with significantly simpler administration. The two caching services use the same API although the Windows Azure version does not implement all the functionality of the Windows Server version.

The caching service provides a central cache, identified by a service namespace, as well as a local cache that reflects its contents. The Windows Azure AppFabric Caching SDK contains a session-state provider for IIS that uses the caching service to persist session state and share it across all instances of the web role. This session state provider is integrated into a web role entirely through changes to the `web.config` file with no code changes. Note that the caching service also supports page-output caching.

In this recipe, we will learn how to share IIS session state using the caching service session-state provider.

How to do it...

The caching service session-state provider is integrated into a web role as follows:

The next stage of the recipe uses the **Service Bus, Access Control & Caching** section of the Windows Azure Portal:

1. On the **Cache** tab, create a new namespace specifying a service name and a cache size.
2. Select the namespace and click on **View Client Configuration** to view the Windows Azure AppFabric Caching configuration needed for the session-state provider.

The next stage of the recipe uses Visual Studio:

3. Use Visual Studio to create an empty cloud project.
4. Add a web role to the project (accept default name of `WebRole1`).
5. Add the Caching service assembly references to the project from the following directory:

   `%ProgramFiles%\Windows Azure AppFabric SDK\V1.0\Assemblies\ NET4.0\Cache`

   Add the following assembly references:

   - ❑ `Microsoft.ApplicationServer.Caching.Client.dll`
   - ❑ `Microsoft.ApplicationServer.Caching.Core.dll`
   - ❑ `Microsoft.Web.DistributedCache.dll`

6. Ensure that the **Copy Local** property for each of them is set to **True**.

7. Add the following within the content of `Default.aspx`:

```
<p>
   Session ID:
     <asp:Label ID="SessionId" runat="server"></asp:Label>
</p>
<p>
   Original instance:
     <asp:Label ID="OriginalInstance" runat="server"></asp:Label>
</p>
<p>
   Current instance:
     <asp:Label ID="CurrentInstance" runat="server"></asp:Label>
</p>
```

8. Add the following `using` statement to `Default.aspx.cs`:

```
using Microsoft.WindowsAzure.ServiceRuntime;
```

9. Replace the existing `Page_Load()` in `Default.aspx.cs` with the following:

```
protected void Page_Load(object sender, EventArgs e)
{
    if (Session["OriginalInstanceId"] == null)
    {
        Session["OriginalInstanceId"] =
            RoleEnvironment.CurrentRoleInstance.Id;
    }
    SessionId.Text = Session.SessionID;
    OriginalInstance.Text =
        Session["OriginalInstanceId"].ToString();
    CurrentInstance.Text =
        RoleEnvironment.CurrentRoleInstance.Id;
}
```

10. Copy the following from the Windows Azure AppFabric Caching configuration, on the Windows Azure Portal, into the `configSections` section of `web.config`:

```
<section name="dataCacheClients" type="Microsoft.
ApplicationServer.Caching.DataCacheClientsSection, Microsoft.
ApplicationServer.Caching.Core" allowLocation="true" allowDefiniti
on="Everywhere"/>
```

11. Copy the following from the Windows Azure AppFabric Caching configuration into the `configuration` section of `web.config`:

```
<dataCacheClients>
  <dataCacheClient name="default">
    <hosts>
```

```
      <host name="{SERVICE_NAMESPACE}.cache.windows.net"
         cachePort="22233" />
   </hosts>

   <securityProperties mode="Message">
      <messageSecurity
        authorizationInfo="{AUTHENTICATION_TOKEN}">
      </messageSecurity>
   </securityProperties>
  </dataCacheClient>
</dataCacheClients>
```

12. Copy the following from the Windows Azure AppFabric Caching configuration, on the Windows Azure Portal, into the `system.web` section of `web.config`:

```
<sessionState mode="Custom"
   customProvider="AppFabricCacheSessionStoreProvider">
   <providers>
      <add name="AppFabricCacheSessionStoreProvider" type="Microsoft.
Web.DistributedCache.DistributedCacheSessionStateStoreProvider,
Microsoft.Web.DistributedCache"
         cacheName="default"
         useBlobMode="true"
         dataCacheClientName="default" />
   </providers>
</sessionState>
```

13. Set the `Instances` count to `2` in `ServiceConfiguration.cscfg`.

14. Build the application and deploy it into the hosted service.

15. In the browser, refresh `Default.aspx` periodically to verify that session state is shared between the two instances.

How it works...

In steps 1 and 2, we create the cache on the Windows Azure Portal. We can perform various administration tasks there, including creating and deleting additional caches and changing the cache size.

In steps 3 and 4, we create a cloud project with a web role. In steps 5 and 6, we set up the assembly references for the project.

In steps 7 through 9, we set up the default web page, so we can verify that the caching is working as expected. In step 7, we add labels in which we will place the session ID, the instance ID of the instance on which the session was created, and the instance ID of the instance serving the current page. We add a required `using` statement in step 8. In step 9, we initialize a session value, `OriginalInstanceId`, and provide values for the labels.

In step 10, we define a custom configuration section in `web.config`. In step 11, we add the custom configuration section to `web.config`. We must replace `{SERVICE_NAMESPACE}` and `{AUTHENTICATION_TOKEN}` with the actual values of the cache service namespace and authentication token from the Windows Azure AppFabric Caching configuration, retrieved from the Windows Azure Portal. In step 12, we configure IIS to use the custom session-state provider we have just configured.

In step 13, we increase the instance count to 2, so that after we deploy the application into the hosted service, in step 14, we can verify that caching works by seeing that the session state is shared between the two instances. In step 15, we use a browser to access the default page of the hosted service. By refreshing the default web page periodically, we can see how the value of *Current instance* varies from one instance to the other while the value of *Original instance* remains the same.

There's more...

The Windows Azure AppFabric Caching API also contains a page-output cache that we implement by adding the following to the `system.web` section of the `web.config` file:

```
<caching>
  <outputCache defaultProvider="DistributedCache">
    <providers>
      <add name="DistributedCache"
        type="Microsoft.Web.DistributedCache.
        DistributedCacheOutputCacheProvider,
        Microsoft.Web.DistributedCache"
         cacheName="default"
         dataCacheClientName="default" />
    </providers>
  </outputCache>
</caching>
```

See also

 ▸ In the *Using the Windows Azure AppFabric Caching* service recipe, we see how to cache data using the caching service.

Using local storage in an instance

The Windows Azure Fabric Controller deploys an instance of a Windows Azure role onto a virtual machine (VM) as three virtual hard disks (VHD). The Guest OS image is deployed to the `D:` drive; the role image is deployed to the `E:` or `F:` drive; while the `C:` drive contains the service configuration and the local storage available to the instance. Only code running with elevated privileges can write anywhere other than local storage.

Each instance has read-write access to a reserved space on the `C:` drive. The amount of space available depends on the instance size, and ranges from 20 GB for an extra small instance to 2,040 GB for an extra large instance. This storage space is reserved by being specified in the service definition file, `ServiceDefinition.csdef`, for the service. Note that `RoleEnvironment.GetLocalResource()` should be invoked to retrieve the actual path to local storage.

The `LocalStorage` element for a role in the service definition file requires a name (`Name`) and, optionally, the size in megabytes to be reserved (`sizeInMb`), and an indication of whether the local storage should be preserved when the role is recycled (`cleanOnRoleRecycle`). This indication is only advisory, as the local storage is not copied if an instance is moved to a new VM.

Multiple local storage resources can be specified for a role as long as the total space allocated is less than the maximum amount available. This allows different storage resources to be reserved for different purposes. Storage resources are identified by name.

The `RoleEnvironment.GetLocalResource()` method can be invoked to retrieve the root path for a local resource with a specific name. The role instance can invoke arbitrary file and directory management methods under this path.

In this recipe, we will learn how to configure and use local storage in an instance.

How to do it...

We are going to access the local storage on an instance and create a file on it. We will write to the file and then read the contents of the file. We do this as follows:

1. Use Visual Studio to create an empty cloud project.

2. Add a worker role to the project (accept default name of `WorkerRole1`).

3. Add the following to the `WorkerRole` section of the `ServiceDefinition.csdef` file for the project:

   ```
   <LocalResources>
     <LocalStorage name="WorkerStorage"
         sizeInMB="10" cleanOnRoleRecycle="false" />
   </LocalResources>
   ```

4. Add a new class named `LocalStorageExample` to the project:

5. Add the following `using` statements to the top of the class file:

   ```
   using Microsoft.WindowsAzure.ServiceRuntime;
   using System.IO;
   ```

6. Add the following private members to the class:

```
static String storageName = "WorkerStorage";
String fileName;
LocalResource localResource =
   RoleEnvironment.GetLocalResource(storageName);
```

7. Add the following constructor to the class:

```
public LocalStorageExample(String fileName)
{
    this.fileName = fileName;
}
```

8. Add the following method, writing to local storage, to the class:

```
public void WriteToLocalStorage()
{
    String path = Path.Combine(
        localResource.RootPath, fileName);

    FileStream writeFileStream = File.Create(path);
    using ( StreamWriter streamWriter =
        new StreamWriter( writeFileStream))
    {
        streamWriter.Write("think but this and all is mended");
    }
}
```

9. Add the following method, reading the file, to the class:

```
public void ReadFromLocalStorage()
{
    String fileContent = string.Empty;
    String path = Path.Combine(
        localResource.RootPath, fileName);
    FileStream readFileStream = File.Open(path, FileMode.Open);
    using (StreamReader streamReader =
        new StreamReader(readFileStream))
    {
        fileContent = streamReader.ReadToEnd();
    }
}
```

10. Add the following method, using the methods added earlier, to the class:

```
public static void UseLocalStorageExample()
{
    String fileName = "WorkerRoleStorage.txt";

    LocalStorageExample example =
        new LocalStorageExample(fileName);
    example.WriteToLocalStorage();
    example.ReadFromLocalStorage();
}
```

11. Add the following at the start of the `Run()` method in `WorkerRole.cs`:

```
LocalStorageExample.UseLocalStorageExample();
```

How it works...

In steps 1 and 2, we create a cloud project with a worker role.

In step 3, we add the definition of the local storage to the service definition file for the hosted service. We provide a name by which it can be referenced and a size. We also specify that the content of local storage should be preserved through an instance recycle.

In steps 4 and 5, we set up the `LocalStorageExample` class. In step 6, we add some private members to store the filename and the local storage resource. We initialize the filename in the constructor we add in step 7.

In step 8, we add a method that creates a file and adds some text to it. In step 9, we open the file and read the text.

In step 10, we add a method that invokes the other methods in the class. In step 11, we invoke this method.

See also

▸ We use local storage in the *Using an Azure Drive in a hosted service* recipe in this chapter.

Using startup tasks in a Windows Azure Role

Windows Azure provides a locked-down environment for websites hosted in IIS (web roles) and application services (worker roles). While this hardening significantly eases administration, it also limits the ability to perform certain tasks, such as installing software or writing to the registry. Another problem is that any changes to an instance are lost whenever the instance is reimaged or moved to a different server.

The Windows Azure SDK v1.3 release provided two solutions to this problem. The simple solution allows for the creation of startup tasks, which are script files or executable programs that are invoked each time an instance is started. Startup tasks allow a temporary escape from the restrictions of the locked-down web role and worker role while retaining the benefits of these roles. The more complex solution is the creation of a new role type, VM Role, which allows an appropriately configured Guest OS image to be uploaded to a hosted service. This moves Windows Azure into IaaS territory, but in doing so significantly increases administrative responsibility. While VM Roles appear to be an attractive alternative to web and worker roles, the best practice, when faced with a need to relax the hardening of a role, is to use startup tasks in one of these roles, rather than use a VM role.

A startup task must be robust against errors because a failure could cause the instance to recycle. In particular, the effect of a startup task must be idempotent. As a startup task is invoked each time an instance starts, it must not fail when performed repeatedly. For example, when a startup task is used to install software, any subsequent attempt to reinstall the software must be handled gracefully.

Startup tasks are specified with the `Startup` element in the service definition file, `ServiceDefinition.csdef`. This is a child element of the `WebRole` or `WorkerRole` element. Note that startup tasks are not used with a VM role. The child elements in the `Startup` element comprise a sequence of one or more individual `Task` elements, each specifying a single startup task. The following example shows the definition of a single startup task and includes all the attributes for a Task:

```
<Startup>
  <Task
     commandLine="Startup.cmd"
     executionContext="elevated"
     taskType="simple" />
</Startup>
```

The `commandLine` attribute specifies a script or executable and its location relative to `%RoleRoot%\AppRoot\bin` folder for the role. The `executionContext` takes one of two values: `limited` to indicate the startup task runs with the same privileges as the role, and `elevated` to indicate the startup task runs with full administrator privileges. It is the capability that is provided by `elevated` startup tasks that gives them their power. There are three types of startup task:

1. **simple** indicates that the system cannot invoke additional startup tasks until this one completes.

2. **background** initiates the startup task in the background. This is useful in the case of a long-running task, the delay in which could cause the instance to appear unresponsive.

3. **foreground** resembles a background startup task except that the instance cannot be recycled until the startup task completes. This can cause problems if something goes wrong with the startup task.

Windows PowerShell 2 is installed on Windows Azure roles running Guest OS 2.x. This provides a powerful scripting language that is ideal for scripting startup tasks. A PowerShell script named, `StartupTask.ps1` is invoked from the startup task command file as follows:

```
C:\Users\Administrator>PowerShell -ExecutionPolicy Unrestricted .\
StartupTask.ps1
```

The `ExecutionPolicy` parameter specifies that `StartupTask.ps1` can be invoked even though it is unsigned. Note that the *RemoteAccess* pluggable module also uses a startup task with a PowerShell script and a timing conflict may arise with the `ExecutionPolicy` setting in that startup task if the module is installed and enabled.

In startup tasks, we can use `AppCmd` to manage IIS. We can also use the `WebPICmdLine` command-line tool—`WebPICmdLine.exe`—to access the functionality of the Microsoft Web Platform Installer. This allows us to install Microsoft Web Platform components, including PHP (for example).

How to do it...

We are going to use a startup task that uses `AppCmd` to modify the default idle timeout for IIS application pools. We do this as follows:

1. Use Visual Studio to create an empty cloud project.

2. Add a web role to the project (accept the default name of `WebRole1`).

3. Add a text file named `StartupTask.cmd` to the root directory of the web role project.

4. Set its **Copy To Output Directory** property to **Copy always**.

5. Insert the following text in the file:

```
%SystemRoot%\system32\inetsrv\appcmd
set config -section:applicationPools
-applicationPoolDefaults.processModel.idleTimeout:0.01:00:00
exit /b 0
```

6. Add the following, as a child of the `WebRole` element, to `ServiceDefinition.csdef`:

```
<Startup>
  <Task commandLine="StartupTask.cmd"
      executionContext="elevated" taskType="simple"/>
</Startup>
```

7. Build and deploy the application into the hosted service.

8. Open IIS Manager, select **Application Pools**, right click on any application pool, and select **Advanced Settings...**. Verify that the **Idle Timeout (minutes)** setting is 60 minutes for the application pool.

How it works...

In steps 1 and 2, we create a cloud project with a web role. In steps 3 and 4, we add the command file for the startup task to the project and ensure that the build copies the file to the appropriate location in the Windows Azure package. In step 5, we add a command to the file that sets the idle timeout to 1 hour for IIS application pools. The `exit` command ends the batch file with a return code of 0.

In step 6, we add the startup task to the service definition file. We set the execution context of the startup task to `elevated`, so that it has the privilege required to modify IIS settings.

In step 7, we build and deploy the application into a hosted service. We verify that the startup task worked in step 8.

There's more...

Note that the Windows Azure SDK v1.3 introduced a feature whereby a web or worker role can run with elevated privileges. In a web role, full IIS runs in its own process that continues to have limited privileges—only the role-entry code (in `WebRole.cs`) runs with elevated privileges. This privilege elevation is achieved by adding the following as a child element of the `WebRole` or `WorkerRole` element in the service definition file, `ServiceDefinition.csdef`:

```
<Runtime executionContext="elevated"/>
```

The default value for `executionContext` is `limited`.

Having done this, we can set the application pool idle timeout in code by invoking the following from the `OnStart()` method for the web role:

```
private void SetIdleTimeout(TimeSpan timeout)
{
    using (ServerManager serverManager = new ServerManager())
    {
        serverManager.ApplicationPoolDefaults.ProcessModel.IdleTimeout
            = timeout;
        serverManager.CommitChanges();
    }
}
```

The `ServerManager` class is in the `Microsoft.Web.Administrator` namespace contained in the following assembly:

`%SystemRoot%\System32\inetsrv\Microsoft.Web.Administration.dll`

Developing startup tasks

When developing startup tasks, it can be useful to log the output of commands to some known location for further analysis. When using the development environment, another trick is to set the startup task script to be the following:

```
start /w cmd
```

This pops up a command window in which we can invoke the desired startup command and see any errors.

Managing upgrades and changes to a hosted service

Windows Azure instances and the Guest OS they reside in have to be upgraded occasionally. The hosted service may need a new software deployment or a configuration change. The Guest OS may need a patch or an upgrade to a new version. To ensure that a hosted service can remain online 24*7, Windows Azure provides an upgrade capability that allows upgrades to be performed without stopping the hosted service completely, as long as each role in the service has two or more instances.

Windows Azure supports two types of upgrade: in-place upgrade and Virtual IP (VIP) swap. An in-place upgrade applies changes to the configuration and code of existing virtual machines (VM) hosting instances of the hosted service. A VIP swap modifies the load-balancer configuration, so that the VIP address of the production deployment is pointed at the instances currently in the staging slot and the VIP address of the staging deployment is pointed at the instances currently in the production slot. A VIP swap is never used to upgrade the Guest OS, which is always performed using an in-place upgrade.

There are two types of in-place upgrades: *configuration change* and *deployment upgrade*. A configuration change can be applied on the Windows Azure Portal by editing the existing configuration directly on the portal. A configuration change or a deployment upgrade can be performed on the Windows Azure Portal by uploading a replacement service configuration file, `ServiceConfiguration.cscfg`, or a service package respectively. They can also be performed by invoking the appropriate operations in the Windows Azure Service Management REST API. Visual Studio contains tools allowing a deployment upgrade to be initiated directly from Visual Studio. Note that it is possible to do an in-place upgrade of an individual role in an application package.

A configuration change supports only modifications to the service configuration file, including changing the Guest OS, changing the value of configuration settings such as connection strings, and changing the actual X.509 certificates used by the hosted service. Note that a configuration change cannot be used to change the names of configuration settings as they are specified in the service definition file.

A deployment upgrade supports changes to the application package, as well as all the changes allowed in a configuration change. Additionally, a deployment upgrade supports some modifications to the service definition file, `ServiceDefinition.csdef`, including:

- Changing the role type
- Changing the local resource definitions
- Changing the available configuration settings
- Changing the certificates defined for the hosted service

A hosted service has an associated set of upgrade domains that control the phasing of upgrades during an in-place upgrade. The instances of a role are distributed evenly among upgrade domains. During an in-place upgrade, all the instances in a single upgrade domain are stopped, reconfigured, and then restarted. This process continues one upgrade domain at a time until all the upgrade domains have been upgraded. This phasing ensures that the hosted service remains available during an in-place upgrade, albeit with roles being served by fewer instances than usual. By default, there are five upgrade domains for a hosted service although this number can be reduced in the service definition file.

The only distinction between the production and staging slots of a hosted service is that the load balancer forwards to the production slot any network traffic arriving at the service VIP address and forwards to the staging slot any network traffic arriving at the staging VIP address. In a VIP swap, the production and staging slots to which the load balancer forwards the network traffic are swapped. This has no effect on the actual VMs running the service—it is entirely a matter of where inbound network traffic is forwarded to. A VIP swap affects the entire service simultaneously and does not use upgrade domains. Nevertheless, since a hosted service is a distributed system, there may be a small overlap during a VIP swap where the inbound traffic is forwarded to some instances running the old version of the service and some instances running the new version. The only way to guarantee that old and new versions are never simultaneously in production is to stop the hosted service while performing the upgrade.

Windows Azure currently has two families of Guest OS, v1.x and v2.x. These correspond substantially to Windows Server 2008 SP2 and Windows Server 2008 R2 respectively. Microsoft releases upgraded versions of these each Guest OS family on a monthly cadence mirroring, so-called **patch Tuesday**. A hosted service can be configured for automatic upgrade to the latest version of the currently installed Guest OS. Alternatively, if more control is required, the Guest OS upgrade can be performed manually using either the Windows Azure Portal or the Windows Azure Service Management REST API. The Windows Azure Portal has a button allowing easy access to the upgrade Guest OS functionality. A manual upgrade can cross from one Guest OS family to another. As the Guest OS family is specified in the service configuration file, a Guest OS upgrade is similar to an in-place upgrade.

Note that Microsoft occasionally has to upgrade the root OS of a server hosting an instance. This type of upgrade is always automatic and Microsoft provides no ability for it to be performed manually.

In this recipe, we will learn how to upgrade a deployment to a hosted service.

Getting ready

We need to deploy an application to the production and staging slots of a hosted service. We could use, for example, the hosted service we created in the *Using startup tasks in a Windows Azure Role* recipe in this chapter.

How to do it...

We are going to use the Windows Azure Portal to perform an in-place upgrade, a VIP swap, and a manual Guest OS upgrade. We do this as follows:

In this stage, we perform an in-place upgrade of the production deployment.

1. On the Windows Azure Portal, select the production slot of the hosted service and click on the **Upgrade** button.

2. Select **Automatic**, and provide the `package location` and `configuration file location` either on the local machine or in Windows Azure blob storage. Then, click on **OK**.

In this stage, we perform a VIP swap.

3. Deploy the upgraded application to the staging slot of the hosted service.

4. On the Windows Azure Portal, select the hosted service and click on the **Swap VIP** button.

In this stage, we perform a manual Guest OS upgrade of the production deployment.

5. On the Windows Azure Portal, select the production slot of the hosted service and click on the **Configure OS** button.

6. Select the desired **OS Family** and **OS Version**, and click on **OK**.

How it works...

We can perform in-place upgrades of the production and staging slots independently of each other. In step 1, we indicate that we want to perform an in-place upgrade of the production slot (or *environment* as the Windows Azure Portal refers to it). In step 2, we specify a location for the upgraded application package and service configuration file and indicate that we want the Windows Azure Portal to manage the in-place upgrade for us. We could have chosen a manual in-place upgrade in which case, we would have had to step manually through the upgrade of each upgrade domain until the in-place upgrade completes. This can be useful if we want to verify the in-place upgrade has worked in each upgrade domain prior to moving onto the next one.

We can perform a VIP swap only if there is a hosted service deployed to the staging slot, and we ensure this in step 3. We initiate the VIP swap in step 4.

We can perform Guest OS upgrades of the production and staging slots independently of each other. In step 5, we indicate that we want to upgrade the Guest OS of the production slot. We initiate the Guest OS upgrade in step 6.

There's more...

In *Chapter 7*, we will see how to use the Windows Azure Service Management REST API to manage deployments including performing upgrades.

Using PowerShell cmdlets to upgrade a hosted service

Both Microsoft and Cerebrata provide PowerShell **cmdlets** that can be used to manage a hosted service, including performing the various upgrades.

Changing the number of endpoints in a hosted service

Neither an in-place upgrade nor a VIP swap can modify the number and nature of role endpoints, including adding an HTTPS endpoint not already present. This can be achieved only by deleting the existing deployment and uploading a new deployment package.

Version issue when performing in-place upgrades

One consequence of using upgrade domains to control the phasing of in-place upgrades is that during the upgrade, some instances will be running the old version of the service and some will be running the new version. Consequently, care must be taken that the hosted service runs successfully in this mixed condition of old and new versions.

Limitations on in-place upgrades

Microsoft has announced that it will remove many of the restrictions on in-place upgrades. As of this writing, these changes have not yet been implemented.

Handling changes to the configuration and topology of a hosted service

A Windows Azure hosted service has to detect and respond to changes to its service configuration. Two types of changes are exposed to the service: changes to the `ConfigurationSettings` element of the service configuration file, `ServiceConfiguration.cscfg`, and changes to service topology. The latter refers to changes in the number of instances of the various roles that comprise the service.

The `RoleEnvironment` class exposes four events to which a role can register a callback method to be notified about these changes:

- ▶ Changing
- ▶ Changed
- ▶ Stopping
- ▶ StatusCheck

The `Changing` event is raised before the change is applied to the role. For configuration setting changes, the `RoleEnvironmentChangingEventArgs` parameter to the callback method identifies the existing value of any configuration setting being changed. For a service topology change, the argument specifies the names of any roles whose instance count is changing. The `RoleEnvironmentChangingEventArgs` parameter has a `Cancel` property that can be set to true to recycle an instance in response to specific configuration setting or topology changes.

The `Changed` event is raised after the change is applied to the role. For configuration setting changes, the `RoleEnvironmentChangedEventArgs` parameter to the callback method identifies the new value of any changed configuration setting. For a service topology change, the argument specifies the names of any roles whose instance count has changed. Note that the `Changed` event is not raised on any instance recycled in the `Changing` event.

The `Stopping` event is raised on an instance being stopped. The `OnStop()` method is also invoked. Either of them can be used to implement an orderly shutdown of the instance. However, this must complete within 30 seconds. In a web role, the `Application_End()` method is invoked before the `Stopping` event is raised and `OnStop()` method invoked. It can also be used for shutdown code.

The `StatusCheck` event is raised every 15 seconds. The `RoleInstanceStatusCheckEventArgs` parameter to the callback method for this event specifies the status of the instance as either `Ready` or `Busy`. The callback method can respond to the `StatusCheck` event by invoking the `SetBusy()` method on the parameter to indicate that the instance should be taken out of the load-balancer rotation temporarily. This is useful if the instance is sufficiently busy that it is unable to process additional inbound requests.

The `csrun` command in the Windows Azure SDK can be used to test configuration changes in the development fabric. The service configuration file can be modified and `csrun` invoked to apply the change. Note that it is not possible to test topology changes that reduce the number of instances. However, when the hosted service is started without debugging it is possible to increase the number of instances by modifying the service configuration file and using `csrun`.

In this recipe, we will learn how to manage service configuration and topology changes to a hosted service.

How to do it...

We are going to configure callback methods for the four `RoleEnvironment` events. We do this as follows:

1. Use Visual Studio to create an empty cloud project.

2. Add a worker role to the project (accept default name of `WorkerRole1`).

3. Add the following to the `ConfigurationSettings` element of `ServiceDefinition.csdef`:

   ```
   <Setting name="EnvironmentChangeString"/>
   <Setting name="SettingRequiringRecycle"/>
   ```

4. Add the following to the `ConfigurationSettings` element of `ServiceConfiguration.cscfg`:

   ```
   <Setting name="EnvironmentChangeString"
       value="OriginalValue"/>
   <Setting name="SettingRequiringRecycle"
       value="OriginalValue"/>
   ```

5. Add a new class named `EnvironmentChangeExample` to the project.

6. Add the following `using` statements to the top of the class file:

```
using Microsoft.WindowsAzure.ServiceRuntime;
using System.Collections.ObjectModel;
using System.Diagnostics;
```

7. Add the following callback method to the class:

```
private static void RoleEnvironmentChanging(object sender,
RoleEnvironmentChangingEventArgs e)
{
   Boolean recycle = false;
   foreach (RoleEnvironmentChange change in e.Changes)
   {
      RoleEnvironmentTopologyChange topologyChange =
         change as RoleEnvironmentTopologyChange;
      if (topologyChange != null)
      {
         String roleName = topologyChange.RoleName;
         ReadOnlyCollection<RoleInstance> oldInstances =
            RoleEnvironment.Roles[roleName].Instances;
      }
      RoleEnvironmentConfigurationSettingChange settingChange
        = change as RoleEnvironmentConfigurationSettingChange;
      if (settingChange != null)
      {
         String settingName =
            settingChange.ConfigurationSettingName;
         String oldValue =
            RoleEnvironment.GetConfigurationSettingValue(
               settingName);
         recycle |= settingName == "SettingRequiringRecycle";
      }
   }

   // Recycle when e.Cancel = true;
   e.Cancel = recycle;
}
```

8. Add the following callback method to the class:

```
private static void RoleEnvironmentChanged(object sender,
   RoleEnvironmentChangedEventArgs e)
{
   foreach (RoleEnvironmentChange change in e.Changes)
   {
      RoleEnvironmentTopologyChange topologyChange =
         change as RoleEnvironmentTopologyChange;
```

```
        if (topologyChange != null)
        {
            String roleName = topologyChange.RoleName;
            ReadOnlyCollection<RoleInstance> newInstances =
                RoleEnvironment.Roles[roleName].Instances;
        }
        RoleEnvironmentConfigurationSettingChange settingChange
            = change as RoleEnvironmentConfigurationSettingChange;
        if (settingChange != null)
        {
            String settingName =
                settingChange.ConfigurationSettingName;
            String newValue =
                RoleEnvironment.GetConfigurationSettingValue(
                    settingName);
        }
    }
}
```

9. Add the following callback method to the class:

```
private static void RoleEnvironmentStatusCheck(object sender,
    RoleInstanceStatusCheckEventArgs e)
{
    RoleInstanceStatus status = e.Status;
    // Uncomment next line to take instance out of the
    // load balancer rotation.
    //e.SetBusy();
}
```

10. Add the following callback method to the class:

```
private static void RoleEnvironmentStopping(object sender,
    RoleEnvironmentStoppingEventArgs e)
{
    Trace.TraceInformation("In RoleEnvironmentStopping");
}
```

11. Add the following method, associating the callback methods with the
    RoleEnvironment events, to the class:

```
public static void UseEnvironmentChangeExample()
{
    RoleEnvironment.Changing += RoleEnvironmentChanging;
    RoleEnvironment.Changed += RoleEnvironmentChanged;
    RoleEnvironment.StatusCheck += RoleEnvironmentStatusCheck;
    RoleEnvironment.Stopping += RoleEnvironmentStopping;
}
```

12. If the application is deployed to the local Compute Emulator, then the `ServiceConfiguration.cscfg` file can be modified. It can then be applied to the running service using the following command in a Windows Azure SDK Command prompt:

```
csrun /update:{DEPLOYMENT_ID};ServiceConfiguration.cscfg
```

13. If the application is deployed to the cloud, the service configuration can be modified directly on the Windows Azure Portal.

How it works...

In steps 1 and 2, we create a cloud project with a worker role. In steps 3 and 4, we add two configuration settings to the service definition file and provide initial values for them in the service configuration file.

In steps 5 and 6, we create a class to house our callback methods.

In step 7, we add a callback method for the `RoleEnvironment.Changing` event. This method iterates over the list of changes looking for any topology or configuration settings changes. In the latter case, we specifically look for changes to the `SettingRequiringRecycle` setting, and on detecting one initiate a recycle of the instance.

In step 8, we add a callback method for the `RoleEnvironment.Changed` event. We iterate over the list of changes and look at any topology changes and configuration settings changes.

In step 9, we add a callback method for the `RoleEnvironment.StatusCheck` event. We look at the current status of the instance and leave commented out the `SetBusy()` call that would take the instance out of the load balancer rotation.

In step 10, we add a callback method for the `RoleEnvironment.Stopping` event. In this callback, we use `Trace.TraceInformation()` to log invocation of the method.

In step 11, we add a method that associates the callback methods with the appropriate event.

In step 12, we see how to modify the service configuration in the development environment. We must replace `{DEPLOYMENT_ID}` with the deployment ID of the current deployment. The deployment ID in the Computer Emulator is a number incremented with each deployment. It is displayed on the Compute Emulator UI. In step 13, we see how to modify the service configuration in a cloud deployment.

There's more...

The `RoleEntryPoint` class also exposes the following virtual methods that allow various changes to be handled:

- ▸ `RoleEntryPoint.OnStart()`
- ▸ `RoleEntryPoint.OnStop()`
- ▸ `RoleEntryPoint.Run()`

These virtual methods are invoked when an instance is started, stopped, or reaches a *Ready* state. An instance of a worker role is recycled whenever the `Run()` method exits.

Using an Azure Drive in a hosted service

The Windows Azure Blob Service supports page blobs providing random read-write access to individual pages. The primary use case for a page blob is to store an NTFS-formatted virtual hard disk (VHD) that can be mounted in an instance of a Windows Azure role. The mounted NTFS drive is referred to as an Azure Drive.

An important limitation of an Azure Drive is that only one instance at a time can mount a VHD page blob as a writable Azure Drive. This means that two instances cannot write simultaneously to the same mounted Azure Drive, so it cannot be used to share real-time data between the two instances. The blob-leasing capability is used to ensure that the Azure Drive has exclusive write access to its backing VHD page blob until the Azure Drive is un-mounted.

The Blob Service supports read-only snapshots of blobs. Multiple instances can mount the same VHD snapshot simultaneously as a read-only Azure Drive. However, as a page blob snapshot backs the Azure Drive, none of the instances can write to it.

Before an instance can mount an Azure Drive, it must initialize a local cache on the local storage of the instance, even if this cache will not be used. This is a read cache, to which pages are added when they are retrieved from the page blob backing the Azure Drive. An un-buffered, flushed NTFS write to an Azure Drive is saved immediately to the VHD page blob backing the Azure Drive. The read cache is located in the local storage of the instance. It is preserved during a role recycle if the local storage containing it is configured with `cleanOnRoleRecycle` set to `false`. Note that the read cache survives through a role upgrade, but is swapped out with its instance during a VIP swap.

The `CloudDrive.Create()` method creates and formats a VHD page blob with a minimum size of 16 MB and a maximum size of 1 TB. Alternatively, a VHD can be uploaded to a page blob. As with other page blobs, only the pages actually used by the page blob are billed. Consequently, when a VHD is uploaded, it is not necessary to upload empty pages.

Note that a VHD page blob stored in the cloud cannot be mounted as an Azure Drive from the development fabric, and vice versa.

In this recipe, we will learn how to use an Azure Drive.

How to do it...

We are going to attach a VHD page blob and mount it as an Azure Drive. We will create and use a file on the drive. Finally, we will disconnect the Azure Drive volume. We do this as follows:

1. Use Visual Studio to create an empty Cloud project.

2. Add a worker role to the project (accept default name of `WorkerRole1`).

3. Add the following assembly reference to the `WorkerRole1` project:

   `Microsoft.WindowsAzure.CloudDrive`

4. Add the following local resource declaration to the `WorkerRole` element of `ServiceDefinition.csdef`:

   ```
   <LocalResources>
      <LocalStorage name="AzureDriveCache"
         sizeInMB="50" cleanOnRoleRecycle="false" />
   </LocalResources>
   ```

5. Add the following to the `ConfigurationSettings` element of `ServiceDefinition.csdef`:

   ```
   <Setting name="DataConnectionString"/>
   ```

6. Add the following to the `ConfigurationSettings` element of `ServiceConfiguration.cscfg` file for the service:

   ```
   <Setting name="DataConnectionString"
        value="{DATA_CONNECTION_STRING}"/>
   <Setting name="Microsoft.WindowsAzure.Plugins.Diagnostics.
   ConnectionString" value="="{DIAGNOSTICS_CONNECTION_STRING}" />
   ```

7. Add a new class named `AzureDriveExample` to the project.

8. Add the following `using` statements to the top of the class:

   ```
   using Microsoft.WindowsAzure;
   using Microsoft.WindowsAzure.StorageClient;
   using Microsoft.WindowsAzure.ServiceRuntime;
   using System.IO;
   using System.Diagnostics;
   ```

9. Add the following private members to the class:

   ```
   private CloudDrive cloudDrive;
   private Int32 cacheSizeInMegabytes;
   ```

10. Add the following constructor to the class:

```
public AzureDriveExample(
  String containerName, String pageBlobName)
{
   CloudStorageAccount cloudStorageAccount =
     CloudStorageAccount.Parse(
     RoleEnvironment.GetConfigurationSettingValue(
     "DataConnectionString"));
   CloudBlobClient cloudBlobClient =
     cloudStorageAccount.CreateCloudBlobClient();
   CloudBlobContainer cloudBlobContainer =
     cloudBlobClient.GetContainerReference(containerName);
   cloudBlobContainer.CreateIfNotExist();

   Char[] forwardSlash = { '/' };
   String trimmedUri =
     cloudStorageAccount.BlobEndpoint.ToString().TrimEnd(
       forwardSlash);
   String pageBlobUri = String.Format("{0}/{1}/{2}",
     trimmedUri, containerName, pageBlobName);
   cloudDrive = cloudStorageAccount.CreateCloudDrive(
     pageBlobUri);
}
```

11. Add the following method, creating a 16 MB VHD page blob, to the class:

```
public void CreateDrive()
{
   Int32 driveSize = 16; //MB
   try
   {
      cloudDrive.Create(driveSize);
   }
   catch (CloudDriveException e)
   {
      Trace.TraceError("CreateDrive error: " + e.Message);
   }
}
```

12. Add the following method, initializing the local cache, to the class:

```
public void InitializeCache()
{
   LocalResource localCache =
     RoleEnvironment.GetLocalResource("AzureDriveCache");
   String localCachePath = localCache.RootPath;
   cacheSizeInMegabytes = localCache.MaximumSizeInMegabytes;
```

```
CloudDrive.InitializeCache(
    localCachePath, cacheSizeInMegabytes);
}
```

13. Add the following method, mounting the drive, to the class:

```
public void MountDrive()
{
    String driveLetter =
        cloudDrive.Mount(cacheSizeInMegabytes,
        DriveMountOptions.None);
}
```

14. Add the following method, writing to a file on the drive, to the class:

```
public void WriteToDrive(String fileName)
{
    String path = Path.Combine(cloudDrive.LocalPath, fileName);
    FileStream fileStream = new FileStream(
        path, FileMode.OpenOrCreate);
    using (StreamWriter streamWriter =
        new StreamWriter(fileStream))
    {
        streamWriter.Write("has been changed glorious summer");
    }
}
```

15. Add the following method, reading from the file, to the class:

```
public void ReadFromDrive(String fileName)
{
    String path = Path.Combine(cloudDrive.LocalPath, fileName);
    FileStream fileStream = new FileStream(
        path, FileMode.Open);
    using (StreamReader streamReader =
        new StreamReader(fileStream))
    {
        String text = streamReader.ReadToEnd();
    }
}
```

16. Add the following method, disconnecting the drive, to the class:

```
public void UnmountDrive()
{
    cloudDrive.Unmount();
}
```

17. Add the following method, using the methods added earlier, to the class:

```
public static void UseAzureDriveExample()
{
    String containerName = "chapter5";
    String pageBlobName = "Chapter5Vhd";
    String fileName = "File.txt";

    AzureDriveExample example =
        new AzureDriveExample(containerName, pageBlobName);
    example.CreateDrive();
    example.InitializeCache();
    example.MountDrive();
    example.WriteToDrive(fileName);
    example.ReadFromDrive(fileName);
    example.UnmountDrive();
}
```

18. Add the following at the start of the `Run()` method in `WorkerRole.cs`:

```
AzureDriveExample.UseAzureDriveExample();
```

19. Replace the `OnStart()` method with the following in `WorkerRole.cs`:

```
public override bool OnStart()
{
    ServicePointManager.DefaultConnectionLimit = 12;

    String connectionString = "Microsoft.WindowsAzure.Plugins.
Diagnostics.ConnectionString";
    DiagnosticMonitorConfiguration configuration =
        DiagnosticMonitor.GetDefaultInitialConfiguration();
    configuration.Logs.ScheduledTransferPeriod =
        TimeSpan.FromMinutes(1.0);
    configuration.Logs.ScheduledTransferLogLevelFilter =
        LogLevel.Verbose;
    DiagnosticMonitor.Start(connectionString, configuration);

    return base.OnStart();
}
```

How it works...

In steps 1 and 2, we create a cloud project with a web role. In step 3, we add the assembly reference required for using an Azure Drive.

In step 4, we define the local resource used for the Azure Drive cache. In steps 5 and 6, we configure the connection string used to access the VHD page blob backing the Azure Drive and the connection string used by Windows Azure diagnostics. We must replace `{DATA_CONNECTION_STRING}` and `{DIAGNOSTICS_CONNECTION_STRING}` with valid connection strings. Note that the Azure Drive connection string **must** use HTTP while the Windows Azure diagnostics connection string **must** use HTTPS. Furthermore, the Azure Drive connection string must be to the same location as the hosted service, that is, compute emulator / storage emulator or cloud / cloud.

In steps 7 and 8, we set up the class. In step 9, we add a private member to store the `CloudDrive` instance, which we initialize in the constructor we add in step 10, and a private member to store the size of the local cache. We also use the constructor to create the container for the VHD page blob. Note that we trim the endpoint to take account of a difference in the way the Windows Azure Storage Client Library handles local and cloud endpoints.

In step 11, we create a 16 MB VHD page blob in a container named *chapter5*. Typically, this blob would be either created out-of-band or uploaded.

In step 12, we initialize the local cache to the maximum size of the local resource named `AzureDriveCache`. Note that not invoking `InitializeCache()` before using the `CloudDrive` instance causes an error.

In step 13, we mount the Azure Drive. We create a file on the Azure Drive and write some text to it in step 14. We read the file in step 15 before disconnecting the Azure Drive in step 16. Note that this leaves the VHD page blob in Windows Azure Blob Storage.

In step 17, we add a method that invokes the other methods in the class. In step 18, we invoke this method. We configure Windows Azure diagnostics in step 19.

See also

> ▸ The code used in this recipe works as is in the development fabric. However, the Azure Drive simulation in the development fabric uses `subst` on a directory to back an Azure Drive, instead of the VHD page blob used in the cloud. We describe this in the *Using an Azure Drive simulation in the development environment* recipe in this chapter.

Using the Azure Drive simulation in the development environment

The virtual hard disk (VHD) used with Azure Drive is a fixed hard disk image formatted as a single NTFS volume. A VHD has a data portion followed by a 512-byte footer. The minimum size for the data portion of the VHD is 16 MB. The maximum size for the entire VHD is 1 TB.

A VHD used as the backing page blob for an Azure Drive can be created on a local system, filled with data, and then uploaded as a page blob to the Windows Azure Blob Service. The Windows Azure development fabric provides an Azure Drive simulation, so that Windows Azure roles using an Azure Drive can be developed and tested. The Azure Drive simulation is implemented independently of the Storage Emulator and consequently does not use VHD page blobs as the backing store for an Azure Drive. Instead, an Azure Drive is backed by an empty directory into which the VHD is mounted, and the `subst` command is used to associate a drive letter with the directory.

The Disk Management snap-in can be used to manage VHDs on the local system. Specifically, it can be used to create and format a VHD and then attach the VHD to an empty directory in the local data area (`%LOCALAPPDATA%\`) on a disk.

In this recipe, we will learn how to use an Azure Drive in the development environment.

Getting ready

We need to create a directory hierarchy `chapter5/chapter5Vhd` to mimic the *container/page blob* structure. This hierarchy is located in the local storage area for the Windows Azure development storage account (`devstoreaccount1`). Specifically, it is directly under:

```
%LOCALAPPDATA%\dftmp\wadd\devstoreaccount1\
```

For the Administrator, this path expands to the following:

```
c:\Users\Administrator\AppData\Local\dftmp\wadd\devstoreaccount1\
chapter5\Chapter5Vhd
```

How to do it...

We use the Disk Management snap-in to create and attach a VHD on the local system. There is more documentation on the Disk Management snap-in at the following URL:

```
http://technet.microsoft.com/en-us/library/dd979539(WS.10).aspx.
```

We launch Disk Management by clicking on **Start**, typing `diskmgmt.msc` in the **Run** box, and then pressing *Enter*. The **Create VHD** and **Attach VHD** operations are on the **Actions** menu. The Disk Management snap-in is displayed in the following screenshot:

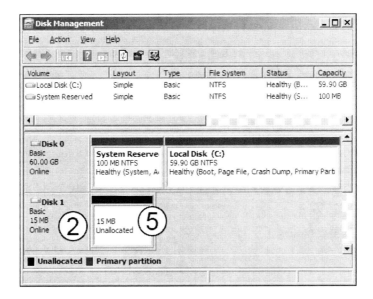

We use the Disk Management snap-in to create (and attach) a VHD as follows:

1. On the **Action** menu, select **Create VHD**:
    - ❑ Browse to the location for the VHD
    - ❑ Specify the size of the VHD
    - ❑ Select **Fixed Size**
    - ❑ Click on **OK**

2. On the disk area, right click on the name of the newly created disk (number 2 in the preceding screenshot):
    - ❑ Select **Initialize Disk**
    - ❑ On the **Initialize Disk** popup, select **MBR** and click on **OK**

3. On the disk area, right click on the uninitialized volume window for the newly created disk:
    - ❑ Select **New Simple Volume** to start the wizard

    In the Wizard:

    - ❑ Specify the desired **Volume size**, select **Do not assign a drive letter or drive path**

> ❑ Under the **Format Partition** pane, use the default selections: that is, use **NTFS,** with the default **Allocation unit size** and **Perform a quick format**
>
> ❑ Click on **Finish**

The Disk Management snap-in is used to attach an existing VHD as follows:

4. On the **Action** menu, select **Attach VHD***:*

> ❑ Browse to the location of the VHD
>
> ❑ Click on **OK**

The Disk Management snap-in is used to mount an attached VHD as follows:

5. On the disk area, right click on the volume window for the attached VHD (number 5 in the preceding screenshot):

> ❑ Right click on volume and select **Change Drive Letter and Paths....**
>
> ❑ Click on **Add.**
>
> ❑ Select **Mount** in the following empty NTFS folder.
>
> ❑ Specify the path we created in the *Getting Ready* section. This resembles:
>
> ```
> c:\Users\Administrator\AppData\Local\dftmp\wadd\
> devstoreaccount1\chapter5\Chapter5Vhd
> ```

6. Click on **OK** twice to mount the VHD in the desired path.

How it works...

In steps 1 through 3, we create a VHD with the required characteristics: fixed size, master boot record, NTFS formatted. In step 4, we attach the VHD. In step 5, we mount the drive in the appropriate directory, so that the Azure Drive simulation can use it as if it were a VHD page blob.

In a Windows Azure hosted service running in the compute emulator, we would use the Azure Drive simulation by invoking `CloudDrive.Mount()` on this "VHD page blob" using a container name of `chapter5` and a page blob name of `chapter5vhd`.

Using a VM Role

Windows Azure is the paradigm for the platform-as-a-Service (PaaS) model for cloud services. It provides a high-level, service-hosting environment into which services can be inserted. The hosting environment is modeled on services, roles, and instances.

Only two role types are available prior to Windows Azure SDK v1.3: web roles and worker roles. The primary difference between them is that web roles are designed to host web applications in IIS whereas worker roles are for other types of applications. However, both roles share the same restrictions on the software that can be installed on them.

The Windows Azure SDK v1.3 release added support for a new role type, VM role. This role allows a Guest OS image to be uploaded into a hosted service. The image can have any desired software installed on it prior to upload. However, it is important to remember that VM roles are still stateless and any changes made to instances after they are deployed will not survive an instance failure. Even with this limitation, the addition of VM roles significantly enhances the flexibility of the Windows Azure service model.

VM roles are intended to provide an interim step in the migration of an application into Windows Azure when the environment is too complex to use a web or worker role. The best practice is to use a web or worker role with, if necessary, startup tasks to configure the environment.

There are two steps involved in the use of a VM role: the production of the Guest OS image, and the addition of the VM role to the service model of the hosted service. The former is essentially an IT task while the latter is a development task.

The Guest OS image is created locally as a Windows Server 2008 R2 (Enterprise or Standard) image to which is added some Windows Azure integration software. Then any other software installation and configuration is performed before the image is sys-prepped to generalize the image. Finally, the image is uploaded to the Windows Azure image repository for the Windows Azure subscription. This Guest OS image is the *base image* for the VM role.

The VM role is added to the service model of a hosted service by adding a `VirtualMachineRole` element to the service definition file, `ServiceDefinition.csdef`. As with `WorkerRole` and `WebRole` elements, the `VirtualMachineRole` element specifies input and internal endpoints; configuration settings; public key certificates; pluggable modules (diagnostics, remote access, and so on); and local storage. The name of the base image uploaded to the Windows Azure image repository is specified in the service configuration file, `ServiceConfiguration.cscfg`.

The base image deployed to a VM role is updated using a differencing disk. This is a specially created virtual hard disk (VHD) derived from the base image and which contains any updates to it. A differencing disk is uploaded to the Windows Azure image repository and associated with the base image. The base image for the VM role is then updated by specifying the differencing disk in the service configuration file.

The differencing disk should be kept as small as possible. If the differencing disk has grown to a size close to that of the base image, then a new base image should be created and configured for the hosted service. When multiple VM roles are needed, a useful technique is to create a single base image with distinct differencing disks for each VM Role. These differencing disks can then be updated independently of each other.

In this recipe, we will learn how to use a VM Role.

How to do it...

Most of the work required to deploy a VM Role is in the IT task of creating and uploading the base image and subsequent differencing disks. The service model for a VM Role is essentially the same as for web roles and worker roles.

The outline of the task of using a VM Role is as follows:

1. Use Hyper-V Manager to create a base Windows Server 2008 R2 Guest OS image.

2. Install the Windows Azure Integration Components on the image. The location of these is described in `http://msdn.microsoft.com/en-us/library/gg465409.aspx`.

3. Install and configure any software required on the image.

4. Use `Sysprep` to generalize the image for deployment.

5. Use the `csupload` utility to upload the base image to the Windows Azure image repository.

6. Use Visual Studio to create an empty Cloud project.

7. In the Visual Studio Solution Explorer, right click on **Roles** and select **Add**, then **New Virtual Machine Role**.

8. Add and configure the `VirtualMachineRole` element in the `ServiceDefinition.csdef`.

9. Add and configure the `VirtualMachineRole` element in `ServiceConfiguration.cscfg`.

How it works...

In step 1, Hyper-V Manager is used to create the Guest OS image just as it would be for any other image. There is nothing specific to Windows Azure.

In step 2, we install the Windows Azure integration components, such as the Windows Azure agent software that interacts with the Windows Azure Fabric Controller.

In step 3, we install and configure the software that requires us to use a VM Role. If necessary, we must configure the firewall. We can also install a VM Role Adapter service if we need to perform any configuration when an instance starts up, such as assigning the correct endpoint ports. The development of a VM Role Adapter service is described at the following URL:

`http://technet.microsoft.com/en-us/library/gg466226.aspx`.

In step 4, we use `Sysprep` to generalize the image by stripping out things such as the computer name. The Windows Azure Fabric Controller will specialize the image during initial deployment to each instance of the role.

In step 5, we use the `csupload` utility from the `bin` directory of the Windows Azure SDK.

In steps 6 and 7, we create a Windows Azure project and add a VM Role to it.

In steps 8 and 9, we perform the traditional service model configuration just as we do for a web or worker role.

Differencing disks

We follow more or less the same steps in creating a differencing disk. In step 1, we use Hyper-V Manager to create a differencing disk from the Guest OS image. We skip step 2 and complete steps 3 through 5, as before. After we upload the differencing disk, we use `csupload` again to associate the differencing disk with the existing base image. We skip steps 6 thorough 8. In step 9, we modify the service configuration file to specify the new differencing disk image rather than the original base image.

See also

▸   Complete instructions for creating an image for a VM Role can be found on the MSDN website at the following URL:

   http://msdn.microsoft.com/en-us/library/gg671907.aspx.

Using Windows Azure Connect

Windows Azure Connect provides a way to create a secure, IPSEC protected virtual network that connects computers inside an organization with role instances in a Windows Azure hosted service. An obvious use for Windows Azure Connect is to allow a hosted service to access a Microsoft SQL Server database resident behind a corporate firewall. This allows a service to benefit from the elasticity of a hosted service for the frontend while keeping data tightly controlled in a corporate datacenter.

Windows Azure Connect is a pluggable module that, like Windows Azure diagnostics, must be imported into a role by adding an `Import` element as a child to the `Imports` element of the service definition file, `ServiceDefinition.csdef`. For example:

```
<Imports>
   <Import moduleName="Diagnostics" />
   <Import moduleName="Connect" />
</Imports>
```

There are a number of Windows Azure Connect configuration settings in the service configuration file, `ServiceConfiguration.cscfg`. Almost all of these settings are related to adding the role instances to an Active Directory domain inside the corporate network. These settings need to be in the service configuration file with a value of an empty string even if the instances are not being added to a domain. The only configuration setting for which a value must be provided is `ActivationToken` which provides an authentication token for Windows Azure Connect. This is specified as follows:

```
<Setting
 name="Microsoft.WindowsAzure.Plugins.Connect.ActivationToken"
 value="9C0af1ee-a758-4237-8edf-f524a30De153" />
```

Note that the entire namespace must be provided for the setting name. The `ActivationToken` itself is provided in the Windows Azure Connect section of the Windows Azure Portal.

The Windows Azure Connect Endpoint software is a Windows service that must be installed on each local machine, server, or PC that is going to access a Windows Azure Connect virtual network. This service is specific to the Windows Azure subscription as it contains the activation token specified in the service configuration file. It can be installed directly from the Windows Azure Portal onto the local machine.

The **Virtual Network** section of the Windows Azure Portal is used to configure the network topology of the Windows Azure Connect virtual network. The configuration is at the subscription level, so it is shared by all hosted services associated with that subscription. The **Virtual Network** section has two pages: **Activated Endpoints**, and **Groups and Roles**.

The **Activated Endpoints** page lists the activated endpoints—the instances of Windows Azure roles configured for Windows Azure Connect. The page provides the names and IPv6 addresses of the instances and local endpoints configured to use Windows Azure Connect. Note that a local endpoint has an IPv6 address only when it is assigned to a group since otherwise it is not associated with a virtual network and has nothing to connect to.

The **Groups and Roles** page defines the virtual network topology by associating local endpoints and roles into groups. A local endpoint can only be in one group but a role can be in multiple groups. A group can be added to another group.

For example, a Windows Azure role could be added to an `Admin` group containing local endpoints on PCs used for administration and added to a `SqlServer` group containing local endpoints on servers running Microsoft SQL Server. The PCs in the `Admin` group would then be in a virtual network with the role instances, but not the `SqlServer` machines. Similarly, the `SqlServer` endpoints would be in a virtual network with the role instances, but not the `Admin` PCs. This distribution of local endpoints among different groups supports a separation of responsibility.

While a group can be configured to allow connections between local endpoints in the group, it does not provide connections between role instances but this can be achieved using internal endpoints. Windows Azure Connect cannot be used to connect role instances from multiple services or across multiple Windows Azure data centers.

In this recipe, we will learn how to use Windows Azure Connect.

Getting ready

To use this recipe, we need to create a new hosted service on the Windows Azure Portal.

How to do it...

We are going to see how to use Windows Azure Connect to connect a PC with a Windows Azure web role. We do this as follows:

The first stage is performed on the PC:

1. Access the Windows Azure Portal and navigate to the **Virtual Network** section.
2. Click on **Install Local Endpoint** and follow the directions.

The second stage is adding Windows Azure Connect to a web role:

3. Use Visual Studio to create an empty Cloud project.
4. Add a web role to the project (accept default name of `WorkerRole1`).In Visual Studio, double click on the **WebRole** in the **Roles** folder to access the service configuration wizard.
5. Select the **Virtual Network** tab in the configuration wizard.
6. Select **Activate Windows Azure Connect**.
7. Get the activation token from the **Virtual Network** section of the Windows Azure Portal and paste it into the activation text box in the **Virtual Network** tab in the configuration wizard.
8. Add a file named `StartupTask.cmd` to the web role and set its **Copy to Output Directory** property to **Copy Always**.
9. Insert the following text in the `StartupTask.cmd` file:
   ```
   netsh advfirewall firewall add rule name="ICMPv6" dir=in
       action=allow enable=yes protocol=icmpv6:128,any
   exit /b 0
   ```

10. Add the following to the `WebRole` section of the `ServiceDefinition.csdef` file for the project:

```
<Startup>
  <Task commandLine="StartupTask.cmd"
     executionContext="elevated" taskType="background"/>
</Startup>
```

11. Publish and deploy the application into the hosted service.

In the next stage, we configure the virtual network in the **Virtual Network** section of the Windows Azure Portal:

12. Ensure that the PC and the role instance are listed on the **Activated Endpoints** page.

13. Click on the **Create Group** button and provide a name for the group.

14. In the **Connect From** section, click on **Add**, select the local endpoint for the PC, and click on **OK**.

15. Under the **Connect To** section, click on **Add**, select the endpoint for the role, and click on **OK**.

16. Click on **Create** to create the group.

The final step is to verify the connection on the local PC:

1. Right click on the **Windows Azure Connect** Software on the task bar and select **Refresh**.

2. Open a command window and `ping` the role instance by name. For example, if the instance is named `RD12345A678B90`, use:

```
ping RD12345A678B90
```

How it works...

In steps 1 and 2, we install the Windows Azure Connect Service on the PC. By default, the service is configured for Automatic start, but we can change this in the **Services** section of the Computer Management application.

In steps 3 and 4, we create a cloud project with a web role. In steps 5 through 7, we use Visual Studio tooling to configure Windows Azure Connect in both the service definition and service configuration files. As we are not adding the web role to an Active Directory domain, the only configuration setting needed is the activation token. If we wanted to add the web role instances to an Active Directory domain, then we would need to configure manually various settings in the service configuration file.

In steps 8 through 10, we create a startup task that modifies the firewall on the web role instance to permit inbound ICMP v6 echo requests (that is, `ping`). The second line of `StartupTask.cmd` cleanly exits `netsh` and the command file.

In step 11, we deploy the application into the hosted service.

In steps 12 through 16, we create the virtual network containing the PC and the role by adding them to the same group. In step 17, we refresh the policy on the local endpoint to ensure that it is aware of the new virtual network.

In step 18, we ping the web role instance to test the virtual network from the local PC. We should get a response similar to the following:

```
Reply from 2a01:111:3f00:1084:e891:889a:1172:f5a6: time=105ms
```

The IPv6 address in the response, `2a01:111:3f00:1084:e891:889a:1172:f5a6`, confirms that the virtual network is using IPv6.

Windows Azure AppFabric Service Bus

The Windows Azure AppFabric Service Bus provides a way to expose internal services through a public-facing endpoint hosted in a Windows Azure data center without exposing the actual location of the service. Both the service and the client connect to the service bus using outbound connections and the service bus splices these outbound connections into a connection between the client and the service. Under certain circumstances, the service bus can upgrade this connection into a direct connection between the client and service. The service bus provides a secure way to expose an internal service to the public without opening an inbound port on a firewall.

Windows Azure Connect and the Windows Azure AppFabric Service Bus are complementary in that the former exposes internal services to a hosted service over a private network, while the latter provides a public endpoint for internal services.

Moving connection to another Windows Azure subscription

The activation key is tied to a Windows Azure subscription. Consequently, a local endpoint on a computer can participate in a virtual network associated with only one Windows Azure subscription at a time. The Windows Azure Connect Service must be uninstalled and then reinstalled if the local endpoint is to join a virtual network for another subscription.

Consuming data from the Windows Azure MarketPlace DataMarket

The Windows Azure MarketPlace DataMarket is the Data-as-a-Service offering in the Windows Azure Platform. It provides a marketplace where data providers can make their data available in a standardized manner that simplifies the consumption of that data. Commercial providers of data, typically charge a subscription for their data while government entities may make it freely available. The DataMarket already contains a wide variety of data from commercial and government providers, varying from house-price data in the USA to gross domestic product expenditures in Afghanistan.

The DataMarket benefits providers of datasets by giving them a standard way of exposing these datasets and generating revenue from them. It benefits consumers of datasets by simplifying the process of accessing data without the need to negotiate individually with providers. The DataMarket therefore serves to democratize access to large datasets that may previously have been inaccessible.

The data in the DataMarket is accessed using an OData interface against a dataset-dependent endpoint under `https://api.datamarket.azure.com`. By default, the data is provided as an *AtomPub* feed, but it can also be retrieved in JSON format. Access to the data is protected using a basic `Authorization` header sent with each data request. This header requires a username/password combination. The username is the Windows Live ID of the DataMarket account and the password is an account key generated on the DataMarket.

There are two types of queries for accessing datasets in the DataMarket: flexible query and fixed query. In a flexible query, various filtering parameters can be attached to each query. In a fixed query, all REST calls must be against one of a set of fixed queries and any filtering desired must be performed on the client. For flexible queries, the DataMarket provides a service reference that can be used inside Visual Studio to generate strongly-typed classes for use with the data. The DataMarket does not do this for fixed queries. Instead, it generates a proxy class that can be downloaded and added to a project.

The LINQ-REST capability of WCF Data Services provides a high-level .NET interface to datasets. The DataMarket provides a strongly-typed class specific to each dataset, which simplifies access to the dataset. Standard LINQ operators such as `Where`, `Select`, `Take`, `Skip`, and so on can be used to control what data is retrieved. The service and proxy classes generated by the DataMarket include, for each dataset, a class derived from `DataServiceContext` that is used for connecting to the datasets. These context classes have various `DataServiceQuery` properties that facilitate the creation of queries against the datasets.

In this recipe, we will learn how to retrieve data from the Windows Azure MarketPlace DataMarket using both flexible and fixed queries.

How to do it...

We are going to retrieve data from the Windows Azure MarketPlace DataMarket using both fixed and flexible queries. We do this as follows:

The first stage is performed on the Windows Azure MarketPlace DataMarket:

1. Subscribe to the following datasets:

    ❑   National Accounts Official Country Data—United Nations Statistics Division published by the United Nations

    ❑   World Development Indicators published by the World Bank

2. Under the **Details** tab of the **National Accounts Official Country Data** page, copy and save the Service root URL:

    ```
    https://api.datamarket.azure.com/Data.ashx/UnitedNations/
    NationalAccounts/
    ```

3. Under the **Details** tab of the **World Development Indicators** page, copy and save the Service root URL:

    ```
    https://api.datamarket.azure.com/Data.ashx/WorldBank/
    WorldDevelopmentIndicators/
    ```

4. Under the **World Development Indicators** page, click on **.Net C# Class Library** and save the generated proxy file:

    ```
    WorldDevelopmentIndicatorsContainer.cs
    ```

The next stage uses a Visual Studio project:

5. Use Visual Studio to create a WPF project.

6. Add a new class named `DataMarketExample`.

7. Add the `WorldDevelopmentIndicatorsContainer.cs` file to the project.

8. Add a Service Reference to the Service root URL for the National Accounts Official Country Data.

9. Add the following `using` statements:

    ```
    using System.Net;
    using System.Data.Services.Client;
    using WorldBank;
    using AzureDataMarketExample.UnitedNationsData;
    ```

10. Add the following members to the class:

```
private Uri worldBankUri = new Uri("https://api.datamarket.azure.
com/Data.ashx/WorldBank/WorldDevelopmentIndicators/");

private Uri unitedNationsUri = new Uri("https://api.datamarket.
azure.com/Data.ashx/UnitedNations/NationalAccounts/");

private String userName = "{WINDOWS_LIVE_ID}";
private String password = "{ACCOUNT_KEY}";
```

11. Add the following property, exposing United Nations data, to the class:

```
public IEnumerable<Values> UnitedNationsValues
{
   get
   {
      UnitedNationsNationalAccountsContainer context =
        new UnitedNationsNationalAccountsContainer(
          unitedNationsUri);
      context.Credentials =
        new NetworkCredential(userName, password);

      IEnumerable<Values> query =
        (from entity in context.Values
         where entity.DataSeriesId == "101"
         && entity.ItemCode == 21
         && entity.FiscalYear == 2005
         select entity);

      return query;
   }
}
```

12. Add the following property, exposing World Bank data, to the class:

```
public IEnumerable<CountryEntity> WorldBankData
{
   get
   {
      WorldDevelopmentIndicatorsContainer context =
        new WorldDevelopmentIndicatorsContainer(worldBankUri);
      context.Credentials =
        new NetworkCredential(userName, password);

      DataServiceQuery<CountryEntity> dataServiceQuery =
        context.GetCountries("en");
```

```
          IEnumerable<CountryEntity> countryQuery =
            dataServiceQuery.Skip<CountryEntity>(50);

          return countryQuery;
      }
   }
```

13. In the `MainWindows.xaml` file, set the `Height` to 600 and `Width` to 700 in the `Window` element.

14. Insert the following `Grid` definition into the `Window` element in `MainWindows.xaml`:

```xml
<Grid Height="600" Width="700">
   <Grid.RowDefinitions>
      <RowDefinition Height="40"/>
      <RowDefinition/>
      <RowDefinition Height="40"/>
      <RowDefinition/>
   </Grid.RowDefinitions>

   <Label Content="Country Information (Fixed Query)"
      FontSize="20" Grid.Row="0" Margin="30,0,0,0"/>

   <DataGrid AutoGenerateColumns="False" Height="200"
      Width="600" HorizontalAlignment="Left" Grid.Row="1"
      Margin="30,0,0,0" Name="WorldBank"
      VerticalAlignment="Top" ItemsSource="{Binding}">
      <DataGrid.Columns>
         <DataGridTextColumn Header="Name"
            Binding="{Binding Path=Name}"/>
         <DataGridTextColumn Header="Iso Code"
            Binding="{Binding Path=CodeIso3Letter}"/>
         <DataGridTextColumn Header="Capital"
            Binding="{Binding Path=CapitalCity}"/>
         <DataGridTextColumn Header="Region"
            Binding="{Binding Path=RegionName}"/>
      </DataGrid.Columns>
   </DataGrid>

   <Label Content="Imports of Goods in FY95 (Flexible Query)"
      FontSize="20" Grid.Row="2" Margin="30,0,0,0"/>

   <DataGrid AutoGenerateColumns="False" Height="200"
      Width="450" HorizontalAlignment="Left" Grid.Row="3"
      Margin="30,0,0,0" Name="UnitedNations"
      VerticalAlignment="Top" ItemsSource="{Binding}">
```

```
      <DataGrid.Columns>
         <DataGridTextColumn Header="Country"
            Binding="{Binding Path=CountryName}"/>
         <DataGridTextColumn Header="Currency"
            Binding="{Binding Path=Currency}"/>
         <DataGridTextColumn Header="Value"
            Binding="{Binding Path=Value}"/>
      </DataGrid.Columns>
   </DataGrid>
</Grid>
```

15. In `MainWindows.xaml.cs`, replace `MainWindow()` with the following:

```
public MainWindow()
{
    InitializeComponent();

    DataMarketExample example = new DataMarketExample();
    WorldBank.DataContext = example.WorldBankData;
    UnitedNations.DataContext = example.UnitedNationsValues;
}
```

How it works...

In step 1, we subscribe to two datasets: one from the World Bank and one from the United Nations. The former requires fixed queries while the latter uses flexible queries. In steps 2 and 3, we save the root URL for the services for each dataset. In step 4, we generate the proxy file for the fixed queries used for the World Bank data.

In step 5, we create the WPF application for the project and in step 6, we create a class for it. In step 7, we add the proxy file for the fixed queries and in step 8, we generate the service reference for the flexible queries used for the United Nations dataset. In step 9, we add the `using` statements.

In step 10, we add some static members to store the root URL for the two services. We also provide static members for the username and password used in basic authentication. We must replace `{WINDOWS_LIVE_ID}` with the Windows Live ID used to sign in to the Windows Azure MarketPlace DataMarket and `{ACCOUNT_KEY}` with the account key generated there.

The `UnitedNationsValues` property, we add in step 11, retrieves data for the imports of goods in fiscal 95 for various countries from the United Nations dataset. This property invokes a fixed query.

In step 12, we add a `WorldBankData` property that retrieves geographical information about various countries from the World Bank dataset. We skip the first 50 entries in the dataset and then retrieve the next page of data (100 entries by default). This property invokes a flexible query.

In step 13, we set the size of the main window for the WPF application. In step 14, we add a grid with four rows. The first row provides a label for the grid, exposing the World Bank dataset we add in the second row. We explicitly display some fields from the dataset as columns of the grid. The third row provides a label for the grid, exposing the United Nations dataset we add in the fourth row. We explicitly display some fields from the dataset as columns of the grid.

In step 15, we bind the `WorldBank` grid to the `WorldBankData` property and the `UnitedNations` grid to the `UnitedNationsValues` property.

Using Web Deploy with Windows Azure

A Windows Azure application is deployed into a hosted service by publishing the application package and its associated service configuration file, `ServiceConfiguration.cscfg`. The package is a compressed, encrypted file containing the assemblies comprising the application. The Windows Azure Fabric Controller allocates the components of the package to the instances of each role in the hosted service. A similar process is used when the hosted service is upgraded.

This process can take 10 minutes or more, depending on the size and complexity of the hosted service. There has been much demand that the deployment process be speeded up. This is particularly true for web roles where developers have become used to seeing their changes deployed almost as soon as they are made.

The IIS Web Deployment Tool (Web Deploy) provides tooling for Visual Studio that supports the rapid deployment of changes to an IIS website. The introduction of Remote Access for Windows Azure allowed Web Deploy to be used with a web role. The Windows Azure SDK v1.4 release simplified the integration of Web Deploy with Windows Azure by providing tooling that handled the necessary configuration. This means that a change to a page in a web role can be deployed using Web Deploy in only a few seconds instead of the 10 minutes or more required previously.

The regular Windows Azure publish process must be used for initial deployment and for subsequent upgrades of the hosted service. Web Deploy can then be used for upgrading individual pages of a website hosted in a Windows Azure web role. As with other changes made following deployment, any changes made using Web Deploy are lost if the instance is reimaged or moved to a new virtual machine (VM). Consequently, Web Deploy is intended for use during development and is specifically not intended for use in a production environment. Web Deploy can be used only with a deployment where there is only a single instance of the web role.

The Visual Studio tooling supports two distinct publishing processes. An application is deployed as a Windows Azure hosted service by invoking Publish on the Windows Azure project. A website is published through Web Deploy by invoking Publish on the website.

In this recipe, we will learn how to use Web Deploy to upload a modified website to a Windows Azure web role.

Getting ready

We need to create a hosted service on the Windows Azure Portal. We also need to create a storage account that Visual Studio tooling can deploy the application through.

We need to upload an X.509 public key certificate to the Management Certificate section of the Windows Azure Portal. The Visual Studio tooling uses this management certificate for authentication when it publishes the Windows Azure package.

We need to upload an X.509 public key certificate to the Certificates section of the hosted service we just created. The Visual Studio tooling uses this service certificate for authentication when it publishes the website using Web Deploy. The tooling can be used to create this certificate, but it must be uploaded separately to the Windows Azure Portal.

How to do it...

We are going to create a Windows Azure application and configure it for Web Deploy when we publish it to Windows Azure. After it is deployed, we will change the `Default.aspx` page and use Web Deploy to upload the change to the web role. We do this as follows:

1. Use Visual Studio to create an empty Cloud project.
2. Add a web role to the project (accept default name of `WebRole1`).

The next few steps implement the initial deployment of the application as a Windows Azure hosted service:

3. Right click on the Windows Azure project and select **Publish** to bring up the **Deploy Windows Azure project** dialog, as shown in the following screenshot:

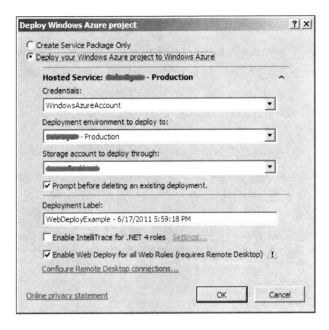

On the **Deploy Windows Azure project** dialog:

4. For **Credentials**, provide the management certificate uploaded in the
    Getting ready section.

5. For **Deployment environment**, select the hosted service created in the
    Getting ready section.

6. For **Storage account**, select the storage account created in the *Getting ready* section.

7. Provide a unique **Deployment Label** for the deployment.

8. Click on **Configure Remote Desktop connections...** to bring up the **Remote Desktop
    Configuration** dialog.

Under the **Remote Desktop Configuration** dialog:

9. Select **Enable connections for all roles**.

10. Select the service certificate uploaded during the *Getting ready* phase.

11. Provide a username and password that Web Deploy uses when it publishes the
    website to the Windows Azure hosted service.

12. Click on **OK**.

On the **Deploy Windows Azure project** dialog:

13. Select the **Enable Web Deploy for all Web Roles** which should now be enabled.

14. Click on **OK** to start deploying the application to the Windows Azure hosted service.

Wait for the deployment to complete and the hosted service to enter the `Ready` state:

15. Open a browser on `Default.aspx` for the web role to confirm it is available.

16. Add the following to the end of the `asp:Content` section of `Default.aspx`:

```
<p>
   Web Deploy in action.
</p>
```

17. In Visual Studio, right click on the website and select **Publish**.

18. Under the **Publish Web** dialog, provide the password created in step 11 and click on **Publish**.

19. Wait a few seconds for Web Deploy to complete.

20. Refresh the browser on `Default.aspx` to verify that the Web Deploy was successful and that the page now displays the text *Web Deploy in action*.

How it works...

In steps 1 and 2 we set up the recipe.

In steps 3 through 7, we configure the initial deployment of the application to the Windows Azure hosted service. In step 4, we provide the management certificate that Visual Studio uses to authenticate when uploading the application package to Windows Azure. In step 5, we specify the hosted service and deployment slot we are deploying the application into. In step 6, we specify the storage account that Visual Studio uses to upload the application package to Windows Azure. In step 7, we provide a unique name for the deployment. Web Deploy uses the Remote Desktop feature of Windows Azure, so it is necessary to configure that before we turn on Web Deploy. We launch the **Remote Desktop Configuration** dialog in step 8.

We configure Remote Desktop in steps 9 through 12. In step 9, we turn on Remote Desktop for all roles. In step 10, we specify the service certificate used to encrypt the username and password we add in steps 11 and 12. These credentials are used for authenticating the Web Deploy upload.

In step 13, we enable Web Deploy. In step 14, we start the initial deployment of the application to the Windows Azure hosted service. We confirm its success in step 15 by demonstrating that we can access the web site hosted by the web role.

In steps 16 through 20, we demonstrate Web Deploy in action by modifying a web page and using Web Deploy to publish it to the web role hosted in Windows Azure. We make a simple modification to a web page in step 16. We initiate the Web Deploy publish process in step 17, and provide the required password in step 18. After waiting a few seconds for Web Deploy to complete, we verify that the change has been deployed in step 20.

6
Digging into Windows Azure Diagnostics

In this chapter, we will cover:

- ▶ Initializing the configuration of Windows Azure Diagnostics
- ▶ Using a configuration file with Windows Azure Diagnostics
- ▶ Using the Windows Azure Diagnostics trace listener
- ▶ Performing an on-demand transfer
- ▶ Implementing custom logging
- ▶ Accessing data persisted to Windows Azure Storage
- ▶ Using the Windows Azure Platform PowerShell cmdlets to configure Windows Azure Diagnostics
- ▶ Using IntelliTrace to diagnose problems with a hosted service

Introduction

A Windows Azure hosted service may comprise multiple instances of multiple roles. These instances all run in a remote Windows Azure data center—typically 24*7. The ability to monitor these instances non-intrusively is essential both in detecting failure and in capacity planning.

Windows Azure Diagnostics provides for the non-intrusive capture of diagnostic data and its subsequent persistence to the Windows Azure Storage Service. It supports various standard sources, allowing for their extensibility where appropriate. Windows Azure Diagnostics also integrates custom logs directly into its normal operational mode.

Diagnostic data can be used to identify problems with a hosted service. The ability to view the data from several sources and across different instances eases the task of identifying a problem.

Diagnostic data can be used to identify when service capacity is either too high or too low for the expected workload. This can guide capacity decisions such as whether to scale up or down the number of instances.

The configuration of Windows Azure Diagnostics is performed at the instance level. The code to do that configuration is at the role level, but the diagnostics configuration for each instance is stored in individual blobs in a container named `wad-control-container` located in the storage service account configured for Windows Azure Diagnostics.

There is no need for application data and diagnostics data to be located in the same storage service account. Indeed, a best practice from both security and performance perspectives would be to host application data and diagnostic data in separate storage service accounts.

The configuration of Windows Azure Diagnostics is centered on the concept of data buffers with each data buffer representing a specific type of diagnostic information. Some of the data buffers have associated data sources which represent a further refining of the data captured and persisted. For example, the performance counter data buffer has individual data sources for each configured performance counter. Windows Azure Diagnostics supports record-based data buffers that are persisted to Windows Azure tables and file-based data buffers that are persisted to Windows Azure blobs. In the *Accessing data persisted to Windows Azure Storage* recipe we see that we can access the diagnostic data in the same way we access other data in Windows Azure storage.

Windows Azure Diagnostics supports the following record-based data buffers:

- ▶ Windows Azure basic logs
- ▶ Performance counters
- ▶ Windows Event Logs
- ▶ Windows Azure Diagnostic infrastructure logs

The Windows Azure basic logs data buffer captures information written to a Windows Azure trace listener. In the *Using the Windows Azure Diagnostics trace listener* recipe, we see how to configure and use the basic logs data buffer. The performance counters data buffer captures the data of any configured performance counters. The Windows Event Logs data buffer captures the events form any configured Windows Event Log. The Windows Azure Diagnostic infrastructure logs data buffer captures diagnostic data produced by the Windows Azure Diagnostics process.

Windows Azure Diagnostics supports the following file-based data sources for the *Directories* data buffer:

- IIS logs
- IIS Failed Request Logs
- Crash dumps
- Custom directories

The *Directories* data buffer copies new files in a specified directory to blobs in a specified container in the Windows Azure Blob Service. The data captured by IIS Logs, IIS Failed Request Logs, and crash dumps is self-evident. With the custom directories data source, Windows Azure Diagnostics supports the association of any directory on the instance with a specified container in Windows Azure storage. This allows for the coherent integration of third-party logs into Windows Azure Diagnostics. We see how to do this in the *Implementing custom logging* recipe.

The implementation of Windows Azure Diagnostics was changed in Windows Azure SDK v1.3 and it is now one of the pluggable modules that have to be explicitly imported into a role in the service definition file. As Windows Azure Diagnostics persists both its configuration and data to Windows Azure storage, it is necessary to specify a storage service account for diagnostics in the service configuration file.

The default configuration for Windows Azure Diagnostics captures some data but does not persist it. Consequently, the diagnostics configuration should be modified at role startup. In the *Initializing the configuration of Windows Azure Diagnostics* recipe, we see how to do this programmatically, which is the normal way to do it. In the *Using a configuration file with Windows Azure Diagnostics* recipe, we see how to use a configuration file to do this, which is necessary in a VM role.

In normal use, diagnostics data is captured all the time and is then persisted to the storage service according to some schedule. In the event of a problem, it may be necessary to persist diagnostics data before the next scheduled transfer time. We see how to do this in the *Performing an on-demand transfer* recipe.

Both Microsoft and Cerebrata have released PowerShell cmdlets that facilitate the remote administration of Windows Azure Diagnostics. We see how to do this in the *Using the Windows Azure Platform PowerShell cmdlets to configure Windows Azure Diagnostics* recipe.

There are times, especially early in the development process, when non-intrusive diagnostics monitoring is not sufficient. In the *Using IntelliTrace to diagnose problems with a hosted service* recipe, we see the benefits of intrusive monitoring of a Windows Azure role instance.

Initializing the configuration of Windows Azure Diagnostics

The Windows Azure Diagnostics module is imported into a role by the specification of an `Import` element with a `moduleName` attribute of `Diagnostics` in the `Imports` section of the service definition file (`ServiceDefinition.csdef`). This further requires the specification, in the service configuration file (`ServiceConfiguration.cscfg`), of a Windows Azure Storage Service account that can be used to access the instance configuration for diagnostics. This configuration is stored as an XML file in a blob, named for the instance, in a container named `wad-control-container` in the storage service account configured for diagnostics.

The Diagnostics Agent service is started automatically when a role instance starts provided the diagnostics module has been imported into the role. Note that in Windows Azure SDK versions prior to v1.3, this is not true in that the Diagnostics Agent must be explicitly started through the invocation of `DiagnosticMonitor.Start()`.

On instance startup, the diagnostics configuration for the instance can be set as desired in the overridden `RoleEntryPoint.OnStart()` method. The general idea is to retrieve the default initial configuration using `DiagnosticMonitor.GetDefaultInitialConfiguration()` and modify it as necessary before saving it using `DiagnosticMonitor.Start()`. This name is something of a relic, since Windows Azure SDK v1.3 and later, the Diagnostics Agent service is started automatically.

Another way to modify the diagnostics configuration for the instance is to use `RoleInstanceDiagnosticManager.GetCurrentConfiguration()` to retrieve the existing instance configuration from `wad-control-container`. This can be modified and then saved using `RoleInstanceDiagnosticManager.SetCurrentConfiguration()`. This method can be used both inside and outside the role instance. For example, it can be implemented remotely to request that an on-demand transfer be performed. An issue is that using this technique during instance startup violates the principal that the environment on startup is always the same, as the existing instance configuration may already have been modified. Note that it is not possible to modify the diagnostics configuration for an instance if there is a currently active on-demand transfer.

In this recipe, we will learn how to initialize programmatically the configuration of Windows Azure Diagnostics.

How to do it...

We are going to see how to initialize the configuration for Windows Azure Diagnostics using code. We do this as follows:

1. Use Visual Studio to create an empty cloud project.

2. Add a web role to the project (accept the default name of `WebRole1`).

3. Add the following assembly reference to the project:

   ```
   System.Data.Services.Client
   ```

4. In the `WebRole` class, replace `OnStart()` with the following:

   ```
   public override bool OnStart()
   {
       WadManagement wadManagement = new WadManagement();
       wadManagement.InitializeConfiguration();

       return base.OnStart();
   }
   ```

5. In the `Default.aspx` file, replace the `asp:Content` element named BodyContent with the following:

   ```
   <asp:Content ID="BodyContent" runat="server"
       ContentPlaceHolderID="MainContent">
     <div id="xmlInner">
        <pre>
           <asp:label id="xmlLabel" runat="server"/>
        </pre>
     </div>
   </asp:Content>
   ```

6. Add the following `using` statements to the `Default.aspx.cs` file:

   ```
   using Microsoft.WindowsAzure.ServiceRuntime;
   ```

7. In the `Default.aspx.cs` file, add the following private members to the `_Default` class:

   ```
   private String deploymentId = RoleEnvironment.DeploymentId;
   private String roleName =
     RoleEnvironment.CurrentRoleInstance.Role.Name;
   private String instanceId =
     RoleEnvironment.CurrentRoleInstance.Id;
   ```

8. In the `Default.aspx.cs` file, replace `Page_Load()` with the following:

   ```
   protected void Page_Load(object sender, EventArgs e)
   {
       WadManagement wad = new WadManagement();
       String wadConfigurationForInstance =
         wad.GetConfigurationBlob(
           deploymentId, roleName, instanceId);
       xmlLabel.Text =
         Server.HtmlEncode(wadConfigurationForInstance);
   }
   ```

9. Add a class named `WadManagement` to the project.

10. Add the following `using` statements to the `WadManagement` class:

```
using Microsoft.WindowsAzure;
using Microsoft.WindowsAzure.Diagnostics;
using Microsoft.WindowsAzure.Diagnostics.Management;
using Microsoft.WindowsAzure.ServiceRuntime;
using Microsoft.WindowsAzure.StorageClient;
```

11. Add the following private members to the `WadManagement` class:

```
private String wadConnectionString =
"Microsoft.WindowsAzure.Plugins.Diagnostics.ConnectionString";
private String wadControlContainerName =
  "wad-control-container";
private CloudStorageAccount cloudStorageAccount;
```

12. Add the following constructor to the `WadManagement` class:

```
public WadManagement()
{
   cloudStorageAccount = CloudStorageAccount.Parse(
     RoleEnvironment.GetConfigurationSettingValue(
       wadConnectionString));
}
```

13. Add the following methods, retrieving the instance configuration blob from Windows Azure Storage, to the `WadManagement` class:

```
public String GetConfigurationBlob(
  String deploymentId, String roleName, String instanceId)
{
   DeploymentDiagnosticManager deploymentDiagnosticManager =
     new DeploymentDiagnosticManager(
       cloudStorageAccount, deploymentId);

   String wadConfigurationBlobNameForInstance =
     String.Format("{0}/{1}/{2}", deploymentId, roleName,
       instanceId);
   String wadConfigurationForInstance =
     GetWadConfigurationForInstance(
       wadConfigurationBlobNameForInstance);

   return wadConfigurationForInstance;
}

private String GetWadConfigurationForInstance(
  String wadConfigurationInstanceBlobName)
{
```

```
  CloudBlobClient cloudBlobClient =
    cloudStorageAccount.CreateCloudBlobClient();
  CloudBlobContainer cloudBlobContainer =
    cloudBlobClient.GetContainerReference(
      wadControlContainerName);
  CloudBlob cloudBlob = cloudBlobContainer.GetBlobReference(
    wadConfigurationInstanceBlobName);

  String wadConfigurationForInstance =
    cloudBlob.DownloadText();

  return wadConfigurationForInstance;
}
```

14. Add the following method, initializing the configuration of Windows Azure Diagnostics, to the `WadManagement` class:

```
public void InitializeConfiguration()
{
  String eventLog = "Application!*";
  String performanceCounter =
    @"\Processor(_Total)\% Processor Time";

  DiagnosticMonitorConfiguration dmc =
    DiagnosticMonitor.GetDefaultInitialConfiguration();

  dmc.DiagnosticInfrastructureLogs.BufferQuotaInMB = 100;
  dmc.DiagnosticInfrastructureLogs.ScheduledTransferPeriod =
    TimeSpan.FromHours(1);
  dmc.DiagnosticInfrastructureLogs.
    ScheduledTransferLogLevelFilter = LogLevel.Verbose;

  dmc.WindowsEventLog.BufferQuotaInMB = 100;
  dmc.WindowsEventLog.ScheduledTransferPeriod =
    TimeSpan.FromHours(1);
  dmc.WindowsEventLog.ScheduledTransferLogLevelFilter =
    LogLevel.Verbose;
  dmc.WindowsEventLog.DataSources.Add(eventLog);

  dmc.Logs.BufferQuotaInMB = 100;
  dmc.Logs.ScheduledTransferPeriod = TimeSpan.FromHours(1);
  dmc.Logs.ScheduledTransferLogLevelFilter =
    LogLevel.Verbose;

  dmc.Directories.ScheduledTransferPeriod =
    TimeSpan.FromHours(1);
```

```
PerformanceCounterConfiguration perfCounterConfiguration
    = new PerformanceCounterConfiguration();
perfCounterConfiguration.CounterSpecifier =
    performanceCounter;
perfCounterConfiguration.SampleRate =
    System.TimeSpan.FromSeconds(10);
dmc.PerformanceCounters.DataSources.Add(
    perfCounterConfiguration);
dmc.PerformanceCounters.BufferQuotaInMB = 100;
dmc.PerformanceCounters.ScheduledTransferPeriod =
    TimeSpan.FromHours(1);

DiagnosticMonitor.Start(cloudStorageAccount, dmc);
}
```

How it works...

In steps 1 and 2, we create a cloud project with a web role. We add the required assembly reference in step 3.

In step 4, we modify `OnStart()`, so that it initializes the configuration of Windows Azure Diagnostics.

In step 5, we modify the default web page, so that it displays the content of the blob storing the instance configuration for Windows Azure Diagnostics. In step 6, we add the required using statement to `Default.aspx.cs`. In step 7, we add some private members to store the deployment ID, the role name, and the instance ID of the current instance. In step 8, we modify the `Page_Load()` event handler to retrieve the blob content and display it on the default web page.

In step 9, we add the `WadManagement` class that interacts with the Windows Azure Blob Service. In step 10, we add the required `using` statements. In step 11, we add some private members to contain the name of the connection string in the service configuration file, and the name of the blob container containing the instance configuration for Windows Azure Diagnostics. We also add a `CloudStorageAccount` instance, which we initialize in the constructor we add in step 12.

We then add, in step 13, the two methods we use to retrieve the content of the blob containing the instance configuration for Windows Azure Diagnostics. In `GetConfigurationBlob()`, we first create the name of the blob. We then pass this into the `GetWadConfigurationForInstance()` method, which invokes various Windows Azure Storage Client Library methods to retrieve the content of the blob.

In step 14, we add the method to initialize the configuration of Windows Azure Diagnostics for the instance. We first specify the names of the event log and performance counter we want to capture and persist. We then retrieve the default initial configuration and configure capture of the Windows Azure infrastructure logs, Windows Event Logs, basic logs, directories, and performance counters. For each of them, we specify a data buffer size of 100 MB and schedule an hourly transfer of logged data.

For Windows Event Logs, we specify that the `Application!*` event log should be captured locally and persisted to the storage service. The event log is specified using an **XPath** expression allowing the events to be filtered, if desired. We can add other event logs if desired. We configure the capture and persistence of only one performance counter—the `\Processor(_Total)\% Processor Time`. We can add other performance counters if desired. Two sections at the end of this recipe provide additional details on the configuration of event logs and performance counters.

We specify a transfer schedule for the directories data buffer. The Diagnostics Agent automatically inserts special directories into the configuration: crash dumps for all roles, and IIS logs and IIS failed request logs for web roles. The Diagnostics Agent does this because the actual location of the directories is not known until the instance is deployed. Note that even though we have configured a persistence schedule for crash dumps, they are not captured by default. We would need to invoke the `CrashDumps.EnableCollection()` method to enable the capture of crash dumps.

There's more...

We can also modify an existing diagnostics configuration for an instance. We do this by adding the following method to `WadManagement` class, and then invoking it in the same way we invoked `InitializeConfiguration()`:

```
public void ModifyConfiguration(
    String deploymentId, String roleName, String instanceId)
{
    String eventLog =
        @"Application!*[System[Provider[@Name='.NET Runtime']]]";
    String performanceCounter = @"\ASP.NET\Requests Rejected";

    RoleInstanceDiagnosticManager ridm =
        cloudStorageAccount.CreateRoleInstanceDiagnosticManager(
            deploymentId, roleName, instanceId);
    DiagnosticMonitorConfiguration dmc =
        ridm.GetCurrentConfiguration();

    Int32 countDataSources =
        dmc.WindowsEventLog.DataSources.Count(
            item => item == eventLog);
    if (countDataSources == 0)
```

```
    {
       dmc.WindowsEventLog.DataSources.Add(eventLog);
       dmc.WindowsEventLog.ScheduledTransferPeriod =
          TimeSpan.FromHours(1);
    }


    countDataSources =
       dmc.PerformanceCounters.DataSources.Count(
          item => item.CounterSpecifier == performanceCounter);
    if (countDataSources == 0)
    {
       PerformanceCounterConfiguration perfConfiguration =
          new PerformanceCounterConfiguration()
          {
             CounterSpecifier = performanceCounter,
             SampleRate = System.TimeSpan.FromHours(1)
          };
       dmc.PerformanceCounters.DataSources.Add(
          perfConfiguration);
    }


    IDictionary<DataBufferName, OnDemandTransferInfo>
       activeTransfers = ridm.GetActiveTransfers();
    if (activeTransfers.Count == 0)
    {
       ridm.SetCurrentConfiguration(dmc);
    }
 }
```

This method can be used locally inside a role, or remotely, to modify the diagnostics configuration for the instance identified by the `deploymentId`, `roleName`, and `instanceId` with which the method is parameterized.

If the method is invoked remotely from an application, then the code to create the `CloudStorageAccount` must be modified to the following:

```
CloudStorageAccount cloudStorageAccount =
   CloudStorageAccount.Parse(
   ConfigurationManager.AppSettings["DataConnectionString"]);
```

This assumes that `DataConnectionString` specified in the following canonical format is an `app.config` file setting:

```
<Setting name="DataConnectionString"
value="DefaultEndpointsProtocol=http;AccountName=ACCOUNT;AccountKey=K
EY" />
```

We also need to add an assembly reference to `System.configuration.dll` and the related `using` statement.

In the method, we initialize variables to specify the Windows Event Log and the performance counter we wish to configure. Note that we use an XPath expression to filter the event log to persist only events coming from the .NET Runtime source.

We create a `RoleInstanceDiagnosticManager` object for the instance and use it to retrieve its `DiagnosticMonitorConfiguration`. Having ensured that we have not already added the event log and performance counter, we add them to the diagnostics configuration for the instance.

Finally, we invoke `RoleInstanceDiagnosticManager.SetCurrentConfiguration()` to save the modified configuration to the diagnostics configuration for the instance stored in `wad-control-container`. We save the configuration only if there is no active on-demand transfer, as `SetCurrentConfiguration()` throws an exception if an on-demand transfer is in progress.

Configuring the Event Log data buffer

An XPath expression can be used to filter the Windows Event Log events that Windows Azure Diagnostics persists to `WADWindowsEventLogsTable` table. This recipe contains the following two examples of the filter expression:

1. `Application!*`
2. `Application!*[System[Provider[@Name='.NET Runtime']]]`

The first persists all events, while the second persists only those events from the .NET Runtime source.

Steve Marx has written a blog post in which he shows how to use the Event Viewer to generate a filter expression at the following URL:

`http://blog.smarx.com/posts/capturing-filtered-windows-events-with-windows-azure-diagnostics`

Configuring the performance counter data buffer

There are a large number of performance counters which Windows Azure Diagnostics can capture and persist to the `WADPerformanceCountersTable` table. It is also possible to add custom performance counters to an instance. The `typeperf` command can be used at the command prompt to generate a list of available performance counters. The following lists all performance counters on the current system:

```
C:\Users\Administrator>typeperf -q
```

The following command filters the list to only those performance counters for the `ASP.NET` object:

```
C:\Users\Administrator>typeperf -q ASP.NET
```

Note that there are also performance counters for objects, such as `ASP.NET Applications`.

Using a configuration file with Windows Azure Diagnostics

Windows Azure Diagnostics stores the diagnostics configuration for an instance as an XML file in a blob, named for the instance, in a container named `wad-control-container` in the Windows Azure Storage Service account configured for diagnostics. When an instance is started for the first time, a default instance configuration is inserted in the container. This can be modified programmatically, either local to the instance or remotely using methods in the Windows Azure SDK.

Local configuration typically occurs in the `OnStart()` method for the role and is used to further specify the information captured by Windows Azure Diagnostics and the schedule with which diagnostic data is persisted in the Windows Azure Storage Service. By default, some diagnostics data is captured, but none of it is persisted to the storage service. Remote configuration can also be used to modify the information captured. However, it is used normally to initiate an on-demand transfer of data from an instance when a problem must be investigated before the next scheduled transfer of data to the storage service.

Windows Azure SDK v1.3 introduced a way to specify declaratively the initial configuration of Windows Azure Diagnostics for a role. This requires the placement of a file, named `diagnostics.wadcfg`, in a specific location in the role package. When an instance is started for the first time, the Diagnostic Agent reads the file and initializes the diagnostic configuration for the instance in `wad-control-container` with it, instead of using the default configuration.

During instance startup, the Diagnostics Agent uses the following sequence to search for a diagnostics configuration to use:

1. Diagnostic configuration for the instance in `wad-control-container`.
2. Configuration specified programmatically when the instance is started.
3. Configuration specified in `diagnostics.wadcfg`.
4. Default configuration.

The physical location of `diagnostics.wadcfg` in a hosted service depends on the role type. For a worker role, the location is `%RoleRoot%` while for a web role, the location is `%RoleRoot%\bin`. For a VM role, `diagnostics.wadcfg` must be in the following directory in the uploaded Guest OS image:

```
%ProgramFiles%\Windows Azure Integration Components\v1.0\Diagnostics
```

The information contained in `diagnostics.wadcfg` mirrors that stored in the instance configuration in `wad-control-container` and exposed through the `DiagnosticsMonitorConfiguration` class in the Windows Azure SDK.

The intended use of the `diagnostics.wadcfg` file is in situations where programmatic configuration is not possible. The primary use case is in a VM role where there is no `RoleEntryPoint` and no `OnStart()` method in which to perform programmatic configuration. Another example is when special logging is required during a startup task.

In this recipe, we will learn how to configure Windows Azure Diagnostics using the `diagnostics.wadcfg` file.

How to do it...

We are going to see how to use a configuration file to configure Windows Azure Diagnostics. We do this as follows:

1. Create a `diagnostics.wadcfg` file in the root directory of the role.
2. In the Visual Studio Properties for the `diagnostics.wadcfg` file, set the **Build Action** to **Content** and the **Copy to Output Directory** to **Copy Always**.
3. Insert the following root element in the file:

```
<DiagnosticMonitorConfiguration
xmlns="http://schemas.microsoft.com/ServiceHosting/2010/10/
DiagnosticsConfiguration"
    configurationChangePollInterval="PT1M"
    overallQuotaInMB="4096" />
```

4. Insert the following as a child element of the `DiagnosticMonitorConfiguration` element:

```
<DiagnosticInfrastructureLogs
    bufferQuotaInMB="100"
    scheduledTransferLogLevelFilter="Verbose"
    scheduledTransferPeriod="PT1H"/>
```

5. Insert the following as a child element of the `DiagnosticMonitorConfiguration` element:

```
<WindowsEventLog
    bufferQuotaInMB="100"
    scheduledTransferLogLevelFilter="Verbose"
    scheduledTransferPeriod="PT1H">
    <DataSource name="Application!*"/>
</WindowsEventLog>
```

6. Insert the following as a child element of the `DiagnosticMonitorConfiguration` element:

```
<Logs
    bufferQuotaInMB="100"
    scheduledTransferLogLevelFilter="Verbose"
    scheduledTransferPeriod="PT1H"/>
```

7. Insert the following as a child element of the `DiagnosticMonitorConfiguration` element:

```
<Directories
    bufferQuotaInMB="1024"
    scheduledTransferPeriod="PT1H">
    <CrashDumps container="wad-crash-dumps"
        directoryQuotaInMB="256"/>
    <FailedRequestLogs container="wad-frq"
        directoryQuotaInMB="256"/>
    <IISLogs container="wad-iis-test"
        directoryQuotaInMB="256"/>

    <DataSources>
        <DirectoryConfiguration
            container="wad-custom"
            directoryQuotaInMB="20">
            <LocalResource name="CustomLoggingLocation"
                relativePath="Logs"/>
        </DirectoryConfiguration>
    </DataSources>
</Directories>
```

8. Insert the following as a child element of the `DiagnosticMonitorConfiguration` element:

```
<PerformanceCounters
    bufferQuotaInMB="100" scheduledTransferPeriod="PT20M">
    <PerformanceCounterConfiguration
        counterSpecifier="\Processor(_Total)\% Processor Time"
        sampleRate="PT10S"/>
</PerformanceCounters>
```

9. Add the following as a child element of the `WebRole` or `WorkerRole` element in the service definition file, `ServiceDefinition.csdef`:

```
<LocalResources>
  <LocalStorage name="CustomLoggingLocation"
    sizeInMB="20" cleanOnRoleRecycle="false"/>
</LocalResources>
```

How it works...

In steps 1 and 2, we create the `diagnostics.wadcfg` file and set the Visual Studio build action. The appropriate location for the file depends on the role. The Visual Studio tooling ensures that the file is copied to the correct location when the project is built.

In step 3, we create the root element of the file and set the maximum size of the diagnostics data buffer to 4 GB. The `configurationChangePollInterval` specifies the interval at which the Diagnostics Agent polls the storage service for diagnostic configuration changes. This is provided in ISO 8601 format. For example, with a `configurationChangePollInterval` of PT1M, the P indicates duration, the T indicates time, and the 1M indicates one minute. The same format is used for other intervals and periods in the configuration file.

In step 4, we configure the diagnostics infrastructure logs into which the Diagnostic Agent logs data about itself. We specify that this data is stored locally in a 100 MB data buffer and that the information is persisted to the storage service once an hour (PT1H). We also filter the persistence of data, so that all events with a level of *verbose* or higher are transferred.

In step 5, we configure the capture and persistence of the Windows Event Logs. We specify that all *verbose* or higher events in the Application event log should be transferred once an hour. We can add more `DataSource` elements to specify the capture and persistence of additional Windows Event Logs. In step 6, we configure the capture and persistence of basic logs from the Windows Azure Diagnostics trace listener.

In step 7, we configure the capture and persistence of data located in directories on the local file system. For crash dumps, failed (IIS) request logs, and IIS logs, we specify the Windows Azure Blob Service container in which the data is persisted, but we don't specify the directory in which the data is located because that is not known until the hosted service starts. The Diagnostics Agent fixes the configuration of these logs when it writes the diagnostics configuration for the instance to `wad-control-container`.

For custom directories, we must specify the name of a local resource, configured in the service definition file, where we write the logs to. We use the `relativePath` attribute to specify a directory under the root path of the local resource. We also specify the Windows Azure Blob Service container into which the logs are persisted. We can add more `DirectoryConfiguration` elements to specify the capture and persistence of files in other directories.

In step 8, we configure the capture and persistence of performance counters data. We specify that the % processor time should be captured every 10 seconds (PT10S) and persisted to the storage service once an hour. We can add more `PerformanceCounterConfiguration` elements to specify the capture and persistence of other performance counters.

In step 9, we add the definition for the local resource, used in custom logging, to the service definition file.

There's more...

Andy Cross has written a blog post in which he describes how to perform XML validation on the `diagnostics.wadcfg` file at the following URL:

`http://blog.bareweb.eu/2011/02/file-based-diagnostics-config-with-intellisense-in-azure-sdk-1-3/`

Using the Windows Azure Diagnostics trace listener

Windows Azure Diagnostics supports the use of `Trace` to log messages. The Windows Azure SDK provides the `DiagnosticMonitorTraceListener` trace listener to capture the messages. The Windows Azure Diagnostics basic logs data buffer is used to configure their persistence to the Windows Azure Table Service.

The trace listener must be added to the `Listeners` collection for the Windows Azure hosted service. This is typically done through configuration in the appropriate `app.config` or `web.config` file, but it can also be done in code. When it creates a worker or web role, the Windows Azure tooling for Visual Studio adds the `DiagnosticMonitorTraceListener` to the list of trace listeners specified in the `Configuration` section of the relevant configuration file.

Methods of the `System.Diagnostics.Trace` class can be used to write error, warning and informational messages. When persisting the messages to the storage service, the Diagnostics Agent can filter the messages if a `LogLevel` filter is configured for the `BasicLogsBufferConfiguration`.

The Compute Emulator in the development environment adds an additional trace listener, so that trace messages can be displayed in the Compute Emulator UI.

In this recipe, we will learn how to trace messages using the Windows Azure trace listener.

How to do it...

We are going to see how to use the trace listener provided in the Windows Azure SDK to trace messages and persist them to the storage service. We do this as follows:

1. Ensure that the `DiagnosticMonitorTraceListener` has been added to the appropriate configuration file: `app.config` for a worker role and `web.config` for a web role.

2. If necessary, add the following to the `Configuration` section of `app.config` or `web.config` file:

```
<system.diagnostics>
  <trace>
    <listeners>
      <add type="Microsoft.WindowsAzure.Diagnostics.
        DiagnosticMonitorTraceListener,
        Microsoft.WindowsAzure.Diagnostics, Version=1.0.0.0,
        Culture=neutral, PublicKeyToken=31bf3856ad364e35"
        name="AzureDiagnostics">
        <filter type="" />
      </add>
    </listeners>
  </trace>
</system.diagnostics>
```

3. Use the following to write an informational message:

```
System.Diagnostics.Trace.TraceInformation("Information");
```

4. Use the following to write a warning message:

```
System.Diagnostics.Trace.Warning("Warning ");
```

5. Use the following to write an error message:

```
System.Diagnostics.Trace.TraceError("Error");
```

6. Ensure that the `DiagnosticMonitorConfiguration.Logs` property is configured with an appropriate `ScheduledTransferPeriod` and `ScheduledTransferLogLevelFilter` when `DiagnosticMonitor.Start()` is invoked.

How it works...

In steps 1 and 2, we ensure that the `DiagnosticMonitorTraceListener` is added to the collection of trace listeners for the web role or worker role.

In steps 3 through 5, we see how to write messages to the trace listener.

In step 6, we ensure that the Diagnostic Agent has been configured to persist the messages to the storage service. Note that they can also be persisted through an on-demand transfer. This configuration is described in the *Initializing the configuration of Windows Azure Diagnostics* recipe in this chapter.

There's more...

The Windows Azure SDK v1.3 introduced full IIS in place of the hosted web core used previously for web roles. With full IIS, the web role entry point and IIS are hosted in separate processes. Consequently, the trace listener must be configured separately for each process. The configuration using `web.config` configures the trace listener for IIS, not the web role entry point. Note that Windows Azure Diagnostics needs to be configured only once in each role, even though the trace listener is configured separately in both the web role entry point and in IIS.

The web role entry point runs under a process named `WaIISHost.exe`. Consequently, one solution is to create a special configuration file for this process named `WaIISHost.exe.config` and add the trace listener configuration to it.

A more convenient solution is to add the `DiagnosticMonitorTraceListener` trace listener programmatically to the list of trace listeners for the web role entry point. The following demonstrates an overridden `OnStart()` method in a web role entry point modified to add the trace listener and write an informational message:

```
public override bool OnStart()
{
    System.Diagnostics.Trace.Listeners.Add(new Microsoft.WindowsAzure.
        Diagnostics.DiagnosticMonitorTraceListener());
    System.Diagnostics.Trace.AutoFlush = true;
    System.Diagnostics.Trace.TraceInformation("Information");

    return base.OnStart();
}
```

The `AutoFlush` property is set to `true` to indicate that messages should be flushed through the trace listener as soon as they are written.

See also

A more sophisticated way to trace messages is to use trace sources and trace switches to control the capture of messages. Typically, this control can be configured through the `app.config` file for an application. This file can only be modified in a hosted service by redeploying the service package rendering the technique less useful. Mike Kelly published an article, *Take Control of Logging and Tracing in Windows Azure*, in the June 2010 issue of MSDN Magazine that shows how to use the service configuration file to handle this configuration (http://msdn.microsoft.com/en-us/magazine/ff714589.aspx)

Performing an on-demand transfer

The Windows Azure Diagnostics configuration file specifies a schedule in which the various data buffers are persisted to the Windows Azure Storage Service. The on-demand transfer capability in Windows Azure Diagnostics allows a transfer to be requested outside this schedule. This is useful if a problem occurs with an instance and it becomes necessary to look at the captured logs before the next scheduled transfer.

An on-demand transfer is requested for a specific data buffer in a specific instance. This request is inserted into the diagnostics configuration for the instance stored in a blob in `wad-control-container`. This is an asynchronous operation whose completion is indicated by the insertion of a message in a specified notification queue. The on-demand transfer is configured using an `OnDemandTransferOptions` instance that specifies the `DateTime` range for the transfer, a `LogLevelFilter` that filters the data to be transferred, and the name of the notification queue. The `RoleInstanceDiagnosticeManager.BeginOnDemandTransfer()` method is used to request the on-demand transfer with the configured options for the specified data buffer.

Following the completion of an on-demand transfer, the request must be removed from the diagnostics configuration for the instance by using the `RoleInstanceDiagnosticManager.EndOnDemandTransfer()` method. The completion message in the notification queue should also be removed. The `GetActiveTransfers()` and `CancelOnDemandTransfers()` methods of the `RoleInstanceDiagnosticManager` class can be used to enumerate and cancel active on-demand transfers. Note that it is not possible to modify the diagnostics configuration for the instance if there is a current request for an on-demand transfer, even if the transfer has completed.

Note that requesting an on-demand transfer does not require a direct connection with the hosted service. The request merely modifies the diagnostic configuration for the instance. This change is then picked up when the Diagnostic Agent on the instance next polls the diagnostic configuration for the instance. The default value for this polling interval is 1 minute. This means that a request for an on-demand transfer needs to be authenticated only against the storage service account containing the diagnostic configuration for the hosted service.

In this recipe, we will learn how to request an on-demand transfer and clean up after it completes.

How to do it...

We are going to see how to request an on-demand transfer and clean up after it completes. We do this as follows:

1. Use Visual Studio to create a WPF project.

2. Add the following assembly references to the project:

   ```
   Microsoft.WindowsAzure.Diagnostics.dll
   Microsoft.WindowsAzure.ServiceRuntime.dll
   Microsoft.WindowsAzure.StorageClient.dll
   System.configuration.dll
   ```

3. Add a class named `OnDemandTransferExample` to the project.

4. Add the following `using` statements to the class:

   ```
   using Microsoft.WindowsAzure;
   using Microsoft.WindowsAzure.Diagnostics;
   using Microsoft.WindowsAzure.Diagnostics.Management;
   using Microsoft.WindowsAzure.ServiceRuntime;
   using Microsoft.WindowsAzure.StorageClient;
   using System.Configuration;
   ```

5. Add the following private member to the class:

   ```
   String wadNotificationQueueName = "wad-transfer-queue";
   ```

6. Add the following method, requesting an on-demand transfer, to the class:

   ```
   public void RequestOnDemandTransfer(
     String deploymentId, String roleName, String roleInstanceId)
   {
     CloudStorageAccount cloudStorageAccount =
       CloudStorageAccount.Parse(
       ConfigurationManager.AppSettings[
       "DiagnosticsConnectionString"]);

     OnDemandTransferOptions onDemandTransferOptions =
       new OnDemandTransferOptions()
     {
       From = DateTime.UtcNow.AddHours(-1),
       To = DateTime.UtcNow,
       LogLevelFilter =
         Microsoft.WindowsAzure.Diagnostics.LogLevel.Verbose,
       NotificationQueueName = wadNotificationQueueName
     };
   ```

```
    RoleInstanceDiagnosticManager ridm =
      cloudStorageAccount.CreateRoleInstanceDiagnosticManager(
      deploymentId, roleName, roleInstanceId);

    IDictionary<DataBufferName, OnDemandTransferInfo>
      activeTransfers = ridm.GetActiveTransfers();
    if (activeTransfers.Count == 0)
    {
      Guid onDemandTransferId = ridm.BeginOnDemandTransfer(
        DataBufferName.PerformanceCounters,
        onDemandTransferOptions);
    }
  }
}
```

7. Add the following method, cleaning up after an on-demand transfer, to the class:

```
public void CleanupOnDemandTransfers()
{
    CloudStorageAccount cloudStorageAccount =
      CloudStorageAccount.Parse(
      ConfigurationManager.AppSettings[
      "DiagnosticsConnectionString"]);
    CloudQueueClient cloudQueueClient =
      cloudStorageAccount.CreateCloudQueueClient();

    CloudQueue cloudQueue = cloudQueueClient.GetQueueReference(
      wadNotificationQueueName);
    CloudQueueMessage cloudQueueMessage;
    while ((cloudQueueMessage =  cloudQueue.GetMessage())
      != null)
    {
      OnDemandTransferInfo onDemandTransferInfo =
        OnDemandTransferInfo.FromQueueMessage(
        cloudQueueMessage);
      String deploymentId = onDemandTransferInfo.DeploymentId;
      String roleName = onDemandTransferInfo.RoleName;
      String roleInstanceId =
        onDemandTransferInfo.RoleInstanceId;
      Guid requestId = onDemandTransferInfo.RequestId;

      RoleInstanceDiagnosticManager ridm =
      cloudStorageAccount.CreateRoleInstanceDiagnosticManager(
        deploymentId, roleName, roleInstanceId);
      Boolean result = ridm.EndOnDemandTransfer(requestId);
      cloudQueue.DeleteMessage(cloudQueueMessage);
    }
}
```

8. Add the following `Grid` declaration to the `Window` element of `MainWindow.xaml`:

```xml
<Grid>
  <Label Content="DeploymentId:" Height="28"
    HorizontalAlignment="Left"
    VerticalAlignment="Top" Margin="30,60,0,0"
    Name="label1"  />
  <Label Content="Role name:" Height="28"
    HorizontalAlignment="Left" VerticalAlignment="Top"
    Margin="30,110,0,0" Name="label2" />
  <Label Content="Instance Id:" Height="28"
    HorizontalAlignment="Left" VerticalAlignment="Top"
    Margin="30,160,0,0" Name="label3" />
  <TextBox HorizontalAlignment="Left" VerticalAlignment="Top"
    Margin="120,60,0,0" Name="DeploymentId" Height="23"
    Width="120" Text="24447326eed3475ca58d01c223efb778" />
  <TextBox HorizontalAlignment="Left" VerticalAlignment="Top"
    Margin="120,110,0,0" Width="120"  Name="RoleName"
    Text="WebRole1" />
  <TextBox Height="23" HorizontalAlignment="Left"
    VerticalAlignment="Top" Margin="120,160,0,0" Width="120"
    Name="InstanceId" Text="WebRole1_IN_0" />
  <Button Content="Request On-Demand Transfer" Height="23"
    HorizontalAlignment="Left" VerticalAlignment="Top"
    Margin="60,220,0,0" Width="175" Name="RequestTransfer"
    Click="RequestTransfer_Click" />
  <Button Content="Cleanup On-Demand Transfers" Height="23"
    HorizontalAlignment="Left" VerticalAlignment="Top"
    Margin="300,220,0,0" Width="175" Name="CleanupTransfers"
    Click="CleanupTransfers_Click" />
</Grid>
```

9. Add the following event handler to `MainWindow.xaml.cs`:

```csharp
private void RequestTransfer_Click(
  object sender, RoutedEventArgs e)
{
    String deploymentId = DeploymentId.Text;
    String roleName = RoleName.Text;
    String roleInstanceId = InstanceId.Text;

    OnDemandTransferExample example =
      new OnDemandTransferExample();
    example.RequestOnDemandTransfer(
      deploymentId, roleName, roleInstanceId);
}
```

10. Add the following event handler to `MainWindow.xaml.cs`:

```
private void CleanupTransfers_Click(
  object sender, RoutedEventArgs e)
{
    OnDemandTransferExample example =
      new OnDemandTransferExample();
    example.CleanupOnDemandTransfers();
}
```

11. Add the following to the `configuration` element of `app.config`:

```
<appSettings>
    <add key="DiagnosticsConnectionString"
      value="DefaultEndpointsProtocol=https;AccountName={
      ACCOUNT_NAME};AccountKey={ACCESS_KEY}"/>
</appSettings>
```

How it works...

We create a WPF project in step 1 and add the required assembly references in step 2.

We set up the `OnDemandTransferExample` class in steps 3 and 4. We add a private member to hold the name of the Windows Azure Diagnostics notification queue in step 5.

In step 6, we add a method requesting an on-demand transfer. We create an `OnDemandTransferOptions` object configuring an on-demand transfer for data captured in the last hour. We provide the name of the notification queue Windows Azure Diagnostics inserts a message indicating the completion of the transfer. We use the deployment information captured in the UI to create a `RoleInstanceDiagnosticManager` instance. If there are no active on-demand transfers, then we request an on-demand transfer for the performance counters data buffer.

In step 7, we add a method cleaning up after an on-demand transfer. We create a `CloudStorageAccount` object that we use to create the `CloudQueueClient` object with which we access to the notification queue. We then retrieve the transfer-completion messages in the notification queue. For each transfer-completion message found, we create an `OnDemandTransferInfo` object describing the `deploymentID`, `roleName`, `instanceId`, and `requestId` of a completed on-demand transfer. We use the `requestId` to end the transfer and remove it from the diagnostics configuration for the instance allowing on-demand transfers to be requested. Finally, we remove the notification message from the notification queue.

In step 8, we add the UI used to capture the deployment ID, role name, and instance ID used to request the on-demand transfer. We can get this information from the Windows Azure Portal or the Compute Emulator UI. This information is not needed for cleaning up on-demand transfers, which uses the transfer-completion messages in the notification queue.

In steps 9 and 10, we add the event handlers for the **Request On-Demand Transfer** and **Cleanup On-Demand Transfers** buttons in the UI. These methods forward the requests to the methods we added in steps 6 and 7.

In step 11, we add the `DiagnosticsConnectionString` to the `app.config` file. This contains the connection string used to interact with the Windows Azure Diagnostics configuration. We must replace `{ACCOUNT_NAME}` and `{ACCESS_KEY}` with the storage service account name and access key for the storage account in which the Windows Azure Diagnostics configuration is located.

Implementing custom logging

Windows Azure Diagnostics can be used to persist third-party log files in the same way it persists IIS logs, failed request logs, and crash dumps. These are all configured through the directories data buffer.

The directories data buffer comprises a set of data sources. These are instances of the `DirectoryConfiguration` class that exposes the following properties:

- ▶ Container
- ▶ DirectoryQuotaInMB
- ▶ Path

A data source maps a path in the local file system with a container in the Windows Azure Blob Service. The `DirectoryQuotaInMB` reserves a specified amount of space in local storage for the specified data source. A scheduled transfer period is specified at the level of the directories data buffer. The Diagnostics Agent persists to the configured container any files added to the specified path since the last transfer.

In this recipe, we will learn how to use Windows Azure Diagnostics to persist custom logs to the Windows Azure Blob Service.

How to do it...

We are going to see how to configure custom logging with Windows Azure Diagnostics. We do this as follows:

1. Use Visual Studio to create an empty cloud project.
2. Add a worker role to the project (accept default name of `WorkerRole1`).
3. Add the following local storage definition, as a child of the `WorkerRole` element, to `ServiceDefinition.csdef`:

```
<LocalResources>
  <LocalStorage name="CustomLoggingLocation"
     sizeInMB="100" cleanOnRoleRecycle="false"/>
</LocalResources>
```

4. Add the following `using` statement to `WorkerRole.cs`:

```
using System.IO;
```

5. Add the following private member to the `WorkerRole` class:

```
private String localResourceName = "CustomLoggingLocation";
```

6. In the `WorkerRole` class, replace the `Run()` method with the following:

```
public override void Run()
{
    Trace.WriteLine("WorkerRole1 entry point called",
      "Information");

    while (true)
    {
      Thread.Sleep(10000);
      Trace.WriteLine("Working", "Information");

      CreateLogFile();
    }
}
```

7. In the `WorkerRole` class, replace `OnStart()` with the following:

```
public override bool OnStart()
{
    ServicePointManager.DefaultConnectionLimit = 12;

    InitializeWadConfiguration();

    return base.OnStart();
}
```

8. Add the following method, configuring Windows Azure Diagnostics, to the `WorkerRole` class:

```
private void InitializeWadConfiguration()
{
    String wadConnectionString =
      "Microsoft.WindowsAzure.Plugins.Diagnostics.ConnectionString";
    String customContainerName = "wad-custom-container";

    DiagnosticMonitorConfiguration dmc =
      DiagnosticMonitor.GetDefaultInitialConfiguration();

    LocalResource localResource =
      RoleEnvironment.GetLocalResource(localResourceName);
    String logPath =
      Path.Combine(localResource.RootPath, "Logs");
```

```
DirectoryConfiguration directoryConfiguration =
  new DirectoryConfiguration()
{
    Container = customContainerName,
    DirectoryQuotaInMB =
      localResource.MaximumSizeInMegabytes,
    Path = logPath
};
dmc.Directories.DataSources.Add(directoryConfiguration);
dmc.Directories.ScheduledTransferPeriod =
  TimeSpan.FromHours(1);

dmc.Logs.BufferQuotaInMB = 100;
dmc.Logs.ScheduledTransferPeriod = TimeSpan.FromHours(1);
dmc.Logs.ScheduledTransferLogLevelFilter =
  LogLevel.Verbose;

CloudStorageAccount cloudStorageAccount =
  CloudStorageAccount.Parse(
    RoleEnvironment.GetConfigurationSettingValue(
      wadConnectionString));
DiagnosticMonitor.Start(wadConnectionString, dmc);
}
```

9. Add the following method, writing a file in the custom logging directory, to the WorkerRole class:

```
private void CreateLogFile()
{
    LocalResource localResource =
      RoleEnvironment.GetLocalResource(localResourceName);
    String logPath =
      Path.Combine(localResource.RootPath, "Logs");
    String fileName =
      Path.Combine(logPath, Path.GetRandomFileName());

    if (!Directory.Exists(logPath))
    {
        Directory.CreateDirectory(logPath);
    }

    using (StreamWriter streamWriter =
      new StreamWriter(fileName))
    {
        streamWriter.Write("If we shadows have offended");
    }
}
```

How it works...

In steps 1 and 2, we create a cloud project with a worker role.

In step 3, we add the definition of the local storage, used for the custom log files, to the service definition file for the hosted service. We provide a name by which it can be referenced and a size. We also specify that the content of local storage should be preserved through an instance recycle.

In step 4, we add the `using` statement required for file handling. In step 5, we add a private member to store the name of the local resource. In step 6, we replace the existing `Run()` method with one that creates a log file every 10 seconds to simulate actual logging. In step 7, we replace the `OnStart()` method with one that configures Windows Azure Diagnostics.

In step 8, we configure Windows Azure Diagnostics to support custom logging. We create the full path to the directory where we store the logs—the `Logs` directory under the `RootPath` for the local storage resource. Then, we create and configure the `DirectoryConfiguration` data source we use to map the log directory to the container in the Blob service into which the Diagnostics Agent transfers the files as blobs. We then add the data source to the `Directories` data buffer and specify a scheduled transfer period. We also configure the `Logs` data buffer. Finally, we invoke `Start()` to update the configuration of Windows Azure Diagnostics.

In step 9, we add a simple method that writes a randomly named file to the custom logging directory.

Accessing data persisted to Windows Azure Storage

Windows Azure Diagnostics captures diagnostic information for an instance then persists it to the Windows Azure Storage Service. The persistence location depends on the data buffer.

The `Directories` data buffer is configured as a set of data sources each of which maps a path on the local file system with a container in the Windows Azure Blob Service. The Diagnostics Agent persists files in that path as blobs in the configured container. Note that the Diagnostics Agent inserts a record in the `WADDirectoriesTable` each time it persists a file to a container.

The Diagnostics Agent persists the data in the other data buffers as records in the Windows Azure Table Service. The following tables are used:

Records	Table
Diagnostic Infrastructure Logs	WADDiagnosticInfrastructureLogsTable
Performance Counters	WADPerformanceCountersTable
Windows Azure Logs	WADLogsTable
Windows Event Logs	WADWindowsEventLogsTable

The tables are partitioned by minute. Specifically, when a record is inserted in a table, the `PartitionKey` is set to the `Tick` count of the current UTC time with the seconds discarded, with the entire value prepended by a `0`. Discarding the seconds has the effect of setting the last 8 characters of the `PartitionKey` to `0`. The `RowKey` combines the deployment ID, the role name, and the instance ID along with a key to ensure uniqueness. The `Timestamp` represents the time the event was inserted in the table.

While each table contains some properties specific to the data being logged, all of them contain the following properties:

- `EventTickCount`
- `DeploymentId`
- `Role`
- `RoleInstance`

The `EventTickCount` is an `Int64` representing the time the event was generated, to an accuracy of 100 nanoseconds. The `DeploymentId` identifies the specific deployment, while the `Role` and `RoleInstance` specify the role instance which generated the event.

The `WADPerformanceCountersTable`, for example, contains the following additional properties:

- `CounterName`
- `CounterValue`

The Windows Azure Diagnostics tables can be queried just like any other table in the Table service. A model class derived from `TableServiceEntity` can be created from the properties of interest. As the only index on a table is on `PartitionKey` and `RowKey`, it is important that the `PartitionKey`, rather than the `Timestamp` or `EventTickCount`, be used for time-dependent queries. An appropriate value for the `PartitionKey` can be created from a `DateTime`. Unless strict equality is desired, it is not necessary to mimic the construction of the `PartitionKey` by setting the last eight characters to `0`.

In this recipe, we will learn how to query data that Windows Azure Diagnostics has persisted to the Table service.

How to do it...

We are going to see how to query performance counter data that Windows Azure Diagnostics persisted in the `WADPerformanceCountersTable` table. We do this as follows:

1. Use Visual Studio to create an empty cloud project.
2. Add an ASP.NET web role to the project (accept default name of `WebRole1`).
3. Add the following assembly reference to the project:

   ```
   System.Data.Services.Client
   ```

4. In the `WebRole` class, replace `OnStart()` with the following:

```
public override bool OnStart()
{
    ConfigureDiagnostics();

    return base.OnStart();
}
```

5. Add the following method, configuring Windows Azure Diagnostics, to the `WebRole` class:

```
private void ConfigureDiagnostics()
{
    String wadConnectionString =
      "Microsoft.WindowsAzure.Plugins.Diagnostics.ConnectionString";

    CloudStorageAccount cloudStorageAccount =
      CloudStorageAccount.Parse(
        RoleEnvironment.GetConfigurationSettingValue(
          wadConnectionString));

    DiagnosticMonitorConfiguration dmc =
      DiagnosticMonitor.GetDefaultInitialConfiguration();

    PerformanceCounterConfiguration pmc =
      new PerformanceCounterConfiguration()
    {
      CounterSpecifier =
        @"\Processor(_Total)\% Processor Time",
      SampleRate = System.TimeSpan.FromSeconds(10)
    };
    dmc.PerformanceCounters.DataSources.Add( pmc);
    dmc.PerformanceCounters.BufferQuotaInMB = 100;
    dmc.PerformanceCounters.ScheduledTransferPeriod =
      TimeSpan.FromMinutes(1);

    DiagnosticMonitor.Start(cloudStorageAccount, dmc);
}
```

6. In the `Default.aspx` file, replace the `asp:Content` element named `BodyContent` with the following:

```
<asp:Content ID="BodyContent" runat="server"
   ContentPlaceHolderID="MainContent">
    <asp:GridView ID="GridView1" runat="server"
       AutoGenerateColumns="false">
        <Columns>
            <asp:BoundField DataField="RoleInstance"
               HeaderText="Role Instance" />
            <asp:BoundField DataField="CounterName"
               HeaderText="Counter Name" />
```

```
        <asp:BoundField DataField="CounterValue"
           HeaderText="Counter Value" />
        <asp:BoundField DataField="EventDateTime"
           HeaderText="Event DateTime" />
    </Columns>
  </asp:GridView>
</asp:Content>
```

7. Add the following `using` statements to the `Default.aspx.cs` file:

```
using Microsoft.WindowsAzure;
using Microsoft.WindowsAzure.ServiceRuntime;
using Microsoft.WindowsAzure.StorageClient;
```

8. In the `Default.aspx.cs` file, add the following private member to the `_Default` class:

```
private String wadConnectionString = "Microsoft.WindowsAzure.
Plugins.Diagnostics.ConnectionString";
```

9. In the `Default.aspx.cs` file, replace `Page_Load()` with the following:

```
protected void Page_Load(object sender, EventArgs e)
{
   CloudStorageAccount cloudStorageAccount =
     CloudStorageAccount.Parse(
       RoleEnvironment.GetConfigurationSettingValue(
         wadConnectionString));
   CloudTableClient cloudTableClient =
     cloudStorageAccount.CreateCloudTableClient();

   DateTime now = DateTime.UtcNow;
   DateTime fiveMinutesAgo = now.AddMinutes(-5);
   String partitionKeyNow =
     String.Format("0{0}", now.Ticks.ToString());
   String partitionKey5MinutesAgo =
     String.Format("0{0}", fiveMinutesAgo.Ticks.ToString());

   TableServiceContext tableServiceContext =
     cloudTableClient.GetDataServiceContext();
   CloudTableQuery<WadPerformanceCountersTable>
     cloudTableQuery =
     (from entity in tableServiceContext.CreateQuery<WadPerformanc
      eCountersTable>(WadPerformanceCountersTable.Name)
     where entity.PartitionKey.CompareTo(partitionKeyNow) < 0
     && entity.PartitionKey.CompareTo(partitionKey5MinutesAgo)
     > 0
     select entity).AsTableServiceQuery();

   GridView1.DataSource = cloudTableQuery;
   GridView1.DataBind();
}
```

10. Add a model class to the project and name it `WadPerformanceCountersTable`.

11. Replace the declaration of the `WadPerformanceCountersTable` class with the following:

```
public class WadPerformanceCountersTable
{
    public static String Name = "WadPerformanceCountersTable";

    public String PartitionKey { get; set; }
    public String RowKey { get; set; }
    public Int64 EventTickCount { get; set; }
    public String DeploymentId { get; set; }
    public String Role { get; set; }
    public String RoleInstance { get; set; }
    public String CounterName { get; set; }
    public Double CounterValue { get; set; }

    public DateTime EventDateTime
    {
        get { return new DateTime(EventTickCount); }
    }
}
```

12. Build the project and run it in the Windows Azure Compute Emulator.

13. Refresh the `Default.aspx` page several times over the next few minutes until the page displays some performance counter data.

How it works...

In steps 1 and 2, we create a cloud project with a worker role. We add the required assembly reference in step 3.

In steps 4 and 5, we configure Windows Azure Diagnostics. Specifically, we create a `PerformanceCounterConfiguration` instance for a performance counter for total processor time with a sampling periodicity of 10 seconds. We add the `PerformanceCounterConfiguration` to the Windows Azure Diagnostics `PerformanceCounters` data buffer specifying that it should be persisted once a minute. Finally, we update Windows Azure Diagnostics with this configuration.

In step 6, we add a `GridView` to contain the performance counter data we retrieve from the Windows Azure Diagnostics tables in the Windows Azure Table Service.

In steps 7 through 9, we modify the `Default.aspx.cs` to retrieve the data we display in the `GridView`. In step 7, we add the required using statements. In step 8, we add a private member to store the name of the connection string setting in the service configuration file, `ServiceConfiguration.cscfg`. In step 9, we initialize the `CloudStorageAccount` and `CloudTableClient` objects we use to access the storage service. We initialize two `String` objects representing the `PartitionKey` representation of the UTC time now and five minutes ago. Note that we prepend the String objects with a `0`, as required by the format used in the Windows Azure Diagnostics table. We then create a `CloudTableQuery` object to query the `WADPerformanceCountersTable` and retrieve data from the last 5 minutes, and set the query as a `DataSource` for the `GridView` and bind the data to the `GridView`.

In steps 10 and 11, we create the model class we use to contain the results of querying the `WadPerformanceCountersTable` that Windows Azure Diagnostics persists diagnostics data in.

In steps 12 and 13, we run the web role and wait for Windows Azure Diagnostics to persist data to the Storage Emulator. This data is then displayed in the `Default.aspx` web page.

Using the Windows Azure Platform PowerShell cmdlets to configure Windows Azure Diagnostics

The Windows Azure team has created a set of PowerShell cmdlets (the Windows Azure Platform PowerShell cmdlets) that can be used to manage Windows Azure hosted services and storage. These cmdlets primarily wrap the Windows Azure Service Management REST API. However, some of the cmdlets use the Windows Azure Diagnostics API to support the remote configuration of Windows Azure Diagnostics.

The cmdlets provide get and set operations for each of the diagnostics data buffers. They also provide operations to request and end an on-demand transfer.

In this recipe, we will learn how to use the Windows Azure Platform PowerShell cmdlets to configure Windows Azure Diagnostics.

Getting ready

If necessary, we can download PowerShell 2 from the Microsoft download center at the following URL:

```
http://www.microsoft.com/download/en/details.aspx?id=11829
```

We need to download and install the Windows Azure Platform PowerShell Cmdlets. The package with the cmdlets can be downloaded from the following URL:

```
http://wappowershell.codeplex.com/
```

Once the package has been downloaded, the cmdlets need to be built and installed. The installed package contains a `StartHere` file explaining the process.

How to do it...

We are going to modify the configuration of the Windows Azure basic logs data buffer. We do this as follows:

1. Create a PowerShell script named `Set-WindowsAzureBasicLogs.ps1` and insert the following text:

```
$account = "{STORAGE_ACCOUNT}"
$key = "{STORAGE_ACCOUNT_KEY}"
$deploymentId = "{DEPLOYMENT_ID}"
$roleName = "{WEB_ROLE_NAME}"
$bufferQuotaInMB = 100
$transferPeriod = 60
$logLevelFilter = 5

Add-PSSnapin AzureManagementToolsSnapIn

Set-WindowsAzureLog -BufferQuotaInMB $bufferQuotaInMB
-TransferPeriod $transferPeriod
-LogLevelFilter $logLevelFilter
-DeploymentId $deploymentId -RoleName $roleName
-StorageAccountname $account -StorageAccountKey $key
```

2. Launch PowerShell.
3. Navigate to the directory containing `Set-WindowsAzureBasicLogs.ps1`.
4. Invoke the cmdlet to modify the configuration:

```
.\SetWindowsAzureLogs.ps1
```

How it works...

In step 1, we create the PowerShell script that changes the configuration of the Windows Azure Diagnostics basic logs data buffer. This is configured in code through the `BasicLogsBufferConfiguration` class. In the diagnostics configuration for an instance stored in *wad-control-container*, it is specified in the `Logs` element. In the Windows Azure Service Management cmdlets, it is specified by `WindowsAzureLog`.

In the script, we must provide actual values for the {STORAGE_ACCOUNT}, {STORAGE_ACCOUNT_KEY}, {DEPLOYMENT_ID}, and {WEB_ROLE_NAME}. Note that we don't need to specify the instance ID, as the PowerShell cmdlet updates all instances of the role.

We add the AzureManagementToolsSnapin to make the cmdlets available. The final action of step 1 is the actual invocation of the cmdlet. We provide desired values for the size of the data buffer, the scheduled transfer period, and the log-level filter. Verbose has a value of 5, Information has a value of 4, and so on.

In steps 2 and 3, we set up PowerShell.

In step 4, we invoke our script using a . \ syntax to demonstrate that we want to invoke an unsigned script in the current directory.

Azure Management cmdlets

Cerebrata has released a commercially supported set of Windows Azure Management Cmdlets that are more extensive than the Windows Azure Platform PowerShell cmdlets. Using the Cerebrata version, the Windows Azure Diagnostics basic logs buffer can be configured using the following script:

```
$account = "{STORAGE_ACCOUNT}"
$key = "{STORAGE_ACCOUNT_KEY}"
$deploymentId = "{DEPLOYMENT_ID}"
$roleName = "{WEB_ROLE_NAME}"
$instanceId = "{INSTANCE_ID}";
$bufferQuotaInMB = 100
$scheduledTransferPeriod = 60
$logLevelFilter = "Verbose"

Add-PSSnapin AzureManagementCmdletsSnapIn

Set-WindowsAzureLog -BufferQuotaInMB $bufferQuotaInMB -
ScheduledTransferPeriod $scheduledTransferPeriod -LogLevelFilter
$logLevelFilter -DeploymentId $deploymentId -RoleName $roleName -
InstanceId $instanceId -AccountName $account -AccountKey $key
```

In the script, we must provide actual values for {STORAGE_ACCOUNT}, {STORAGE_ACCOUNT_KEY}, {DEPLOYMENT_ID}, {WEB_ROLE_NAME}, and {INSTANCE_ID}. Note that the Cerebrata cmdlet updates the diagnostic configuration for an individual instance whereas the Windows Azure team version updates the diagnostic configuration for all instances. The Cerebrata version also provides a more detailed feedback while executing.

Using IntelliTrace to diagnose problems with a hosted service

Windows Azure Diagnostics provides non-intrusive support for diagnosing problems with a Windows Azure hosted service. This non-intrusion is vital in a production service. However, when developing a hosted service, it may be worthwhile to get access to additional diagnostics information even at the cost of intruding on the service.

The Visual Studio 2010 Ultimate Edition supports the use of IntelliTrace with an application deployed to the cloud. This can be particularly helpful when dealing with problems, such as missing assemblies. It also allows for the easy identification and diagnosis of exceptions. Note that IntelliTrace has a significant impact on the performance of a hosted service. Consequently, it should never be used in a production environment and, in practice, should only be used when needed during development.

IntelliTrace is configured when the application package is published. This configuration includes specifying the events to trace and identifying the modules and processes for which IntelliTrace should not capture data. For example, the Storage Client module is removed by default from IntelliTrace since otherwise, storage exceptions could occur due to timeouts.

Once the application package has been deployed, the Windows Azure Compute node in the Visual Studio Server Explorer indicates the Windows Azure hosted service, roles, and instances which are capturing IntelliTrace data. From the instance level in this node, a request can be made to download the current IntelliTrace log. This lists:

- Threads
- Exceptions
- System info
- Modules

The threads section provides information about when particular threads were running. The exceptions list specifies the exceptions that occurred, and provides the call stack when they occurred. The system info section provides general information about the instance, such as number of processors and total memory. The modules section lists the loaded assemblies.

The IntelliTrace logs will probably survive an instance crash, but they will not survive if the virtual machine is moved due to excessive failure. The instance must be running for Visual Studio to be able to download the IntelliTrace logs.

In this recipe, we will learn how to use IntelliTrace to identify problems with an application deployed to a hosted service in the cloud.

Getting ready

Only Visual Studio Ultimate Edition supports the use of IntelliTrace with an application deployed to a hosted service in the cloud.

How to do it...

We are going to use IntelliTrace to investigate an application deployed to a hosted service in the cloud. We do this as follows:

The first few steps occur before the application package is deployed to the cloud:

1. Use Visual Studio 2010 Ultimate Edition to build a Windows Azure project.
2. Right click on the Solution and select **Publish...**.
3. Select **Enable IntelliTrace for .Net 4 roles**.
4. Click on **Settings...** and make any changes desired to the IntelliTrace settings for modules excluded, and so on.
5. Click on **OK** to continue the deployment of the application package.

The remaining steps occur after the package has been deployed and the hosted service is in the Ready (that is, running) state:

1. Open the Server Explorer in Visual Studio.
2. On the Windows Azure Compute node, right click on an instance node and select **View IntelliTrace logs**.
3. Investigate the downloaded logs, looking at exceptions and their call stacks, and so on.
4. Right click on individual lines of code in a code file and select **Search For This Line In IntelliTrace**.
5. Select one of the located uses and step through the code from the line.

How it works...

Steps 1 through 5 are a normal application package deployment except for the IntelliTrace configuration.

In steps 6 and 7, we use Server Explorer to access and download the IntelliTrace logs. Note that we can refresh the logs through additional requests to **View IntelliTrace logs**.

In steps 8 through 10, we look at various aspects of the downloaded IntelliTrace logs.

7
Managing Hosted Services with the Service Management API

In this chapter, we will cover:

- ▶ Creating a Windows Azure hosted service
- ▶ Deploying an application into a hosted service
- ▶ Upgrading an application deployed to a hosted service
- ▶ Retrieving the properties of a hosted service
- ▶ Autoscaling with the Windows Azure Service Management REST API
- ▶ Using the Windows Azure Platform PowerShell Cmdlets

Introduction

The Windows Azure Portal provides a convenient and easy-to-use way of managing the hosted services and storage account in a Windows Azure subscription, as well as any deployments into these hosted services. The Windows Azure Service Management REST API provides a programmatic way of managing the hosted services and storage accounts in a Windows Azure subscription, as well as any deployments into these hosted services. These techniques are complementary and, indeed, it is possible to use the Service Management API to develop an application that provides nearly all the features of the Windows Azure Portal.

The Service Management API provides almost complete control over the hosted services and storage accounts contained in a Windows Azure subscription. All operations using this API must be authenticated using an X.509 management certificate. We see how to do this in the *Authenticating against the Windows Azure Service Management REST API* recipe in *Chapter 1, Controlling Access in the Windows Azure Platform*.

In Windows Azure, a hosted service is an administrative and security boundary for an application. A hosted service specifies a name for the application, as well as specifying a Windows Azure datacenter or affinity group into which the application is deployed. In the *Creating a Windows Azure hosted service* recipe, we see how to use the Service Management API to create a hosted service.

A hosted service has no features or functions until an application is deployed into it. An application is deployed by specifying a deployment slot, either production or staging, and by providing the application package containing the code, as well as the service configuration file used to configure the application. We see how to do this using the Service Management API in the *Deploying an application into a hosted service* recipe.

Once an application has been deployed, it probably has to be upgraded occasionally. This requires the provision of a new application package and service configuration file. We see how to do this using the Service Management API in the *Upgrading an application deployed to a hosted service* recipe.

A hosted service has various properties defining it as do the applications deployed into it. There could, after all, be separate applications deployed into each of the production and staging slots. In the *Retrieving the properties of a hosted service* recipe, we see how to use the Service Management API to get these properties.

An application deployed as a hosted service in Windows Azure can use the Service Management API to modify itself while running. Specifically, an application can autoscale by varying the number of role instances to match anticipated demand. We see how to do this in the *Autoscaling with the Windows Azure Service Management REST API* recipe.

We can use the Service Management API to develop our own management applications. Alternatively, we can use one of the PowerShell cmdlets libraries that have already been developed using the API. Both the Windows Azure team and Cerebrata have developed such libraries. We see how to use them in the *Using the Windows Azure Platform PowerShell Cmdlets* recipe.

Creating a Windows Azure hosted service

A hosted service is the administrative and security boundary for an application deployed to Windows Azure. The hosted service specifies the service name, a label, and either the Windows Azure datacenter location or the affinity group into which the application is to be deployed. These cannot be changed once the hosted service is created. The service name is the subdomain under `cloudapp.net` used by the application, and the label is a human-readable name used to identify the hosted service on the Windows Azure Portal.

The Windows Azure Service Management REST API exposes a **create hosted service** operation. The REST endpoint for the **create hosted service** operation specifies the subscription ID under which the hosted service is to be created. The request requires a payload comprising an XML document containing the properties needed to define the hosted service, as well as various optional properties. The service name provided must be unique across all hosted services in Windows Azure, so there is a possibility that a valid **create hosted service** operation will fail with a 409 Conflict error if the provided service name is already in use. As the **create hosted service** operation is asynchronous, the response contains a request ID that can be passed into a **get operation status** operation to check the current status of the operation.

In this recipe, we will learn how to use the Service Management API to create a Windows Azure hosted service.

Getting ready

The recipes in this chapter use the `ServiceManagementOperation` utility class to invoke operations against the Windows Azure Service Management REST API. We implement this class as follows:

1. Add a class named `ServiceManagementOperation` to the project.

2. Add the following assembly reference to the project:

   ```
   System.Xml.Linq.dll
   ```

3. Add the following `using` statements to the top of the class file:

   ```
   using System.Security.Cryptography.X509Certificates;
   using System.Net;
   using System.Xml.Linq;
   using System.IO;
   ```

4. Add the following private members to the class:

   ```
   String thumbprint;
   String versionId = "2011-02-25";
   ```

5. Add the following constructor to the class:

```
public ServiceManagementOperation(String thumbprint)
{
    this.thumbprint = thumbprint;
}
```

6. Add the following method, retrieving an X.509 certificate from the certificate store, to the class:

```
private X509Certificate2 GetX509Certificate2(
    String thumbprint)
{
    X509Certificate2 x509Certificate2 = null;
    X509Store store =
        new X509Store("My", StoreLocation.LocalMachine);
    try
    {
        store.Open(OpenFlags.ReadOnly);
        X509Certificate2Collection x509Certificate2Collection =
            store.Certificates.Find(
                X509FindType.FindByThumbprint, thumbprint, false);
        x509Certificate2 = x509Certificate2Collection[0];
    }
    finally
    {
        store.Close();
    }
    return x509Certificate2;
}
```

7. Add the following method, creating an `HttpWebRequest`, to the class:

```
private HttpWebRequest CreateHttpWebRequest(
    Uri uri, String httpWebRequestMethod)
{
    X509Certificate2 x509Certificate2 =
        GetX509Certificate2(thumbprint);

    HttpWebRequest httpWebRequest =
        (HttpWebRequest)HttpWebRequest.Create(uri);
    httpWebRequest.Method = httpWebRequestMethod;
    httpWebRequest.Headers.Add("x-ms-version", versionId);
    httpWebRequest.ClientCertificates.Add(x509Certificate2);
    httpWebRequest.ContentType = "application/xml";
    return httpWebRequest;
}
```

8. Add the following method, invoking a GET operation on the Service Management API, to the class:

```
public XDocument Invoke(String uri)
{
    XDocument responsePayload;
    Uri operationUri = new Uri(uri);
    HttpWebRequest httpWebRequest =
        CreateHttpWebRequest(operationUri, "GET");
    using (HttpWebResponse response =
        (HttpWebResponse)httpWebRequest.GetResponse())
    {
        Stream responseStream = response.GetResponseStream();
        responsePayload = XDocument.Load(responseStream);
    }
    return responsePayload;
}
```

9. Add the following method, invoking a POST operation on the Service Management API, to the class:

```
public String Invoke(String uri, XDocument payload)
{
    Uri operationUri = new Uri(uri);
    HttpWebRequest httpWebRequest =
        CreateHttpWebRequest(operationUri, "POST");
    using (Stream requestStream =
        httpWebRequest.GetRequestStream())
    {
        using (StreamWriter streamWriter =
            new StreamWriter(requestStream,
                System.Text.UTF8Encoding.UTF8))
        {
            payload.Save(streamWriter,
                SaveOptions.DisableFormatting);
        }
    }

    String requestId;
    using (HttpWebResponse response =
        (HttpWebResponse)httpWebRequest.GetResponse())
    {
        requestId = response.Headers["x-ms-request-id"];
    }
    return requestId;
}
```

How it works...

In steps 1 through 3, we set up the class. In step 4, we add a version ID for service management operations. Note that Microsoft periodically releases new operations for which it provides a new version ID, which is usually applicable for operations added earlier. In step 4, we also add a private member for the X.509 certificate thumbprint that we initialize in the constructor we add in step 5.

In step 6, we open the Personal (My) certificate store on the local machine level and retrieve an X.509 certificate identified by thumbprint. If necessary, we can specify the current user level, instead of the local machine level, by using `StoreLocation.CurrentUser` instead of `StoreLocation.LocalMachine`.

In step 7, we create an `HttpWebRequest` with the desired HTTP method type, and add the X.509 certificate to it. We also add various headers including the required `x-ms-version`.

In step 8, we invoke a `GET` request against the Service Management API and load the response into an XML document which we then return. In step 9, we write an XML document, containing the payload, into the request stream for an `HttpWebRequest` and then invoke a `POST` request against the Service Management API. We extract the request ID from the response and return it.

How to do it...

We are now going to construct the payload required for the **create hosted service** operation, and then use it when we invoke the operation against the Windows Azure Service Management REST API. We do this as follows:

1. Add a new class named `CreateHostedServiceExample` to the WPF project.
2. If necessary, add the following assembly reference to the project:

   ```
   System.Xml.Linq.dll
   ```

3. Add the following `using` statement to the top of the class file:

   ```
   using System.Xml.Linq;
   ```

4. Add the following private members to the class:

   ```
   XNamespace wa =
       "http://schemas.microsoft.com/windowsazure";
   String createHostedServiceFormat =
   "https://management.core.windows.net/{0}/services/hostedservices";
   ```

5. Add the following method, creating a base-64 encoded string, to the class:

```
private String ConvertToBase64String(String value)
{
    Byte[] bytes = System.Text.Encoding.UTF8.GetBytes(value);
    String base64String = Convert.ToBase64String(bytes);
    return base64String;
}
```

6. Add the following method, creating the payload, to the class:

```
private XDocument CreatePayload(
  String serviceName, String label, String description,
  String location, String affinityGroup)
{
    String base64LabelName = ConvertToBase64String(label);

    XElement xServiceName =
      new XElement(wa + "ServiceName", serviceName);
    XElement xLabel =
      new XElement(wa + "Label", base64LabelName);
    XElement xDescription =
      new XElement(wa + "Description", description);
    XElement xLocation =
      new XElement(wa + "Location", location);
    XElement xAffinityGroup =
      new XElement(wa + "AffinityGroup", affinityGroup);
    XElement createHostedService =
      new XElement(wa +"CreateHostedService");

    createHostedService.Add(xServiceName);
    createHostedService.Add(xLabel);
    createHostedService.Add(xDescription);
    createHostedService.Add(xLocation);
    //createHostedService.Add(xAffinityGroup);
    XDocument payload = new XDocument();
    payload.Add(createHostedService);
    payload.Declaration =
      new XDeclaration("1.0", "UTF-8", "no");
    return payload;
}
```

7. Add the following method, invoking the create hosted service operation, to the class:

```
private String CreateHostedService(String subscriptionId,
   String thumbprint, String serviceName, String label,
   String description, String location, String affinityGroup)
{
   String uri =
     String.Format(createHostedServiceFormat, subscriptionId);

   XDocument payload = CreatePayload(serviceName, label,
     description, location, affinityGroup);
   ServiceManagementOperation operation =
     new ServiceManagementOperation(thumbprint);
   String requestId = operation.Invoke(uri, payload);
   return requestId;
}
```

8. Add the following method, invoking the methods added earlier, to the class:

```
public static void UseCreateHostedServiceExample()
{
   String subscriptionId = "{SUBSCRIPTION_ID}";
   String thumbprint = "{THUMBPRINT}";
   String serviceName = "{SERVICE_NAME}";
   String label = "{LABEL}";
   String description = "Newly created service";
   String location = "{LOCATION}";
   String affinityGroup = "{AFFINITY_GROUP}";
   CreateHostedServiceExample example =
     new CreateHostedServiceExample();
   String requestId = example.CreateHostedService(
     subscriptionId, thumbprint, serviceName, label,
     description, location, affinityGroup);
}
```

How it works...

In steps 1 through 3, we set up the class. In step 4, we add private members to define the XML namespace used in creating the payload and the String format used in generating the endpoint for the **create hosted service** operation. In step 5, we add a helper method to create a base-64 encoded copy of a String.

We create the payload in step 6 by creating an XElement instance for each of the required and optional properties, as well as the root element. We add each of these elements to the root element and then add this to an XML document. Note that we do not add an AffinityGroup element because we provide a Location element and only one of them should be provided.

In step 7, we use the `ServiceManagementOperation` utility class, described in the *Getting ready* section, to invoke the **create hosted service** operation on the Service Management API. The `Invoke()` method creates an `HttpWebRequest`, adds the required X.509 certificate and the payload, and then sends the request to **the create hosted services** endpoint. It then parses the response to retrieve the request ID which can be used to check the status of the asynchronous **create hosted services** operation.

In step 8, we add a method that invokes the methods added earlier. We need to provide the subscription ID for the Windows Azure subscription, a globally unique service name for the hosted service, and a label used to identify the hosted service in the Windows Azure Portal. The location must be one of the official location names for a Windows Azure datacenter, such as *North Central US*. Alternatively, we can provide the GUID identifier of an existing affinity group and swap the commenting out in the code, adding the `Location` and `AffinityGroup` elements in step 6. We see how to retrieve the list of locations and affinity groups in the *Locations and affinity groups* section of this recipe.

There's more...

Each Windows Azure subscription can create six hosted services. This is a soft limit that can be raised by requesting a quota increase from Windows Azure Support at the following URL:

`http://www.microsoft.com/windowsazure/support/`

There are also soft limits on the number of cores per subscription (20) and the number of Windows Azure storage accounts per subscription (5). These limits can also be increased by request to Windows Azure Support.

Locations and affinity groups

The list of locations and affinity groups can be retrieved using the **list locations** and **list affinity groups** operations respectively in the Service Management API. We see how to do this in the *Using the Windows Azure Platform PowerShell Cmdlets* recipe in this chapter.

As of this writing, the locations are:

- Anywhere US
- South Central US
- North Central US
- Anywhere Europe
- North Europe
- West Europe
- Anywhere Asia
- Southeast Asia
- East Asia

The affinity groups are specific to a subscription.

Deploying an application into a hosted service

An application is deployed into a Windows Azure hosted service to provide its features and functionality. The deployment comprises the package containing the code to be deployed into the instances of the roles in the application, as well as the service configuration file specifying the configuration for the application. Each deployment is into either the production or staging slot of the hosted service. The result of a deployment is the creation of all the roles and instances specified in the service configuration file. By default, these instances are initially in the stopped state.

The Windows Azure Service Management REST API exposes a **create deployment** operation. The REST endpoint for the **create deployment** operation specifies the subscription ID, the name of the hosted service, and the deployment slot into which the application is to be deployed. The operation requires a payload comprising an XML document specifying the Windows Azure blob containing the application package and a base-64 encoded version of the service configuration file. Each deployment has a name used to distinguish it from other deployments into the same-hosted service. As the **create deployment** operation is asynchronous, the response contains a request ID that can be passed into a **get operation status** operation to check the current status of the operation.

In this recipe, we will learn how to use the Windows Azure Service Management REST API to deploy an application into a hosted service.

How to do it...

We are going to construct the payload required for the **create deployment** operation and then use it when we invoke the operation against the Windows Azure Service Management REST API. Then, we invoke a **get operation status** operation to retrieve the status of the asynchronous **create deployment** operation. We do this as follows:

1. Add a new class named `CreateDeploymentExample` to the project.

2. If necessary, add the following assembly reference to the project:
   `System.Xml.Linq.dll`

3. Add the following `using` statements to the top of the class file:
   ```
   using System.Xml.Linq;
   using System.IO;
   ```

4. Add the following private members to the class:

```
XNamespace wa = "http://schemas.microsoft.com/windowsazure";
String createDeploymentFormat =
"https://management.core.windows.net/{0}/services/
hostedservices/{1}/deploymentslots/{2}";
String getOperationStatusFormat =
"https://management.core.windows.net/{0}/operations/{1}";
```

5. Add the following method, creating a base-64 encoded `String`, to the class:

```
private String ConvertToBase64String(String value)
{
    Byte[] bytes = System.Text.Encoding.UTF8.GetBytes(value);
    String base64String = Convert.ToBase64String(bytes);
    return base64String;
}
```

6. Add the following method, creating the payload, to the class:

```
private XDocument CreatePayload(
  String deploymentName, String packageUrl,
  String pathToConfigurationFile, String label)
{
    String configurationFile =
      File.ReadAllText(pathToConfigurationFile);
    String base64ConfigurationFile =
      ConvertToBase64String(configurationFile);

    String base64Label = ConvertToBase64String(label);

    XElement xName = new XElement(wa + "Name", deploymentName);
    XElement xPackageUrl =
      new XElement(wa + "PackageUrl", packageUrl);
    XElement xLabel = new XElement(wa + "Label", base64Label);
    XElement xConfiguration =
     new XElement(wa+"Configuration", base64ConfigurationFile);
    XElement xStartDeployment =
      new XElement(wa + "StartDeployment", "true");
    XElement xTreatWarningsAsError =
      new XElement(wa + "TreatWarningsAsError", "false");
    XElement createDeployment =
      new XElement(wa + "CreateDeployment");

    createDeployment.Add(xName);
    createDeployment.Add(xPackageUrl);
    createDeployment.Add(xLabel);
    createDeployment.Add(xConfiguration);
```

```
createDeployment.Add(xStartDeployment);
createDeployment.Add(xTreatWarningsAsError);

XDocument payload = new XDocument();
payload.Add(createDeployment);
payload.Declaration =
  new XDeclaration("1.0", "UTF-8", "no");

return payload;
}
```

7. Add the following method, invoking the **create deployment** operation, to the class:

```
private String CreateDeployment( String subscriptionId,
  String thumbprint, String serviceName,
  String deploymentName, String deploymentSlot,
  String packageUrl, String pathToConfigurationFile,
  String label)
{
  String uri = String.Format(createDeploymentFormat,
    subscriptionId, serviceName, deploymentSlot);

  XDocument payload = CreatePayload( deploymentName,
    packageUrl, pathToConfigurationFile, label);
  ServiceManagementOperation operation =
    new ServiceManagementOperation(thumbprint);
  String requestId = operation.Invoke(uri, payload);
  return requestId;
}
```

8. Add the following method, retrieving the operation status, to the class:

```
public String GetOperationStatus(
  String subscriptionId, String thumbprint, String requestId)
{
  String uri = String.Format(
    getOperationStatusFormat, subscriptionId, requestId);

  ServiceManagementOperation operation =
    new ServiceManagementOperation(thumbprint);
  XDocument operationStatus = operation.Invoke(uri);

  String status = operationStatus.Element(
    wa + "Operation").Element(wa + "Status").Value;
  return status;
}
```

9. Add the following method, invoking the methods added earlier, to the class:

```
public static void UseCreateDeploymentExample()
{
    String subscriptionId = "{SUBSCRIPTION_ID}";
    String thumbprint = "{THUMBPRINT}";
    String serviceName = "{SERVICE_NAME}";
    String deploymentName = "{DEPLOYMENT_NAME}";
    String deploymentSlot = "{SLOT_NAME}";
    String packageUrl = "{PACKAGE_URL}";
    String pathToConfigurationFile =
        "{CONFIGURATION_FILE_PATH}";
    String label = "{DEPLOYMENT_LABEL}";

    CreateDeploymentExample example =
        new CreateDeploymentExample();
    String requestId = example.CreateDeployment(
        subscriptionId, serviceName, deploymentName,
        deploymentSlot, packageUrl, pathToConfigurationFile,
        label);
    String operationStatus =
        example.GetOperationStatus(subscriptionId, thumbprint,
            requestId);
}
```

How it works...

In steps 1 through 3, we set up the class. In step 4, we add private members to define the XML namespace used in creating the payload and the `String` formats used in generating the endpoints for the **create deployment** and **get operation status** operations. In step 5, we add a helper method to create a base-64 encoded copy of a `String`.

We create the payload in step 6 by creating an `XElement` instance for each of the required and optional properties, as well as the root element. We load the service configuration file from disk and add a base-64 encoded version of its content to the `Configuration` element. We add each of these elements to the root element and then add this to an XML document. We specify that the deployed application should be started and that warnings should not be treated as errors.

In step 7, we use the `ServiceManagementOperation` utility class, described in the *Getting ready* section of the *Creating a Windows Azure hosted service* recipe in this chapter, to invoke the *create deployment* operation on the Service Management API. The `Invoke()` method creates an `HttpWebRequest`, adds the required X.509 certificate and the payload, and then sends the request to *the create deployment* endpoint. It then parses the response to retrieve the request Id. In step 8, we again use the `ServiceManagementOperation` utility class to invoke the **get operation status** operation. We parameterize this operation with the request ID, so that we can find the current status of the asynchronous **create deployment** operation.

In step 9, we add a method that invokes the methods added earlier. We need to provide the subscription ID for the Windows Azure subscription, the name of the hosted service, a name identifying this deployment, the deployment slot (*production* or *staging*) in which the deployment is created, as well as a label identifying this deployment in the Windows Azure Portal. We have to specify the complete URL to the application package, which is contained in a blob hosted by a storage account under the Windows Azure subscription. We also need to provide the file-system path to the service configuration file for the application.

There's more...

The Windows Azure Service Management REST API exposes a **get operation status** operation that can be used to retrieve the current status of an asynchronous operation using the API. The REST endpoint for the **get operation status** operation specifies the subscription ID and the request ID for the asynchronous operation. The request has no payload. The response contains an XML document specifying the current status of the specified operation, as well as any error information.

Upgrading an application deployed to a hosted service

An application deployed into a Windows Azure hosted service can be upgraded using the Windows Azure Service Management REST API. The upgrade includes both the application package and the service configuration file. Although the entire application package must be uploaded, it is possible to specify that only a single role be upgraded.

The Service Management API exposes an **upgrade deployment** operation. The REST endpoint for the upgrade deployment operation specifies the subscription ID, the name of the hosted service, and the slot of the application to be deployed. The operation requires a payload comprising an XML document specifying the Windows Azure blob containing the application package and a base-64 encoded version of the service configuration file. Each deployment upgrade has a name used to distinguish it from other deployments into the same-hosted service. As the upgrade deployment operation is asynchronous, the response contains a request ID that can be passed into a get operation status operation to check the current status of the operation.

In this recipe, we will learn how to use the Windows Azure Service Management REST API to upgrade an application in a hosted service.

How to do it...

We are going to construct the payload required for the upgrade deployment operation and then use it when we invoke the operation against the Windows Azure Service Management REST API. We do this as follows:

1. Add a new class named `UpgradeDeploymentExample` to the project.

2. If necessary, add the following assembly reference to the project:

   ```
   System.Xml.Linq.dll
   ```

3. Add the following `using` statements to the top of the class file:

   ```
   using System.Xml.Linq;
   using System.IO;
   ```

4. Add the following private members to the class:

   ```
   XNamespace wa = "http://schemas.microsoft.com/windowsazure";
   String upgradeDeploymentFormat = "https://management.core.
   windows.net/{0}/services/hostedservices/{1}/deploymentslots/{2}/
   ?comp=upgrade";
   ```

5. Add the following method, creating a base-64 encoded `String`, to the class:

   ```
   private String ConvertToBase64String(String value)
   {
       Byte[] bytes = System.Text.Encoding.UTF8.GetBytes(value);
       String base64String = Convert.ToBase64String(bytes);
       return base64String;
   }
   ```

6. Add the following method, creating the payload, to the class:

   ```
   private XDocument CreatePayload(
     String roleName, String packageUrl,
     String pathToConfigurationFile, String label)
   {
       String configurationFile =
         File.ReadAllText(pathToConfigurationFile);
       String base64ConfigurationFile =
         ConvertToBase64String(configurationFile);

       String base64Label = ConvertToBase64String(label);

       XElement xMode = new XElement(wa + "Mode", "auto");
       XElement xPackageUrl =
         new XElement(wa + "PackageUrl", packageUrl);
       XElement xConfiguration = new XElement(
         wa + "Configuration", base64ConfigurationFile);
   ```

```
XElement xLabel = new XElement(wa + "Label", base64Label);
XElement xRoleToUpgrade =
  new XElement(wa + "RoleToUpgrade", roleName);
XElement upgradeDeployment =
  new XElement(wa + "UpgradeDeployment");

upgradeDeployment.Add(xMode);
upgradeDeployment.Add(xPackageUrl);
upgradeDeployment.Add(xConfiguration);
upgradeDeployment.Add(xLabel);
upgradeDeployment.Add(xRoleToUpgrade);

XDocument payload = new XDocument();
payload.Add(upgradeDeployment);
payload.Declaration =
  new XDeclaration("1.0", "UTF-8", "no");

return payload;
}
```

7. Add the following method, invoking the `upgrade deployment` operation, to the class:

```
private String UpgradeDeployment(String subscriptionId,
  String thumbprint, String serviceName,
  String deploymentSlot, String roleName, String packageUrl,
  String pathToConfigurationFile, String label )
{
  String uri = String.Format(upgradeDeploymentFormat,
    subscriptionId, serviceName, deploymentSlot);

  XDocument payload = CreatePayload(roleName, packageUrl,
    pathToConfigurationFile, label);
  ServiceManagementOperation operation =
    new ServiceManagementOperation(thumbprint);
  String requestId = operation.Invoke(uri, payload);
  return requestId;
}
```

8. Add the following method, invoking the methods added earlier, to the class:

```
public static void UseUpgradeDeploymentExample()
{
  String subscriptionId = "{SUBSCRIPTION_ID}";
  String thumbprint = "{THUMBPRINT}";
  String serviceName = "{SERVICE_NAME}";
  String deploymentSlot = "{SLOT_NAME}";
```

```
String roleName = "{ROLE_NAME}";
String packageUrl = "{PACKAGE_URL}";
String pathToConfigurationFile =
    "{CONFIGURATION_FILE_PATH}";
String label = "{DEPLOYMENT_LABEL}";

UpgradeDeploymentExample example =
    new UpgradeDeploymentExample();
String requestId = example.UpgradeDeployment(
    subscriptionId, thumbprint, serviceName, deploymentSlot,
    roleName, packageUrl, pathToConfigurationFile, label );
}
```

How it works...

In steps 1 through 3, we set up the class. In step 4, we add private members to define the XML namespace used in creating the payload and the `String` formats used in generating the endpoints for the upgrade deployment operation. In step 5, we add a helper method to create a base-64 encoded copy of a `String`.

We create the payload in step 6 by creating an `XElement` instance for each of the required and optional properties, as well as the root element. We load the service configuration file from disk and add a base-64 encoded version of its content to the `Configuration` element. We add each of these elements to the root element and then add this to an XML document. We specify that the deployed application should be started and that warnings should not be treated as errors. We also specify which role in the package should be upgraded.

In step 7, we use the `ServiceManagementOperation` utility class, described in the _Getting ready_ section of the _Creating a Windows Azure hosted service_ recipe, to invoke the upgrade deployment operation on the Windows Azure Service Management REST API. The `Invoke()` method creates an `HttpWebRequest`, adds the required X.509 certificate and the payload, and then sends the request to the upgrade deployment endpoint. It then parses the response to retrieve the request ID.

In step 8, we add a method that invokes the methods added earlier. We need to provide the subscription ID for the Windows Azure subscription, the name of the hosted service, the name of the role to upgrade, a name identifying this deployment, the deployment slot (_production_ or _staging_) of the deployment to be upgraded, as well as a label used to identify this upgraded deployment in the Windows Azure Portal. We have to specify the complete URL to the application package, which is contained in a blob hosted by a storage account under the subscription. We also need to provide the filesystem path to the service configuration file for the application.

Retrieving the properties of a hosted service

The Windows Azure Service Management REST API exposes a **get hosted service properties** operation that can be used to retrieve the properties of a Windows Azure hosted service and any deployments to it. The REST endpoint for the get hosted service properties operation specifies the subscription ID and the name of the hosted service. The URL can be parameterized to specify that information about all deployments in the hosted service should also be returned. The request has no payload. The response contains an XML document comprising the properties of the hosted service, as well as information on the current status of all deployments in the hosted service.

In this recipe, we will learn how to use the Windows Azure Service Management REST API to retrieve the full set of properties for a hosted service.

How to do it...

We are going to invoke the get hosted service properties operation of the Windows Azure Storage Management REST API to retrieve the deployment status, as well as the role count and the instance count of a hosted service. We do this as follows:

1. Add a new class named `GetHostedServicePropertiesExample` to the project.

2. If necessary, add the following assembly reference to the project:

   ```
   System.Xml.Linq.dll
   ```

3. Add the following `using` statement to the top of the class file:

   ```
   using System.Xml.Linq;
   ```

4. Add the following private members to the class:

   ```
   XNamespace wa = "http://schemas.microsoft.com/windowsazure";
   String serviceOperationFormat = "https://management.core.windows.
   net/{0}/services/hostedservices/{1}?embed-detail=true";
   ```

5. Add the following method, retrieving the desired properties, to the class:

   ```
   private void GetHostedServiceProperties(
     String subscriptionId, String thumbprint,
     String serviceName)
   {
     String uri = String.Format(
       serviceOperationFormat, subscriptionId, serviceName);
     ServiceManagementOperation operation =
       new ServiceManagementOperation(thumbprint);
     XDocument hostedServiceProperties = operation.Invoke(uri);
   ```

```
var deploymentInformation =
  (from t in hostedServiceProperties.Elements()
   select new
   {
      DeploymentStatus = (
        from deployments in
            t.Descendants(wa + "Deployments")
          select deployments.Element(
              wa + "Deployment").Element(
              wa + "Status").Value).First(),
      RoleCount = (
        from roles in t.Descendants(wa + "RoleList")
        select roles.Elements()).Count(),
      InstanceCount = (
        from instances in
            t.Descendants(wa +"RoleInstanceList")
        select instances.Elements()).Count()
   }).First();

String deploymentStatus =
  deploymentInformation.DeploymentStatus;
Int32 roleCount = deploymentInformation.RoleCount;
Int32 instanceCount = deploymentInformation.InstanceCount;
}
```

6. Add the following method, using the method we added previously, to the class:

```
public static void UseGetHostedServicePropertiesExample()
{
   String subscriptionId = "{SUBSCRIPTION_ID}";
   String thumbprint = "{THUMBPRINT}";
   String serviceName = "{SERVICE_NAME}";
   GetHostedServicePropertiesExample example =
     new GetHostedServicePropertiesExample();

   example.GetHostedServiceProperties(
     subscriptionId, thumbprint, serviceName);
}
```

How it works...

In steps 1 through 3, we set up the class. In step 4, we add private members to define the XML namespace used in processing the response and the `String` format used in generating the endpoint for the get hosted service properties operation. Note that we append a parameter to this endpoint indicating that we want the complete list of properties for the hosted service.

In step 5, we use the `ServiceManagementOperation` utility class, described in the *Creating a Windows Azure hosted service* recipe, to invoke the get hosted service properties operation on the Service Management API. The `Invoke()` method creates an `HttpWebRequest`, adds the required X.509 certificate, and then sends the request to the get hosted services properties endpoint. It then loads the response into an XML document and returns it. We then invoke a LINQ-to-XML query on the document to retrieve the deployment status, as well as the number of roles and instances in the hosted service. This query fails if there is no application deployed into the hosted service.

In step 6, we add a method that invokes the methods added earlier. We need to provide the subscription ID for the Windows Azure subscription, the thumbprint of a management certificate, and the service name for the hosted service for which we want the properties.

There's more...

The Windows Azure Service Management REST API exposes an operation named **list subscription operations** that can be used to retrieve information on the operations performed on the subscription. The REST endpoint for the list subscription operations operation specifies the subscription ID. It can be parameterized by a timeframe used to filter the list of operations retrieved. The request has no payload. The response contains an XML document describing the operations performed on the subscription in the specified timeframe.

See also

> ▶ We see how to retrieve the properties of a hosted service in the *Using the Windows Azure Platform PowerShell Cmdlets* recipe in this chapter.

Autoscaling with the Windows Azure Service Management REST API

One of the attractions of cloud computing is the financial saving gained through the elastic provision of compute services, that is, the ability to scale up and down the number of instances of a hosted service. Windows Azure charges by the hour for each compute instance, so the appropriate number of instances should be deployed at all times.

A hosted service may have a predictable pattern such as heavy use during the week and limited use at the weekend. Alternatively, it may have an unpredictable pattern identifiable through various performance characteristics. The Windows Azure Service Management REST API can be used to autoscale a hosted service, so that it can handle the current and predicted load. By *autoscale* we mean the ability of a hosted service to scale itself elastically by modifying automatically the number of running instances.

The basic idea is that the number of instances for the various roles in the hosted service is modified to a value appropriate to a schedule or to the performance characteristics of the hosted service. We use the Service Management API to retrieve the service configuration for the hosted service, modify the instance count as appropriate, and then upload the service configuration.

In this recipe, we will learn how to use the Windows Azure Service Management REST API to autoscale a hosted service depending on the day of the week.

Getting ready

We need to create a hosted service. We must create an X.509 certificate and upload it to the Windows Azure Portal twice: once as a management certificate and once as a service certificate to the hosted service. We see how to create and upload a management certificate in the *Authenticating against the Windows Azure Service Management REST API* recipe. We see how to create and upload a service certificate in the *Implementing HTTPS in a web role* recipe.

How to do it...

We are going to vary the instance count of a web role deployed to the hosted service by using the Windows Azure Service Management REST API to modify the instance count in the service configuration. We are going to use two instances of the web role from Monday through Friday and one instance on Saturday and Sunday, where all days are calculated in UTC. We do this as follows:

1. Create a Windows Azure Project and add an ASP.Net Web Role to it.

2. Add the following `using` statements to the top of `WebRole.cs`:

   ```
   using System.Threading;
   using System.Xml.Linq;
   using System.Security.Cryptography.X509Certificates;
   ```

3. Add the following members to the `WebRole` class in `WebRole.cs`:

   ```
   XNamespace wa = "http://schemas.microsoft.com/windowsazure";
   XNamespace sc = "http://schemas.microsoft.com/
   ServiceHosting/2008/10/ServiceConfiguration";

   String changeConfigurationFormat = "https://management.core.
   windows.net/{0}/services/hostedservices/{1}/deploymentslots/{2}/
   ?comp=config";
   String getConfigurationFormat = "https://management.core.windows.
   net/{0}/services/hostedservices/{1}/deploymentslots/{2}";
   ```

```
String subscriptionId = RoleEnvironment.GetConfigurationSettingVal
ue("SubscriptionId");
String serviceName = RoleEnvironment.GetConfigurationSettingValue(
"ServiceName");
String deploymentSlot = RoleEnvironment.GetConfigurationSettingVal
ue("DeploymentSlot");
String thumbprint = RoleEnvironment.GetConfigurationSettingValue("
Thumbprint");
String roleName = "WebRole1";
String instanceId = "WebRole1_IN_0";
```

4. Add the following method, implementing `RoleEntryPoint.Run()`, to the `WebRole` class:

```
public override void Run()
{
    Int32 countMinutes = 0;
    while (true)
    {
        Thread.Sleep(60000);
        if (++countMinutes == 20)
        {
            countMinutes = 0;
            if (
            RoleEnvironment.CurrentRoleInstance.Id == instanceId)
            {
                ChangeInstanceCount();
            }
        }
    }
}
```

5. Add the following method, controlling the instance count change, to the `WebRole` class:

```
private void ChangeInstanceCount()
{
    XElement configuration = LoadConfiguration();
    Int32 requiredInstanceCount =
      CalculateRequiredInstanceCount();
    if (GetInstanceCount(configuration) !=
          requiredInstanceCount)
    {
        SetInstanceCount(configuration, requiredInstanceCount);
        String requestId = SaveConfiguration(configuration);
    }
}
```

6. Add the following method, calculating the required instance count, to the
   `WebRole` class:

```
private Int32 CalculateRequiredInstanceCount()
{
    Int32 instanceCount = 2;
    DayOfWeek dayOfWeek = DateTime.UtcNow.DayOfWeek;
    if (dayOfWeek == DayOfWeek.Saturday ||
        dayOfWeek == DayOfWeek.Sunday)
    {
        instanceCount = 1;
    }
    return instanceCount;
}
```

7. Add the following method, retrieving the instance count from the service
   configuration, to the `WebRole` class:

```
private Int32 GetInstanceCount(XElement configuration)
{
    XElement instanceElement =
        (from s in configuration.Elements(sc + "Role")
        where s.Attribute("name").Value == roleName
        select s.Element(sc + "Instances")).First();

    Int32 instanceCount = (Int32)Convert.ToInt32(
        instanceElement.Attribute("count").Value);

    return instanceCount;
}
```

8. Add the following method, setting the instance count in the service configuration, to
   the `WebRole` class:

```
private void SetInstanceCount(
  XElement configuration, Int32 value)
{
    XElement instanceElement =
        (from s in configuration.Elements(sc + "Role")
        where s.Attribute("name").Value == roleName
        select s.Element(sc + "Instances")).First();

    instanceElement.SetAttributeValue("count", value);
}
```

9. Add the following method, creating the payload for the change deployment configuration operation, to the `WebRole` class:

```
private XDocument CreatePayload(XElement configuration)
{
    String configurationString = configuration.ToString();
    String base64Configuration =
      ConvertToBase64String(configurationString);

    XElement xConfiguration =
      new XElement(wa + "Configuration", base64Configuration);
    XElement xChangeConfiguration =
      new XElement(wa + "ChangeConfiguration", xConfiguration);

    XDocument payload = new XDocument();
    payload.Add(xChangeConfiguration);
    payload.Declaration =
      new XDeclaration("1.0", "UTF-8", "no");

    return payload;
}
```

10. Add the following method, loading the service configuration, to the `WebRole` class:

```
private XElement LoadConfiguration()
{
    String uri = String.Format(getConfigurationFormat,
      subscriptionId, serviceName, deploymentSlot);
    ServiceManagementOperation operation =
      new ServiceManagementOperation(thumbprint);
    XDocument deployment = operation.Invoke(uri);

    String base64Configuration = deployment.Element(
      wa + "Deployment").Element(wa + "Configuration").Value;
    String stringConfiguration =
      ConvertFromBase64String(base64Configuration);

    XElement configuration =
      XElement.Parse(stringConfiguration);
    return configuration;
}
```

11. Add the following method, saving the service configuration, to the `WebRole` class:

```
private String SaveConfiguration(XElement configuration)
{
    String uri = String.Format(changeConfigurationFormat,
      subscriptionId, serviceName, deploymentSlot);
```

```
      XDocument payload = CreatePayload(configuration);
      ServiceManagementOperation operation =
        new ServiceManagementOperation(thumbprint);
      String requestId = operation.Invoke(uri, payload);
      return requestId;
   }
```

12. Add the following utility methods, converting a `String` to and from its base-64 encoded version, to the `WebRole` class:

```
private String ConvertToBase64String(String value)
{
   Byte[] bytes = System.Text.Encoding.UTF8.GetBytes(value);
   String base64String = Convert.ToBase64String(bytes);
   return base64String;
}

private String ConvertFromBase64String(String base64Value)
{
   Byte[] bytes = Convert.FromBase64String(base64Value);
   String value = System.Text.Encoding.UTF8.GetString(bytes);
   return value;
}
```

13. Add the `ServiceManagementOperation` class described in the _Getting ready_ section of the _Creating a Windows Azure hosted service_ recipe to the `WebRole1` project.

14. Set the `ConfigurationSettings` element in the `ServiceDefinition.csdef` file to:

```
<ConfigurationSettings>
   <Setting name="DeploymentSlot" />
   <Setting name="ServiceName" />
   <Setting name="SubscriptionId" />
   <Setting name="Thumbprint" />
</ConfigurationSettings>
```

15. Set the `ConfigurationSettings` element in the `ServiceDefinition.cscfg` file to the following:

```
<ConfigurationSettings>
   <Setting name="Microsoft.WindowsAzure.Plugins.Diagnostics.
ConnectionString" value="DefaultEndpointsProtocol=https;AccountNam
e=ACCOUNT_NAME;AccountKey=ACCOUNT_KEY" />
   <Setting name="DeploymentSlot" value="production" />
   <Setting name="ServiceName" value="SERVICE_NAME" />
   <Setting name="SubscriptionId" value="SUBSCRIPTION_ID" />
   <Setting name="Thumbprint" value="THUMBPRINT" />
</ConfigurationSettings>
```

How it works...

In steps 1 and 2, we set up the `WebRole` class. In step 3, we add private members to define the XML namespace used in processing the response and the `String` format used in generating the endpoint for the change deployment configuration and get deployment operations. We then initialize several values from configuration settings in the service configuration file deployed to each instance.

In step 4, we implement the `Run()` class. Every 20 minutes, the thread this method runs in wakes up and, only in the instance named `WebRole1_IN_0`, invokes the method controlling the instance count for the web role. This code runs in a single instance to ensure that there is no race condition with multiple instances trying to change the instance count simultaneously.

In step 5, we load the service configuration. If we detect that the instance count should change we modify the service configuration to have the desired instance count and then save the service configuration. Note that the service configuration used here is downloaded and uploaded using the Service Management API.

Step 6 contains the code where we calculate the needed instance count. In this example, we choose an instance count of 2 from Monday through Friday and 1 on Saturday and Sunday. All days are specified in UTC. This is the step where we should insert the desired scaling algorithm.

In step 7, we retrieve the instance count for the web role from the service configuration. In step 8, we set the instance count to the desired value in the service configuration.

In step 9, we create the payload for the change deployment configuration operation. We create a `Configuration` element and add a base-64 encoded copy of the service configuration to it. We add the `Configuration` element to the root `ChangeConfiguration` element which we then add to an XML document.

In step 10, we use the `ServiceManagementOperation` utility class, described in the *Creating a Windows Azure hosted service* recipe, to invoke the get deployment operation on the Service Management API. The `Invoke()` method creates an `HttpWebRequest`, adds the required X.509 certificate, and sends the request to the get deployment endpoint. We load the response into an XML document from which we extract the base-64 encoded service configuration. We then convert this into its XML format and load this into an `XElement` which we return.

In step 11, we use the `ServiceManagementOperation` utility class to invoke the change deployment configuration operation on the Service Management API. The `Invoke()` method creates an `HttpWebRequest`, adds the required X.509 certificate and the payload, and then sends the request to the change deployment configuration endpoint. It then parses the response to retrieve the request ID.

In step 12, we add two utility methods to convert to and from a base-64 encoded String.

In step 13, we add the `ServiceManagementOperation` utility class that we use to invoke operations against the Service Management API.

In steps 14 and 15, we define some configuration settings in the service definition file and specify them in the service configuration file. We provide values for the Windows Azure Storage Service account name and access key. We also provide the subscription ID for the Windows Azure subscription, as well as the service name for current hosted service. We also need to add the thumbprint for the X.509 certificate we uploaded as a management certificate to the Windows Azure subscription and a service certificate to the hosted service we are deploying this application into. Note that this thumbprint is the same as that configured in the `Certificate` section of the `ServiceConfiguration.cscfg` file. This duplication is necessary because the `Certificate` section of this file is not accessible to the application code.

Using the Windows Azure Platform PowerShell cmdlets

The Windows Azure Platform PowerShell cmdlets use the Windows Azure Service Management REST API to expose service management operations as PowerShell cmdlets. The cmdlets provide a convenient way to manage hosted services, including retrieving the properties of current deployments and uploading new and upgraded deployments.

In this recipe, we will learn how to use the Windows Azure Platform PowerShell cmdlets to invoke various service operations in the Windows Azure Service Management REST API.

Getting ready

If necessary, we can download PowerShell 2 from the Microsoft download center at the following URL:

`http://www.microsoft.com/download/en/details.aspx?id=11829`

We need to download and install the Windows Azure Platform PowerShell cmdlets. The package with the cmdlets can be downloaded from the following URL:

`http://wappowershell.codeplex.com/`

Once the package has been downloaded, the cmdlets need to be built and installed. The installed package contains a `StartHere` file explaining the process.

How to do it...

We are going to use the Windows Azure Platform cmdlets to retrieve various properties of a Windows Azure subscription and a hosted service in it.

1. Create a PowerShell script named `Get-Properties.ps1` and insert the following text:

```
$subscriptionId = 'SUBSCRIPTION_ID'
$serviceName = 'SERVICE_NAME'
$thumbprint = 'THUMBPRINT'
$getCertificate = Get-Item cert:\LocalMachine\My\$thumbprint

Add-PSSnapin AzureManagementToolsSnapIn

Get-HostedServices -SubscriptionId $subscriptionId
  -Certificate $getCertificate
Get-AffinityGroups -SubscriptionId $subscriptionId
  -Certificate $getCertificate
Get-HostedProperties -SubscriptionId $subscriptionId
  -Certificate $getCertificate -ServiceName $serviceName
```

2. Launch PowerShell.

3. Navigate to the directory containing `Get-Properties.ps1`.

4. Invoke the cmdlets to retrieve the properties:

```
.\Get-Properties.ps1
```

How it works...

In step 1, we create the PowerShell script to invoke the get hosted service properties, list affinity groups, and get hosted service properties operations in the Windows Azure Service Management REST API. We need to provide the subscription ID for the Windows Azure subscription, the name of the hosted service, and the thumbprint for a management certificate uploaded to the Windows Azure subscription. In the script, we retrieve the X.509 certificate from the Personal (My) certificate store on the local machine level. If necessary, we can specify the current user level, instead of the local machine level, by using `CurrentUser` in place of `LocalMachine` when we define `$getCertificate`.

In steps 2 and 3, we set up PowerShell.

In step 4, we invoke the script using a `.\` syntax to demonstrate that we really want to invoke an unsigned script in the current directory.

There's more...

PowerShell supports an execution policy to restrict the PowerShell scripts that can be run on a system. If the current execution policy does not permit the Windows Azure Service Management cmdlets to run, then the execution policy can be changed to `remote signed` by invoking the following at the command prompt:

```
C:\Users\Administrator>PowerShell -command "Set-ExecutionPolicy
RemoteSigned"
```

This sets the global PowerShell execution context. PowerShell 2 introduced a command-line switch allowing it to be set only for the current invocation:

```
C:\Users\Administrator>PowerShell -ExecutionPolicy RemoteSigned
```

Azure Management cmdlets

Cerebrata has released a commercial set of Azure Management cmdlets that are more extensive than the Windows Azure Service Management cmdlets. The following PowerShell script retrieves the list of affinity groups for a Windows Azure subscription, including the GUID identifier not available on the Windows Azure Portal:

```
$subscriptionId = 'SUBSCRIPTION_ID'
$thumbprint = 'THUMBPRINT'
$getCertificate = Get-ChildItem
  -path cert:\LocalMachine\My\$thumbprint

Add-PSSnapin AzureManagementCmdletsSnapIn

Get-AffinityGroup -SubscriptionId $subscriptionId
  -Certificate $getCertificate
```

We need to provide the subscription ID for the Windows Azure subscription, and the thumbprint for a management certificate uploaded to the Windows Azure subscription. In the script, we retrieve the X.509 certificate from the Personal (My) certificate store on the local machine level. If necessary, we can specify the current user level, instead of the local machine lever, by using `CurrentUser` in place of `LocalMachine` when we define `$getCertificate`.

We can use the following command to retrieve the list of Windows Azure locations:

```
Get-AzureDataCenterLocation -SubscriptionId $subscriptionId
  -Certificate $getCertificate
```

8

Using SQL Azure

In this chapter, we will cover:

- ▸ Provisioning a SQL Azure Server
- ▸ Creating a SQL Azure database
- ▸ Migrating a database to SQL Azure
- ▸ Measuring SQL Azure usage
- ▸ Connecting to SQL Azure with ADO.NET
- ▸ Handling connection failures to SQL Azure
- ▸ Scaling out SQL Azure into the Windows Azure Blob Service

Introduction

SQL Azure provides relational database technology to the Windows Azure Platform. It is essentially a hosted version of SQL Server. However, Microsoft provides all management of the physical server leaving the customer responsible for managing individual databases on a logical, but not a physical, level.

The SQL Azure administrator must provision a SQL Azure Server which is the administrative and security boundary for a collection of SQL Azure databases. This is a logical server not a physical server, as the SQL Azure customer has no access to the physical servers on which SQL Azure databases are stored. In the *Provisioning a SQL Azure server* recipe, we see how to create one using the Windows Azure Portal.

The next step after creating a SQL Azure server is to create some SQL Azure databases in it. We can do this either by using the Windows Azure Portal or by invoking a Transact SQL operation. This is almost the same as with traditional Microsoft SQL Server except that there are constraints on database size and location. Furthermore, any attempt to specify physical placement of data and logs is forbidden because the SQL Azure administrator has no control over physical placement. We see how to do this in the *Creating a SQL Azure database* recipe.

Having created a SQL Azure database, we may need to create tables in it and populate it with data from an existing Microsoft SQL Server database. We see how to use the SQL Azure Migration Wizard to do this in the *Migrating a database to SQL Azure* recipe.

SQL Azure is a shared, multitenant database system in which the databases of many customers may coexist on the same physical hardware. This causes resource constraints on maximum size and operational throughput. Monitoring these is consequently important. In the *Measuring SQL Azure usage* recipe, we see how to use dynamic management views to look at current resource consumption.

An important feature of SQL Azure is its similarity to Microsoft SQL Server. Often code that works against Microsoft SQL Server can be used against SQL Azure merely by changing the connection string to point to the SQL Azure database. We see how to do this in the *Connecting to SQL Azure with ADO.NET* recipe. An increased likelihood of dropped connections is an important consequence on the resource constraints imposed by the shared nature of SQL Azure. These dropped connections are really transient errors that vanish when another connection is opened and the operation retried. It is important that an application have some easy mechanism to do this. In the *Handling connection failures to SQL Azure* recipe, we see how to do this using the **Transient Fault Handling Framework for Azure Storage, Service Bus and SQL Azure**.

One drawback of SQL Azure is that it is far more costly to store data in it than it is to store data using the Windows Azure Storage Service. A solution is to use the storage service to store blobs while keeping pointers to them, that is, blob name, in SQL Azure. This marries the cost-effective scalable storage of the storage service with the query capability of SQL Azure. We see how to do this in the *Scaling out SQL Azure into the Windows Azure Blob Service* recipe.

Note that the SQL Azure Management REST API provides a RESTful interface to manage aspects of SQL Azure. Use of this API is almost identical to use of the Windows Azure Service Management REST API covered in *Chapter 7, Managing Hosted Services with the Service Management API*. The only differences are in the service endpoint and the value of the `x-ms-version` header, which need to be changed to the following:

service endpoint: `management.database.windows.net:8443`

x-ms-version: `1.0`

Provisioning a SQL Azure Server

A SQL Azure Server is the administrative and security boundary for a collection of SQL Azure databases hosted in a single Windows Azure datacenter (region). All connections to a database hosted by the server go through the service endpoint provided by the SQL Azure Server. A Windows Azure subscription can create up to six SQL Azure Servers, each of which can host up to 150 databases (including the master database). These SQL Azure Servers can be in different Windows Azure datacenters. These are soft limits that can be increased by arrangement with Microsoft.

The SQL Azure Server is provisioned on the Windows Azure Portal. The Windows Azure datacenter location, as well as the administrator login and password must be specified during the provisioning process. The rules for the SQL Azure firewall, used to restrict access to the SQL Azure databases associated with the SQL Azure Server, can also be configured as part of the provisioning process. After the SQL Azure Server has been provisioned, the firewall rules can be modified: on the Windows Azure Portal; by using Transact SQL; or by using the SQL Azure Service Management REST API.

The result of the provisioning process is a SQL Azure Server identified by a fully qualified DNS name, such as `SERVER_NAME.database.windows.net` where `SERVER_NAME` is an automatically generated (random) string that differentiates this SQL Azure Server from any other. The provisioning process also creates the master database for the SQL Azure Server and adds a login and user for the administrator specified during the provisioning process. This user has the authorization to create the actual databases associated with this SQL Azure Server, as well as any logins needed to access them.

In this recipe, we will learn how to create a SQL Azure Server using the Windows Azure Portal.

How to do it...

We are going to create a SQL Azure server using the Windows Azure Portal. We do this as follows:

1. On the Windows Azure Portal, go to the **Database** section.
2. Select a subscription.
3. On the **Server** menu, click on **Create** to start the **Create Server** wizard.
4. On the **Create a new server** dialog, choose a region for the server from the list of allowed Windows Azure datacenter locations and click on **Next**.
5. Provide an administrator login and password and click on **Next**.
6. If necessary, check the box to **Allow other Windows Azure services to access this server**.
7. If necessary, click on **Add** to add other IP ranges to the SQL Azure firewall. Then, provide a rule name and the start and end IP addresses for any new firewall rule required and click on **OK**.
8. Click on **Finish** to complete the creation of the SQL Azure Database Server.

How it works...

We use the Windows Azure Portal to create a SQL Azure Server. We access the portal in step 1 and choose the appropriate subscription in step 2. The process uses the **Create Server** wizard, which we start in step 3 and then work through in the remaining steps of the recipe.

In step 4, we specify the Windows Azure datacenter (region) in which the SQL Azure Server is to be created.

In step 5, we provide the administrator credentials for the SQL Azure server.

In steps 6 and 7, we configure the firewall used to restrict access to databases hosted by the SQL Azure Server. In step 6, we add a special firewall rule allowing a Windows Azure hosted service to access the SQL Azure Server. In step 7, we add firewall rules for other IP ranges. This dialog provides the IP address of the current connection making it convenient to add a rule for it.

In step 8, we complete the **Create Server** wizard and create the SQL Azure Server.

Creating a SQL Azure database

SQL Azure is a multi-tenanted database system in which many distinct databases are hosted on a single physical server managed by Microsoft. SQL Azure administrators have no control over the physical provisioning of a database to a particular physical server. Indeed, to maintain high-availability, a primary and two secondary copies of each SQL Azure database are stored on separate physical servers.

Consequently, SQL Azure does not provide a way for the administrator to specify the physical layout of a database and its logs when creating a SQL Azure database. The administrator merely has to provide a name and maximum size for the database. An administrator can create a SQL Azure database either on the Windows Azure Portal or by using the CREATE DATABASE Transact SQL statement.

SQL Azure supports two classes of database: web edition for small databases under 5 GB, and business edition for databases of 10 GB and larger. There is no difference in these editions other than the maximum size and the billing increment. Web edition databases are billed in 1 GB increments while business edition databases are billed in 10 GB increments. Once a SQL Azure database has been created, the ALTER DATABASE Transact SQL statement can be used to alter either the edition or the maximum size of the database. The maximum size is important as the database is made read-only once it reaches that size.

In this recipe, we will learn how to create a SQL Azure database using both the Windows Azure Portal and Transact SQL.

How to do it...

We are going to create a database on a SQL Azure Server using the Windows Azure Portal and by using Transact SQL. We do this as follows:

Using the Window Azure Portal:

1. On the Windows Azure Portal, go to the **Database** section.

2. Select a subscription.

3. On the **Database** menu, click on **Create** to open the **Create Database** dialog.

4. On the **Create Database** dialog, specify a database name and choose both an edition and maximum size, and then click on **OK**.

Using Transact SQL:

1. Launch Microsoft SQL Server 2008 R2 Management Studio.

2. Connect to the `master` database for the SQL Azure Database Server.

3. Invoke the following Transact SQL command:

```
CREATE DATABASE DATABASE_NAME
(
    MAXSIZE = 1 GB
)
```

How it works...

In steps 1 through 3, we open the **Create Database** dialog on the Windows Azure Portal.

In step 4, we specify the database name and size and create it.

In steps 5 and 6, we use Microsoft SQL Server 2008 Management Studio to get a connection to the `master` database on the SQL Azure server.

In step 7, we create a 1 GB database. In specifying a size, we must provide one of the allowable values which are: 1, 5, 10, 20, 30, 40, and 50.

There's more...

We can also use the web-based Data Manager to invoke Transact SQL commands against a SQL Azure database. We launch Data Manager as follows:

1. On the Windows Azure Portal, go to the **Database** section.

2. On the **Database** menu, click on **Manage** to launch the Database Manager.

3. Specify the master database and provide the requested username and password.

Copying a database

We can use the `COPY DATABASE` command to create a transactionally-consistent copy of a SQL Azure database by connecting to the `master` database and invoking the following Transact SQL command:

```
CREATE DATABASE NEW_DATABASE_NAME
AS COPY OF DATABASE_NAME
```

We can also use this command to copy a database to another SQL Azure Database Server located in the same Windows Azure datacenter. We do this by connecting to the `master` database in the destination server and invoking the following Transact SQL command:

```
CREATE DATABASE NEW_DATABASE_NAME
AS COPY OF SERVER_NAME.DATABASE_NAME
```

The copy is performed asynchronously. The `sys.dm_database_copies` system view can be queried to check on its status.

Note that when performing an inter-server copy, the login used must have the same name and password on both the source and destination servers. This login becomes the **DBO** of the copied database. The source database users are copied, and the `ALTER USER` statement can be used to associate these users with logins on the destination server.

Increasing the size of a database

We can use the `ALTER DATABASE` command to increase the size of a SQL Azure database by connecting to the `master` database and invoking the following Transact SQL command:

```
ALTER DATABASE DATABASE_NAME
MODIFY
(
    MAXSIZE = 5 GB
)
```

We must use one of the allowable database sizes.

Migrating a database to SQL Azure

SQL Azure supports many, but not all the features of Microsoft SQL Server. For example, all SQL Azure tables must have a clustered index as SQL Azure does not support heap tables. Consequently, although it is not difficult to migrate a Microsoft SQL Server database to SQL Azure, some attention must be paid when doing so. This involves identifying non-supported features and modifying the Transact SQL script so that it can run correctly in SQL Azure.

The SQL Azure Migration Wizard is a CodePlex project that can be used to analyse a Microsoft SQL Server database to identify features not supported in SQL Azure. It generates a Transact SQL script that can recreate the database and modifies, to a valid form, any statement not supported by SQL Azure. The **SQL Azure Migration Wizard** can then migrate the database by applying the script to a SQL Azure database and using `bcp`, a bulk-copy utility, to copy the data from the Microsoft SQL Server database and upload it to the SQL Azure database.

The default mode of the SQL Azure Migration Wizard works well. The method it uses to identify non-supported features is configurable and can be changed, if necessary. The **SQL Azure Migration Wizard** can also be used to analyse an arbitrary Transact SQL script to ensure that it is valid when used with SQL Azure.

In this recipe, we will learn how to use the **SQL Azure Migration Wizard** to migrate a Microsoft SQL Server database to SQL Azure.

Getting ready

The **SQL Azure Migration Wizard** only uploads data into an existing SQL Azure database. If necessary, we must create the SQL Azure database before we invoke the **SQL Azure Migration Wizard**. We see how to do this in the *Creating a SQL Azure database* recipe.

How to do it...

We are going to migrate a Microsoft SQL Server database to SQL Azure using the **SQL Azure Migration Wizard**. We do this as follows:

1. Download the **SQL Azure Migration Wizard** from CodePlex from the following URL:

   `http://sqlazuremw.codeplex.com/`

2. Extract the files from the compressed download file.

3. Start the `SQLAZureMW` executable to bring up the **Script Wizard** dialog.

4. In the **Select Process** dialog, select **Analyze and Migrate**, **SQL Database**, and click on **Next**.

5. On the **Connect** dialog, specify the source Microsoft SQL Server name (or leave as `localhost`) and click on **Connect**.

6. On the **Select Source** dialog, select the source database and click on **Next**.

7. On the **Choose Object** dialog, click on **Next**.

8. On the **Script Database Summary** dialog, click on **Next**.

9. On the **Generate Script** popup, click on **Yes**.

10. In the **Result Summary** dialog, click on **Next** to continue with the migration.

11. On the **Connect** pop-up:

   ❑ Select **Use a specific user ID and password**

   ❑ Specify a user name

   ❑ Specify a password

   ❑ Select **Specify database**

   ❑ Specify a database name

12. Click on **Next**.

13. On the **Execute Script** pop-up dialog, click on **Yes**.

14. In the **Target Server Response** dialog, we can view the summary of the database migration and verify its success.

How it works...

In step 1, we download the latest version of the SQL Azure Migration Wizard from CodePlex. In step 2, we extract it to a suitable location.

In step 3, we launch the **SQL Azure Migration Wizard**. This progresses in two phases: analysis and migration—through the remaining steps in the recipe. In the analysis phase, we specify the source Microsoft SQL Server database. The **SQL Server Migration Wizard** analyses it, and generates scripts that can recreate the database tables on SQL Azure and use bcp to extract the data. In the migration phase, we specify the SQL Azure database to which we are going to migrate the database, and then the Server Migration Wizard extracts the data and uploads it to newly created tables in the destination SQL Azure database.

In step 4, we specify that we want to analyse and migrate a Microsoft SQL Server database to SQL Azure. We have other choices here including specifying that we only want to perform the analysis. In steps 5 through 9, we specify the source Microsoft SQL Server instance and the source database and start the analysis process.

On completion of the analysis phase, we can see both the Transact SQL script required to regenerate the tables in a SQL Azure database and a summary showing the modifications required to handle limitations of SQL Azure. We then specify that we want to continue with the migration process.

In step 11, we provide the information required to connect to the destination SQL Azure database. In steps 12 and 13, we complete the configuration and start the migration process.

We view the result of the migration phase in step 14.

Measuring SQL Azure usage

A SQL Azure database resides on a physical server shared with many other SQL Azure databases. This sharing leads to resource constraints on the maximum size and operational throughput of a SQL Azure database. No data can be written to a SQL Azure database that has reached its maximum size. Connections are terminated when operational throughput limits are breached. It is therefore important that SQL Azure usage is measured to avoid the consequences of hitting resource constraints. SQL Azure exposes various dynamic management views that can be queried to measure resource usage.

SQL Azure allocates one partition for a table, and one partition for each non-clustered index in a database. As SQL Azure manages the physical allocation of a database, it does not provide operations supporting partition management. However, the `sys.dm_db_partition_stats` dynamic management view contains one row for each partition allocated in the database. Consequently, the view can be queried to find the current size of the database, as well as the objects in it. These queries are useful in ensuring that the database is not approaching its maximum size and in identifying which objects are consuming the most space.

The `sys.dm_exec_sessions` dynamic management view contains information about all connections on the SQL Azure server. It can be used to observe current usage of the server. The `sys.dm_exec_query_stats` dynamic management view contains information on the performance of cached queries. It can be used to identify those queries consuming the most resources with regard to CPU, time, as well as logical and physical data access.

In this recipe, we will see how to measure usage of SQL Azure.

How to do it...

We are going to invoke various queries against dynamic management views of a SQL Azure database to collect information that helps us manage our use of the database. We do this as follows:

1. Connect to the SQL Azure database.

2. We invoke the following query to calculate the total size in MB of the current database:

```
SELECT
  DB_NAME() AS [Database],
  SUM(reserved_page_count) * 8.0 / 1024 AS [Size in MB]
FROM
  sys.dm_db_partition_stats;
```

3. We invoke the following query to calculate the total size in MB of each object in the current database:

```
SELECT
    OBJECT_NAME(object_id) AS [Name],
    SUM(reserved_page_count) * 8.0 / 1024 AS [Size in MB]
FROM
    sys.dm_db_partition_stats
GROUP BY
    object_id
ORDER BY
2 DESC
```

4. We invoke the following query to calculate the total size in MB of each partition in the current database:

```
SELECT
    OBJECT_NAME(object_id) AS [Name],
    index_id AS [Index Id],
    row_count AS [Row Count],
    used_page_count * 8.0 / 1024 AS [Used in MB],
    reserved_page_count * 8.0 / 1024 as [Reserved in MB]
FROM
    sys.dm_db_partition_stats
ORDER BY
    1
```

5. We invoke the following query to view CPU usage of active connections to the current database:

```
SELECT
    ec.connection_id AS [Connection ID],
    es.session_id AS [Session ID],
    es.cpu_time AS [CPU in ms] ,
    es.last_request_end_time AS [Last Used]
FROM
    sys.dm_exec_sessions AS [es]
INNER JOIN
    sys.dm_exec_connections AS [ec]
ON
    es.session_id = ec.session_id
```

6. We invoke the following query to view the top five queries, by average worker time, in the current database:

```
SELECT TOP 5
    query_stats.query_hash AS [Query Hash],
    SUM(query_stats.total_worker_time) /
```

```
           (1000000.0 * SUM(query_stats.execution_count))
             AS [Avg CPU Time (s)],
         SUM(query_stats.total_logical_reads) /
             (1000000.0 * SUM(query_stats.execution_count))
             AS [Avg Logical Reads (s)],
         SUM(query_stats.total_logical_writes) /
             (1000000.0 * SUM(query_stats.execution_count))
             AS [Avg Logical Writes (s)],
         MIN(query_stats.statement_text) AS [Statement Text]
    FROM
       (SELECT
           qs.*,
           SUBSTRING(st.text, (qs.statement_start_offset/2) + 1,
           ((CASE statement_end_offset
           WHEN -1 THEN DATALENGTH(st.text)
           ELSE qs.statement_end_offset END
           - qs.statement_start_offset)/2) + 1) AS [statement_text]
       FROM
           sys.dm_exec_query_stats AS [qs]
       CROSS APPLY
           sys.dm_exec_sql_text(qs.sql_handle) AS [st])
             AS [query_stats]
    GROUP BY
       query_stats.query_hash
    ORDER BY
       2 DESC
```

How it works...

In step 1, we connect to the desired SQL Azure database. Note that the queries do not work against the `master` database.

In step 2, we invoke a query to retrieve the total size of the current SQL Azure database. We can use this query to check how close we are to hitting the size limit for the database.

In step 3, we invoke a query to retrieve the total size of each object in the current SQL Azure database. We can use this query to find out which objects are taking up the most space in the database.

In step 4, we invoke a query to retrieve the total size of each partition used by each object in the current SQL Azure database. We can use this query to identify when it may be useful to rebuild non-clustered indexes, in particular, since each of these is in its own partition. A large difference between the used and reserved page count indicates that an index rebuild may help free up space.

In step 5, we invoke a query to retrieve the total CPU time used by current connections to the database, as well as the last time each of them was used. We can use this information to find out current usage of our SQL Azure database.

In step 6, we invoke a query to retrieve the five queries with the highest average CPU time. We can use this information to focus our attention on optimizing these queries. This query also returns the average logical reads and writes for these queries. The query uses a standard technique, using `sys.dm_exec_sql_text()`, for generating the query text from the query handle.

Connecting to SQL Azure with ADO.NET

An application communicates with SQL Azure using the same tabular data stream (TDS) format used in communicating with Microsoft SQL Server. This simplifies the task of migrating from Microsoft SQL Server to SQL Azure as an application need only change to the appropriate connection string to use SQL Azure.

When a SQL Azure server is provisioned, it is assigned a fully qualified DNS name of the form: `SERVER_NAME.database.windows.net`. A database name must be provided when the SQL Azure database is created. SQL Azure logins are created in precisely the same way they are in Microsoft SQL Server. It is conventional to specify SQL Azure logins in the form `LOGIN@SERVER_NAME`. All communication with SQL Azure is over an encrypted channel and it is recommended that the server certificate used with this channel not be trusted. This leads to a connection string like:

```
Data Source=SERVER_NAME.database.windows.net;Initial Catalog=DATABASE_
NAME;
User ID=LOGIN@SERVER_NAME;Password=PASSWORD;
Encrypt=True;TrustServerCertificate=False
```

This connection string can be retrieved from the application configuration or created using the `SqlConnectionStringBuilder` class. Note that SQL Azure forces the connection to be encrypted, even if the client does not specify encryption. The `TrustServerCertificate` parameter forces the client to validate the server certificate, helping to avoid man-in-the-middle attacks.

In this recipe, we will learn how to connect to SQL Azure using ADO.NET.

How to do it...

We are going to connect to SQL Azure using ADO.NET and perform various data-definition language (DDL) and data-manipulation language (DML) operations. We do this as follows:

1. Add a new class named `StandardConnectionExample` to the project.

2. Add the following `using` statements to the top of the class file:

```
using System.Data;
using System.Data.SqlClient;
```

3. Add the following private member to the class:

```
String connectionString;
```

4. Add the following constructor to the class:

```
public StandardConnectionExample( String server,
  String database, String login, String password)
{
    SqlConnectionStringBuilder connStringBuilder;
    connStringBuilder = new SqlConnectionStringBuilder();
    connStringBuilder.DataSource =
      String.Format("{0}.database.windows.net", server);
    connStringBuilder.InitialCatalog = database;
    connStringBuilder.Encrypt = true;
    connStringBuilder.TrustServerCertificate = false;
    connStringBuilder.UserID = String.Format("{0}@{1}",
      login, server);
    connStringBuilder.Password = password;
    connectionString = connStringBuilder.ToString();
}
```

5. Add the following method, retrieving the session tracing Id, to the class:

```
public String GetSessionTracingId()
{
    String commandText =
      "SELECT CONVERT(NVARCHAR(36), CONTEXT_INFO())";
    String sessionTracingId;
    using (SqlConnection connection =
      new SqlConnection(connectionString))
    {
        connection.Open();
        using (SqlCommand sqlCommand =
          connection.CreateCommand())
        {
            sqlCommand.CommandText = commandText;
            sessionTracingId =
              sqlCommand.ExecuteScalar() as String;
        }
    }
    return sessionTracingId;
}
```

6. Add the following method, creating the `Writer` table, to the class:

```csharp
public void CreateTable()
{
    String commandText =
      @"CREATE TABLE Writer (
        Id int PRIMARY KEY NOT NULL,
        Name nvarchar(20) NOT NULL,
        CountBooks int NULL)";

    using (SqlConnection connection =
      new SqlConnection(connectionString))
    {
      connection.Open();
      using (SqlCommand sqlCommand =
        connection.CreateCommand())
      {
        sqlCommand.CommandText = commandText;
        sqlCommand.ExecuteNonQuery();
      }
    }
}
```

7. Add the following method, dropping the `Writer` table, to the class:

```csharp
public void DropTable()
{
    String commandText = "DROP TABLE Writer";
    using (SqlConnection connection =
      new SqlConnection(connectionString))
    {
      connection.Open();
      using (SqlCommand sqlCommand =
        connection.CreateCommand())
      {
        sqlCommand.CommandText = commandText;
        sqlCommand.ExecuteNonQuery();
      }
    }
}
```

8. Add the following method, querying the `Writer` table, to the class:

```csharp
public void QueryTable()
{
    String commandText = "SELECT * FROM Writer";
    using (SqlConnection connection =
      new SqlConnection(connectionString))
    {
      connection.Open();
```

```
using (SqlCommand sqlCommand =
  new SqlCommand(commandText, connection))
{
  using (SqlDataReader reader =
    sqlCommand.ExecuteReader())
  {
    Int32 idColumn = reader.GetOrdinal("Id");
    Int32 nameColumn = reader.GetOrdinal("Name");
    Int32 countBooksColumn =
      reader.GetOrdinal("CountBooks");
    while (reader.Read())
    {
      Int32 id = (Int32)reader[idColumn];
      String name = reader[nameColumn] as String;
      Int32? countBooks =
        reader[countBooksColumn] as Int32?;
    }
  }
}
}
```

9. Add the following method, inserting rows in the `Writer` table, to the class:

```
public Int32 InsertRows()
{
  String commandText =
    @"INSERT INTO Writer
        (Id, Name, CountBooks)
      VALUES
        (1, N'Cervantes', 2),
        (2, N'Smollett', null),
        (3, 'Beyle', 4)";

  Int32 rowsAffected;
  using (SqlConnection connection =
    new SqlConnection(connectionString))
  {
    connection.Open();
    using (SqlCommand sqlCommand =
      new SqlCommand(commandText, connection))
    {
      rowsAffected = sqlCommand.ExecuteNonQuery();
    }
  }
  return rowsAffected;
}
```

10. Add the following method, updating a row in the `Writer` table, to the class:

```
public Int32 UpdateRow()
{
    String commandText =
      @"UPDATE Writer
        SET Name=@Name
        WHERE Id=3";

    Int32 rowsAffected;
    using (SqlConnection connection =
      new SqlConnection(connectionString))
    {
        connection.Open();
        using (SqlCommand sqlCommand =
          new SqlCommand(commandText, connection))
        {
            SqlParameter sqlParameter = new SqlParameter()
            {
                ParameterName = "@Name",
                Value = "Stendhal",
                SqlDbType = SqlDbType.NVarChar,
                Size = 20
            };
            sqlCommand.Parameters.Add(sqlParameter);
            rowsAffected = sqlCommand.ExecuteNonQuery();
        }
    }
    return rowsAffected;
}
```

11. Add the following method, using the methods added earlier, to the class:

```
public static void UseStandardConnectionExample()
{
    String server = "SERVER_NAME";
    String database = "DATABASE_NAME";
    String login = "LOGIN";
    String password = "PASSWORD";

    StandardConnectionExample example =
      new StandardConnectionExample(
        server, database, login, password);

    example.GetSessionTracingId();
    example.CreateTable();
```

```
         example.InsertRows();
         example.QueryTable();
         example.UpdateRow();
         example.QueryTable();
         example.DropTable();
    }
```

How it works...

In steps 1 and 2, we set up the class. In step 3, we add a private member for the connection string that we initialize in the constructor we add in step 4 using a `SqlConnectionStringBuilder` instance. Configuring a connection string for SQL Azure is precisely the same as for Microsoft SQL Server, apart from the way in which the `DataSource` is specified—using the fully qualified DNS name. We turn encryption on, as this is required, and set `TrustServerCertificate` to `false`, so that the server certificate is validated. Instead of building the connection string like this, we could have loaded it from a configuration file.

In step 5, we create and open a `SqlConnection` which we use to create `SqlCommand`. The connection is closed automatically when we exit the `using` block. We use `SqlCommand` to retrieve the session tracing ID for the connection. This is a `GUID`, identifying a particular connection, which can be provided to SQL Azure Support when its help is sought in debugging a problem.

In step 6, we invoke a `CREATE TABLE` operation on SQL Azure to create a table named `Writer`. The table has three columns: the Primary Key is the ID column; the remaining columns store the name of a writer and the number of books they wrote. In step 7, we invoke a `DROP TABLE` operation on SQL Azure to drop the `Writer` table.

In step 8, we retrieve all rows from the `Writer` table and then iterate over them to examine the content of each column. In step 9, we insert three rows into the `Writer` table and we update one of the rows in step 10.

In step 11, we add a method that invokes the methods added earlier. We need to provide the server name, the database name, the login, and the password.

Note that, with an appropriately configured connection string, all the code in this recipe can be run against Microsoft SQL Server—with the exception of the retrieval of the session tracing ID in step 5.

Handling connection failures to SQL Azure

SQL Azure database is a distributed system in which each physical server hosts many databases. This sharing of resources leads to capacity constraints on operational throughput. SQL Azure handles these capacity constraints by throttling operations and closing connections that are using too many resources. SQL Azure also closes connections when it alleviates operational hot spots by switching from a primary SQL Azure database to one of its two backup copies. Furthermore, connectivity to a SQL Azure database is likely to be less reliable than connectivity to a Microsoft SQL Server database on a corporate LAN. It is imperative therefore that applications using SQL Azure be designed to withstand the connection failures that are far more likely to occur than with Microsoft SQL Server.

One of the mantras of cloud development is *design for failure*. It is important that applications using SQL Azure be designed to handle failures appropriately. There are two kinds of error: permanent errors indicating a general failure of part of the system and transient errors existing only for a brief time. Permanent errors perhaps indicate a logical problem with the application—and handling them may require code changes. However, an application should handle transient errors gracefully by retrying the operation that led to the error in the hope that it does not recur. A dropped connection should be regarded as transient, and an application should respond to a dropped connection by opening a new connection and retrying the operation.

There remains the problem of distinguishing permanent from transient errors. This can be done by comparing the error returned from a failed operation with a known list of transient errors. An application can therefore include a retry mechanism that checks the status of operations and retries any operations that experienced a transient error.

The Windows Azure AppFabric Customer Advisory Team has made available on the MSDN Code Gallery the source code and pre-compiled assemblies for the *Transient Fault Handling Framework for Azure Storage, Service Bus, and SQL Azure*. This comprises a set of classes that can be used to detect transient failures and retry SQL operations. It contains an extensible way to identify transient failures, with various examples including one that compares an error with a list of known transient failures. The Transient Fault Handling Framework provides various built-in retry backoff techniques that specify how often and frequently an operation should be retried following a transient failure. These include both a fixed interval and an exponential delay between retries. The classes in the Transient Fault Handling Framework include various extension methods that simplify the use of the framework, thereby minimizing the work required to add the handling of dropped connections and other transient failures to an application using SQL Azure.

In this recipe, we will learn how to use the *Transient Fault Handling Framework for Azure Storage, Service Bus*, and *SQL Azure* to handle dropped connections and other transient failures when using SQL Azure.

Getting ready

The recipe uses the Transient Fault Handling Framework for Azure Storage, Service Bus, and SQL Azure. It can be downloaded from the following URL:

```
http://archive.msdn.microsoft.com/appfabriccat
```

This download is a Visual Studio solution with precompiled output assemblies that are referenced in the project used in the recipe.

How to do it...

We are going to connect to SQL Azure using ADO.NET and perform various DDL and DML operations taking advantage of the transient-error handling provided by the Transient Fault Handling library. We do this as follows:

1. On the **Project Properties** dialog in Visual Studio, set the Target Framework to .NET Framework 4.

2. Add the following assembly references to the project:

   ```
   Microsoft.AppFabricCAT.Samples.Azure.TransientFaultHandling.dll
   System.configuration.dll
   ```

3. Add a new class named `RetryConnectionExample` to the project.

4. Add the following `using` statements to the top of the class file:

   ```
   using System.Data;
   using System.Data.SqlClient;
   using Microsoft.AppFabricCAT.Samples.Azure.TransientFaultHandling;
   using Microsoft.AppFabricCAT.Samples.Azure.TransientFaultHandling.SqlAzure;
   using Microsoft.AppFabricCAT.Samples.Azure.TransientFaultHandling.Configuration;
   ```

5. Add the following private members to the class:

   ```
   String connectionString;
   RetryPolicy connectionRetryPolicy;
   RetryPolicy commandRetryPolicy;
   ```

6. Add the following constructor to the class:

   ```
   public RetryConnectionExample(String server, String database,
     String login, String password)
   {
     SqlConnectionStringBuilder connStringBuilder;
     connStringBuilder = new SqlConnectionStringBuilder();
     connStringBuilder.DataSource =
       String.Format("{0}.database.windows.net", server);
   ```

```
connStringBuilder.InitialCatalog = database;
connStringBuilder.Encrypt = true;
connStringBuilder.TrustServerCertificate = false;
connStringBuilder.UserID =
  String.Format("{0}@{1}", login, server);
connStringBuilder.Password = password;
connectionString = connStringBuilder.ToString();

connectionRetryPolicy =
  new RetryPolicy<SqlAzureTransientErrorDetectionStrategy>(
    5, TimeSpan.FromMilliseconds(100));
connectionRetryPolicy.RetryOccurred +=
  RetryConnectionCallback;

RetryPolicyConfigurationSettings retryPolicySettings =
  ApplicationConfiguration.Current.GetConfigurationSection<
    RetryPolicyConfigurationSettings>(
      RetryPolicyConfigurationSettings.SectionName);
RetryPolicyInfo retryPolicyInfo =
  retryPolicySettings.Policies.Get("FixedIntervalDefault");
commandRetryPolicy = retryPolicyInfo.CreatePolicy<
  SqlAzureTransientErrorDetectionStrategy>();
commandRetryPolicy.RetryOccurred += RetryCallbackCommand;
}
```

7. Add the following callback methods to the class:

```
private void RetryConnectionCallback(Int32 currentRetryCount,
  Exception lastException, TimeSpan delay)
{
    Int32 retryCount = currentRetryCount;
}

private void RetryCallbackCommand(Int32 currentRetryCount,
  Exception lastException, TimeSpan delay)
{
    Int32 retryCount = currentRetryCount;
}
```

8. Add the following method, retrieving the session tracing Id, to the class:

```
public String GetSessionTracingId()
{
    String commandText =
      "SELECT CONVERT(NVARCHAR(36), CONTEXT_INFO())";
    String sessionTracingId;
    using (ReliableSqlConnection connection =
      new ReliableSqlConnection(connectionString))
```

```
    {
        connection.Open();
        using (SqlCommand sqlCommand =
          connection.CreateCommand())
        {
            sqlCommand.CommandText = commandText;
            sessionTracingId =
              sqlCommand.ExecuteScalarWithRetry() as String;
        }
    }
    return sessionTracingId;
}
```

9. Add the following method, creating the `Writer` table, to the class:

```
public void CreateTable()
{
    String commandText =
      @"CREATE TABLE Writer (
          Id int PRIMARY KEY NOT NULL,
          Name nvarchar(20) NOT NULL,
          CountBooks int NULL)";
    using (ReliableSqlConnection connection =
      new ReliableSqlConnection(connectionString,
        connectionRetryPolicy))
    {
        connection.Open();
        using (SqlCommand sqlCommand =
          connection.CreateCommand())
        {
            sqlCommand.CommandText = commandText;
            sqlCommand.ExecuteNonQueryWithRetry();
        }
    }
}
```

10. Add the following method, dropping the `Writer` table, to the class:

```
public void DropTable()
{
    String commandText = "DROP TABLE Writer";
    using (ReliableSqlConnection connection =
      new ReliableSqlConnection(connectionString))
    {
        connection.Open(connectionRetryPolicy);
        using (SqlCommand sqlCommand =
          connection.CreateCommand())
```

```
      {
          sqlCommand.CommandText = commandText;
           sqlCommand.ExecuteNonQueryWithRetry(
              commandRetryPolicy);
      }
    }
  }
```

11. Add the following method, querying the `Writer` table, to the class:

```
public void QueryTable()
{
    String commandText = "SELECT * FROM Writer";
    using (ReliableSqlConnection connection =
      new ReliableSqlConnection(connectionString,
        connectionRetryPolicy, commandRetryPolicy))
    {
      connection.Open();
      using (SqlCommand sqlCommand =
        new SqlCommand(commandText, connection.Current))
      {
        using (IDataReader reader =
          connection.ExecuteCommand<IDataReader>(
            sqlCommand))
        {
          Int32 idColumn = reader.GetOrdinal("Id");
          Int32 nameColumn = reader.GetOrdinal("Name");
          Int32 countBooksColumn =
            reader.GetOrdinal("CountBooks");
          while (reader.Read())
          {
            Int32 id = (Int32)reader[idColumn];
            String name = reader[nameColumn] as String;
            Int32? countBooks =
              reader[countBooksColumn] as Int32?;
          }
        }
      }
    }
}
```

12. Add the following method, inserting rows in the `Writer` table, to the class:

```
public Int32 InsertRows()
{
    String commandText =
      @"INSERT INTO Writer
```

```
            (Id, Name, CountBooks)
            VALUES
                (1, N'Cervantes', 2),
                (2, N'Smollett', null),
                (3, 'Beyle', 4)";
        Int32 rowsAffected;
        using (SqlConnection connection =
          new SqlConnection(connectionString))
        {
            connection.OpenWithRetry();
            using (SqlCommand sqlCommand =
              new SqlCommand(commandText, connection))
            {
                rowsAffected = sqlCommand.ExecuteNonQueryWithRetry();
            }
        }
        return rowsAffected;
    }
```

13. Add the following method, updating a row in the `Writer` table, to the class:

```
    public Int32 UpdateRow()
    {
        RetryPolicy exponentialRetryPolicy =
          RetryPolicy.DefaultExponential;

        String commandText =
            @"UPDATE Writer
              SET Name=@Name
              WHERE Id=3";
        Int32 rowsAffected;
        using (SqlConnection connection =
          new SqlConnection(connectionString))
        {
            connection.OpenWithRetry(exponentialRetryPolicy);
            using (SqlCommand sqlCommand =
              new SqlCommand(commandText, connection))
            {
                SqlParameter sqlParameter = new SqlParameter()
                {
                    ParameterName = "@Name",
                    Value = "Stendhal",
                    SqlDbType = SqlDbType.NVarChar,
                    Size = 20
                };
                sqlCommand.Parameters.Add(sqlParameter);
```

```
            rowsAffected = sqlCommand.ExecuteNonQueryWithRetry(
                exponentialRetryPolicy);
        }
    }
    return rowsAffected;
}
```

14. Add the following method, using the methods added earlier, to the class:

```
public static void UseRetryConnectionExample()
{
    String server = "SERVER_NAME";
    String database = "DATABASE_NAME";
    String login = "LOGIN";
    String password = "PASSWORD";
    RetryConnectionExample example =
        new RetryConnectionExample(
            server, database, login, password);

    example.GetSessionTracingId();
    example.CreateTable();
    example.InsertRows();
    example.QueryTable();
    example.UpdateRow();
    example.QueryTable();
    example.DropTable();
}
```

15. Add the following Transient Fault Handling Framework configuration to the `app.config` file for the project:

```
<configSections>
    <section name="RetryPolicyConfiguration" type="Microsoft.
AppFabricCAT.Samples.Azure.TransientFaultHandling.Configuration.
RetryPolicyConfigurationSettings,
Microsoft.AppFabricCAT.Samples.Azure.TransientFaultHandling"/>
</configSections>

<RetryPolicyConfiguration
        defaultPolicy="FixedIntervalDefault">
    <add name="FixedIntervalDefault"
        maxRetryCount="10" retryInterval="100"/>
</RetryPolicyConfiguration>
```

How it works...

In step 1, we modify the output target of the project to make it consistent with the requirements of the Transient Fault Handling Framework. In step 2, we add references to the Transient Fault Handling Framework assembly and to the `System.configuration` assembly used to access the Transient Fault Handling configuration in the `app.config` file.

In steps 3 and 4, we set up the class. In step 5, we add private members for the connection string and two `RetryPolicy` instances. In the constructor, we add in step 6, we initialize the connection string using a `SqlConnectionStringBuilder` instance. Configuring a connection string for SQL Azure is precisely the same as for Microsoft SQL Server apart from the way in which the `DataSource` is specified—with the fully qualified host name. We turn encryption on, as this is required, and set `TrustServerCertificate` to `false`, so that the server certificate is validated. Instead of building the connection string like this, we could have loaded it from a configuration file.

For demonstration purposes, we initialize the `RetryPolicy` private members using different techniques. We create the `connectionRetryPolicy` member directly by providing initialization values in its constructor. We associate the `RetryOccurred` callback method with the `connectionRetryPolicy` member. We create the `commandRetryPolicy` member by retrieving a `FixedIntervalDefault` policy from the `app.config` file. We associate the `RetryOccurred` callback method with the `commandRetryPolicy` member. In both cases, we use `SqlAzureTransientErrorDetectionStrategy` to identify transient errors. This compares an error with a list of pre-defined transient errors.

In step 7, we add two `RetryOccurred` callback methods the class. These have a trivial implementation that in a real application could be replaced by logging that a retry had occurred.

In step 8, we create and open a `ReliableSqlConnection` which we use to create a `SqlCommand`. The connection is closed automatically when we exit the `using` block. We use `SqlCommand` to retrieve the session tracing ID for the connection. This is a GUID, identifying a particular connection, which can be provided to SQL Azure Support when its help is sought in debugging a problem. We use the default `RetryPolicy` when we open the connection and when we invoke the `ExecuteScalarWithRetry()` extension method. Note that the default `RetryPolicy` identifies all errors as being transient.

In step 9, we invoke a CREATE TABLE operation on SQL Azure to create a table named `Writer`. The table has three columns: the Primary Key is the `Id` column; the remaining columns store the name of a writer and the number of books they wrote. We use the `connectionRetryPolicy`, configured in the constructor, when the connection is opened and the default `RetryPolicy` when we invoke the `ExecuteNonQueryWithRetry()` extension method.

In step 10, we invoke a `DROP TABLE` operation on SQL Azure to drop the `Writer` table. We use the default `RetryPolicy` when the connection is opened and the `commandRetryPolicy` when we invoke the `ExecuteNonQueryWithRetry()` extension method.

In step 11, we retrieve all rows from the `Writer` table and then iterate over them to examine the content of each column. We use the `connectionRetryPolicy` when the connection is opened and the `commandRetryPolicy` when we invoke the `ExecuteComman<IDataReader>()` extension method.

We insert three rows in the `Writer` table in step 12. We invoke the `OpenWithRetry()` and `ExecuteNonQueryWithRetry()` extension methods to use the default `RetryPolicy` when we open and use the connection respectively. In step 13, we use the same extension methods when we update a row in the `Writer` table. In this case, however, we parameterize them, so that we use the `DefaultExponential` retry policy when we open and use the connection. This default policy identifies all errors as transient.

In step 14, we add a method that invokes the methods added earlier. We need to provide the server name, the database name, the login, and the password.

In step 15, we add the configuration used to configure a `RetryPolicy` instance in step 6. In doing so, we need to add a `configSection` element specifying the assembly used to access the configuration and then we add a `RetryPolicyConfiguration` element in which we specify a configuration we name `FixedIntervalDefault`.

Note that, with an appropriately configured connection string, all the code in this recipe can be run against Microsoft SQL Server—with the exception of the retrieval of the session tracing ID in step 8.

There's more...

The *Transient Fault Handling Framework for Azure Storage, Service Bus, and SQL Azure* can also be used for retrying operations against the Windows Azure Storage Service and the Windows Azure Service Bus.

See also

> ▶ Valery Mizonov of the Windows Azure AppFabric Customer Advisory Team has written a blog post on *Best practices for handling transient conditions in SQL Azure client applications*. He explains how to use the Transient Fault Handling Framework. The post is available at the following URL:
>
> `http://blogs.msdn.com/b/appfabriccat/archive/2010/10/28/best-practices-for-handling-transient-conditions-in-sql-azure-client-applications.aspx`

Scaling out SQL Azure into the Windows Azure Blob Service

The Windows Azure Platform contains two storage technologies: relational with SQL Azure, and NoSQL with the Windows Azure Storage Service. These are complementary, in that storage service provides cost-effective, scalable storage while SQL Azure provides powerful query capability.

The amount of data stored in SQL Azure can be increased through sharding, in which data is distributed among several SQL Azure databases. This distribution is based on some value in the data. Although improving the scalability of SQL Azure, sharding does not address cost effectiveness.

One technique to addresses this is to scale-out data from SQL Azure into the Windows Azure Blob Service (or Windows Azure Table Service). In this technique, large data objects are stored in the Blob service and a pointer to the data stored, along with other queryable data, in SQL Azure. This effectively marries cost-effective scalable storage with a powerful query capability. Another view of this technique is that it uses SQL Azure to index the Blob service

In this recipe, we will learn how to scale out data, so that it is stored partially in SQL Azure and partially in the Windows Azure Blob Service.

How to do it...

We are going to connect to upload an "image" to the Windows Azure Blob Service and store its location using SQL Azure. We do this as follows:

1. Add the following reference to the project:

   Microsoft.WindowsAzure.StorageClient

2. Add the following Windows Azure Storage Client library configuration to the
   `app.config` file for the project:

   ```
   <appSettings>
     <add key="DataConnectionString"
       value="UseDevelopmentStorage=true"/>
   </appSettings>
   ```

3. Add a new class named `BlobShardingExample` to the project.

4. Add the following `using` statements to the top of the class file:

   ```
   using System.Data;
   using System.Data.SqlClient;
   using Microsoft.WindowsAzure;
   using Microsoft.WindowsAzure.StorageClient;
   using System.Configuration;
   using System.IO;
   ```

5. Add the following private members to the class:

```
String connectionString;
String containerName = "image";
```

6. Add the following constructor to the class:

```
public BlobShardingExample(String server, String database,
  String login, String password)
{
   SqlConnectionStringBuilder connStringBuilder;
   connStringBuilder = new SqlConnectionStringBuilder();
   connStringBuilder.DataSource =
     String.Format("{0}.database.windows.net", server);
   connStringBuilder.InitialCatalog = database;
   connStringBuilder.Encrypt = true;
   connStringBuilder.TrustServerCertificate = false;
   connStringBuilder.UserID =
     String.Format("{0}@{1}", login, server);
   connStringBuilder.Password = password;
   connectionString = connStringBuilder.ToString();
}
```

7. Add the following method, creating the `Image` table, to the class:

```
public void CreateTable()
{
   String commandText =
     @"CREATE TABLE Image (
         Id int PRIMARY KEY NOT NULL,
         Tag nvarchar(64) NOT NULL,
         ImageName nvarchar(64) NOT NULL)";
   using (SqlConnection connection =
     new SqlConnection(connectionString))
   {
      connection.Open();
      using (SqlCommand sqlCommand =
        connection.CreateCommand())
      {
         sqlCommand.CommandText = commandText;
         sqlCommand.ExecuteNonQuery();
      }
   }
}
```

8. Add the following method, dropping the `Image` table, to the class:

```
public void DropTable()
{
    String commandText = "DROP TABLE Image";
    using (SqlConnection connection =
      new SqlConnection(connectionString))
    {
        connection.Open();
        using (SqlCommand sqlCommand =
          connection.CreateCommand())
        {
            sqlCommand.CommandText = commandText;
            sqlCommand.ExecuteNonQuery();
        }
    }
}
```

9. Add the following method, retrieving the image name from the `Image` table, to the class:

```
public String RetrieveImageName(String tag)
{
    String commandText =
        @"SELECT TOP 1 ImageName
          FROM Image
          WHERE
          Tag = @Tag";

    String imageName = String.Empty;
    using (SqlConnection connection =
      new SqlConnection(connectionString))
    {
        connection.Open();
        using (SqlCommand sqlCommand =
          new SqlCommand(commandText, connection))
        {
            sqlCommand.Parameters.Add(
              "@Tag", SqlDbType.NVarChar, 64).Value = tag;
            using (SqlDataReader reader =
              sqlCommand.ExecuteReader())
            {
                Int32 blobNameColumn =
                  reader.GetOrdinal("ImageName");
                while (reader.Read())
                {
                    imageName = reader[blobNameColumn] as String;
```

```
                    }
                }
            }
        }
        return imageName;
    }
```

10. Add the following method, saving the image name in the `Image` table, to the class:

```
public void SaveImageName(
  Int32 Id, String tag, String imageName)
{
    String commandText =
      @"INSERT INTO Image
        (Id, Tag, ImageName)
        VALUES
        ( @Id, @Tag, @ImageName)";
    using (SqlConnection connection =
      new SqlConnection(connectionString))
    {
        connection.Open();
        using (SqlCommand sqlCommand =
          new SqlCommand(commandText, connection))
        {
            sqlCommand.Parameters.Add(
              "@Id", SqlDbType.Int).Value = Id;
            sqlCommand.Parameters.Add(
               "@Tag", SqlDbType.NVarChar, 64).Value = tag;
            sqlCommand.Parameters.Add(
              "@ImageName", SqlDbType.NVarChar, 64).Value
                 = imageName;
            sqlCommand.ExecuteNonQuery();
        }
    }
    return;
}
```

11. Add the following method, uploading the "image" to the Blob service, to the class:

```
public void UploadImage(String imageName)
{
    CloudStorageAccount cloudStorageAccount =
      CloudStorageAccount.Parse(
        ConfigurationManager.AppSettings[
          "DataConnectionString"]);
    CloudBlobClient cloudBlobClient =
      cloudStorageAccount.CreateCloudBlobClient();
```

```
CloudBlobContainer cloudBlobContainer =
  cloudBlobClient.GetContainerReference(containerName);
cloudBlobContainer.CreateIfNotExist();
CloudBlockBlob cloudBlockBlob =
  cloudBlobContainer.GetBlockBlobReference(imageName);

String shouldBeAnImage = new String('z', 1000);
UTF8Encoding utf8Encoding = new UTF8Encoding();
using (MemoryStream memoryStream =
  new MemoryStream(utf8Encoding.GetBytes(shouldBeAnImage)))
{
    cloudBlockBlob.UploadFromStream(memoryStream);
}

return;
}
```

12. Add the following method, coordinating the use of SQL Azure and the Blob service, to the class:

```
public void Save(String tag, String imageName)
{
    UploadImage(imageName);
    SaveImageName(1, tag, imageName);
}
```

13. Add the following method, using the methods added earlier, to the class:

```
public static void UseBlobShardingExample()
{
    String server = "SERVER_NAME";
    String database = "DATABASE_NAME";
    String login = "tolsta";
    String password = "PASSWORD";
    String tag = "Grand Canyon";
    String imageName = "SomeImage";

    BlobShardingExample example = new
      BlobShardingExample(server, database, login, password);
    example.CreateTable();
    example.Save(tag, imageName);
    String retrievedBlobName = example.RetrieveImageName(tag);
    example.DropTable();
}
```

How it works...

In steps 1 and 2, we add the Windows Azure Storage Client library to the project and add its configuration to the application configuration file.

In steps 3 and 4, we set up the class. In step 5, we add private members for the connection string and the container name. In the constructor we add in step 6, we initialize the connection string using a `SqlConnectionStringBuilder` instance.

In step 7, we invoke a `CREATE TABLE` operation on SQL Azure to create a table named `Image`. The table has three columns: the Primary Key is the `Id` column; the remaining columns store a tag and the name of the blob in which the "image" is stored. In step 8, we invoke a `DROP TABLE` operation on SQL Azure to drop the `Image` table.

In step 9, we retrieve the blob name from the first row in the `Image` table with the specified tag. In step 10, we insert a row in the `Image` table to associate an image name with a tag. In step 11, we create an in-memory "image" and upload it the blob with the specified `imageName`. In step 12, we add a method to coordinate the uploading of the "image" with the saving of its location in the `Image` table.

In step 13, we add a method that invokes the methods added earlier. We need to provide the server name, the database name, the login, and the password. We also provide a tag and a name for the "image" we upload.

There's more...

SQL Azure Federations supports the automated sharding of data among multiple SQL Azure databases, referred to as federation members, as well as the automated routing of Transact SQL commands to the appropriate federation member. A federated database can have multiple federations, identified by federation key, allowing different classes of data in the federated database to scale independently. SQL Azure Federations provides a single connection endpoint for a federated database, so that a client application does not need to route SQL statements to a specific federation member.

A federation is created by invoking a `CREATE FEDERATION` statement in a root database, and providing a federation name and a federation key. This creates a federation with a single federation member into which all federated data is stored. As data is added to the federation member, the `ALTER FEDERATION` statement can be used with a `SPLIT` keyword to split the federation at a specific value of the federation key. The outcome of this statement is a federation with two federation members, one containing data from below the split value and the other containing data from above the split value. This process can be repeated to create additional federation members, as required.

SQL Azure Federations supports three types of table:

1. `Federated tables` exist in all federation members, and federated data is allocated to them depending on the value of the federation key.

2. `Reference tables` exist in all federation members, and store the same reference data in each federation member.

3. `Root tables` exist only in the root database for the federation.

The records with the same federation key in a federation comprise an atomic unit, as they represent an indivisible set of records that are always allocated to the same federation member. An application can invoke the `USE FEDERATION` statement, specifying a federation key, to indicate that subsequent SQL statements should apply only to the specified federation member and filtered to the atomic unit identified by the federation key. This feature is useful in the migration of single-tenant Microsoft SQL Server databases to a multitenant federated solution.

As of this writing, SQL Azure Federations is in limited CTP. Cihan Biyikoglu, of the SQL Azure team, has published various posts on SQL Azure Federations to his blog at the following URL:

`http://blogs.msdn.com/b/cbiyikoglu/`

9
Looking at the Windows Azure AppFabric

In this chapter, we will cover:

- ► Creating a namespace for the Windows Azure AppFabric
- ► Using the Service Bus as a relay service
- ► Using Service Bus events
- ► Using a Service Bus message buffer
- ► Using the Windows Azure AppFabric Caching service

Introduction

The Windows Azure AppFabric adds middleware services to the Windows Azure Platform. The initial focus extended **Windows Communication Foundation** (**WCF**) services into the cloud. However, the Windows Azure AppFabric now provides many higher-level services that simplify the use of the Windows Azure Platform. It provides a Service Bus that services can use to host public endpoints acting as rendezvous addresses for various capabilities. It provides a Caching service that Windows Azure hosted services can use to cache and share frequently used data. It provides an **Access Control Service** that exposes a cloud-based **Secure Token Service** (STS) that various services in the Windows Azure Platform use to facilitate claims-based authentication.

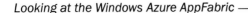

The Windows Azure AppFabric provides a labs environment where new features can be tried out as **Community Technology Previews** (**CTP**). Two very powerful features currently being previewed are **Windows Azure AppFabric Queues and Topics**, and **Windows Azure AppFabric Applications**. AppFabric Queues and Topics supports sophisticated publish/subscribe scenarios. AppFabric Applications simplifies the development and deployment of sophisticated applications created through the composition of services.

The Windows Azure AppFabric services use a namespace for identification. This namespace must be included as the first part of the URL when accessing these services. We see how to use the Windows Azure Portal to configure a namespace in the *Creating a namespace for the Windows Azure AppFabric* recipe.

The basic extension of WCF to the cloud is provided by the Windows Azure AppFabric Service Bus. This provides various bindings that allow a service to create a public listening endpoint on a Service Bus located in a Windows Azure datacenter, and have a client access that endpoint. The Service Bus relays all traffic across the connection to and from the client and the service. As both service and client connect to the Service Bus through outbound connections, there is no need to open inbound ports on a firewall to use the Service Bus. It therefore provides a secure way to expose services normally hidden behind a firewall. The different Service Bus bindings support various scenarios. In the *Using the Service Bus as a relay service* recipe, we see the basic example of a two-way connection between a client and a service. In the *Using Service Bus events* recipe, we see how to implement a one-way publish/subscribe scenario.

The Service Bus provides message buffers to support disconnected communication between a client and a service. A message buffer is an in-memory queue that can hold a small number of messages for a short time. A client and a service can use multiple message buffers to implement a request and response scenario without there ever being a connection between the two. We see how to do this in the *Using a Service Bus message buffer* recipe. The Windows Azure AppFabric Queues and Topics CTP provide a powerful alternative to Service Bus message buffers.

Caching is an important feature for highly scalable services and websites. The Windows Azure AppFabric Caching service is a cloud-based caching service that supports caches up to 4 GB. The Caching service is based on the Windows Server AppFabric Caching service and provides most of its functionality with none of the management responsibility. We see how to use the Caching service in the *Using the Windows Azure AppFabric Caching service* recipe.

Creating a namespace for the Windows Azure AppFabric

The Windows Azure AppFabric Service Bus supports various features that involve the creation of a relay endpoint at a service-specific *rendezvous address* on the Service Bus. A listening service connects to the Service Bus and creates a listener at the rendezvous address. A client can then connect to the listener at the rendezvous address, and the Service Bus then relays communication between the client and the service.

The Service Bus uses a multi-part name to identify a rendezvous address. This name is constructed from a Service Bus namespace, configured on the Windows Azure Portal, and a service path used to distinguish individual rendezvous addresses within the same namespace. The rendezvous address is in the following form:

```
{SERVICE_NAMESPACE}.servicebus.windows.net/{SERVICE_PATH}
```

The service namespace must be unique across the entire Service Bus. The service path can be multilevel, so that `Chicago/Sales` and `Atlanta/Sales` identify different rendezvous addresses that can be used to distinguish relay endpoints for different services. The Service Bus uses a matching algorithm that causes a rendezvous address to hide another one that merely adds additional characters. For example, a rendezvous address on `Chicago` hides one on `Chicago/Sales`. However, `Chicago/Sales` and `Chicago/Accounts` would both be valid were `Chicago` itself not used as a rendezvous point.

In this recipe, we will learn how to create a namespace for the Windows Azure AppFabric Service Bus.

How to do it...

We are going to create and configure a namespace for the Windows AppFabric Service Bus. We do this as follows:

1. Access the Windows Azure Portal.
2. Click on the **Service Bus, Access Control & Caching** button.
3. Click on the **Service Bus** button.
4. Click on the **New** button.
5. Specify the following values:
   - ❏ `Namespace`
   - ❏ `Country/Region`
   - ❏ `Subscription`
   - ❏ `Connection Pack Size`
6. Click on the **Create Namespace** button.

How it works...

In steps 1 through 3, we go to the correct screen on the Windows Azure Portal to create a Service Bus namespace.

In step 5, we configure the namespace. We need to provide a namespace that is unique across the entire Service Bus. We also have to specify the Windows Azure datacenter, indicated by region, where the Service Bus endpoint will be located for any services that use this namespace. We need to provide the Windows Azure subscription with which the namespace is associated. Finally, we can specify the size of connection pack we want to use to take advantage of discounted pricing offered for pre-committed use.

In step 6, we initiate the creation process which should complete in a few minutes.

Once the Service Bus namespace has been created, we can view its properties on the portal. Specifically, we can click on the **Default Key** button to retrieve the issuer and authentication token we need to authenticate use of the Service Bus. The default issuer name is `owner`, but it is possible to use the Windows Azure AppFabric Access Control Service management service to add other issuers.

There's more...

The Windows Azure AppFabric Caching service and Access Control Service use the same namespace creation dialog used in creating a Service Bus namespace. In fact, if we click on the **Create Namespace** button visible after step 2, we are presented with the same dialog preconfigured to create the same namespace for all three services. The only effect of performing step 3 is that the dialog is preconfigured to create a namespace only for the Service Bus.

Using the Service Bus as a relay service

The Windows Azure AppFabric Service Bus provides a relay service allowing communication between a client and a server even when the server is located behind a firewall. The Service Bus does this by providing a public endpoint for the service. A client, who could not ordinarily punch through the firewall, can connect in a secure manner to the public endpoint and the Service Bus relays this connection through the firewall to the service. The Service Bus implements this capability by fusing an outbound connection from the server with an outbound connection from the client. Consequently, the firewall does need to allow an outbound connection, but it does not need to allow an inbound connection. Under certain circumstances, the Service Bus may upgrade the connection, so that it goes directly between the client and the server bypassing the Service Bus relay endpoint completely, thereby providing a much faster connection. This is similar to the way instant messaging clients transfer files by communicating directly with each other rather than using the instant messaging service.

The Service Bus supports various bindings to support the relay service. These bindings are essentially Service Bus variants of existing Windows Communication Foundation (WCF) bindings. The Microsoft recommended binding for the relay service is the `NetTcpRelayBinding`, which is the Service Bus equivalent of the `NetTcpBinding` binding in WCF. This binding requires both client and server to be using WCF and to use a special "sb" protocol scheme instead of the "tcp" or "http" protocol schemes. Alternatively, the `BasicHttpRelayBinding` supports the WS-I Basic Profile 1.1, while the `WebHttpRelayBinding` supports HTTP messages instead of the SOAP used in the other bindings. Other than the use of a specific Service Bus binding, the code for the client and the service is essentially standard WCF. The Service Bus configuration can be provided either programmatically or through the `app.config` file.

In this recipe, we will learn how to use the Service Bus relay service.

Getting ready

We need to create a Service Bus namespace. We see how to do this in the *Creating a namespace for the Windows Azure AppFabric* recipe in this chapter.

How to do it...

We are going to use a Windows AppFabric Service Bus relay service to connect a client with service. This service exposes a simple contract with an implementation that converts a temperature between Celsius and Fahrenheit and vice versa. In this recipe, we will configure the Service Bus connection programmatically. We do this as follows:

1. Create a Console Application and name the project `Server`.

2. Set the Target Framework for the project to.NET Framework 4.

3. Add the following assembly references to the project:

   ```
   Microsoft.ServiceBus
   System.ServiceModel
   ```

4. Add the following using statements to the top of the `Program.cs`:

   ```
   using Microsoft.ServiceBus;
   using System.ServiceModel;
   using System.ServiceModel.Description;
   ```

5. Add the following members to the top of the `Program` class:

   ```
   static String serviceNamespace = "SERVICE_NAMESPACE";
   static String issuerName = "owner";
   static String issuerKey = "AUTHENTICATION_TOKEN";
   static String serviceName = "TemperatureService";
   ```

6. Replace `Main()` with the following:

```
static void Main(string[] args)
{
    RunService();
}
```

7. Add the following method, setting up the service, to the `Program` class:

```
private static void RunService()
{
    Console.WriteLine("Server");

    ServiceRegistrySettings registryBehavior =
      new ServiceRegistrySettings()
    {
        DiscoveryMode = DiscoveryType.Public,
        DisplayName = "Temperature Service"
    };

    TransportClientEndpointBehavior credentialBehavior =
      new TransportClientEndpointBehavior();
    credentialBehavior.CredentialType =
      TransportClientCredentialType.SharedSecret;
    credentialBehavior.Credentials.SharedSecret.IssuerName =
      issuerName;
    credentialBehavior.Credentials.SharedSecret.IssuerSecret =
      issuerKey;

    Uri serviceUri = ServiceBusEnvironment.CreateServiceUri(
      "sb", serviceNamespace, serviceName);

    using (ServiceHost serviceHost =
      new ServiceHost(typeof(TemperatureService), serviceUri))
    {
        NetTcpRelayBinding binding = new NetTcpRelayBinding();

        serviceHost.AddServiceEndpoint(
          typeof(ITemperatureContract), binding, serviceUri);
        serviceHost.Description.Endpoints[0].Behaviors.Add(
          credentialBehavior);
        serviceHost.Description.Endpoints[0].Behaviors.Add(
          registryBehavior);

        serviceHost.Open();
        Console.WriteLine("Press Enter to exit.");
        Console.ReadLine();
    }
}
```

8. Add a new Interface, named `ITemperatureContract`, to the project.

9. Add the following `using` statement to `ITemperatureContract.cs`:

```
using System.ServiceModel;
```

10. Replace everything inside the declaration with the following service contract:

```
[ServiceContract(Name = "ITemperatureContract")]
interface ITemperatureContract
{
    [OperationContract]
    Double ToCelsius(Double fahrenheit);

    [OperationContract]
    Double ToFahrenheit(Double celsius);
}
```

11. Add a class, named `TemperatureService`, to the project.

12. Add the following `using` statement to the class:

```
using System.ServiceModel;
```

13. Replace everything inside the `namespace` declaration in `TemperatureService.cs` with the following:

```
[ServiceBehavior(Name = "TemperatureService")]
public class TemperatureService : ITemperatureContract
{
    public Double ToCelsius(Double fahrenheit)
    {
        Double celsius = (fahrenheit - 32d) * 5d / 9d;
        Console.WriteLine("{0} Fahrenheit is {1} celsius",
          fahrenheit, celsius);
        return celsius;
    }

    public Double ToFahrenheit(Double celsius)
    {
        Double fahrenheit = 32d + celsius * 9d / 5d;
        Console.WriteLine("{0} celsius is {1} Fahrenheit",
          celsius, fahrenheit);
        return fahrenheit;
    }
}
```

14. Add another Console Application to the project and name it `Client`.

15. Set the Target Framework for the project to .NET Framework 4.

16. Add the following assembly references to the project:

```
Microsoft.ServiceBus
System.ServiceModel
```

17. Add the following `using` statements to the top of `Program.cs`:

```
using Microsoft.ServiceBus;
using System.ServiceModel;
using Server;
```

18. Add the following members to the top of the `Program` class:

```
static String serviceNamespace = "SERVICE_NAMESPACE";
static String issuerName = "owner";
static String issuerKey = "AUTHENTICATION_TOKEN";
static String serviceName = "TemperatureService";
```

19. Replace `Main()` with the following:

```
static void Main(string[] args)
{
    RunClient();
}
```

20. Add the following method, using the service, to the `Program` class:

```
private static void RunClient()
{
    Console.WriteLine("Client");

    TransportClientEndpointBehavior credentialBehavior =
      new TransportClientEndpointBehavior();
    credentialBehavior.CredentialType =
      TransportClientCredentialType.SharedSecret;
    credentialBehavior.Credentials.SharedSecret.IssuerName =
      issuerName;
    credentialBehavior.Credentials.SharedSecret.IssuerSecret =
      issuerKey;

    NetTcpRelayBinding binding = new NetTcpRelayBinding();

    Uri serviceUri = ServiceBusEnvironment.CreateServiceUri(
      "sb", serviceNamespace, serviceName);
    EndpointAddress endpointAddress =
      new EndpointAddress(serviceUri);

    using (ChannelFactory<ITemperatureContract> channelFactory
      = new ChannelFactory<ITemperatureContract>(
          binding, endpointAddress))
```

```
    {
            channelFactory.Endpoint.Behaviors.Add(
              credentialBehavior);

            ITemperatureContract channel =
              channelFactory.CreateChannel();
            ((ICommunicationObject)channel).Open();

            Double boilingPointCelsius = channel.ToCelsius(212);
            Double boilingPointFahrenheit =
              channel.ToFahrenheit(boilingPointCelsius);

            Console.WriteLine("212 Fahrenheit is {0} celsius",
              boilingPointCelsius);
            Console.WriteLine("{0} celsius is {1} Fahrenheit",
              boilingPointCelsius, boilingPointFahrenheit);

            ((ICommunicationObject)channel).Close();

            Console.WriteLine("Press Enter to exit.");
            Console.ReadLine();
    }
    }
```

21. Add a link to the `ITemperatureContract` interface added in step 8.

22. Build the solution.

23. Start the Server program.

24. Start the Client program.

How it works...

In steps 1 through 4, we set up the server program by adding the required references and `using` statements. In step 5, we add private members to store the Service Bus namespace and authentication token, which we need to replace with the actual values for the Service Bus configuration from the Windows Azure Portal. In step 6, we delegate to the `RunService()` method.

In step 7, we configure and create the `TemperatureService` service. We create a `ServiceRegistrySettings` behavior to make the service discoverable with the specified display name. This means that a public feed is generated at `{SERVICE_NAMESPACE}.servicebus.windows.net/`, exposing the name of the service, as well as the name of any other service declared as discoverable for this Service Bus namespace. We then create a `TransportClientEndpointBehavior` specifying that we are using shared secret authentication with the `issuerName` and `issuerKey` members we added in step 5.

Next, we create the service URI, specifying the `sb` service protocol required for the `NetTcpRelayBinding`, from the namespace and name for the service. Then, we create the `ServiceHost` for the `TemperatureService` using the service URI. We add a service endpoint using the `NetTcpRelayBinding`, as well as the `ServiceRegistrySettings` and `TransportClientEndpointBehavior` we created earlier. Finally, we open the service and wait for it to be used.

In steps 8 and 9, we set up the `ITemperatureContract` interface for the service contract. In step 10, we specify the interface, adding two operation contracts: one to convert Fahrenheit to Celsius and the other to convert Celsius to Fahrenheit.

In steps 11 and 12, we set up the `TemperatureContract` class that implements the `ITemperatureContract` interface. In step 13, we provide the actual implementation for the `ToCelsius()` and `ToFahrenheit()` operations exposed by `TemperatureService`.

In steps 14 through 17, we set up the client program by adding the required references and using statements. In step 18, we add private members to store the Service Bus namespace and authentication token, which we need to replace with the actual values for the Service Bus configuration from the Windows Azure Portal. In step 19, we delegate to the `RunClient()` method.

In step 20, we create a `TransportClientEndpointBehavior` specifying that we are using a shared secret credential with the `issuerName` and `issuerKey` members we added in step 18. Next, we create a `NetTcpRelayBinding` instance, and configure an `EndpointAddress` from the service namespace and name. As required for the `NetTcpRelayBinding`, we again specify `sb` as the service protocol.

We then create a `ChannelFactory` for the `ITemperatureContract`, using the just created `NetTcpRelayBinding` and `EndpointAddress`. We add the shared secret credential to it and then open the channel. Finally, we use the channel to invoke the `ToCelsius()` and the `ToFahrenheit()` operations and write the results to the console.

In step 21, we add the `ITemperatureContract` interface to the client project by linking to its definition in the server project.

In step 22, we build the solution. In step 23, we start the server and should wait until the service has started—indicated by the display of `Press Enter to Exit` in the Console—before starting the client in step 24. The results of a conversion from Celsius to Fahrenheit and back should be displayed in the console windows for both the server and the client.

The service must authenticate with the Windows Azure Access Control Service (ACS) using an issuer name and authentication token generated when the Service Bus namespace is created on the Windows Azure Portal. The service can be configured, so that the client does not require authentication. We see how to create the Service Bus namespace and retrieve the issuer and authentication token in the *Creating a namespace for the Windows Azure AppFabric* recipe in this chapter.

Using Service Bus events

The Windows Azure AppFabric Service Bus supports two bindings that have no parallel in traditional Windows Communication Foundation (WCF): `NetOneWayRelayBinding` and `NetEventRelayBinding`. These explicitly support only one-way communication from a client to a service. In the `NetOneWayRelayBinding`, the service connects to the Service Bus which creates a listening endpoint for the service. A client can connect to this relay service endpoint and send messages to it that are relayed to the service. The `NetEventRelayBinding` is derived from the `NetOneWayRelayBinding` and adds the feature that multiple services can listen at the same relay service endpoint. This makes the `NetEventRelayBinding` useful for publish/subscribe scenarios, with the client being the publisher and the subscribers being one or more instances of the service.

In this recipe, we will learn how to use the `NetEventRelayBinding` to implement a publish/subscribe scenario.

We need to create a Service Bus namespace. We see how to do this in the *Creating a namespace for the Windows Azure AppFabric Service Bus* recipe in this chapter.

We are going to use a Windows AppFabric Service Bus `NetEventRelayBinding` to implement a publish/subscribe scenario in which a client publishes events, which one or more instances of a service subscribe to. The initial subscriber creates a Service Bus relay service endpoint to which the publisher and additional subscribers connect. In this recipe, we will configure the Service Bus connection in the `app.config` file. We do this as follows:

1. Create a Console Application and name the project `Subscriber`.

2. Set the Target Framework for the project to .NET Framework 4.

3. Add the following assembly references to the project:

   ```
   Microsoft.ServiceBus
   System.ServiceModel
   ```

4. Add the following `using` statements to the top of `Program.cs`:

```
using Microsoft.ServiceBus;
using Microsoft.ServiceBus.Description;
using System.ServiceModel;
using System.ServiceModel.Description;
```

5. Add the following members to the top of the `Program` class:

```
static String serviceBusNamespace = "SERVICE_NAMESPACE";
static String serviceName = "Subscriber.GossipService";
```

6. Replace `Main()` with the following:

```
static void Main(string[] args)
{
    SubscribeToGossip();
}
```

7. Add the following method, setting up the service, to the `Program` class:

```
private static void SubscribeToGossip()
{
    Console.WriteLine("Subscriber");

    Uri serviceUri = ServiceBusEnvironment.CreateServiceUri(
        "sb", serviceBusNamespace, serviceName);

    using (ServiceHost serviceHost =
        new ServiceHost(typeof(GossipService), serviceUri))
    {
        serviceHost.Open();

        Console.WriteLine("Press Enter to Exit");
        Console.ReadLine();
    }
}
```

8. Add a new interface named `IGossipContract` to the project.

9. Add the following `using` statement to `IGossipContract.cs`:

```
using System.ServiceModel;
```

10. Replace everything inside the `namespace` declaration with the following service contract:

```
[ServiceContract(Name = "IGossipContract")]
public interface IGossipContract
{
    [OperationContract(IsOneWay = true)]
    void ShareGossip( String gossip);
}
```

11. Add a class named `GossipService` to the project.

12. Add the following `using` statement to the class:

```
using System.ServiceModel;
```

13. Replace everything inside the `namespace` declaration in the `GossipService` class:

```
[ServiceBehavior(Name = "GossipService")]
public class GossipService : IGossipContract
{
    public void ShareGossip(String gossip)
    {
        String moreGossip = gossip;
        Console.WriteLine(moreGossip);
    }
}
```

14. Add the following service definition to the `configuration` section of `app.config`:

```
<system.serviceModel>
  <behaviors>
    <endpointBehaviors>
      <behavior name="sharedSecretCredentials">
        <transportClientEndpointBehavior
          credentialType="SharedSecret">
          <clientCredentials>
            <sharedSecret  issuerName="owner"
                issuerSecret="AUTHENTICATION_KEY" />
          </clientCredentials>
        </transportClientEndpointBehavior>
      </behavior>
    </endpointBehaviors>
  </behaviors>
  <services>
    <service name="Subscriber.GossipService">
      <endpoint
        name="RelayEndpoint"
        binding="netEventRelayBinding"
        contract="Subscriber.IGossipContract"
        behaviorConfiguration="sharedSecretCredentials"/>
    </service>
  </services>
</system.serviceModel>
```

15. Add another Console Application to the project and name it `Publisher`.

16. Set the Target Framework for the project to .NET Framework 4.

17. Add the following assembly references to the project:

```
Microsoft.ServiceBus
System.ServiceModel
```

18. Add the following `using` statements to the top of the `Program` class:

```
using Microsoft.ServiceBus;
using Microsoft.ServiceBus.Description;
using System.ServiceModel;
using Subscriber;
```

19. Replace `Main()` with the following:

```
static void Main(string[] args)
{
    PublishGossip();
}
```

20. Add the following method, publishing events, to the `Program` class:

```
private static void PublishGossip()
{
    Console.WriteLine("Publisher");

    using (ChannelFactory<IGossipContract> channelFactory =
      new ChannelFactory<IGossipContract>("RelayEndpoint"))
    {
        IGossipContract channel =
            channelFactory.CreateChannel();
        ((ICommunicationObject)channel).Open();

        channel.ShareGossip("All's well that ends well.");
        channel.ShareGossip("As you like it.");
        channel.ShareGossip("Much ado about nothing.");
        channel.ShareGossip("Measure for measure.");

        ((ICommunicationObject)channel).Close();

        Console.WriteLine("Gossip sent");
        Console.WriteLine("Press Enter to Exit");
        Console.ReadLine();
    }
}
```

21. Add a link to the `IGossipContract` interface added in step 8.

22. Add the following client configuration to the `configuration` section of `app.config`:

```
<system.serviceModel>
  <behaviors>
    <endpointBehaviors>
      <behavior name="sharedSecretCredentials">
       <transportClientEndpointBehavior
          credentialType="SharedSecret">
        <clientCredentials>
          <sharedSecret issuerName="owner"
            issuerSecret="AUTHENTICATION_KEY" />
        </clientCredentials>
       </transportClientEndpointBehavior>
      </behavior>
    </endpointBehaviors>
  </behaviors>
  <client>
    <endpoint name="RelayEndpoint"
       address="sb://SERVICE_NAMESPACE.servicebus.
         windows.net/Subscriber.GossipService"
      binding="netEventRelayBinding"
      contract="Subscriber.IGossipContract"
      behaviorConfiguration="sharedSecretCredentials"/>
    </client>
</system.serviceModel>
```

23. Build the solution.

24. Start the Subscriber program. We can start this multiple times to use multiple subscribers.

25. Start the Publisher program.

How it works...

In steps 1 through 4, we set up the server by adding the required references and `using` statements. In step 5, we add a private member to store the Service Bus namespace (`SERVICE_NAMESPACE`), which we need to replace with the actual value for the Service Bus configuration from the Windows Azure Portal. In step 6, we delegate to the `SubscribeToGossip()` method.

In step 7, we create the service URI, specifying the `sb` service protocol required for the `NetEventRelayBinding`, from the namespace and service name. Then, we create the `ServiceHost` for the `GossipService` using the service URI. The configuration is loaded automatically from `app.config`. Finally, we open the service and wait for it to be used.

In steps 8 and 9, we set up the `IGossipContract` interface for the service contract. In step 10, we specify the interface adding a single operation contract to share gossip. This contract is decorated with the `IsOneWay = true` attribute, as the `NetEventRelayBinding` is one way.

In steps 11 and 12, we set up the `GossipService` class that implements the `IGossipContract` interface. In step 13, we provide the actual implementation for the `ShareGossip()` operation exposed by `IGossipContract`.

In step 14, we configure the `GossipService` service using `app.config`. We first provide an `endpointBehavior` containing the shared key authentication credentials. We then specify the binding, the contract, and the authentication credentials for the `GossipService` service. We need to replace the `AUTHENTICATION_KEY` with the actual value for the Service Bus configuration from the Windows Azure Portal.

In steps 15 through 18, we set up the client program by adding the required references and `using` statements. In step 19, we delegate to the `PublishGossip()` method.

In step 20, we create a `ChannelFactory` for the `IGossipContract`, loading the configuration from `app.config`, and then open the channel. Finally, we use the channel to invoke the `ShareGossip()` operation and log that to the console.

In step 21, we add the `IGossipContract` interface to the client project by linking to its definition in the server project.

In step 22, we configure the `GossipService` client using `app.config`. We first provide an `endpointBehavior` containing the shared key authentication credentials. We then specify the binding, the contract, and the authentication credentials for the `GossipService` client. We need to replace the `AUTHENTICATION_KEY` and `SERVICE_NAMESPACE` with the actual values for the Service Bus configuration from the Windows Azure Portal.

In step 23, we build the solution. In step 24, we start the Subscriber service one or more times. After one of them has started (indicated by the display of `Press Enter to Exit` in the Console) we can start the Publisher client. The gossip should then appear in the console windows of each subscriber.

There's more...

The service must authenticate with the Windows Azure Access Control Service (ACS) using an issuer name and authentication token generated when the Service Bus namespace is created on the Windows Azure Portal. The service can be configured, so that the client does not require authentication. We see how to create the Service Bus namespace and retrieve the issuer and authentication token in the *Creating a namespace for the Windows Azure AppFabric* recipe in this chapter.

See also

The *See also* section of the *Using a service bus message buffer* recipe has a description of Windows Azure Service Bus Queues and Topics, a new feature Microsoft has introduced as a community technology preview (CTP). Service Bus Queues and Topics supports sophisticated publish/subscribe scenarios.

Using a Service Bus message buffer

The Windows Azure AppFabric Service Bus supports disconnected communication between a client and a server through a message buffer implemented as a named endpoint on the Service Bus. A client can insert a message into a message buffer, and the server can later retrieve the message from the buffer. The server can respond to the client by putting a message in another buffer which the client can read.

By default, a message buffer may contain 10 messages, but it can be configured to hold up to 50 messages. A message buffer is transient and is automatically deleted when it has not been used for a configurable amount of time, with a default of 5 minutes and a maximum of 10 minutes. Message buffers are stored in memory and are not persisted to permanent storage. Consequently, it is possible that the contents of a message buffer are lost if the server storing it encounters a problem.

In this recipe, we will learn how to use a message buffer to implement disconnected communication.

Getting ready

We need to create a Service Bus namespace. We see how to do this in the *Creating a namespace for the Windows Azure AppFabric* recipe in this chapter.

How to do it...

We are going to use a Windows AppFabric Service Bus message buffer to connect two services representing the individual players in a game of chess. The services use two message buffers to communicate—one buffer for each player. These message buffers are limited to a single message each, representing the fact that a player can make only one move at a time. The first service that adds a move to the "white" message buffer is declared to be *white*. In this recipe, we will configure the Service Bus connection programmatically. We do this as follows:

1. Create a Console Application and name the project `MessageBufferExample`.
2. Set the Target Framework for the project to be .NET Framework 4.

3. Add the following assembly references to the project:

```
Microsoft.ServiceBus
Microsoft.ServiceModel
System.Runtime.Serialization
```

4. Add the following using statements to the top of `Program.cs`:

```
using Microsoft.ServiceBus;
using System.ServiceModel.Channels;
```

5. Add the following members to the top of the `Program` class:

```
static String serviceNamespace = "SERVICE_NAMESPACE";
static String issuerName = "owner";
static String issuerKey = "AUTHENTICATION_KEY";
static String whiteBufferName = "White";
static String blackBufferName = "Black";
```

6. Replace `Main()` with the following:

```
static void Main(string[] args)
{
    PlayGame();
}
```

7. Add the following method, controlling the game logic, to the `Program` class:

```
private static void PlayGame()
{
    String[] whiteMoves = { "e4", "Nf3", "d4", "Nxd4", "Nc3" };
    String[] blackMoves = { "c5", "d6", "cxd4", "Nf6", "g6" };

    MessageBufferClient whiteBufferClient =
        CreateMessageBufferClient(whiteBufferName);
    MessageBufferClient blackBufferClient =
        CreateMessageBufferClient(blackBufferName);

    Boolean playingBlack = false;
    try
    {
        MakeMove(whiteBufferClient, "BlackOrWhite");
    }
    catch (System.TimeoutException)
    {
        playingBlack = true;
        GetMove(whiteBufferClient);
    }
```

```
    Console.WriteLine("Playing {0}",
      playingBlack ? "black" : "white");
    Console.WriteLine("Press Enter to start");
    Console.ReadLine();

    for (Int32 i = 0; i < whiteMoves.Length; i++)
    {
       if (playingBlack)
       {
          String lastWhiteMove = GetMove(whiteBufferClient);
          MakeMove(blackBufferClient, blackMoves[i]);
       }
       else
       {
          if (i > 0)
          {
             String lastBlackMove = GetMove(blackBufferClient);
          }
          MakeMove(whiteBufferClient, whiteMoves[i]);
       }
    }

    if (playingBlack)
    {
       whiteBufferClient.DeleteMessageBuffer();
       blackBufferClient.DeleteMessageBuffer();
    }

    Console.WriteLine("Press Enter to Exit");
    Console.ReadLine();
}
```

8. Add the following method, creating the message buffer client, to the `Program` class:

```
private static MessageBufferClient
  CreateMessageBufferClient(String bufferName)
{
    TransportClientEndpointBehavior credentialBehavior =
      GetCredentials();

    Uri bufferUri =
      ServiceBusEnvironment.CreateServiceUri(
        "https", serviceNamespace, bufferName);

    MessageBufferPolicy messageBufferPolicy =
      GetMessageBufferPolicy();
```

```
        MessageBufferClient bufferClient =
          MessageBufferClient.CreateMessageBuffer(
            credentialBehavior, bufferUri, messageBufferPolicy);

        return bufferClient;
    }
```

9. Add the following method, creating the Service Buffer credentials, to the `Program` class:

```
private static TransportClientEndpointBehavior GetCredentials()
{
    TransportClientEndpointBehavior credentialBehavior =
      new TransportClientEndpointBehavior();
    credentialBehavior.CredentialType =
      TransportClientCredentialType.SharedSecret;
    credentialBehavior.Credentials.SharedSecret.IssuerName =
      issuerName;
    credentialBehavior.Credentials.SharedSecret.IssuerSecret =
      issuerKey;
    return credentialBehavior;
}
```

10. Add the following method, getting the message buffer policy, to the `Program` class:

```
private static MessageBufferPolicy GetMessageBufferPolicy()
{
    MessageBufferPolicy messageBufferPolicy =
      new MessageBufferPolicy()
    {
        ExpiresAfter = TimeSpan.FromMinutes(10d),
        MaxMessageCount = 1
    };
    return messageBufferPolicy;
}
```

11. Add the following method, sending a move, to the `Program` class:

```
private static void MakeMove(
  MessageBufferClient bufferClient, String move)
{
    Console.WriteLine("{0} -> {1}",
      bufferClient.MessageBufferUri.LocalPath[1], move);
    using (Message moveMessage =
      Message.CreateMessage(
        MessageVersion.Soap12WSAddressing10,
        "urn:Message", move))
    {
        bufferClient.Send(moveMessage,
```

```
            TimeSpan.FromSeconds(1d));
    }
}
```

12. Add the following method, getting the last move, to the `Program` class:

```
private static String GetMove(MessageBufferClient bufferClient)
{
    String move;
    using (Message moveMessage = bufferClient.Retrieve())
    {
        move = moveMessage.GetBody<String>();
    }
    Console.WriteLine("{0} <- {1}",
        bufferClient.MessageBufferUri.LocalPath[1], move);
    return move;
}
```

13. Build the solution.

14. Start the project twice (the first one launched becomes "white").

How it works...

In steps 1 through 4, we set up the server by adding the required references and `using` statements. In step 5, we add a private member to store the Service Bus namespace (`SERVICE_NAMESPACE`), which we need to replace with the actual value for the Service Bus configuration on the Windows Azure Portal. We also provide unique names for each message buffer. In step 6, we delegate to the `PlayGame()` method.

In step 7, we first add the first five moves of a chess game to a pair of `String` arrays. We then invoke the `CreateMessageBufferClient()` method, which we add in the next step, to create the two `MessageBufferClient` instances used for communication with the message buffers.

We then wrap the logic used to choose the white player in a try/catch block. The idea is that both players try to make a white move, but the second player to make a move receives a `TimeOutException` as we set up the message buffers to accept only one message (move) at a time. The second player is then declared to be the black player and removes the dummy first move from the white message buffer.

The game proceeds with each service (player) iterating over the appropriate moves contained in the `String` array we created earlier. We are careful to modify the first move attempt by white to take account of the fact that there is no prior move by black. Once the moves have been completed, the black player deletes the two message buffers.

In step 8, we retrieve an endpoint behavior containing the Service Bus credentials, and then we create the service URI, before getting the `MessageBufferPolicy`. Finally, we use these properties to create the message buffer and return a `MessageBufferClient` we can use to refer to it. Note that an attempt to create the same message buffer is non-destructive and returns a `MessageBufferClient` usable against the existing message buffer.

In step 9, we create a `TransportClientEndpointBehavior` containing the shared secret credentials for the message buffer. In step 10, we create the `MessageBufferPolicy` where we specify that a message buffer allows only one message at a time and that it expires after 10 minutes.

We make the move in step 11, by creating a message containing the move and sending it to the message buffer. In step 12, we retrieve a message from the message buffer and extract the move from it. In both steps, we write the move to the Console window.

In step 13, we build the solution. In step 14, we start the service twice—once for each player. The completion of the game is indicated by the display of `Press Enter to Exit` in the Console windows of both players.

There's more...

Microsoft has released a community technology preview (CTP) of Windows Azure Service Bus Queues and Topics which support sophisticated publish/subscribe scenarios. Service Bus Queues and Topics is a significant feature enhancement over Service Bus message buffers as it supports much larger queues, with messages persisted in a store managed by the Service Bus. Service Bus Queues and Topics also benefit from the much richer API support for these features.

A queue is a persistent message buffer with a single message stream (subscription) to which multiple subscribers compete for messages. Each message can contain a serializable message body, as well as message-specific properties. Messages can be retrieved using either at-most once semantics (receive-and-delete) or at least once semantics (peek-lock). In receive-and-delete, a message is deleted from the queue as soon as a subscriber receives it. In peek-lock, a message must be explicitly deleted before a timeout expires and it once again becomes visible to other subscribers. A queue can be configured to support sessions allowing related messages to be viewed as a single session and delivered to the same subscriber.

A topic is a persistent message buffer with multiple independent message streams (subscriptions) to each of which multiple subscribers compete for messages. Each message published to a topic is delivered independently to all subscriptions to the topic. The semantics of message retrieval for an individual topic subscription is the same as with a queue subscription. However, topics support the association of rules with a subscription. A rule comprises a filter, selecting which messages in the topic are delivered to the subscription, and an optional action allowing message properties to be altered. Filters provide much of the power of topics, as they allow different subscriptions to offer different views of the messages in the topic. For example, regional offices could subscribe to topic messages for their region while a head office could subscribe to all the messages in a topic.

Using the Windows Azure AppFabric Caching service

The Windows Azure AppFabric Caching service provides a fully managed Caching service to services hosted in Windows Azure. The Caching service is essentially a cloud-based version of the Windows Server AppFabric Caching service. The Windows Azure version does not support all the features of the Windows Server version, but it does so in a way that does not require the cluster management needed by the Windows Server version. The Windows Azure AppFabric Caching service uses the same API as the Windows Server AppFabric Caching service. However, it is implemented in separate assemblies, so that authentication and unsupported features are handled appropriately.

The Windows Azure AppFabric Caching service supports cache sizes between 128 MB and 4 GB. The cache size is associated with service quotas on the number of transactions per hour, bandwidth MB per hour, and the number of concurrent connections. Usage exceeding these limits is throttled.

Each cache is identified by a unique namespace which provides the first part of the hostname used to access it. The complete hostname for a cache is constructed as {NAMESPACE}.cache.windows.net. Access to a cache requires the provision of an authentication token. As with other parts of the Windows Azure AppFabric, the Caching service uses the Windows Azure Access Control Service for authentication.

In the initial release, timeout-based expiration is the only supported cache-expiration policy. The default timeout of 10 minutes can be modified when items are added to the cache. It is not possible to disable item eviction on a cache, so an item may be evicted (or removed) from the cache when the cache reaches its configured maximum size. This eviction uses a least-recently used algorithm.

The Caching service supports both optimistic and pessimistic caching. The former uses version identifiers while the latter uses locks. It supports a local cache, which can be used to cache data on the local instance to ensure extremely low latency. Consequently, data can be served from any of three levels: local cache, central cache, and the original datastore.

The cache-aside pattern is a standard way of using the Caching service. In this pattern, data is requested from the cache and if it is not found there, it is retrieved from its originating datastore and then added to the cache. This pattern simplifies the use of the Caching service by the application. It can also be used to hide the source of the data from the application, so that a single cache can be used as a front for data stored in multiple backing datastores.

In this recipe, we will learn how to use the cache-aside pattern with the Windows Azure AppFabric Caching service.

Getting ready

We need to create a Caching service namespace. We see how to do this in the *Creating a namespace for the Windows Azure AppFabric* recipe in this chapter. We also need to have created a Windows Azure Blob Service container and uploaded a blob, containing text, to it.

How to do it...

We are going to use the cache-aside programming pattern to retrieve an item from the Windows Azure Blob Service and cache it using the Windows Azure AppFabric Caching service. Whenever the item is missing from the cache, we will retrieve it again from the Blob service. We do this as follows:

1. Create a Windows Azure Solution and add a Worker Role project to it.

2. Add the following assembly references to the project:

   ```
   Microsoft.ApplicationServer.Caching.Client
   Microsoft.ApplicationServer.Caching.Core
   Microsoft.WindowsFabric.Common
   Microsoft.WindowsFabric.Data.Common
   ```

3. Add the following using statements to the top of `WorkerRole.cs`:

   ```
   using Microsoft.ApplicationServer.Caching;
   using System.Security;
   ```

4. Add the following members to the `WorkerRole` class:

   ```
   DataCache dataCache;
   String containerName = "CONTAINER_NAME";
   String key = "BLOB_NAME";
   ```

5. Replace `Run()` with the following:

   ```
   public override void Run()
   {
       while (true)
       {
           Thread.Sleep(10000);
           String theValue = GetData(key);
       }
   }
   ```

6. Replace `OnStart()` with the following:

```
public override bool OnStart()
{
    ServicePointManager.DefaultConnectionLimit = 12;

    InitializeCache();

    RemoveData(key);

    String value = GetData(key);

    return base.OnStart();
}
```

7. Add the following method, initializing the cache, to the `WorkerRole` class:

```
private void InitializeCache()
{
    String cacheHost =
      RoleEnvironment.GetConfigurationSettingValue(
        "Namespace");
    String cacheService = String.Format(
      "{0}.cache.windows.net", cacheHost);
    Boolean SslEnabled = true;
    Int32 cachePort = SslEnabled ? 22243 : 22233;
    Int32 sizeLocalCache = 100;

    DataCacheLocalCacheProperties localCacheProperties =
      new DataCacheLocalCacheProperties(
        sizeLocalCache, TimeSpan.FromSeconds(60),
        DataCacheLocalCacheInvalidationPolicy.TimeoutBased);

    List<DataCacheServerEndpoint> servers =
      new List<DataCacheServerEndpoint>();
    servers.Add(new DataCacheServerEndpoint(
      cacheService, cachePort));

    DataCacheTransportProperties dataCacheTransportProperties =
      new DataCacheTransportProperties()
        { MaxBufferSize = 10000,
          ReceiveTimeout = TimeSpan.FromSeconds(45)
        };

    DataCacheFactoryConfiguration cacheFactoryConfiguration =
      new DataCacheFactoryConfiguration()
    {
```

```
        LocalCacheProperties = localCacheProperties,
        SecurityProperties = GetSecurityToken(SslEnabled),
        Servers = servers,
        TransportProperties = dataCacheTransportProperties
    };

    DataCacheFactory dataCacheFactory =
      new DataCacheFactory(cacheFactoryConfiguration);

    dataCache = dataCacheFactory.GetDefaultCache();
}
```

8. Add the following method, creating the security token, to the `WorkerRole` class:

```
private DataCacheSecurity GetSecurityToken(Boolean SslEnabled)
{
    DataCacheSecurity dataCacheSecurity;
    using (SecureString secureString = new SecureString())
    {
        String authenticationToken =
          RoleEnvironment.GetConfigurationSettingValue(
            "AuthenticationToken");
        foreach (Char c in authenticationToken)
        {
            secureString.AppendChar(c);
        }
        secureString.MakeReadOnly();
        dataCacheSecurity = new DataCacheSecurity(secureString,
          SslEnabled);
    }
    return dataCacheSecurity;
}
```

9. Add the following method, removing data from the cache, to the `WorkerRole` class:

```
private void RemoveData(String key)
{
    dataCache.Remove(key);
}
```

10. Add the following method, implementing the cache aside functionality, to the `WorkerRole` class:

```
private String GetData(String key)
{
    String blobText = String.Empty;
    blobText = dataCache.Get(key) as String;
    if (String.IsNullOrEmpty(blobText))
```

```
    {
        blobText = GetBlobFromStorage(containerName, key);
        dataCache.Put(key, blobText, TimeSpan.FromMinutes(10d));
    }
    return blobText;
}
```

11. Implement the following method, retrieving the blob content from the Blob service, to the `WorkerRole` class:

```
private String GetBlobFromStorage(
    String container, String blobName)
{
    String blobAddress = String.Format(
        "{0}/{1}", container, blobName);
    CloudStorageAccount cloudStorageAccount =
        CloudStorageAccount.Parse(
            RoleEnvironment.GetConfigurationSettingValue(
            "DataConnectionString"));

    CloudBlobClient cloudBlobClient =
        cloudStorageAccount.CreateCloudBlobClient();
    CloudBlockBlob cloudBlockBlob =
        cloudBlobClient.GetBlockBlobReference(blobAddress);
    String blobText = cloudBlockBlob.DownloadText();
    return blobText;
}
```

12. Replace the `ConfigurationSettings` section of `ServiceDefinition.csdef` with the following:

```
<ConfigurationSettings>
    <Setting name="AuthenticationToken" />
    <Setting name="DataConnectionString" />
    <Setting name="Namespace" />
</ConfigurationSettings>
```

13. Replace the `ConfigurationSettings` section of `ServiceDefinition.cscfg` with the following:

```
<ConfigurationSettings>
    <Setting name=
 "Microsoft.WindowsAzure.Plugins.Diagnostics.ConnectionString"
        value="UseDevelopmentStorage=true" />
    <Setting name="AuthenticationToken"
        value="AUTHENTICATION_TOKEN" />
    <Setting name="DataConnectionString"
        value="UseDevelopmentStorage=true" />
    <Setting name="Namespace" value="CACHE_NAMESPACE" />
</ConfigurationSettings>
```

How it works...

In steps 1 through 3, we set up the class. In step 4, we add private members to store the `DataCache` instance we use to access the cache, as well as the container name and blob name from which we retrieve the data. We need to replace `CONTAINER_NAME` and `BLOB_NAME` with the actual container and blob names. In a more realistic example, we would cache many items rather than the single item used in this sample.

In step 5, we modify the provided `Run()` method, so that it retrieves the cached data every 10 seconds. In step 6, we modify the provided `OnStart()` method, so that it invokes initialization of the local cache. We also refresh the cache, which exists independently of this instance, by removing the existing entry and adding a fresh copy to the cache. The latter is implicit in the use of `GetData()` to retrieve data from the cache.

In step 7, we initialize the cache. We retrieve the Caching service namespace from the service configuration file and then select the correct port for the cache depending on whether or not we are going to use SSL. We specify that we are going to use a local cache with a 60-second timeout and timeout-based cache invalidation. In the initial release, this is the only supported cache-invalidation technique. We then create the desired Caching service endpoint.

We need to specify the `DataCacheTransportProperties` to provide a buffer size for cached objects and to provide a `ReceiveTimeout`. This needs to be 60 seconds or less as Windows Azure destroys connections which have been idle for more than 60 seconds, which can cause an error when a stale connection is used to access the Caching service.

We then use these configuration properties to create a `DataCacheFactoryConfiguration` instance which we use to initialize a `DataCacheFactory` instance. Finally, we use this to retrieve the default cache, which is the only cache currently supported in the Caching service.

In step 8, we retrieve the Caching service authentication token from the service configuration file. We use it to create the `SecureString` instance we need to initialize the `DataCacheSecurity` instance required to initialize the `DataCacheFactoryConfiguration` in step 7.

In step 9, we add a simple method to remove an item from the cache. The method we add in step 10 implements the cache-aside functionality. We attempt to retrieve an item from the cache and, if it is not present, we retrieve it from blob storage and add it to the cache before returning it. In step 11, we retrieve the specified blob from blob storage and return its contents.

In steps 12 and 13, we define and specify the configuration settings in the service definition files. We must replace the `CACHE_NAMESPACE` and `AUTHENTICATION_TOKEN` with the appropriate values for the cache. These can be found on the Windows Azure Portal. Before deploying the application to Windows Azure, we need to replace the `Microsoft.WindowsAzure.Plugins.Diagnostics.ConnectionString` and `DataConnectionString` settings with values representing an actual storage account and key.

There's more...

The Caching service can also be configured using the `app.config` and `web.config` files. The latter is essential when configuring the session-state provider or output-cache provider for a website.

Using a configuration file to configure the Caching service

The Caching service can also be configured using the `app.config` file. We need to add the following configuration `section` definition to the `configSections` section of the `app.config` file, as follows:

```
<section name="dataCacheClient" type=
"Microsoft.ApplicationServer.Caching.DataCacheClientSection,
Microsoft.ApplicationServer.Caching.Core"
       allowLocation="true" allowDefinition="Everywhere"/>
```

We can replicate the earlier programmatic configuration by adding the following data-cache client declaration under the `configuration` element as follows:

```
<dataCacheClient>
    <localCache isEnabled="true" sync="TimeoutBased"
      ttlValue="60" objectCount="100"/>
    <hosts>
      <host name="CACHE_NAMESPACE.cache.windows.net"
        cachePort="22243" />
    </hosts>
    <securityProperties mode="Message" sslEnabled="true" >
      <messageSecurity
       authorizationInfo="AUTHENTICATION_TOKEN">
      </messageSecurity>
    </securityProperties>
    <transportProperties maxBufferSize="10000"
       receiveTimeout="45000"/>
</dataCacheClient>
```

We need to provide appropriate values for `CACHE_NAMESPACE` and `AUTHENTICATION_TOKEN`.

We can then replace `InitializeCache()` with the following:

```
private void InitializeCache()
{
   DataCacheFactoryConfiguration cacheFactoryConfiguration =
     new DataCacheFactoryConfiguration();
   DataCacheFactory dataCacheFactory =
     new DataCacheFactory(cacheFactoryConfiguration);
   dataCache = dataCacheFactory.GetDefaultCache();
}
```

The disadvantage of this technique is that we need to redeploy the application package to change `app.config`.

 Note that the basic version of this configuration can be found by selecting **View Client Configuration** on the **Cache** section of the Windows Azure Portal.

Session-state provider and output-cache provider

In Windows Azure, traffic to input endpoints for a role is load balanced across all instances of the role. This means that there is explicitly no session affinity for web roles, and different web pages may be served from different instances during a single user session. This means that session management for a web role must be handled off the instance. There is a similar issue with output caching for web pages.

The Windows Azure AppFabric Caching service can be used to store session state and the output cache for a web role. This can be done entirely through configuration, by changing `web.config`, with no code change whatsoever. The required configuration can be found by selecting **View Client Configuration** on the **Cache** section of the Windows Azure Portal.

 Note that the Windows Azure Platform Training Kit contains, in the *Building ASP.NET Applications with Windows Azure* hands-on lab, a sample session-state provider using the Windows Azure Table Service. The Windows Azure Platform Training Kit can be downloaded from the Windows Azure website (http://www.microsoft.com/windowsazure/).

Index

L

LINQ-REST 228
ListBlobs() method 53
ListBlobsSegmented() method 53
local storage
  using, in instance 196-199
LocalStorage element 197
LocalStorageExample class 199

M

makecert command 42, 192
master database 313
MergeOption.NoTracking context 120
MergeOption.OverwriteChanges context 120
MergeOption.PreserveChanges context 121
MergeOption enumeration 121
MergeOption property 121, 124
MergeOption values 122
message
  adding, to queue 154, 159
  CloudQueue class 154, 156
  CloudQueueMessage.DeleteMessage()
      method 156
  CloudQueueMessage object 155
  CloudQueue object 155
  EncodeMessage property 154
  GetMessage() method 156
  GetMessages() method 156
  large amounts data, storing 159-161
  PeekMessage() method 156
  PeekMessages() method 156
  queue, creating 154, 155
Microsoft.WindowsAzure.Plugins.Diagnostics.
      ConnectionString 10
Microsoft.WindowsAzure.StorageClient.Proto-
      col namespace 93
Microsoft.WindowsAzure.StorageClient name-
      space 92
Microsoft.WindowsAzure namespace 11
Microsoft Management Console (MMC) 42
Microsoft SQL Server database, migrating to
      SQL Azure
  about 308, 309
  steps 309, 310
MixedBatch() method 117
ModelContextExample class 110-112

ModifyEntity() method 124
multiple websites
  hosting, in web role 183-187

N

namespace
  creating, for Windows Azure AppFabric
      339, 340
NetTcpRelayBinding instance 346
NoSQL systems 102

O

on-demand transfer
  performing 255
  performing, steps 256-259
  working 259, 260
OnDemandTransferOptions instance 255
OnDemandTransferOptions object 259
OnStart() method 17, 216, 248, 249, 254,
      263, 364
OnStop() method 208
OptimisticConcurrencyExample class 123

P

Page_Load() 241, 266
Page_Load() event handler 244
page blob
  VHD, uploading 66-72
Parallel.ForEach method 76
Parallel.For loop 79
Parallel.For method 76
ParallelizationExample class 79
PartitionKey
  about 112
  selecting, for table 125-128
patch Tuesday 205
PeekMessage() method 156, 159
PeekMessages() method 156
Platform-as-a-Service model (PaaS) 172, 174
poison messages
  about 150
  handling 166, 170
  identifying 166, 170
  identifying, steps 166-169
PoisonMessagesExample class 167, 168

Thank you for buying
Microsoft Windows Azure Development Cookbook

About Packt Publishing

Packt, pronounced 'packed', published its first book "*Mastering phpMyAdmin for Effective MySQL Management*" in April 2004 and subsequently continued to specialize in publishing highly focused books on specific technologies and solutions.

Our books and publications share the experiences of your fellow IT professionals in adapting and customizing today's systems, applications, and frameworks. Our solution-based books give you the knowledge and power to customize the software and technologies you're using to get the job done. Packt books are more specific and less general than the IT books you have seen in the past. Our unique business model allows us to bring you more focused information, giving you more of what you need to know, and less of what you don't.

Packt is a modern, yet unique publishing company, which focuses on producing quality, cutting-edge books for communities of developers, administrators, and newbies alike. For more information, please visit our website: www.PacktPub.com.

About Packt Enterprise

In 2010, Packt launched two new brands, Packt Enterprise and Packt Open Source, in order to continue its focus on specialization. This book is part of the Packt Enterprise brand, home to books published on enterprise software – software created by major vendors, including (but not limited to) IBM, Microsoft and Oracle, often for use in other corporations. Its titles will offer information relevant to a range of users of this software, including administrators, developers, architects, and end users.

Writing for Packt

We welcome all inquiries from people who are interested in authoring. Book proposals should be sent to author@packtpub.com. If your book idea is still at an early stage and you would like to discuss it first before writing a formal book proposal, contact us; one of our commissioning editors will get in touch with you.

We're not just looking for published authors; if you have strong technical skills but no writing experience, our experienced editors can help you develop a writing career, or simply get some additional reward for your expertise.

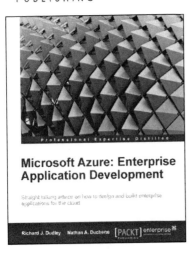

Microsoft Azure: Enterprise Application Development

ISBN: 978-1-849680-98-1   Paperback: 248 pages

Straight talking advice on how to design and build enterprise applications for the cloud using Microsoft Azure with this book and eBook

1. Build scalable enterprise applications using Microsoft Azure

2. The perfect fast-paced case study for developers and architects wanting to enhance core business processes

3. Packed with examples to illustrate concepts

4. Written in the context of building an online portal for the case-study application

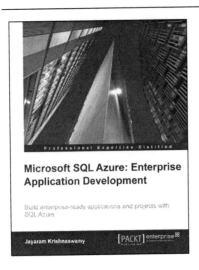

Microsoft SQL Azure: Enterprise Application Development

ISBN: 978-1-849680-80-6   Paperback: 420 pages

Build enterprise-ready applications and projects with Microsoft SQL Azure using this book and eBook

1. Develop large scale enterprise applications using Microsoft SQL Azure

2. Understand how to use the various third party programs such as DB Artisan, RedGate, ToadSoft etc developed for SQL Azure

3. Master the exhaustive Data migration and Data Synchronization aspects of SQL Azure

4. Includes SQL Azure projects in incubation and more recent developments including all 2010 updates

Please check **www.PacktPub.com** for information on our titles

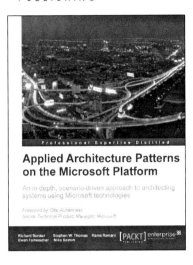

Applied Architecture Patterns
on the Microsoft Platform

An in-depth, scenario-driven approach to architecting
systems using Microsoft technologies

Foreword by Otto Aukkensaas
Azure Technical Product Manager, Microsoft

Richard Seroter   Stephen W. Thomas   Rama Ramani
Ewan Fairweather   Mike Sexton

Applied Architecture Patterns on the Microsoft Platform

ISBN: 978-1-849680-54-7   Paperback: 544 pages

An in-depth scenario-driven approach to architecting
systems using Microsoft technologies with this book
and eBook

1. Provides an architectural methodology for
   choosing Microsoft application platform
   technologies to meet the requirements of your
   solution

2. Examines new technologies such as Windows
   Server AppFabric, StreamInsight, and Windows
   Azure Platform and provides examples of how they
   can be used in real-world solutions

3. Considers solutions for messaging, workflow, data
   processing, and performance scenarios

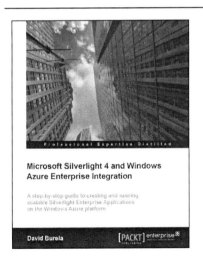

Microsoft Silverlight 4 and Windows
Azure Enterprise Integration

A step-by-step guide to creating and running
scalable Silverlight Enterprise Applications
on the Windows Azure platform

David Burela

Microsoft Silverlight 4 and Windows Azure Enterprise Integration

ISBN: 978-1-84968-3-12-8   Paperback: 446 pages

A step-by-step book and eBook guide to creating and
running scalable Silverlight 4 Enterprise Applications on
the Windows Azure platform

1. This book and e-book details how enterprise
   Silverlight applications can be written to take
   advantage of the key features of Windows Azure
   to create scalable applications

2. Provides an overview of the Windows Azure
   platform and how the different technologies can
   be integrated within your enterprise application

Please check **www.PacktPub.com** for information on our titles

CPSIA information can be obtained at www.ICGtesting.com
Printed in the USA
LVOW130243051111

253636LV00018B/161/P